I0884997

Apps Management and E-Commerce Transactions in Real-Time

Sajad Rezaei
Taylor's University, Malaysia

A volume in the Advances in E-Business Research (AEBR) Book Series

IGI GLOBAL
DISSEMINATOR OF KNOWLEDGE
www.igi-global.com

Published in the United States of America by
IGI Global
Business Science Reference (an imprint of IGI Global)
701 E. Chocolate Avenue
Hershey PA 17033
Tel: 717-533-8845
Fax: 717-533-8661
E-mail: cust@igi-global.com
Web site: http://www.igi-global.com

Copyright © 2017 by IGI Global. All rights reserved. No part of this publication may be reproduced, stored or distributed in any form or by any means, electronic or mechanical, including photocopying, without written permission from the publisher.
Product or company names used in this set are for identification purposes only. Inclusion of the names of the products or companies does not indicate a claim of ownership by IGI Global of the trademark or registered trademark.

Library of Congress Cataloging-in-Publication Data

Names: Rezaei, Sajad, 1984- editor.
Title: Apps management and e-commerce transactions in real-time / Sajad Rezaei, editor.
Description: Hershey, PA : Business Science Reference, [2017] | Includes bibliographical references.
Identifiers: LCCN 2017003170| ISBN 9781522524496 (h/c) | ISBN 9781522524502 (eISBN)
Subjects: LCSH: Electronic commerce. | Mobile commerce. | Application software--Management. | Mobile apps--Management.
Classification: LCC HF5548.32 .A669 2017 | DDC 658.8/72--dc23 LC record available at https://lccn.loc.gov/2017003170

This book is published in the IGI Global book series Advances in E-Business Research (AEBR) (ISSN: 1935-2700; eISSN: 1935-2719)

British Cataloguing in Publication Data
A Cataloguing in Publication record for this book is available from the British Library.

All work contributed to this book is new, previously-unpublished material. The views expressed in this book are those of the authors, but not necessarily of the publisher.

Advances in E-Business Research (AEBR) Book Series

ISSN:1935-2700
EISSN:1935-2719

Mission

Technology has played a vital role in the emergence of e-business and its applications incorporate strategies. These processes have aided in the use of electronic transactions via telecommunications networks for collaborating with business partners, buying and selling of goods and services, and customer service. Research in this field continues to develop into a wide range of topics, including marketing, psychology, information systems, accounting, economics, and computer science.

The **Advances in E-Business Research (AEBR) Book Series** provides multidisciplinary references for researchers and practitioners in this area. Instructors, researchers, and professionals interested in the most up-to-date research on the concepts, issues, applications, and trends in the e-business field will find this collection, or individual books, extremely useful. This collection contains the highest quality academic books that advance understanding of e-business and addresses the challenges faced by researchers and practitioners.

Coverage

- E-business technology investment strategies
- E-business systems integration
- Outsourcing and e-business technologies
- E-Services
- Web 2.0
- Virtual Collaboration
- Valuing e-business assets
- Sustainable E-business
- Online consumer behavior
- Economics of e-business

IGI Global is currently accepting manuscripts for publication within this series. To submit a proposal for a volume in this series, please contact our Acquisition Editors at Acquisitions@igi-global.com or visit: http://www.igi-global.com/publish/.

The Advances in E-Business Research (AEBR) Book Series (ISSN 1935-2700) is published by IGI Global, 701 E. Chocolate Avenue, Hershey, PA 17033-1240, USA, www.igi-global.com. This series is composed of titles available for purchase individually; each title is edited to be contextually exclusive from any other title within the series. For pricing and ordering information please visit http://www.igi-global.com/book-series/advances-business-research/37144. Postmaster: Send all address changes to above address. Copyright © 2017 IGI Global. All rights, including translation in other languages reserved by the publisher. No part of this series may be reproduced or used in any form or by any means – graphics, electronic, or mechanical, including photocopying, recording, taping, or information and retrieval systems – without written permission from the publisher, except for non commercial, educational use, including classroom teaching purposes. The views expressed in this series are those of the authors, but not necessarily of IGI Global.

Titles in this Series

For a list of additional titles in this series, please visit: www.igi-global.com

Driving Innovation and Business Success in the Digital Economy
Ionica Oncioiu (Titu Maiorescu University, Romania)
Business Science Reference • copyright 2017 • 321pp • H/C (ISBN: 9781522517795) • US $200.00 (our price)

Social Media Listening and Monitoring for Business Applications
N. Raghavendra Rao (FINAIT Consultancy Services, India)
Business Science Reference • copyright 2017 • 470pp • H/C (ISBN: 9781522508465) • US $205.00 (our price)

Analyzing the Strategic Role of Social Networking in Firm Growth and Productivity
Vladlena Benson (Kingston University, UK) Ronald Tuninga (Kingston Business School, UK) and George Saridakis (Kingston University, UK)
Business Science Reference • copyright 2017 • 525pp • H/C (ISBN: 9781522505594) • US $220.00 (our price)

Securing Transactions and Payment Systems for M-Commerce
Sushila Madan (University of Delhi, India) and Jyoti Batra Arora (Banasthali Vidyapeeth University, India)
Business Science Reference • copyright 2016 • 349pp • H/C (ISBN: 9781522502364) • US $205.00 (our price)

E-Retailing Challenges and Opportunities in the Global Marketplace
Shailja Dixit (Amity University, India) and Amit Kumar Sinha (Amity University, India)
Business Science Reference • copyright 2016 • 358pp • H/C (ISBN: 9781466699212) • US $215.00 (our price)

Successful Technological Integration for Competitive Advantage in Retail Settings
Eleonora Pantano (Middlesex University London, UK)
Business Science Reference • copyright 2015 • 405pp • H/C (ISBN: 9781466682979) • US $200.00 (our price)

Strategic E-Commerce Systems and Tools for Competing in the Digital Marketplace
Mehdi Khosrow-Pour (Information Resources Management Association, USA)
Business Science Reference • copyright 2015 • 315pp • H/C (ISBN: 9781466681330) • US $185.00 (our price)

IGI GLOBAL
DISSEMINATOR OF KNOWLEDGE
www.igi-global.com

701 E. Chocolate Ave., Hershey, PA 17033
Order online at www.igi-global.com or call 717-533-8845 x100
To place a standing order for titles released in this series,
contact: cust@igi-global.com
Mon-Fri 8:00 am - 5:00 pm (est) or fax 24 hours a day 717-533-8661

Table of Contents

Detailed Table of Contents

Social Mobile Analytics and Cloud – SMAC the new abbreviation that every business leader is thinking off. It is also part of everyone's lives these days. SMAC technologies are creating enormous opportunities across industries while the consumer willingly gives up personal information. Cloud technologies have made it possible to collect and store such large amounts of data. While each of these four technologies are able to enhance the business on its own, using these four technologies together as a stack has changed the way businesses are looking to maximize their customer base, enhance brand value and off course, increase company profit. For example, SMAC has forced businesses leaders to make analytics part of their marketing strategy and business operation as a whole.

Digital marketing has put mobile and social into the center of the vision. Mobile and social interactions have transformed marketing activities and imposed a new paradigm on consumer behaviors based on real-time customer relationship management, peer-to-peer social influence and idea co-creation with consumers. Extensive research has been conducted in both mobile and social media domain, however few research has led a systematic approach by illustrating the marketing evolution and identifying mobile and social features. In this chapter, we fill this research gap through a literature review approach by first presenting the new marketing paradigm created by social networks, and then analyzing the marketing evolution

Applications for mobile devices – apps – have seen unprecedented growth in importance. Ever better apps keep propelling the proliferation of mobile computing. App development is rather easy, particularly if it is based on Web technology. However, implementing apps that are user friendly and useful in the long-run is cumbersome. Thereby, it typically is expensive for corporate developers. Nonetheless, business apps are embraced by enterprises. To overcome the overhead of developing separately for multiple platforms and to mitigate the problems of device fragmentation, cross-platform development approaches are employed. While many such approaches exist, few have found widespread usage. In this chapter, we argue what the path towards future solutions could look like. We thereby take a rather technological look, but always keep business-orientation in mind. Our findings suggest that much effort is needed to enable the next generations of business apps. However, such apps will provide many merits and possibilities. Moreover, they provide the chance to master several of today's challenges.

Consumer behaviors and attitudes represent a continuously evolving field, thus, by understanding consumer behavior towards Apps from marketing strategy standpoint, managers can benefit from acquiring much information from applying and translating new insights into strategies and tactics that could be helpful for retailer's decision makers. Furthermore, the buying behavior of online shoppers is substantial in the prosperity of Apps marketing strategies and by identifying and understanding the factors that influence the consumer's buying decision, Apps retailers can design their online marketing strategy accordingly to maximize customer satisfaction and ultimately increase the sales volume. This chapter mainly proposed an integration of Internet consumer attitudes, behavior and Apps marketing strategy. This chapter is twofold in terms of having implications both in theory and practice. Indeed, this study helps in understanding consumer decision-making process in Apps environment and

The importance of relationship between customer and retailer has become prevalent in the ever-increasing competitive online market. The customers buying process often begin with the downloading of the required Apps in relation to the products they intended to purchase. Hence, customer satisfaction depends on customers' post-purchase evaluation on their experience with the use of the Apps. The aim of this chapter is to conceptualize the apps usage for online shopping, by examining the role of trust and satisfaction gained from the market interaction between the customers and retailers. Customers rely heavily on the information as well as the experiences encountered from the use of the apps. The retailers need to gain insights from the customer's perspective on the apps usage in order to improve customer relationship. This has impact on retailers' marketing efforts for winning the customers' loyalty.

The development of Apps usage in the tourism industry is along with the rise of relevant technologies that has affected the tourism industry all around the world. In order to build a competitive brand, firms are forced to implement the information technology related functions in their core business model. This chapter mainly focuses on the impact of Apps implementation in hospitality and tourism sector and conceptually propose that how branded Apps could yield tourist satisfaction and loyalty. Apps awareness, Apps quality and Apps image are proposed as several indicators of traveler's satisfaction and loyalty. The chapter argue that branding makes a business advantage; the brand follows indication of quality and assurance to the buyer and also special characteristics that could inspire consumers to buy products or services that are branded.

Current chapter focuses on the effectiveness of Augmented Reality (AR) supported applications for mobile and wearable devices during the visitation of tourist destinations. AR as an innovative technology tool becomes inseparable part of destinations' marketing in different countries across the world. However, the use of AR for marketing purpose in tourism destinations is fully dependent on access and resource availabilities. Hence the effective of AR application in tourism destination marketing remains a subject to detailed and accurate information availability of a

Preface

The emergence of the new marketing environment affects marketing/business science and practice (Kotler, 2011) in which the traditional marketing principle is influenced by the emergence of the electronic commerce applications such as Apps. E-commerce is a form of trade that has gained increasing attention from consumers and sellers; however, despite high growth rates, E-Commerce still has low levels of consumers (Rezaei et al., 2016). "E-commerce is defined as the process of buying and selling over the Internet" (Ramayah et al., 2009, p. 1223) and the process might include several online transactions like retailing, banking, tourism, and stock trading. As such "Apps commerce is a series of business efforts in utilizing apps for the distribution of information, sustaining and conducting relationships, communications, and transactions within an individual organization" (Rezaei et al., 2016, p. 409). Apps-commerce has deeply altered the way in which individual consumers conduct their business activities as the E-commerce is defined as the usage of the Internet to sell products or services to consumers.

Apps commerce have grown to be progressively efficient in a series of aspects along with the highest feature that is the performance along with accuracy and reliability involving transferring information. The E-commerce has advantages such as decreasing business transaction costs and also saving time, which makes it more feasible and effective. Apps and the related technologies are the platforms, through which organizations are struggling to implement their core business activities. Semantic Web, Internet of Things, Web 2.0, Web 3.0, Web mining, Social Computing, and Cloud Computing technologies, as a medium in Apps, empower organizations by providing a wider stand to information which is related to firm offering/products and services. Therefore, the traditional retail channel, as well as online direct channel, are dual channels in which recently, producers are progressively selling their products due to the establishment of the Internet.

Furthermore, Apps-Management is involved with business approaches via executing Apps in organizations to create and to enhance the communications channels, the Apps experience and distribution of information, to sustain and to conduct the relationships with stakeholders that are aiming for strategic results.

This new phenomenon of E-commerce is becoming a strategic tool to enhance the firm's total value chain in business domains such as education, IS, IT, marketing, hospitality, tourism, education, and even human resource management. Apps-Commerce business models, includes Apps-Intermediaries, Apps-Auction, Apps-Game, Apps-Tourism, Apps-Product, Apps-Dating, and so on and so forth. Accordingly, Apps-Commerce management includes several aspects of a business, including Apps-CRM, Apps-HRM, Apps-Marketing, Apps-Advertising, Apps-Retailing, Apps-Telecommunication, Apps-Security, Apps-Privacy, Apps-Cyber Law, Apps-Services, Apps-Location Map, Apps-Banking, and Apps-Payment. A successful management of Apps utilization is supposed to enhance E-commerce transactions in real-time. As a result, this book discusses trends, issues, and implications in Apps-Commerce development, implementation, and management as new phenomena of E-Commerce.

This book aims to contribute high-quality and original works that are highlighting the most important research topics, concepts, trends, issues, and practice implications in Apps-commerce development, implementation, and management. Throughout different discipline of business management, the book offers profound theoretical and practical foundations, regarding the current and future implementation of Apps-Commerce. The book would serve as a source of knowledge for researchers, educators, students, and industry practitioners all around the world.

THE CHALLENGES

E-Commerce advancement shifts the power of the supplier to the consumer, which contributes to important changes in the way firms relate to their clients and compete with each another; thus, there are no difficulties for customers to shift to an alternative online retailer if the performance of that retailer in unacceptable. Additionally, the emerging influence of the internet considerably magnifies the scope and impact of "sensory satisfactions" in marketing management (Achrol & Kotler, 2012; Holbrook & Schindler, 2003). Although some researchers advocated the importance of online experience in a commercial context and some others claimed that online experience is irrelevant for marketing, empirical evidence for these claims is lacking (van Noort et al., 2012). As such, consumers' churn behavior is an issue to be considered for businesses (Heinemann & Schwarzl, 2010) and the management of customer's Apps churn behavior or turnover is one of the top agenda for marketing managers within industries. This sensory experience and satisfaction might control individual Apps patronage intention. In the mobile environment, (See-To et al., 2012) it was found that sensory experience is a significant element for the enjoyment and engagement with the video. For an Apps market, the sensory shopping experience should be perceived (Rosen & Purinton, 2004), in which the motivation for sensual satisfaction during the shopping process must not be overlooked.

Despite the fact that the overall marketing cost is high (Copeland, 1923), in the time of recession, marketers should understand that the customer will reduce spending and relatively, companies will cut the marketing budgets (Kotler & Caslione, 2009; Shankar et al., 2011). Specifically, churn issue and management of churn behavior is a fundamental concern for businesses with the emergence of the digital economy (Lejeune, 2001). Churn behavior has become an issue and is considered as one of the primary challenges that many retailers and organizations have to face, globally (Yu et al., 2011). The churn behavior rate in saturated markets (churn rates: the percentage of customers quitting their relationship with a company) might be more than 30% per year (Zorn et al., 2010), thus, retailers should acquire new customers continually to survive in the market. For this reason, as Apps markets become totally and dramatically saturated, firms have confirmed that their key strategies should focus on recognizing those consumers who are likely to churn and shift to another Apps supplier.

SEARCHING FOR A SOLUTION

More experienced Apps users might find the Apps commerce interface as more predictable, quicker and easier to use compared to inexperienced online shoppers (McGoldrick et al., 2008), thus, it is crucial for online retailers to recognize that a customer's experience is not only limited to their interaction in the store. It has been documented that "for every four purchases made through the Internet, at least one results in dissatisfaction" (Cristiane & Daniel, 2011) and only a very small minority of website visitors return to make purchases (Harris & Goode, 2004). Virtual environments using Apps can generate changes in the affective states of consumers, influencing consumer's attitude toward the firm and their participation in value creation. Kotler (1965) believes that some of the major features of the marketing environments could be usefully deployed in computer model terms. As the role of the technology continues to increase (Becerra et al., 2013; Drucker, 1966, 1967), studies of online commercial retail are crucial to academic research (Allen et al., 2006).

Small businesses and large corporations spend a substantial amount of budget a year, yet many of these businesses fail to reach the organization's goals and are uncertain how to use this technology to gain competitive advantage or market advantages (Bevan & Murphy, 2001; Lam et al., 2004). According to Bulu (2012), throughout the evolution of the web, the focus has moved from "access and find" (Web 1.0), "share, participate, and collaborate" (Web 2.0) to "immersive collaboration and co-creation" (Web 3.0). Moreover, regarding the evolution of information technology, the attractiveness of immersive online settings revolutionizing the expression of human behaviors (Guitton, 2012), which intensifies retail competition, needs more sophisticated management practices.

ORGANIZATION OF THE BOOK

The book is organized into 14 chapters. A brief description of each of the chapters follows:

Chapter 1 discusses on Social Mobile Analytics and Cloud and introduces SMAC as a new abbreviation that every business leader is thinking off. SMAC technologies are creating enormous opportunities across industries while the consumer willingly gives up personal information. Cloud technologies have made it possible to collect and store such large amounts of data. While each of these four technologies is able to enhance the business on its own, using these four technologies together as a stack has changed the way businesses are looking to maximize their customer base, enhance brand value and off course, increase company profit. The objective of this chapter is to provide an overview of SMAC. The importance of implementing SMAC in a business to remain competitive in the future will be emphasized. The different technologies will be introduced, and the benefits and opportunities of SMAC trends will be pointed out. The solution and recommendation, future research directions, and conclusion follow this section.

Chapter 2 discusses applications in the marketing evolution from social networks to mobile social networks. Digital marketing has put mobile and social into the center of the vision. Mobile and social interactions have transformed marketing activities and imposed a new paradigm on consumer behaviors based on real-time customer relationship management, peer-to-peer social influence and idea co-creation with consumers. Extensive research has been conducted in both mobile and social media domain, however, few types of research have led a systematic approach by illustrating the marketing evolution and identifying mobile and social features. In this chapter, authors fill this research gap through a literature review approach by first presenting the new marketing paradigm created by social networks, and then analyzing the marketing evolution from web-based social networks to mobile social networks. The mobile and social features are identified to guide marketers for application design. Finally, four case studies are presented to show how these features are distributed in applications to lead a better consumer experience. This chapter brings both theoretical and practical implications in this new trends.

Chapter 3 discusses the Apps-commerce in emerging markets and provides insights and future business models perspectives. The Internet and Apps related technologies are considered as information ‘‘super highway” since they are able to connect people, computers, and data to one another. Because of them, a new communication medium has risen, which provides an access to the large flow of information across various broad extensions. As a consequence, there has been a need for understanding the behaviors of online consumers, since Information Technology and its usage have had a massive impact on shopping behaviors as well as the rate of market success. Therefore, this chapter's aim will be to sanitize the current understanding of Apps/ online consumer behavior to shape Apps marketing strategies and implementations.

Chapter 4 discusses the Security Problems in Cloud Computing Environments using Deep Analysis and a Secure Framework. Cloud computing technology is a relatively new concept of providing scalable and virtualized resources, software and hardware on demand to consumers. It presents a new technology to deliver computing resources as a service. It offers a variety of benefits like services on demand and provisioning and suffers from several weaknesses. In fact, security presents a major obstacle in cloud computing adoption. In this chapter, authors discussed security problems in cloud computing systems and show how to solve these problems using a quantitative security risk assessment model named Multi-dimensional Mean Failure Cost (M2FC). In fact, this chapter presents first a deep analysis of security issues related to cloud computing environments and then propose a generic framework that analysis and evaluate cloud security problems and then propose appropriate countermeasures to solve these problems.

Chapter 5 discusses how cross-platform technology can facilitate the easier creation of business Apps. Applications for mobile devices – apps – have seen unprecedented growth in importance. Ever better apps keep propelling the proliferation of mobile computing. App development is rather easy, particularly if it is based on Web technology. However, implementing apps that are user-friendly and useful in the long-run is cumbersome. Thereby, it typically is expensive for corporate developers. Nonetheless, business apps are embraced by enterprises. To overcome the overhead of developing separately for multiple platforms and to mitigate the problems of device fragmentation, cross-platform development approaches are employed. While many such approaches exist, few have found widespread usage. In this chapter, authors argue what the path towards future solutions could look like. They thereby take a rather technological look, but always keep business-orientation in mind. Their findings suggest that much effort is needed to enable the next generations of business apps. However, such apps will provide many merits and possibilities. Moreover, they provide the chance to master several of today's challenges.

Chapter 6 elaborates on the essential of Apps marketing implementation and E-commerce strategies and discusses Apps users' decision-making process. Consumer behaviors and attitudes represent a continuously evolving field, thus, by understanding consumer behavior towards Apps from marketing strategy standpoint, managers can benefit from acquiring much information from applying and translating new insights into strategies and tactics that could be helpful for retailer's decision makers. This chapter mainly proposed an integration of Internet consumer attitudes, behavior and Apps marketing strategy. This chapter is twofold in terms of having implications both in theory and practice. Indeed, this study helps in understanding consumer decision-making process in Apps environment and produce new knowledge to online and Apps retailers, marketing managers as well as marketing and IT scholars. The Apps related technologies have developed as an important medium for marketing in various areas, including expanded geographic scope, novel opportunities for appreciating customers and offering cost efficiencies.

Chapter 7 discusses Mobile Social Commerce. S-commerce and M-commerce become buzz word recent years. The social and mobile elements have brought new ways of thinking as well as challenging opportunities in e-commerce. In this chapter, authors firstly introduce the concepts of online social commerce, its classifications, and social shopping behaviors. Secondly, they analyze the evolution from online social commerce to mobile social commerce. Different case studies are given to demonstrate the concept of mobile social commerce, to precisely define how mobile and social feathers add value to traditional e-commerce.

Chapter 8 discusses on brand personality, social status and physical vanity in building luxury fashion branded Apps. While there have been an increasing number of researches done on branding and consumer behavior especially on brand personality, social status and vanity and its influence on purchase intention, there are little studies that focus on the influence of all these factors collectively on Apps purchase intention. This chapter conceptually argues that brand personality, social status, and physical vanity are important in building luxury fashion branded Apps. While brand personality and luxury fashion branded Apps as an internal factor plays an important role in deciphering if it has an influence on an individual's Apps purchase intention for luxury fashion brands; therefore, it is important to look into how external factors have an influence on an individual.

Chapter 9 discusses on post-purchase apps usage attitudes to revisit trust, customer satisfaction and loyalty of apps usage. The importance of the relationship between customer and retailer has become prevalent in the ever-increasing competitive online market. The customers buying process often begin with the downloading of the required Apps in relation to the products they intended to purchase. Hence, customer satisfaction depends on customers' post-purchase evaluation on their experience with the use of the Apps. The aim of this chapter is to conceptualize the usage of the Apps for online shopping, by examining the role of trust and satisfaction gained from the market interaction between the customers and retailers. Customers rely heavily on the information as well as the experiences encountered from the use of the apps. The retailers need to gain insights from the customer's perspective on the usage of the app in order to improve customer relationship. This has an impact on retailers' marketing efforts for winning the customers' loyalty.

Chapter 10 discusses Apps in hospitality and tourism to conceptualize branded Apps in building traveler satisfaction and loyalty. The development of Apps usage in the tourism industry is along with the rise of relevant technologies that has affected the tourism industry all around the world. In order to build a competitive brand, firms are forced to implement the information technology related functions in their core business model. This chapter mainly focuses on the impact of Apps implementation in hospitality and tourism sector and conceptually propose that how branded Apps could yield tourist satisfaction and loyalty. Apps awareness, Apps quality, and Apps image are proposed as several indicators of traveler's satisfaction and loyalty. The chapter argues that branding makes a business advantage; the brand follows the indication of quality and assurance to the buyer and also special characteristics that could inspire consumers to buy products or services that are branded.

Chapter 11 discusses augmented reality apps for tourism destination promotion. This chapter focuses on the effectiveness of Augmented Reality (AR) supported applications for mobile and wearable devices during the visitation of tourist destinations. AR as an innovative technology tool becomes an inseparable part of destinations' marketing in different countries across the world. However, the use of AR for marketing purpose in tourism destinations is fully dependent on access and resource availabilities. Hence the effective of AR application in tourism destination marketing remains a subject to detailed and accurate information availability of a particular destination or a region. This chapter draws particular reference to the AR supported 'Mobile guides' that replaced conventional human tourist guides. The chapter is indebted to AR literature written Turkish. Results demonstrate that AR as an innovative technology can be applied for tourism destination promotion.

Chapter 12 proposes antecedents of apps channel selection in form of a research proposal. Hence, this chapter aims to propose a research proposal in the determinants and the factors influencing App channel selection. It is essential to building an understanding of concepts of social enterprise regarding the Apps marketing and to design an empirically based research to cultivate an understanding in terms of the perceptions and practices of Apps enterprises within the context of marketing. The significance of this research is to provide the undergraduate researcher a guideline in proposing a research and forming strategic marketing and tactical decision-making when defining the roles of Apps channel.

Chapter 13 proposes value and risk as the dual pillars of apps usefulness. The rapid expansion of Apps and subsequently Apps marketing have now entered into a post-adoption stage, where technical characteristics and qualities such as visual design, user interfaces, and navigation become the determinants of consumer's intentions. However, very few studies have looked into the perceptions related to usefulness and "post-adoption" or acceptance of Apps-commerce. Building on risk and value concept, the aim of this chapter is to expand an understanding of the decision-making of those potential Apps customers to adopt Apps usage for the first time and also re-purchase decisions of experienced e-customers. As the concept of customer value has received increasing attention from both marketing, managers, researchers and practitioners, more originalities are encouraged to start incorporating the elements of Apps value, Apps risk, Apps usefulness elements in their strategies to sustain their core businesses activities. Besides, customers are likely to perceive a higher level of risk in using Apps than in traditional in-store setting. Thus, this chapter proposes that the risk concern of user information given to the vendors has an impact on the amount of consumption in Apps market. The practical and conceptual implications are discussed.

Chapter 14 finalizes the book by proposing the future of apps as a smart investment for business. Today consumers are demanding apps that can fulfill many different needs and are much more individualized. This high and consuming demand forces the developers the use large amounts of data before they can be able to meet these needs. The objective of this chapter is to look at the implications apps have on society. Current apps are not going to be around forever, so future potential modifications will be discussed as changes are needed to keep the users engaged. Benefits, challenges, and solutions will be discussed along with examples.

Sajad Rezaei
Taylor's University, Malaysia

REFERENCES

Achrol, R., & Kotler, P. (2012). Frontiers of the marketing paradigm in the third millennium. *Journal of the Academy of Marketing Science*, *40*(1), 35–52. doi:10.1007/s11747-011-0255-4

Allen, G. N., Burk, D. L., & Davis, G. B. (2006). Academic data collection in electronic environments: Defining acceptable use of internet resources. *Management Information Systems Quarterly*, *30*(3), 599–610.

Becerra, E. P., Badrinarayanan, V., & Kim, C.-H. (2013). Influence of thinking tendencies on online transaction of hybrid retailers. *Journal of Business Research*, *66*(3), 336–344. doi:10.1016/j.jbusres.2011.08.014

Bevan, J., & Murphy, R. (2001). The nature of value created by uk online grocery retailers. *International Journal of Consumer Studies*, *25*(4), 279–289. doi:10.1046/j.1470-6431.2001.00195.x

Bulu, S. T. (2012). Place presence, social presence, co-presence, and satisfaction in virtual worlds. *Computers &amp. Education*, *58*(1), 154–161. doi:10.1016/j.compedu.2011.08.024

Copeland, M. T. (1923). Relation of consumers' buying habits to marketing methods. *Harvard Business Review*, *1*(3), 282–289.

Cristiane, P. S., & Daniel, V. H. F. (2011). Perceptions of justice after recovery efforts in internet purchasing: The impact on consumer trust and loyalty toward retailing sites and online shopping in general. *Brazilian Administration Review*, *8*(3), 225–246. doi:10.1590/S1807-76922011000300002

Drucker, P. F. (1966). What computers will be telling you. *Management Review*, *55*(10), 30.

Drucker, P. F. (1967). The manager and the moron. *Management Review*, *56*(7), 20.

Guitton, M. J. (2012). Living in the hutt space: Immersive process in the star wars role-play community of second life. *Computers in Human Behavior*, *28*(5), 1681–1691. doi:10.1016/j.chb.2012.04.006

Harris, L. C., & Goode, M. M. (2004). The four levels of loyalty and the pivotal role of trust: A study of online service dynamics. *Journal of Retailing*, *80*(2), 139–158. doi:10.1016/j.jretai.2004.04.002

Heinemann, G., & Schwarzl, C. (2010). *New online retailing — what does it mean?. In New online retailing* (pp. 19–91). Gabler.

Holbrook, M. B., & Schindler, R. M. (2003). Nostalgic bonding: Exploring the role of nostalgia in the consumption experience. *Journal of Consumer Behaviour*, *3*(2), 107–127. doi:10.1002/cb.127

Kotler, P. (1965). The competitive marketing simulatora new management tool. *California Management Review*, *7*(3), 49–60. doi:10.2307/41165632

Kotler, P. (2011). Reinventing marketing to manage the environmental imperative. *Journal of Marketing*, *75*(4), 132–135. doi:10.1509/jmkg.75.4.132

Kotler, P., & Caslione, J. A. (2009). How marketers can respond to recession and turbulence. *Journal of Customer Behaviour*, *8*(2), 187–191. doi:10.1362/147539209X459804

Lam, S., Shankar, V., Erramilli, M. K., & Murthy, B. (2004). Customer value, satisfaction, loyalty, and switching costs: An illustration from a business-to-business service context. *Journal of the Academy of Marketing Science*, *32*(3), 293–311. doi:10.1177/0092070304263330

Lejeune, M. A. (2001). Measuring the impact of data mining on churn management. *Internet Research, 11*(5), 375–387. doi:10.1108/10662240110410183

McGoldrick, P. J., Keeling, K. A., & Beatty, S. F. (2008). A typology of roles for avatars in online retailing. *Journal of Marketing Management, 24*(3/4), 433–461. doi:10.1362/026725708X306176

Ramayah, T., Rouibah, K., Gopi, M., & Rangel, G. J. (2009). A decomposed theory of reasoned action to explain intention to use internet stock trading among malaysian investors. *Computers in Human Behavior, 25*(6), 1222–1230. doi:10.1016/j.chb.2009.06.007

Rezaei, S., Shahijan, M. K., Amin, M., & Ismail, W. K. W. (2016). Determinants of app stores continuance behavior: A pls path modelling approach. *Journal of Internet Commerce, 15*(4), 408–440. doi:10.1080/15332861.2016.1256749

Rosen, D. E., & Purinton, E. (2004). Website design: Viewing the web as a cognitive landscape. *Journal of Business Research, 57*(7), 787–794. doi:10.1016/S0148-2963(02)00353-3

See-To, E. W. K., Papagiannidis, S., & Cho, V. (2012). User experience on mobile video appreciation: How to engross users and to enhance their enjoyment in watching mobile video clips. *Technological Forecasting and Social Change, 79*(8), 1484–1494. doi:10.1016/j.techfore.2012.03.005

Shankar, V., Inman, J. J., Mantrala, M., Kelley, E., & Rizley, R. (2011). Innovations in shopper marketing: Current insights and future research issues. *Journal of Retailing, 87. Supplement, 1*(0), S29–S42. doi:10.1016/j.jretai.2011.04.007

van Noort, G., Voorveld, H. A. M., & van Reijmersdal, E. A. (2012). Interactivity in brand web sites: Cognitive, affective, and behavioral responses explained by consumers online flow experience. *Journal of Interactive Marketing, 26*(4), 223–234. doi:10.1016/j.intmar.2011.11.002

Yu, X., Guo, S., Guo, J., & Huang, X. (2011). An extended support vector machine forecasting framework for customer churn in e-commerce. *Expert Systems with Applications, 38*(3), 1425–1430. doi:10.1016/j.eswa.2010.07.049

Zorn, S., Jarvis, W., & Bellman, S. (2010). Attitudinal perspectives for predicting churn. *Journal of Research in Interactive Marketing, 4*(2), 157–169. doi:10.1108/17505931011051687

Chapter 1
Let's Talk SMAC:
The Status of Business Today

Cathrine Linnes
Østfold University College, Norway

ABSTRACT

Social Mobile Analytics and Cloud – SMAC the new abbreviation that every business leader is thinking off. It is also part of everyone's lives these days. SMAC technologies are creating enormous opportunities across industries while the consumer willingly gives up personal information. Cloud technologies have made it possible to collect and store such large amounts of data. While each of these four technologies are able to enhance the business on its own, using these four technologies together as a stack has changed the way businesses are looking to maximize their customer base, enhance brand value and off course, increase company profit. For example, SMAC has forced businesses leaders to make analytics part of their marketing strategy and business operation as a whole.

INTRODUCTION

Social, mobile, analytics, and cloud (SMAC) is among the hottest developments in IT enterprise architecture. Its foremost goal is to get closer to the consumer by exploiting these four technologies (Shelton, 2013). There are three business units that are particularly suited for applying the principle of SMAC: business products, business processes, and business models (Chen et al., 2012). Use of all four SMAC principles to these business units goes beyond simply being competitive–these tools allow for a business to become a disruptive force in their respective market segment (Ackx, 2014).

DOI: 10.4018/978-1-5225-2449-6.ch001

Copyright ©2017, IGI Global. Copying or distributing in print or electronic forms without written permission of IGI Global is prohibited.

Products become personalized through the application of social media (Dewan & Jena, 2014). When linked with a mobile platform, the architecture enables collection of who, what, where, when, and even why the product is being used - as opposed to the traditional transaction data normally available to non-SMAC products (i.e., who bought which product, from where and when as opposed to who used which product where, when, and why). The cloud is conceivably the most viable procedure through which to direct these types of data for further analytics. This analysis provides deeper insights that help steer the decisions of business leaders.

A product that is integrated with social, mobile, analytics, and cloud is also a product that provides a significantly improved customer experience that is more capable of self-service and is more in line with the times. Consumers expect a certain type of convenience and service therefore SMAC has gained such a position in business today. Business methods that are implemented in the cloud and on social platforms gain an efficiency with which it is hard to compete traditionally (Dewan & Jena, 2014). Social and cloud architecture enables the IT raw materials behind the process to be scaled out - that is, adding less expensive hardware, as opposed to scaling up, which means replacing hardware with larger, more high-priced specifications. This allows the business to outlay funds on an as-needed basis. The addition of mobile technologies facilitates collaboration and knowledge sharing from anywhere, anytime. Storing the data (and metadata) behind SMAC-enabled business processes facilitates an easier analysis that allows for data driven decision-making. Besides, a corporate method that is driven by SMAC is better situated to have its mundane tasks automated, and to be more agile and adaptable. Note that in this case, the customer to be closer to is in fact the employee. An enterprise can also base the model of an entire line of business on providing a SMAC technology infrastructure to others (Dewan & Jena, 2014). For example, a traditional software product can be reshaped and offered as a service product in the form of a platform. Interestingly, the best way to provide a SMAC infrastructure is through tools that are themselves SMAC-enabled. This will result in long term growth for the organization and reduce costs, streamline inefficiencies, and improve quality. In fact, even a divided industry can become unified and sustainable again through the utilization of these principles (Thecka, 2014). Ultimately, the SMAC places the small and medium enterprises at the same level with larger organizations.

The objective of this chapter is to provide an overview of SMAC. The importance of implementing SMAC in a business to remain competitive in the future will be emphasized. The different technologies will be introduced, and the benefits and opportunities of SMAC trends will be pointed out. The solution and recommendation, future research directions, and conclusion follow this section.

BACKGROUND

There has been a tremendous push from the U.S. government for schools, universities, businesses, and government agencies to focus on technology, innovation, and effective usage of data. In October 2014, former White House CIO Theresa Payton asked, "Will SMAC hit organizations in the face?" This question should be on the minds of any leader who handles data to meet the demands of his or her job, or for that sake any human being. SMAC is identified as the new set of building blocks for organizations looking ahead to take advantage of internal and external data resources. Theresa Payton warned that implementing SMAC is not a quick shift in mindset or simple investment of hardware and software. It takes time and effort to achieve each pillar of SMAC. Interestingly, the implementation boom of the chief data officer role in the past two years has correlated to how organizations listened to this question, realized they needed to react, and made the changes necessary to realize the benefits (Payton, 2014). One such organization that processes large amounts of data is the United States Government, and President Obama made this clear on June 17, 2014: at TechShop (TechShop is a vibrant, innovative community that provides access to instruction, tools, software and space to its members).

The federal government possesses incredible amounts of data... Essentially, all the weather apps that you have on your phone are all based on data that the government collected. (Obama, 2014)

Less than a year later, the White House hired a professional to manage the amounts of data. Dr. DJ Patil was named the first "deputy chief technology officer for data policy and chief data scientist, making him the first-ever national data scientist" in February 2015 (Smith, 2015). Throughout the United States, organizations are also following the trend of creating chief data officer (CDO) roles. One such city is San Francisco, where Joy Bonaguro was named their first chief data officer in March 2014 (Shueh, 2014). On June 8, 2016 over 96 CDOs and senior level data leaders from North America gathered in Washington D.C.to examine the role of CDOs to better serve the American people and exploit the power of technology and innovation (Bowater, 2016).

Government: Social Application

Social media have provided a platform where the world can use a digital voice to share their concerns and opinions they have at will. Recent data supplied by the Pew Research Center show that the growth of social media has slowed down but the level of user engagement has increased (Duggan et al., 2015). Some interesting facts presented by Duggan et al. (2015) were 52% of online adults use two or more social media sites, 56% of adults older than 65 years of age use Facebook, 53% of adults 18-29 years of age use Instagram, 50% of those with a college degree use LinkedIn, and 42% of women use Pinterest. For instance, the city of San Francisco is concerned about data coming from social media and so are many other city and county officials as well as corporations. Goals set by the city of San Francisco consists of growing and broadening communication and engagement activities and provide mechanisms to elicit and track feedback and knowledge from data users (Bonaguro, 2015). The city of San Francisco currently monitors 33 Facebook accounts, 39 Twitter accounts, and 16 YouTube accounts (Carver, 2013). As one can see, this is quite a bit to keep track of. SMAC helps bring the government closer to its people; however, the use of social media sites requires monitoring and frequent response to be beneficial.

Government: Mobile Application

To detect whether a corporation or government is serious about mobile technologies, simply navigate to its website using a mobile web browser. When navigating to the national award- winning website Hawaii.gov, a web portal spearheaded by former State of Hawaii CIO Sonny Bhagowalia the user is presented with a page that is designed with responsive design in mind. In responsive layout, the page responds to changes in the browser size that go beyond the width scaling of a liquid layout, such as a normal desktop computer (Connolly & Hoar, 2015).

According to Meunier (2015), 82% of Google webmasters claim they use responsive design. However, Meunier states that the percentage fluctuates quite a bit when surveying various webmaster groups. When Meunier analyzed the top tier web sites only 11.8% of these sites used responsive web design. A similar study was conducted in 2013 by Brian Klais of Pure Oxygen Lab, who reported that only 11% of websites were responsive (Klais, 2013). Responsive sites are a must these days to remain competitive and retain users. They certainly give the user a better experience.

Government: Analytics Application

A privately traded company that might want to track its sales exclusively using analytics, the data found at DataSF are to be shared publicly for anyone who wishes to use them. The same goes for data found on other government websites. The Hawaii Open Data Initiative in conjunction with Socrata is a site used to share government data with its citizens. Burt Lum has been extremely active on the open data initiative in Hawaii, which has benefited the public tremendously. The open data initiative has led to many folks getting involved and it has resulted in new ways of presenting' data. An exciting result of DataSF is its Data Academy, the goal of which is to aid data analysts citywide explore, refine, and enhance their skills in data analysis and visualization (DataSF, n.d.). Courses within Data Academy cover everything from analysis, information design, mapping, data management, data visualization and data science. The offering is quite complete and it is certainly one of the better governmental sites. For citizens of San Francisco, links to courses provided by local educational institutions are available (DataSF, n.d.).

Government: Cloud Application

Socrata is the global leader in software solutions that are designed exclusively for digital government and supports the governments open data initiative (Empson, 2012). Socrata's cloud-based, Software as a Service (SaaS) solutions, supported by the Socrata Open Data Network and Socrata Partner Ecosystem, deliver unprecedented data-driven innovation and cost-savings for hundreds of public sector leaders and millions of their constituents around the globe (Socrata, 2016). Further, Socrata provides an astonishing 264 published datasets that are available to the public to use at will (Socrata, 2016). The government gives the public insight to what goes on at the local or federal level. Citizens can freely use the data, analyze it, and find new ways of displaying the data, and the government is embracing the partnership with the general public, who can assist the government in displaying its data. As an example, the former State of Hawaii CIO Sonny Bhagowalia and former Deputy Director at OMIT Randy Baldemor reached out to the author and her class of students at Hawaii Pacific University to build a prototype to help display State of Hawaii's data stored in Socrata. This was a fabulous opportunity for the class to learn more about the government and its operations and to work closely with a great group of state people. The prototype was very well received and was showcased around the state to aid the open data initiative (Linnes et al., 2013). Sonny Bhagowalia and Randy Baldemor are true visionaries and leaders and they have done a tremendous job establishing a comprehensive framework and plan to transform government in Hawaii to improve business processes, modernize the information technology infrastructure and increase transparency and accountability. It has been an honor to collaborate with them both on various projects over last 4 years.

OVERVIEW AND IMPACT OF SMAC TECHNOLOGIES

The IT industry stands at the edge of the most significant revolution in 20 years since client-server architecture and web tier platforms. The merging of social, mobile, analytics and cloud has generated a substantial change in the value that enterprise applications can provide to businesses (Mohapatra, Parisa & Banerjee, 2014).

In January of 2014 it was reported that mobile devices accounted for 55% of the Internet usage in the United States; apps made up 47% of the Internet traffic, and the remaining 8% came from mobile browsers (O'Toole, 2014). Data show that 87% of millennials always have their smartphone by their side, day and night. In addition, 78% of millennials spend over 2 hours a day using their smartphones, while 68% of millennials consider their smartphone to be a personal device (Choen, 2015). According to Cisco (2014), the number of devices that are connected to IP networks will actually be three times bigger than the actual population by 2017. This exponential growth will pose new challenges for data centers, existing information infrastructures, and corporations. As such, within the SMAC area, IT departments will need to supply an infrastructure layer that is capable of dealing with vast amounts of data streaming as well as making informative and intelligent decisions. Gartner predicted that 10% of computers will be learning and not processing by 2017 (Cooney, 2013). Further, according to the National Association of Software and Services Companies (NASSCOM), an additional 10% will be spent on IT to deploy mobile solutions before 2020. This mobility market could be worth $140-150 billion on a worldwide basis (Lawton, 2015). To remain competitive, it is important that corporations incorporate SMAC.

Social

In June 2015, Facebook had an average of 968 million daily and 1.59 billion monthly active users (Facebook, 2015; SocialTimes, 2015). Other popular social networking tools are LinkedIn, Instagram, WhatsApp and Twitter. LinkedIn had 400 million members in 2015 compared to 37 million in 2009 (Statista, 2016b). There were 400 million active users on Instagram in 2015, up from 90 million in 2013 (Statistica, 2016d). WhatsApp is approaching 1 billion active users, up from 200 million in 2013 (Statistica, 2016f). Twitter has 320 million active users every month compared to 30 million in 2010. It is projected to have 111.6 million users by 2019, which will equal 40.7% of the U.S. population (Statistica, 2016e). Many of the social media sites allow cross-posting, which helps organizations and government agencies to reach unlimited numbers of individuals while still achieving one to one contact (Hendricks, 2013). The worldwide magnitude of social media is astonishing.

The broad usage of social media has altered and will continue to change businesses and governments, which are faced with new challenges in terms of reaching and interacting with customers to remain competitive (Rouse, 2014). Social media's exponential growth has not bypassed companies. Many have realized the growth potential for their businesses by paying Facebook to acquire detailed profiles of consumers, so they can then pinpoint likely customers for their products or services. This is common practice of other providers as well. Customer interaction used to mean giving a discount on a customer's birthday, now it means giving a discount on a friend's birthday with recommendations of what that friend would like based on his or her Facebook profile. It has transitioned from an intimate relationship to a borderline intrusive relationship; however, customers are more than willing to give up their privacy for the added perks, discounts, enjoyments and benefits of a personalized shopping experience (Surdak, 2014). Some consumers might not be aware of the trail of information they leave behind every time they visit a website or use a coupon at a store. These organizations are tracking information and running an experiment on us all.

In May 2015, an e-commerce vendor TOMS Shoes used Instagram to help meet its goal to donate a pair of shoes for every pair sold. The campaign resulted in the donation of 296,243 pairs of shoes. TOMS Shoes is active in giving back to the community and those in need (Martin, 2015; TOMS, 2016). A successful campaign that was launched through social media was the Share-a-Coke campaign in the United States. The campaign increased U.S. sales by 11% from prior years as a result of the endorsement from teens via Facebook, Instagram, Twitter, and Tumblr. Another effective campaign were Share Your Ears – with Make A Wish Foundation and Disney where each social media post unlocked a $5 donation from Disney to the Make a Wish Foundation (Gallegos, 2016). Of course there are many more. In cases where budget is limited, social media has the potential to bring marketing creativity to life (Fulgoni, 2015). It is almost impossible to run a business without social media.

On the contrary, consumers have become more empowered than ever. Social media gives consumers a global platform from which to share immediate reviews of experiences with companies and the rest of the world. It has been suggested that the speed at which reviews are posted following a negative experience can be measured in seconds. The social norm is for social media users to bare their souls on any and all issues, and they expect the same from the companies on which they spend their money. Companies must follow suit and bare their souls on social media, especially if they fail in the delivery of their services (Surdak, 2014). To better understand, if 10 people one respects all of a sudden follow the same Twitter account, one should not ignore the signs. Social media is so powerful and the influence people can have on a business is tremendous.

Moreover, large corporations have employees in place whose duty is to go through social data and find emerging clues and patterns and respond to accusations. Vendors like DataSift a leader in human intelligence are going through what people talk about, what they are interested in, what they are looking forward to, as well as identifying the basic family demographics of social network users (Hassell, 2015).

Mobile

The explosion of mobile computing can be evidenced by the 2.27 trillion text messages sent between Americans in 2012 alone. This resulted in mobile data traffic growth of more than 100% that same year, totaling 1.1 billion GB of data (Surdak, 2014). In 2015 people sent 8.3 billion text messages. This is approximately 23 billion messages per day (Teckst, 2015). These numbers support the statistics showing that smartphones connect to the Internet more often than computers do just because users carry their smart devices with them all time. These devices can do pretty much everything a computer can do; they just come with a smaller screen. Companies have realized the power of mobile devices and the potential for consumer personalization and convenience that these technologies can offer. For example, the savviest companies identify when the customer needs to only enter numbers into a form on their website. To accommodate this, a small numeric keypad will appear on the screen as opposed to the unnecessary QWERTY keypad. Mobile users appreciate this added touch.

Mobile computing has grown beyond mobile versions of websites to include applications. Companies allow customers to download their app, usually for free, so their customers have immediate access to the most pertinent company information and opportunities for purchasing and service. Repeat customers have the convenient option of clicking an icon (app) on their device as opposed to having to do a web search for the company website and navigating through countless webpages. In 2012 Apple announced that it had reached 25 billion app downloads, and this number is expected to reach 268.69 billion in 2017 (Statista, 2016c; Surdak, 2014). Moreover, there are 2 million available apps to choose from on the Apple app Store today, and the number of apps and downloads keeps increasing (Statista, 2016a). Such apps provide traveler and commuter services, point of sale, stock trading, emergency medical care, law enforcement, package delivery, education, and insurance (Helal, 2002). For example, FedEx, USPS, and UPS utilize mobile computing to send updates on package tracking, banks send fraud alerts or account balance updates, and hospitals send appointment reminders through text messaging or app notifications.

Nearly 90% of the Facebook users and approximately 80% of the Twitter users are using mobile devices to generate news. According to Rouse (2014), a competitive advantage arises only due to the fact, that all four technologies are used jointly but the mobile trend is more than cellphones connected to the Internet. There are also many technologies such as different kinds of sensors, that are used in mobile devices. Radio-frequency identification (RFID) tags can be attached to cash, clothing, and possessions, or implanted in human beings and pets, and the possibility of reading personally linked information without consent has started to raise serious privacy concerns. Another example is driverless cars or electric vehicles like Tesla, which are able to create more data (e.g. speed, acceleration) in addition to location information. Therefore, continued increasing number of devices will create more data, and that in turn will lead to automatic data exploitation.

Mobile devices make it faster and easier to connect with anyone at any time; they are designed to foster social interactions (PricewaterhouseCoopers, hereafter PwC, 2015). Mobile devices are the cornerstone of how new business is being built. With them, users continue with their personal or business interactions by connecting to various wireless signals and near-field communication (NFC) devices (Hassell, 2015). The spread of affordable 3G, 4G, 4G LTE, and the upcoming 5G networks is driving the growth of mobile apps, and the industry is shifting from the PC/ laptop to mobile devices. There are 4.61 billion mobile subscribers globally, with a projection of 5.07 billion subscribers in 2019 (Statista, 2016). Each generation is supposedly faster, more secure, and more reliable. The reliability factor is of course the hardest obstacle to overcome.

Analytics

Social analytics is defined as the process of collecting, measuring, analyzing and interpreting the results of interactions and associations among people topics and ideas. Social analytics is viewed as an umbrella term that includes a number of specialized analysis techniques, such as social filtering, social network analysis, social channel analysis, sentiment analysis and social media analytics (Rozwell, Sallam & Sussin, 2013). The prevalence of social media creates an enormous amount of unstructured data, or data that are not organized in a pre-defined manner. Social media analytics is the mechanism by which such data are analyzed. The results of these analyses often show an underlined relationship between entities. These relationships are normally unnoticed or unseen by the naked eye. As a communal form social media is often public facing.

Social media moves quicker than the speed of business, and it is the number one item on any CEO's list. An overall strategy must be applied that brings both value and purpose. For example, an Indian food manufacturer leveraged social analytics to identify its brand and product shortcomings in order to make brand and product improvements. By making changes and improvements based upon this insight, the company was able to decrease negative comments by 42% (Sussin, Rozwell & Sallam, 2015). This strategy improved the overall reception of the product, which resulted in a financial windfall. At the minimum this process was able to divert potential loss of sales. More importantly, it improved upon something, that could not be bought: the reputation of the company.

In 2015, more than 30% of analytics projects will deliver insights based on structured and unstructured data (Rozwell, Sallam, & Sussin, 2013). Social media is the clear leader of unstructured data. Whether from a desktop, laptop, tablet, or mobile phone, data are input into social media. The unstructured data arrive in the form of comments, blogs, tweets, or instant messages. This is a bidirectional communication between creators and consumers. Creators are able to reach an abundance of potential clients while consumers are able to voice their opinions and make more informed decisions (Leskovec, 2011). Ultimately, social media analytics will be used as a tool to augment decision-making. The costs of these tools fluctuates. In a recent study it was suggested that the financial responsibility of running social media analytics would begin at $18,000 a year and could exceed six-figures per year (Sussin, Rozwell & Sallam, 2013). Not everyone who does social media analytics has such an expansive budget. There are alternatives that are significantly cheaper or even free. The open source alternatives are robust; however, there is the old adages that you get what you pay for. Buyers beware.

Analytics is the discovery and communication of meaningful patterns in data. These enable organizations to mine public, organizational, and workforce data to generate insights and enable better, faster decision-making and new ways of doing business (PwC, 2015). Billions of gigabytes of data are generated by companies and individuals each year. Companies that analyze and gain insights from such data can emerge as leaders (KPMG, 2013). In fact, 93% of United States executives believe their companies are losing revenue by not leveraging available data (Neistat, 2013). Companies cannot just collect and store information; they must do something with the data to remain in power.

In 2013, organizations worldwide spent $31 billion on Big Data, and the spending is predicted to reach $114 billion in 2018 (Capgemini Consulting, 2014). Analytics can assist companies to understand how people interact with other people, goods, and media. The online blogging service Twitter was launched in 2006. Users can follow other users to become subscribers. Status updates also known as tweets are posted, and followers can read these posts. According to Asur and Huberman (2010), social media data can be used to predict events. The two researchers conducted an interesting study where they analyzed 2.89 million tweets (status posts) from 1.2 million Twitter users and extracted keywords for 24 block buster movies. They showed that a movie with a small average rate of tweets per hour (e.g., 10) will be pulled from theatres in a few weeks. On the other hand, a movie will trigger an enormous splash if it has a large rate of tweets per hour (e.g., over 1000). More precisely, they showed that rate of tweets could be used to predict box office sales of movies with a high accuracy (Liu, 2014). Therefore, user data created with social networks, such as Twitter can be used to predict movie revenue. These are extremely powerful tools that should not be ignored. Network analysis is also powerful in preventing crime and predicting election results.

Cloud

Companies such as Google, Amazon, Microsoft, and FDC Servers saw the business potential in buying server space and reselling it to small and medium-sized companies as cloud services. Take for example FDC Servers, which currently has 13 data centers, over 10,000 customers, and 10 Tbps Internet backbone, and reports 99.995% reliability (FDC Servers, 2016). This brings flexibility, cost effectiveness, and efficiency to businesses purchasing the company's services. Company leaders will then be able to focus on what they are good at and will not necessary need to become IT experts. If a company was just starting out, instead of spending millions on hardware, software, brick-and-mortar storefronts, and IT personnel, it could simply purchase cloud space for thousands of dollars and test its business plan and growth potential on the Internet. In 2013, the annual data center traffic amounted to approximately 3.1 zettabytes (1 zettabyte is equal to 1 billion terabytes), and it will increase to 8.6 zettabytes by the end of 2018 (CISCO, 2014). The rise is caused by new technologies; such as cloud services. Famous applications, such as Google Drive, Amazon Cloud Drive, Dropbox, and iCloud are used in everyday life to share files and provide easy access to the user. There are different reasons why cloud services are becoming more and more important. A compound annual growth rate (CAGR) of 32% was expected for global cloud traffic from 2013 to 2018, according to a technical report of CISCO. Further, in 2015, around 1.387 billion people were expected to use personal cloud storage, and this number was expected to increase to around 2 billion users by 2018 (CISCO, 2014).

Cloud computing offers the flexibility to tailor a company's data needs based on its number of users or take it a step further by adjusting to peak shopping seasons (Surdak, 2014). This pay- per-use framework cuts costs and demands fewer personnel to manage servers. Since cloud space is considered a rental space, creating no asset, it is referred to as an operational expenditure. In other words, it can be subtracted from profits. Additional benefits of cloud computing are abundant. Companies can access applications anywhere on any device, receive software and platform upgrades from the service provider, outsource the headache of IT, increase employee collaboration on projects through the use of Dropbox, iCloud and Google Drive. It is even suggested that cloud computing has lent to an increase in telecommuting and subsequently a reduction in travel and environmental impact, as suggested by the fact that 8% of the UK workforce worked from home in 2005 (William, 2010). The company itself cannot compete with cloud providers, companies like Amazon or FDC Servers mentioned above can customize a new server in no time and they provide excellent security monitoring services.

Abhishek Mehta, a digital marketing evangelist for Google, called today's extremely fast- paced and competitive technology industry the next industrial revolution in suggested that the massive amount of data circulating the digital world will replace raw materials, and that manufacturing factories will be swapped for data factories (Minelli et al., 2013). Then, it will become an absolute necessity for companies to utilize the modern raw material, data, to gain a competitive advantage in today's business environment. According to a study published on cloudcomputing-news.net, as of 2015, 89% of the Fortune 500 companies had changed since 1955. The Fortune 500 list is now increasingly being replaced by the Digital 500 companies. Needless to say, the general public could make a good guess which companies lead this list. By July 2015, Google, Facebook, Amazon, Apple, and Netflix were among the six companies that produced more than half of the NASDAQ market that accounts to $664 billion (Moyse, 2015). These companies are also companies that are responsible for generating the massive amount of data we see today. Netflix alone has reached 81 million subscribers, and 42% of its customer base is outside of the United States (Popper, 2016).

One study found that 89% of the business leaders were convinced that Big Data would have a revolutionary impact on business processes. In this study, 83% of the companies had implemented Big Data projects to earn a competitive advantage in their industries. In addition, Wikibon forecast tells us that by 2025, the global Big Data market will reach $122 billion in revenue (Moyse, 2015). It is important to note that the explosion of Big Data was made possible by the advent of cloud computing. As both technologies continue to grow, more and more people will understand the power of cloud computing. According to a survey by Forbes.com in 2015, 93% of the surveyed organizations were using cloud applications or experimenting with it. The enterprises with a hybrid cloud strategy in 2015 increased by nearly 10% from the previous year, from 74% to 82%. Also, 88% of the organizations were utilizing the public cloud, whereas 63% were utilizing a private cloud (Kepes, 2015).

Certain organizations say that cloud storage is proving to be more flexible and efficient for storing and accessing Big Data (Yasuhiro, 2012). In addition, all scientists are encouraged to place their data on the cloud for easy access, and the Big Query by Google offers the simplicity to make it possible (Dobre & Xhafa, 2014). According to Chandran, Cloud storage is a smart answer to the challenge facing Big Data in terms of efficiency, scalability, and cost as well as providing reliability and concurrent access. Consequently, many CEOs are putting effort into identifying the types of data and workloads transferrable to the cloud as they realize their potential insights (Chandran, 2015). This is backed up by the belief of some of the big players in the industry that the return on investment is great in embracing the cloud (Minelli et al., 2013). Another advantage is that users do not have to estimate the hardware capacity or resources for the future because the cloud structure easily scales up or down, when the need changes. Hassan (2011) also pointed out, that cloud services allow companies to better respond to market fluctuations. The opportunity for large-scale parallel processing appeared with the emergence of cloud computing. This is useful for complex computations or time-consuming tasks. A cloud service provider has one or more data centers that can be accessed by users. Only a credit card is needed to get on-demand access to 100,000+ computers distributed throughout the world (Foster et al., 2008). A similar improvement in speed and agility for organizations was pointed out by Amazon Web Services (2016). The time that is, needed to build new infrastructure for data center or to extend it decreased to just a few hours or minutes. In fact, it is only a few clicks away, and users can access it anytime.

There are also several drawbacks that are inevitable with the extensive use of Big Data and cloud services. High-speed Internet connections are necessary for cloud computing, especially when enormous data sets are used. The downtime problem of servers is another challenge. No cloud service provider claims to have permanent uptime. Apple's iCloud service suffered a seven-hour outage in June 2015, which, in turn, affected 11 of the company's cloud-based services. Approximately 40% of all iCloud users were unable to use the service at that time (Kobialka, 2015). Regarding security, when we deal with data, especially when it is stored centrally on cloud servers, users should keep in mind that all information is accessible from anywhere on the Internet. Computer hackers can get access to every text-message and to phone calls of users, and they can steal sensitive data, such as credit card information, and use it to make money. An even simpler way to hack in is through user passwords to access the cloud, a specific computer software or just a cell phone. According to Cloud Security (2012), passwords such as, "123456" or "password" are very common. Okyle (2015) also mentioned, that 3 out of 4 consumers use duplicate passwords, and many of them have not changed their passwords for 5 or even 10 years. With this knowledge, many users can improve security easily. Cloud computing has an immense potential and can change Internet and user habits. We should be aware, that security and privacy issues should be taken into account, especially when sensitive data are used. The increasing demand of cloud services can also improve security standards. Overall, this summary has shown that advantages are able to outweigh the disadvantages.

SOLUTIONS AND RECOMMENDATIONS

The integration of SMAC requires businesses and governments to create clear policies and guidelines for its organization to be successful. Furthermore, management tools that can automate the business process need to be in place. Organizations need to ask several questions before implementing any social media technologies into their operations.

First, what is the purpose of the social media account, and what is the organization trying to accomplish? Is the purpose aligned with the company goals? It is very important that the social media accounts are aligned with the business's goals. They need to be part of trying to drive the business in a certain direction. For example, it is important to use some time to try to find a proper username when setting up a Twitter account.

Second, who will be responsible for the account? If organizations have a Twitter account, it is important that they post something every day. You see many organizational leaders who create an account and then it is forget about it. Also, when you have a Facebook account, it is important to monitor the conversation. If customers are complaining about the service or products, try to rectify the situation and show them that you care.

Third, it is also important to decide what type of information should be posted. This will help the employees to focus on the strategic plan of the business. Having a communication plan in place might be a good idea, and if the organization is planning to be collecting feedback, strategize around this.

Forth, how will organizations secure their social media account online? This is public face of the organization, so important measures need to be in place.

Netflix is a great example of a corporation that has empowered SMAC. Customers can either log in with their username and password or opt to use their Facebook credentials to begin streaming a movie. It might be convenient but they are of course giving away some privacy. On the website itself, customers can provide social feedback by rating the movie they just watched. Customers may also write a review or share what they have watched with friends on Facebook or Twitter. Netflix stores this information in the cloud, which allows the company to analyze its customers in detail and provide one-on-one marketing. This should be the ultimate goal of every organization.

FUTURE RESEARCH DIRECTIONS

Gartner, Inc. forecasts that 6.4 billion connected things will be in use worldwide in 2016, up 30% from 2015, and number will reach 20.8 billion by 2020. It is estimated that in 2016, 5.5 million new things will get connected every day (Gartner, 2015b). All of these sensors and devices are producing an enormous amount of data and this is commonly referred to as the Internet of Things (IoT). McKinsey & Company (2015) estimated a potential economic impact of as much as $11.1 trillion per year in 2025 for IoT applications. As IoT continues to evolve, it will lead to more robust data analytics.

An opportunity for the analysis of Big Data in a variety of applications is predictive maintenance. Previously, sensors were used to build and run a machine, and that changed the manufacturing process from manual to automatic production. But manufacturers of wearables, computers, equipment, or clothing can improve the efficiency of their machines even more. According to McKinsey & Company (2015), manufacturers that implement analytic software in their daily operations as well as sensors can reduce downtime by 50%. Real-time monitoring of equipment, such as with sensors or other parts of a machine, can help to reduce downtime before the quality of products diminishes. The result is, that a technical service will not only depend on technicians (implying their skills to observe damages) or maintenance plans (which can be imperfect). This can change the maintenance model from repair and replace to predict and prevent (McKinsey & Company, 2015).

Another trend that one can see is analytics being used in the health care industry. Once in a while patients die in the hospital because they get the wrong medication or the wrong diagnosis is put in place. According to the report "To Err Is Human: Building a Safer Health System," it is estimated that these preventable blunders cost between $17 billion and $29 billion (Institute of Medicine, 1999). In 2008 preventable medical errors were reported to cost 19.5 billion in the United States alone (Andel, Davidow, Hollander & Moreno, 2012). In 2014 a survey of health information technology (IT) leaders found that the U.S. healthcare system could save a total of $23.4 billion in 2016 by implementing SMAC. This is a 11% saving from social media, 16% from mobile, 21% from analytics, and 20% from cloud (Deloitte, 2016). On can clearly see that monitoring of people's health can create a financial benefit to society and health providers. Technologies such as smart pills or nanobots could be available in the near future to reduce the errors. The previously mentioned devices can send information via wireless connections, accelerating medical findings. Unnecessary surgeries can be reduced or omitted. The result is a reduction of working hours and costs. According to Casado and Younas (2014), remote monitoring could create around $1.1 trillion a year in savings. In addition, when there is a drug shortage or when faced with counterfeit drugs, or perhaps misplaced equipment mobile analytics and cloud technologies can aid health providers to make their supply chains more data driven, efficient and secure (Deloitte, 2016).

Beside humans, one could also monitor other areas, such as cities, countries or the entire word for that sake. An important and fast-developing research topic is analytical chemistry (e.g., to monitor air pollution). It is reported that a 35% increase of emissions from human activities expressed as carbon dioxide equivalents from 1990 to 2010 totaled nearly 46 billion metric tons (United States Environmental Protection Agency, 2014). Moreover, other cities around the globe, such as Chinese megacities suffer (visible) smog, which also is caused by air pollution. This visible pollution also affects the Earth's climate, forcing governments to limit emissions of greenhouse gases. The Kyoto Protocol is an example of an international treaty to reduce these emissions worldwide. But a drawback is that major polluters- including China, India and the United States-"... will not ratify any treaty that will commit them legally to reduce CO_2 emissions" (United Nations, 2014). Environmental pollution is a major concern both today and in the future. Not only should governments be conscientious, but companies should try to reduce waste that causes pollution. In fact, every human being should have this goal, because we only have one planet to live on.

Some of the major trends in 2015 include advanced analytics, Big Data and the IoT. The Gartner (2015a) Hype Cycle for Emerging Technologies provides a cross-industry perspective on technologies and emerging trends for the future. Another realm, for example, is autonomous vehicles, which are an omnipresent technology in the car industry.

CONCLUSION

Cloud technology is a way to maximize the effectiveness of shared resources. Different types of cloud computing are available to users. There are public clouds, private cloud services, and a mix of both, namely hybrid clouds. An example is the Apache Hadoop product, which was invented for distributed processing and storage. The financial aspect, caused by higher economies of scale, is a main reason for the cloud's success. Therefore, wider ranges of companies are able to use Big Data analytics. According to Hardiman (2013), cloud computing is available for companies of all sizes. Moreover, users can make use of the parallel processing to accelerate computations and calculations. In fact, only a credit card is needed to get on-demand access to 100,000+ computers distributed throughout the world (Foster et al., 2008).

Security and privacy issues should be taken into account, especially when sensitive data are used. The main concern about the cloud can be, that it is easy for criminals to get a lot of information with little effort. When criminals get access to a data warehouse where all the user information is saved, it is much more efficient for them because they only access one data warehouse but get information from several cloud users. There are also risks companies might not think of when using cloud services. According to Hughes (2014), companies cannot see what measures cloud service providers use to secure their data.

Social media tools cover similar opportunities as mobile and cloud computing. Eventually, an increasing number of connected devices and likewise the demand of SMAC technologies can improve these security standards. Overall, the advantages of these tools outweigh the disadvantages. Cloud computing is a network-based service, served by virtual hardware that runs on one or more real machines. Virtual servers do not physically exist and can therefore be easily relocated and scaled up or down, potentially running in a private or public cloud. "The cloud" maximizes the effectiveness of shared resources and increases flexibility and agility in deploying and maintaining enterprise technology (PwC, 2015). Microsoft is using Hadoop in the cloud to make learning available for data scientists so they can filter through data and have the service itself suggest comparisons, predictions, and key points (Hassell, 2015). The positive feedback on SMAC are coming from CEOs and top-performing companies where 86% of US CEOs think that it is important that they themselves champion the use of digital technologies. They are tapping into social networks. In fact, 29% of top-performing companies gather ideas for technology innovation through employee idea marketplaces (PwC, 2015). There are also some less-than- positive effects. The enterprises that are making the most sustained progress with SMAC and a services-enabled future all have great training programs in place. According to Cognizant (2013), "We need to recognize that SMAC and emerging alternative IT delivery vehicles are like 'free puppies.' They are cheap and cute on the front end, but they require funding, health checks, care and support over time." Furthermore, only 13% of organizations have achieved full-scale production for their Big Data implementations, and 60% of senior executives believe that Big Data will disrupt their industry within the next three years (Capgemini Consulting, 2014). According to Deloitte (2016) 50% of IT and technology, 46% if telecommunications, 35% of entertainment, media, and publishing, 34% of automotive, 34 of professional service, 31% of transportation and tourism, but only 22% of education, 16% of government to mention a few sectors are claiming their company is digitally maturing. There is still room for improvements.

Though individuals are enjoying less energy consumption at their homes as they are shying away from PCs, and businesses are moving away from mainframes and towards the cloud, there is still a cost of such business. That cost goes to the huge data centers that provide the source for cloud computing and Big Data collection. According to Berl et al., (2010) Amazon.com reported that expenses related to the cost and operation of its servers account for 53% of the total budget, while energy-related costs amount to 42% of the total. Given the increase in cloud computing, today massive facilities are needed to house servers. Some of these facilities are the size of warehouses, consuming large amounts of energy, and use diesel generators. As a result, major data centers not only consume large amounts of energy but also now emit significant amounts of greenhouse gases. In 2012, Apple's carbon footprint was 30.9 million metric tons, while Facebook's carbon footprint was 384,000 thousand metric tons (Story, 2014). As much as we are saving energy in our homes and business, the carbon footprint is very high in the centralized data centers. CEO's must continue to prepare themselves for the abundance of information they can obtain through SMAC. Every enterprise will use at least one technology of SMAC, and the majority will strive to implement all four, something we can already appreciate. The bottom line is that the four SMAC technologies go hand in hand. SMAC technologies cannot be ignored by organizations. They have changed the way organizations must operate in years to come. IT does not matter whether a corporation is large or small; it is important that organizations pay attention to the upcoming changes and try to implement the technologies into their strategic plans.

REFERENCES

Ackx, S. (2014). Emerging Technologies, Disrupt or be Disrupted. In ISSE 2014 Securing Electronic Business Processes (pp. 177-187). Springer Fachmedien Wiesbaden.

Amazon Web Services. (2016). *What is Cloud Computing?* Retrieved January 31, 2016, from https://aws.amazon.com/what-is-cloud-computing/

Andel, C., Davidow, S. L., Hollander, M., & Moreno, D. A. (2012). The economics of health care quality and medical errors. *Journal of Health Care Finance*, *39*(1), 39–50. PMID:23155743

Asur, S., & Huberman, B. A. (2010). *Predicting the future with social media*. HP Labs. Retrieved January 31, 2016, from http://www.hpl.hp.com/research/scl/papers/socialmedia/socialmedia.pdf

Berl, A. (2010). *Energy-Efficient Cloud Computing*. Retrieved January 31, 2016 from: https://www.researchgate.net/publication/46116227_Energy-Efficient_Cloud_Computing

Bonaguro, J. (2015). *Data in San Francisco: Meeting supply, spurring demand* (FY2015-16). Retrieved January 31, 2016, from https://docs.google.com/document/d/1mqunsT9wXRt-mBbOmY3WcEJmsWSpMOISotZ1WHZ1_IU/edit?usp=embed_facebook

Bowater, J. (2016). *Welcome to the Chief Data Officer Forum, Government*. Retrieved February 10, 2016, from http://www.chiefdataofficergovernment.com

Capgemini Consulting. (2014). *Cracking the Data Conundrum: How Successful Companies Make Big Data Operational*. Retrieved February 10, 2016, from http://www.datascienceassn.org/sites/default/files/Cracking%20the%20Data%20Conundrum%20-%20How%20Successful%20Companies%20Make%20Big%20Data%20Operational.pdf

Carver, S. (2013). *How the City of San Francisco uses Social Media to Connect with Citizens*. Retrieved February 10, 2016, from http://www.exacttarget.com/blog/how-the-city-of-san-francisco-uses-social-media/

Casado, R., & Younas, M. (2014). Emerging trends and technologies in big data processing. *Concurrency and Computation, 27*(8), 2078–2209. doi:10.1002/cpe.3398

Chen, H., Chiang, R. H., & Storey, V. C. (2012). Business Intelligence and Analytics: From Big Data to Big Impact. *Management Information Systems Quarterly, 36*(4), 1165–1188.

Choen, H. (2015). *2015 Mobile Marketing – 19 Research Charts*. Retrieved February 10, 2016, from http://heidicohen.com/2015-mobile-marketing/

CISCO. (2014). *Cisco Global Cloud Index: Forecast and Methodology, 2013–2018*. Retrieved February 10, 2016, from https://www.terena.org/mail-archives/storage/pdfVVqL9tLHLH.pdf

Cloud Security. (2012). *What security lessons can be learned from LinkedIn?* Retrieved February 10, 2016, from http://www.cloudcomputing-news.net/news/2012/jun/18/security-lessons-learned-from-linkedin/

Cognizant. (2013). Keep on Smacking: Taking Social, Mobile, Analytics and Cloud to the Bottom Line. *Cognizanti, 6*(1). Retrieved February 10, 2016, from: https://www.cognizant.com/InsightsWhitepapers/Cognizanti-Journal-XaaS-Code-Halos-SMAC-and-the-Future-of-Work.pdf

Connolly, R., & Hoar, R. (2015). *Fundamentals of Web Development*. Boston: Pearson. Retrieved March 5, 2016, from: https://scanlibs.com/fundamentals-of-web development/

Cooney, M. (2013). *Gartner: Top 10 future strategic IT predictions*. Retrieved March 5, 2016, from http://www.networkworld.com/article/2225521/malware-cybercrime/gartner--top-10-future-strategic-it-predictions.html

Data, S. F. (n.d.). *About*. Retrieved March 5, 2016, from http://datasf.org/about/

Deloitte. (2016). *SMAC: Better together Improving health care efficiency with social, mobile, analytics, and cloud technologies*. Retrieved September 28, 2016, from https://www2.deloitte.com/content/dam/Deloitte/us/Documents/life-sciences-health-care/us-lshc-smac-better-together.pdf

Dewan, B., & Jena, S. R. (2014, December). The State-Of-The-Art of Social, Mobility, Analytics and Cloud Computing an Empirical Analysis. In *High Performance Computing and Applications (ICHPCA), 2014 International Conference on* (pp. 1-6). IEEE.

Duggan, M., Ellison, N. B., Lampe, C., Lenhart, A., & Madden, M. (2015). *Social Media Update 2014*. Retrieved March 5, 2016, from http://www.pewinternet.org/files/2015/01/ PI_SocialMediaUpdate20144.pdf

Empson, R. (2012). *Clouds & APIs: Mayor Lee Unveils The San Francisco Open Data Cloud*. Retrieved March 5, 2016, from http://techcrunch.com/2012/03/09/san-francisco-open-data/

Facebook. (2015). *Our Mission*. Retrieved March 5, 2016, from http://newsroom.fb.com/company-info/

FDC Servers. (2016). *The Bandwidth Authority*. Retrieved September 27, 2016, from https://fdcservers.net

Foster, I., Zhao, Y., Raicu, I., & Lu, S. (2008). *Cloud Computing and Grid Computing 360-Degree Compared*. Retrieved March 5, 2016, from https://arxiv.org/pdf/0901.0131.pdf

Fulgoni, G. M. (2015). How Brands Using Social Media Ignite Marketing and Drive Growth. *Journal of Advertising Research*, 235–236.

Gallegos, J. A. (2016, April). *The Best Social Media Campaigns of 2016*. Retrieved September 28, 2016, from http://www.tintup.com/blog/the-best-social-media-campaigns-of-2016-so-far/

Gartner. (2015a). *Gartner's 2015 Hype Cycle for Emerging Technologies Identifies the Computing Innovations That Organizations Should Monitor*. Retrieved March 5, 2016 from http://www.gartner.com/newsroom/id/3114217

Gartner. (2015b). *Gartner Says 6.4 Billion Connected "Things" Will Be in Use in 2016, Up 30 Percent From 2015*. Retrieved March 5, 2016 from http://www.gartner.com/newsroom/ id/3165317

Hardiman, N. (2013). *Cloud computing and the rise of big data*. Retrieved March 5, 2016, from http://www.techrepublic.com/blog/the-enterprise-cloud/cloud-computing-and-the-rise-of-big-data/

Hassan, Q. F. (2011). *Demystifying cloud computing*. Retrieved March 5, 2016, from http://static1.1.sqspcdn.com/static/f/702523/10181434/1294788395300/201101-Hassan.pdf

Hassell, J. (2015, May 4). *Talking SMAC: Revisiting social, mobile, analytics and cloud*. Retrieved September 26, 2016 from http://www.cio.com/article/2918194/cloud-computing/taking-smac-revisiting-social-mobile-analytics-and-cloud.html

Helal, A. (2002). *Anytime, Anywhere Computing: Mobile Computing Concepts and Technology*. New York, NY: The Springer International Series in Engineering and Computer Science.

Hendricks, D. (2013). *Complete History of Social Media: Then and Now*. Retrieved March 5, 2016, from http://smallbiztrends.com/2013/05/the-complete-history-of-social-media-infographic.html

Hughes, J. (2014). *Data breaches in the cloud: Who's responsible?* Retrieved March 5, 2016, from http://www.govtech.com/security/Data-Breaches-in-the-Cloud-Whos-Responsible.html

Institute of Medicine. (1999). *To err is human: Building a safer health system*. Retrieved March 5, 2016, from https://www.nationalacademies.org/hmd/~/media/Files/Report% 20Files/ 1999/To-Err-is Human/To%20Err%20is%20Human%20 1999%20% 20report%20brief.pdf

Kepes, B. (2015). *New Stats from the State of Cloud Report*. Retrieved March 5, 2016, from http://www.forbes.com/sites/benkepes/2015/03/04/new-stats-from-the-state-of-cloud-report/

Klais, B. (2013, June). *Research: Two-Thirds of the Fortune 100 are not Mobile-Optimized for Google*. Retrieved September 26, 2016, from http://pureoxygenlabs.com/research two thirds-of-the-fortune-100-are-not-mobile-optimized-for-google/

Kobialka, D. (2015). *7 Worst Cloud Outages of 2015 (So Far)*. Retrieved March 5, 2016, from http://talkincloud.com/cloud-computing/06172015/7-worst-cloud-outages-2015-so-far#slide-0-field_images-46431

KPMG. (2013). *The SMAC Code Embracing new technologies for future business*. Retrieved April 10, 2016, from https://www.kpmg.com/IN/en/IssuesAndInsights/ArticlesPublications/ Documents/The-SMAC-code-Embracing-new-technologies-for-future-business.pdf

Lawton, R. (2015). *SMAC – Social, Mobile, Analytics, Cloud: A Guide*. Retrieved March 20, 2016, from http://www.arrkgroup.com/thought-leadership/smac-social-mobile-analytics-cloud-a-guide/

Leskovec, J. (2011). *Social Media Analytics: Tracking, Modeling and Predicting the Flow of Information through Networks*. Retrieved March 10, 2016, from https://pdfs.semanticscholar.org/7ec6/c63dc0b12cb7e00122ffe08daf1cbd28cba9.pdf

Linnes, C., Viwatmanitsakul, B., Ladegaard, M., Cheng, F., Alamran, S., & Befus, N. … Tabor, R. (2013). *Welcome to Open Data for Hawaii*. Retrieved March 10, 2016, from http://data.hpu.edu/index.html

Liu, H. (2014). *How to Mine Social Media*. Retrieved March 10, 2016, from http://theinstitute.ieee.org/ieee-roundup/members/achievements/how-to-mine-social-media

Martin, J. A. (2015). *11 most memorable social media marketing successes of 2015*. Retrieved March 10, 2016 from http://www.cio.com/article/2988313/social-networking/11-most-memorable- social-media-marketing-successes-of-2015.html#slide4

McKinsey & Company. (2015). *The Internet of Things: Mapping the Value Beyond the Hype (Tech. Rep.)*. Mc Kinsey Global Institute.

Meunier, B. (2015, January). *82% Of Sites Use Responsive Web Design In 2015? Try 11.8%?* Retrieved September 26, 2016 from http://marketingland.com/82-sites-use-responsive-web-design-2015-try-11-8-114050

Minelli, M., Chambers, M., & Dhiraj, A. (2013). *Big Data Technology. Big Data, Big Analytics: Emerging Business Intelligence and Analytic Trends for Today's Businesses*. Hoboken, NJ: John Wiley & Sons. doi:10.1002/9781118562260

Mohapatra, B., Parisa, V., & Banerjee, J. (2014). *The Value of Big Data Analytics to the Business* (Vol. 5). ISACA Journal.

Moyse, I. (2015). *Big data, Cloud, Mobility, and Why IT Needs to Move at the Speed of Business*. Retrieved March 15, 2016, from http://www.cloudcomputing-news.net/news/2015/aug/25/big-data-cloud-mobility-and-why-it-needs-move-speed-business

Neistat, M. (2013). *What is the 3rd Platform and How Will It Affect Business?* Retrieved March 15, 2016, from https://technologyfirst.org/magazine-articles/124-may-2013/843-mark-neistat-us-signal-company.html

O'Toole, J. (2014). *Mobile apps overtake PC Internet usage in U.S.* Retrieved March 5, 2016, from http://money.cnn.com/2014/02/28/technology/mobile/mobile-apps-internet/

Obama, B. (2014). *Remarks by the President in Q&A with TechShop Workers*. Presented at the Address at TechShop, Pittsburgh, PA. Retrieved March 11, 2016, from https://www.whitehouse.gov/the-press-office/2014/06/17/remarks-president-qa-techshop-workers

Okyle, C. (2015). *Password statistics: The bad, the worse and the ugly (infographic)*. Retrieved March 11, 2016, from http://www.entrepreneur.com/article/246902

Payton, T. (2014). *Will SMAC Hit You in the Face?* Retrieved March, 15, 2016, from http://www.fortalicesolutions.com/blog/2014/10/27/will-smac-hit-you-in-the-face/

Popper, B. (2016, April). *Netflix passes 81 million subscribers, but predicts slower growth ahead*. Retrieved September 27, 2016, from http://www.theverge.com/2016/4/18/11454362/netflix-q1-2016-earnings-81-million-subscribers

PricewaterhouseCoopers. (2015). *The connected workforce is talking SMAC. Are you ready?* Retrieved March 10, 2016, from: https://www.pwc.com/us/en/people-management/publications/assets/ connected-workforce.pdf

Rouse, M. (2014). *SMAC (social, mobile, analytics and cloud) definition*. Retrieved March 10, 2016, from http://searchcio.techtarget.com/definition/SMAC-social-mobile-analytics-and-cloud

Rozwell, C., Sallam, L, R., & Sussin, J. (2013, September 27). *Who's who in Social Analytics*. Gartner.

Shelton, T. (2013). Appendix: PwC thought leadership on social, mobile, analytics, cloud (SMAC). Business Models for the Social Mobile Cloud: Transform Your Business Using Social Media. In *Mobile Internet, and Cloud Computing*, (pp. 165-216). Retrieved March 10, 2016, from http://adnanalhashmi.weebly.com/uploads/2/3/7/6/23764062/business_models_for_the_social_mobile_cloud.pdf

Shueh, J. (2014). *San Francisco Announces Chief Data Officer Joy Bonaguro*. Retrieved February 5, 2016, from http://www.govtech.com/data/San-Francisco-Announces-Chief-Data-Officer-Joy-Bonaguro.html

Smith, M. (2015, February). *The White House Names Dr. DJ Patil as the First U.S. Chief Data Scientist*. Retrieved September 26, 2016, from https://www.whitehouse.gov/blog/2015/02/18 /white-house-names-dr-dj-patil-first-us-chief-data-scientist

SocialTimes. (2016). *Here's How Many People Are on Facebook, Instagram, Twitter and Other Big Social Networks*. Retrieved September 5, 2016 from http://www.adweek.com/socialtimes/heres-how-many-people-are-on-facebook-instagram-twitter-other-big-social-networks/637205

Socrata. (2016). *Unleashing the Power of Government Data to Improve Society*. Retrieved September 26, 2016, from http://www.socrata.com/company-info/

Statista. (2016a). *Number of apps available in the leading App stores as of June 2016*. Retrieved September 26, 2016, from https://www.statista.com/statistics/276623/number-of-apps-available-in-leading-app-stores/

Statista. (2016b). *Numbers of LinkedIn members from 1st quarter 2009 to 2nd quarter 2016 (in millions)*. Retrieved 26 September 2016 from, https://www.statista.com/statistics/ 274050/ quarterly-numbers-of-linkedin-members/

Statista. (2016c). *Number of mobile app downloads worldwide from 2009 to 2017 (in millions)*. Retrieved September 26, 2016, from https://www.statista.com/statistics/266488/forecast-of-mobile-app-downloads/

Statista. (2016d). *Number of monthly active Instagram users from January 2013 to June 2016 (in millions)*. Retrieved September 26, 2016 from, https://www.statista.com/statistics/ 253577/number-of-monthly-active-instagram-users/

Statista. (2016e). *Number of monthly active Twitter users worldwide from 1st quarter 2010 to 2nd quarter 2016 (in millions)*. Retrieved 26 September, 2016 from https://www.statista.com/statistics/282087/number-of-monthly-active-twitter-users/

Statista. (2016f). *Number of monthly active WhatsApp users worldwide from April 2013 to February 2016 (in millions)*. Retrieved 26 September, 2016 from https://www.statista.com/ statistics/260819/number-of-monthly-active-whatsapp-users/

Surdak, C. (2014). *Data Crush: How the Information Tidal Wave Is Driving New Business Opportunities*. New York: AMACOM.

Sussin, J., Rozwell, C., & Sallam, L, R. (2015, March 12). *Technology Overview for Social Analytics Applications*. Gartner.

Teckst. (2015). *19 Texg Messaging Stats That Will Blow Your Mind*. Retrieved September 25, 2016, from https://teckst.com/19-text-messaging-stats-that-will-blow-your-mind/

Thecka, S. (2014, May). Transforming fragmented industry into sustainable businesses with SMAC technologies. In *IST-Africa Conference Proceedings* (pp. 1-9). IEEE. doi:10.1109/ISTAFRICA.2014.6880615

Toms Shoes. (2016). *About TOMS*. Retrieved September 27, 2016, from http://www.toms.com/about-toms#companyInfo

United Nations. (2014). *Status of Ratifications of the Kyoto Protocol.* Retrieved September 25, 2016, from http://unfccc.int/kyoto_protocol/status_of_ratification/items/2613.php

United States Environmental Protection Agency. (2014). *Climate Change Indicators in the United States.* Retrieved September 25, 2016, from: https://www3.epa.gov/climatechange/ pdfs/climateindicators-full-2014.pdf

William, M. (2010). *A Quick Start Guide to Cloud Computing: Moving Your Business Into the Cloud. New Tools for Business.* London: Kogan Page.

Yasuhiro, T. (2012). Tiering and Prioritizing Big Storage -In-House and in the Cloud. *Document News, 30*(1), 2–4.

KEY TERMS AND DEFINITIONS

Carbon Footprint: The amount of carbon dioxide and other carbon compounds emitted due to the consumption of fossil fuels by a particular person, group, etc.

CO2 Emission: Carbon dioxide (CO2) is a colorless, odorless and non-poisonous gas formed by combustion of carbon and in the respiration of living organisms and is considered a greenhouse gas. Emissions means the release of greenhouse gases and/or their precursors into the atmosphere over a specified area and period of time.

Data Warehouse: An electronic storage that holds large amounts of information for a business.

Internet of Things: (IoT) A computing concept that describes how everyday physical objects will be connected to the Internet and be able to identify themselves to other devices.

Mobile Platform: A mobile platform is also described as an operating system. Example mobile platforms are Windows, BlackBerry, and OS X.

SaaS: A software distribution model where applications are hosted by a vendor or service provider and made available to customers over the Internet.

SMAC: Social, mobile, analytics and cloud is the concept that four technologies are currently changing business.

Socrata: A cloud-based solution, where government and organizations can put their data online for the public to see and use.

Chapter 2
From Social Networks to Mobile Social Networks:
Applications in the Marketing Evolution

Zhenzhen Zhao
ISC Paris Business School, France

Christine Balagué
Telecom Ecole de Management, France

ABSTRACT

Digital marketing has put mobile and social into the center of the vision. Mobile and social interactions have transformed marketing activities and imposed a new paradigm on consumer behaviors based on real-time customer relationship management, peer-to-peer social influence and idea co-creation with consumers. Extensive research has been conducted in both mobile and social media domain, however few research has led a systematic approach by illustrating the marketing evolution and identifying mobile and social features. In this chapter, we fill this research gap through a literature review approach by first presenting the new marketing paradigm created by social networks, and then analyzing the marketing evolution from web-based social networks to mobile social networks. The mobile and social features are identified to guide marketers for application design. Finally, four case studies are presented to show how these features are distributed in applications to lead a better consumer experience. This chapter brings both theoretical and practical implications in this new trends.

DOI: 10.4018/978-1-5225-2449-6.ch002

Copyright ©2017, IGI Global. Copying or distributing in print or electronic forms without written permission of IGI Global is prohibited.

INTRODUCTION

With the emergence of Web 2.0 and mobile technologies, the past more than a dozen years have witnessed end-users' increasing involvement in social networks. More than ever, people today use smartphones and tablets to access all their favorite websites, especially popular social networks. According to Nielsen social media report, the use of mobile applications and mobile internet increased by 63% in the U.S. in 2012. The trend of mobile social media not only changes and impacts people's way of living and thinking, but it also brings huge business opportunities to companies to redefine their marketing strategies: how they market their brands, products and services, and how they listen to consumers (Zhao and Balagué, 2015). The development of marketing applications has represented a challenge and opportunity for companies to market their brands and products through a new channel; however, the applications currently available in the market are far from perfect and existing application designs do not yet have well established in the new marketing trend by using mobile social networks.

Some marketing research has been done on social media and mobile applications. For example, how social media and mobile applications affect consumers' brand/product attitudes and purchase intentions (Bellman, et al., 2011; Christodoulides & Michaelidou, 2011; Kim et al, 2015; Olbrich & Holsing, 2011; Shin and Shin, 2011; Wang, et al., 2012); what factors drive the popularity of brand marketing activities on social media (De Vries, et al., 2012; Singh & Sonneburg, 2012); what factors make mobile marketing strategies accepted by users (Heinonen & Strandvik, 2007; Kourouthanassis, et al., 2010; Picoto, Palma-dos-Reis & Belanger, 2010; Pousttchi & Wiedemann, 2007; Shankar, et al., 2010); and what are the main motives and engagement factors for branded mobile application usage (Bellman, 2011; Ho & Syu, 2010; Wachter, et al., 2012; Kim, et al., 2013; Shen, 2015; Zhao & Balagué, 2014, 2015). However, marketing applications by leveraging mobile social networks have received limited research attention; particularly, how social and mobile aspects have impacted the general marketing strategy has rarely been investigated.

In order to understand the marketing trend of mobile social networks, the first objective of this chapter is to present an overview of marketing strategy given the emergence of social media and mobility. This new trend raises several questions:

- What is social networks? How do social networks affect traditional marketing?
- What is mobile social networks? How is mobile social networks different from web-based social networks in marketing strategy?
- What are the social and mobile features that can be utilized in marketing applications design in this marketing evolution?

The second objective of this chapter is to provide insights for marketers about application design in the this fast-growing trend. For this purpose, four examples of applications are provided to illustrate relevant practices.

The contributions of this chapter are four-fold:

1. We define and classify social networks and mobile social networks in two categories based on marketing dimension, potentially allowing a differentiated marketing approach for each to be developed.
2. We describe social and mobile features in detail based on current literatures and practices.
3. We illustrate the marketing evolution from four perspectives (communication, customer relationship management, market research, and product innovation) and two phases (marketing evolution from traditional approach to social networks, and from web-based social networks to mobile social networks).
4. We evaluate four application case studies to demonstrate how social and mobile features are applied in this marketing evolution.

The rest of the chapter is organized as follows. The background section reviews previous literatures and presents key concepts and related works. Then we describe the marketing evolution from traditional approach to social networks, and from web-based social networks to mobile social networks, by illustrating social and mobile features, respectively. Four case studies of applications are given to further discuss the concepts. Finally, we conclude the chapter with perspectives and future research directions.

BACKGROUND

In this section we present the background in two parts: Firstly, we present the concept of social media and social networks; secondly we illustrate the literature reviews of social media, mobile marketing and branded mobile application.

Concept Evolution

Referring to Kaplan and Haenlein (2010), social media is a group of internet-based applications that builds on the ideological and technological foundations of Web 2.0, and that allows the creation and exchange of user-generated content. Kaplan and Haenlein provided a classification of social media which groups the current applications in the year 2010 into six specific categories according to the degree of social presence, media richness, social representation and self-disclosure, which are: collaborative projects (e.g. Wikipedia), blogs (and microblogs; the term microblogs is added in Kaplan and Haenlein's updated categorization in 2012, after microblogs like Twitter grew popular), content communities (e.g. YouTube, Flickr), social networking sites (e.g. Facebook, MySpace), virtual game worlds (e.g. World of Warcraft), and virtual social worlds (e.g. Second Life). All these different kinds of social media have been used in companies' marketing strategies. For example, most firms have their own Wikipedia pages; many companies are using blogs to update employees, customers, and shareholders on developments they consider to be important (Kaplan and Haenlein, 2010, pp. 63); the high popularity of content communities like YouTube makes it a very attractive advertising channel for many companies; most brands use Facebook to support the creation and interaction of brand communities (named Facebook Fan pages); the high popularity of virtual game worlds can be leveraged in traditional communication campaigns; virtual social worlds offer a multitude of opportunities for companies in marketing like advertising/ communication, virtual product sales etc (Kaplan and Haenlein, 2009).

Social networking site is one category of six social media forms proposed by Kaplan and Haenlein. It is a platform to build social relations among people who share ideas, interests, pictures, posts, activities, or real-life events. In a broader sense, online community is sometimes considered a social network. Social network usually means an individual-centered network whereas online community is group-centered. The first definition of social networks can be traced back more than a dozen years, while the definition from Boyd and Ellison (2007) is widely accepted by current research. In their article published in 2007, social network is defined as web-based applications that allow individuals to (1) construct a public or semi-public profile within a bounded system, (2) articulate a list of other users with whom they share a connection, and (3) view and traverse their list of connections and those made by others within the system. The nature and nomenclature of these connections may vary from site to site. In the year 2013, six years after the first definition, Boyd and Ellison began to reconsider how to define a social network given the shifts in technology and practice. Referring to their definition 2.0, a social network is a networked communication platform in which participants (1) have uniquely identifiable profiles that consist of user-supplied content, content provided by other users, and/or system-provided data; (2) can publicly articulate connections that can be viewed and traversed by others; and (3) can consume, produce, and/or interact with streams of user-generated content provided by their connections on the site (Ellison and Boyd, 2013).

LITERATURE REVIEWS

Recent research has been conducted in the area of social media and mobile applications with a focus on brand marketing. Firstly with regard to social media, Hinchcliffe (2013) predicts that social networking features will be noticeably added to traditional branded apps to allow for enhanced collaboration and sharing. Singh and Sonnenburg (2012) offer a semantic framework that resolves issues in storytelling, demonstrates the necessity of co-creation in storytelling, and identifies the core of an inspiring story. It shows that in social media, brand owners do not tell brand stories alone but co-create brand performances in collaboration with consumers. De Vries, et al. (2012) analyze 355 brand posts from 11 international brands spread across six product categories. The results of the study show that the vividness, interactivity and the position of the post are the key drivers of a brand post's popularity. Furthermore, extensive studies have been conducted on the relationship between social interactions and users' online shopping behaviors. Christodoulides and Michaelidou (2011) showed that social interactions positively impact e-satisfaction and e-loyalty and represent a critical variable in e-commerce. Olbrich and Holsing (2011) demonstrated the positive impact of social functionalities on shopping behavior. Shin and Shin (2011) showed that social presence is a key element of buying on websites, reinforcing security and confidence. Wang, et al. (2012) investigate consumption-related peer communication through social media and its impacts on consumers' product attitudes and purchase intentions.

Secondly we explore the literature field of mobile marketing, defined by Shankar and Balasubramanian (2009) as "the two- or multi-way communication and promotion of an offer between a firm and its customers using a mobile medium, device, or technology". The distinction of mobile marketing as a tool lies in the technological medium and the process it uses in communicating with consumers. A key driver of the success of mobile marketing is the acceptance and use by consumers, since the power of marketing depends on the extent of consumer responsiveness (Heinonen & Strandvik, 2007; Pousttchi & Wiedemann, 2007). A study (Picoto, Palma-dos-Reis & Belanger, 2010) on the organizational effect of mobile offers shows that customer response has an impact on the sales support, customer service, innovation, productivity and flexibility of the firm. One way of evaluating marketing offers via mobile phones is by looking into the extent and characteristics of customer responses. A number of factors can measure customer adoption and responsiveness. Pousttchi and Wiedemann (2007) identified these factors as perceived utility, reward, perceived ease of use, free viral content, initial contacts, first-mover advantage, critical mass and scalability. Additionally,

Kourouthanassis, et al. (2010) identified expected performance as a significant determinant in the acceptance of marketing offers. Shankar, et al. (2010) propose a conceptual framework addressing successful retailer mobile marketing strategies, and identify the customer-related and organizational challenges on this topic.

Finally, with regard to branded mobile applications, defined as software downloadable to a mobile device and prominently displays a brand identity, often via the name of the app and the appearance of a brand logo or icon throughout the user experience (Bellman, 2011). Hinchcliffe (2013) predicts the fusion of mobile will continue to be a major challenge, and the branded mobile applications will make significant progress in the following years. Ho and Syu (2010) found that the main motives and sought-after rewards in using mobile applications are entertainment, functionality, information, socialization, intellectual stimulation, following a trend, and learning. Bellman, et al. (2011) utilize an experimental design to determine whether using popular mobile apps affects brand attitude and brand purchase intention. The results show that using the apps has a positive persuasive impact, increasing interest in the brand and also the brand's product category. Wachter, et al. (2012) and Kim, et al. (2013) investigate mobile users engagement behavior. A model of user engagement behavior is developed to assess engagement factors. The findings show that users' motivation to engage using their smartphones increases users' value and satisfaction. Most significantly, users' hedonic and social motivations influence their perceived value, satisfaction, and continued engagement intention. Kim, et al. (2013) examine 106 branded applications with engagement attributes (i.e., vividness, novelty, motivation, control, customization, feedback etc). The findings suggest that branded apps could be an effective means by which brand communications are integrated into entertainment content. A branded app represents a unique form of branded entertainment because such content makes the app itself the brand message. Zhao and Balagué (2014, 2015) offer systematic guidelines for branded app design by identifying application types and brand identifiers that should be taken into consideration by companies. Kim, et al. (2015) investigate the effects of branded apps on app adopters' subsequent brand purchase behavior. The findings suggest that portable, convenient and interactive engagement allow customers to interact with the brand on a habitual basis. Though companies should prioritize launching a mobile app to communicate with their customers, but they should also keep in mind that a poorly designed app, which customers abandon after only a few users, may hurt their brand experience and company revenues. Shen (2015) develops a conceptual framework to outline users' behavior regarding apps. The findings show that app type (utilitarian and hedonic) and perceived risk moderate reputation source's influence on users' attitude toward using apps.

ISSUES, CONTROVERSIES, PROBLEMS

As illustrated in the background section, though extensive research has been conducted in social media, mobile marketing and mobile applications, limited research has been done on the illustration of the marketing evolution of mobile social networks, and identification of the social and mobile features which can be useful for companies to design their marketing strategy and related applications.

This section present two marketing evolutions: (1) from traditional approach to social networks by adding social features, and (2) from web-based social networks to mobile social networks by adding mobile features. Four case studies are presented afterwards to demonstrate the concepts and features.

MARKETING EVOLUTION

Marketing Evolution from Traditional Approach to Social Networks

In the background section we discussed the concepts and definitions of social media and social networks. In this section we focus on the classifications and the key features of social networks and how they impact traditional marketing.

Classification of Social Networks

Ellison and Boyd (2013) have classified social networks into three categories: profile-centric sites like LinkedIn and MySpace, media-centric sites like Flickr and YouTube, and location-focused sites like Foursquare.

Beyond Ellison and Boyd's classification, in this chapter we create another dimension of classification for the purpose of differentiation of marketing approach. The new dimension is classified based on the scope of audience (Table 1) and marketing strategy execution.

General Social Networks

General social network (GSNs) refers to social networks designed for the general public. The most famous up-to-date general social networks today are Facebook, Twitter, Google+, Instagram and Pinterest. GSNs often offer Application Programming Interfaces (APIs) to allow outside contents to be shared through their applications. With regard to marketing strategy, brands often present on most GSN applications. They regularly post contents, games and contests to interact with their fans and followers.

Specific Social Networks

Specific social network (SSNs) refers to social networks designed for specific/dedicated audience, for example SSNs could be designed for education, government, a sector of business, dating, finance or medicine etc. Examples can be seen as LinkedIn, PatientsLikeMe, or Match.com. SSNs often integrate APIs of general social networks to share internal contents outside. With regard to marketing strategy, brands design their own SSN applications to interact with consumers.

Social Features

Within the definition and classification of social networks, we further identify social features that can be applied in marketing applications. Kietzmann et al. (2011) proposed a consolidated social media framework based on a number of social media bloggers. The honeycomb framework is classified into seven functional building blocks: identity, conversation, sharing, presence, relationships, reputation, and groups. Different social networks are focused on different functionalities, for example LinkedIn emphasizes primarily identity and reputation, Foursquare focuses mainly on presence and relationships, YouTube puts weight on sharing, and Facebook's primary focus is relationships. The honeycomb framework can help to understand how different levels of social media functionality can be configured.

In this chapter, from the perspective of user interaction, we classify social features into two categories by taking into account the interactions among contents and interactions among users respectively (Table 2).

Table 1. Classification of social networks

Social Networks Category	Public	API	Marketing Strategy
General social networks (GSNs)	General public	Provide API for SCNs	Present on GSNs
Specific social networks (SSNs)	Specific public	Integrate API from GSNs	Design own SSNs

Table 2. Social features

Social Features	Description
Interactions among contents	• User-generated-content (UGC) • Content annotation • Content sharing
Interactions among users	• Follow/unfollow people • Online chat • Invite contacts from external social networks

Interactions among contents contain user-generated content (UGC), content annotation and content sharing features.

With regard to UGC, contents have evolved over time with different media formats, from texts to images then to voices, from videos to personalized television channels, and other forms of media. Creative consumers (Berthon et al, 2012), rather than firms, produce much of the value-added content in social media, and it is their networks of friends and associates that constitute the social.

With regard to content annotation, social annotation is online annotation by end users for the following purposes:

1. To improve or adapt its contents by adding/removing materials, e.g. wiki.
2. To rate a web resource. e.g. like/unlike or rate.
3. To discuss the contents of a certain resource. e.g. comment.
4. To categorize the contents. e.g. tag.
5. To enrich resources around a location. e.g. check-in function in Foursquare.

Interactions among users contain features as follow/unfollow people, online chat (peer-to-peer conversation among people) and invite contacts from existing social networks.

Marketing Evolution from Traditional Approach to Social Networks

The rapid growth of use of social networks and the big audience of these applications have required new marketing and communication strategies from companies. Regardless of traditional marketing, social networks constitute a new paradigm, transforming the different aspects of this domain. Table 3 illustrates the evolution from four perspectives: communication, customer relationship management (CRM), marketing research and product innovation.

Table 3. Marketing evolution from traditional approach to social networks

Marketing Perspectives	Evolution
Communication	• Earned media: Information virally spread by web users • Creates a big potential audience at low costs • Markets are conversations and brands become topic of conversations
CRM	• Community centric rather than client one-to-one centric • Social networks and community management • E-reputation by listening to peer-to-peer conversations
Marketing Research	Social networks provide qualitative and quantitative data enriched by network structure and links among consumers
Product Innovation	Crowd innovation: product co-creation by consumers

First of all, social networks provide a new type of communication. Traditionally, companies used two supports: either external media, by purchasing advertising space, or owned media, by providing content (on website or blog). Generally, these two communication types imply big investments and budgets. Social networks constitute a third way to communicate, called earned media. This process consists, on social networks, of posting content that is, in a second step, virally spread by thousands of web users. This system creates therefore a big potential audience at low cost. Communication objectives also change with earned media: strategy focuses on information sharing by social networks users. Content on Twitter needs to be retweeted, or shared and liked on Facebook. In this new paradigm, markets are conversations and brands become one topic of these conversations. Companies no longer manage the whole process as in traditional communication: there are interactive exchanges between people and companies, but also peer-to-peer conversations, without the company presence, diffusing positive information but also sometimes bad buzz. Marketing in social networks requires in this case strategies and tools to manage e-reputation, to listen to web-based conversations, not only by companies but also by brands, product category, or larger topics. These tools capture and analyze conversations (qualitative data in massive quantity). New metrics appear, such as web users' influence or engagement for instance, and marketers need to integrate this new culture.

The second marketing area impacted by social networks is CRM. During the last twenty years, companies have mainly implemented CRM processes and hardware in order to develop one-to-one marketing. The objective was to contact a potential client at a right time, with the right product, through the right distribution channel. Algorithms and models based on consumer behaviors have been developed to achieve this objective. Nowadays, social networks provide new opportunities. On these applications, companies are not client-centric but communities-centric. CRM becomes social networks and communities management. These communities can be created on Facebook, Twitter or on other social networks, and are managed by a community manager whose role consists in animating the communities, facilitating relationships between the communities and the company, or managing complaints. To achieve this last objective, several companies have created a Twitter profile managed by a community manager who manages the complaints and provides recovery satisfaction. One key benefit is real time on Twitter. The consumer's complaint can be sent on Twitter during service provision or product consumption with fast community manager's reaction and conversations. A second benefit is community presence and added value for consumers (events, community values sharing, exclusive offers).

Social networks also impact marketing research. Traditionally, marketers use qualitative studies or quantitative surveys to analyze markets and consumer behavior. Social networks provide big data (both qualitative and quantitative), enriched by networks' structures of friends and links between consumers. Social graphs, open graphs or predictive models allow companies to more deeply understand markets and social influence, and to build efficient recommendation systems.

Finally, social networks provide a new paradigm in marketing for innovation. Instead of doing internal and confidential research and development, companies can develop via open innovation, with external partners (companies, research centers, consumers) on these applications. For instance, in Brazil Fiat developed a specific social network application where thousands of people could post and share ideas for a new car model. They created the concept car "Fiat Mio", based on collective intelligence.

Marketing Evolution From Web-Based Social Networks to Mobile Social Networks

This section addresses the marketing evolution from web-based social networks to mobile social networks. It's important to understand the major differences between mobile social networks and web-based ones.

Mobile Social Networks

In our definition, mobile social networks contain the following categories:

1. The use of social networks on a mobile device. The social networks can be general social networks (e.g., Facebook) or specific social networks (e.g., LinkedIn).
2. Mobile applications with social features or mobile applications connected to existing social networks.

Mobile Features

Followed by literature review, we list up-to-date mobile interaction features which can be applied for mobile marketing strategies (Table 4).

Location awareness is one of the most prominent features through all mobile functionalities. Today, location awareness and mobility have added context to even the most ordinary actions, while social media and the mobile web have added a layer of immediate human connection to seemingly straightforward commercial transactions (Romanov, 2012, pp. 31).

There is a new buzzword currently being thrown around by marketing teams: SoLoMo, which stands for Social-Local-Mobile, and refers to the integration of social, location-based, and mobile marketing tools into new acquisition applications.

Table 4. Mobile features

Mobile Features	Description
Location awareness	Provide user information based on location
Multi-touch gestures	Sway, shake, click, swipe, pinch, spread, etc
Voice sensor	Recognize human voices
Augmented reality	Allow users to perceive virtual products in the real environment.
Camera	• Take a snap • Scan a barcode/QR code to get information
Mobile video	Short and smart viral video contents
Mobile payments	Allow users to pay for products directly from their mobile devices, anytime and anywhere

Examples of famous SoLoMo applications are Foursquare and Groupon. SoLoMo search relies on the real-time location of a mobile device to provide the user with a stream of information based on their location and interests.

The technology of various mobile sensors creates rich interaction between end users and mobile devices (Lane et al., 2010). Hinckley et al. (2000) introduced set a framework that points researchers towards functionality of sensors in handheld devices. For example, a touch sensor, tilt sensor and proximity sensor inside a device allow users to carry out single and multi-touch gestures like sway, shake, click, swipe, etc. These gestures have been widely used in various games including branded games.

Voice sensor (Bijani et al., 2013) allows mobile to recognize the human voice and has been used in customer relationship marketing to answer questions from clients by direct speaking.

Furthermore, augmented reality (AR) technology (Olsson & Salo, 2012) combines virtual data with the physical real world, allowing users to perceive virtual products in the real environment. The term "virtual mirror" (Cho and Schwarz, 2012) is created in the marketing field and is widely used in e-commerce application by using AR technology, which adjusts geometrically to reflect the viewers' image in real time.

Other mobile features, for example mobile integrated cameras (Salo & Olsson, 2013), allow users to snap or scan, a feature that gives marketing strategists the possibility to encourage consumers to take photos of branded products to share with friends, or to scan barcodes of products to gain credits. Short and smart mobile advertising videos are used to attract people's attention, while mobile payment systems allow users to pay for a product/service directly from mobile.

Table 5. Marketing evolution from web-based social networks to mobile social networks

Marketing Perspective	Evolution
Communication	Localization provides new information to target consumers
CRM	• Consumer instant action centric than conversation centric • CRM focuses on real time relationships with consumers
Marketing Research	Mobile real-time features provides insights for marketing research
Product Innovation	Mobile real-time features make co-creation of products easier and more flexible

Marketing Evolution From Web-Based Social Networks to Mobile Social Networks

Mobile features provide new opportunities for marketing, as illustrated in Table 5 from four perspectives.

In terms of communication, localization provides new information to target consumers. Several beauty products retailers have developed localized marketing campaigns, sending a specific SMS with product promotions to consumers passing a store. Localized advertising increases the probability of an individual in a specific place choosing the offer. Finally, mobile sensory features constitute fantastic opportunities in terms of marketing and communication about products. Concerning CRM, brands build and manage client communities with new mobile applications, either on general social networks such as Facebook or Twitter, or on specific social networks. Mobile marketing by using social networks is more consumer-instant-action-centric than conversation-centric, and is focused on real-time relationships with consumers. Moreover, mobile social network marketing is more focused on shared content type such as photos and videos than on text. New mobile applications such as Instagram and Pinterest have greatly increased photo sharing behaviors, and marketers have to integrate these new usages in their strategy. Another well-known mobile consumer behavior on mobile and on social networks is playing games, which becomes one key strategy in this emerging marketing trends. The objectives of marketing strategy on mobile games focus not only brand image and awareness, but also database collection. Mobile social networks also constitute new research marketing tools. In the shampoo market, for instance, some companies have asked women to take and share photos with their mobiles to express what good/bad hair appearance is for them personally. This process provides added value information (based on behavioral and not declarative data) for marketers to better understand consumer behaviors, but also implies the emergence of privacy as an issue.

APPLICATION CASE STUDIES IN MARKETING TRENDS OF MOBILE SOCIAL NETWORKS

In this section we select four marketing applications presented as case studies to further explain the concepts illustrated in the above two sections.

1. Marketers though Foursquare: typical SoLoMo application.
2. McDonald's Golden McRib Quest: branded mobile Facebook application.
3. UNIQLO's UNIQLOOKS: branded mobile application with social features.
4. Johnson & Johnson's Band-Aid: branded mobile application connected to existing social networks.

Of these four applications, the first two (Foursquare and Facebook) are designed for the general public, while the last two are designed by company/brand to achieve specific audiences.

Foursquare

Foursquare was created as a location-based social networks for mobile devices in New York in 2009. By December 2015 Foursquare had over 55 million monthly active users. Foursquare describes their service as a mobile application that makes cities easier to use and more interesting to explore. It is a friend-finder, a social city guide, and a game that challenges users to experience new things - and rewards them for doing so. Foursquare allows users to earn points by announcing their presence, and there is a bonus if one reaches a place for the first time. Also, it is possible to earn badges (check-ins) depending on the characteristics of the places, the person who is most assiduously attending a place becoming mayor of this place. Several research studies have been conducted to understand how people use Foursquare, why they check in or don't, why, when, and what people want to share on a mobile location sharing application, and implications of design of SoLoMo applications (Lindqvist et al, 2011, Tang et al, 2010, Tsai et al, 2009, and Consolvo et al, 2005).

For marketers, Foursquare offers great opportunities for companies to advertise their products and services, and its business model is based on the distribution of promotional offers by advertisers through the connected and location-based networks. For example, various attractive promotions and offers are proposed at each "check-in" near a trade partner of Foursquare (Figure 1). By December 2015, Foursquare has reached 7 billion check-ins in total and 7 million most check-ins per day. Applications like Twitter and Facebook have shown that brands can engage with consumers in really interesting ways online, and Foursquare is well poised to take all that engagement offline, providing brands with tools to lead their consumers to

Figure 1. Screenshots of Foursquare application

do things, as opposed to just suggest (Carr., 2010). Foursquare allows consumers to build an even deeper affinity for brands. Said Tristan Walker, head of business development for Foursquare, "We're hoping to offer retailers tools to aid consumer retention and acquisition, telling retailers a little more about their loyal customers: who checks in, when, where, how soon, how often, where they go before, where they go after. And on the acquisition side, geo-tag specials can entice new consumers."

McDonald's Golden McRib Quest

McDonald's Golden McRib Quest is a quiz-based Facebook application (Figure 5). Users are asked with answering various questions in rounds of several challenges before virtually arriving at their local McDonald's. If users answered the questions correctly and had a good chance, they will unlock the mysterious Golden McRib and their names will ascend the leaderboard. This application reflects a common version of a branded social gaming application. According to Rick Wion, McDonald's director of social media, the strategy behind developing this application was to provide McRib fans with "more ways to share". The temporary addition of the McRib to McDonald's menu got a 4.8% sales increase for the month after launching the game. The entertainment perspective of gaming as part of campaigns have brought lots of positive feedback and strong engagement from customers.

Uniqlo's Uniqlooks

Japanese apparel retailer UNIQLO has launched UNIQLOOKS (Figure 6), the brand's global online fashion community that enables people around the world to share their UNIQLO style. The application affords customers, fans and visitors the opportunity to populate the global community with images of themselves wearing UNIQLO clothes in varying combinations. According to the company, "The most

Figure 2. Screenshots of Golden McRib Quest application

popular looks will be recognized by specialists from a variety of fields such as fashion and design." A global audience determines each "Look of the Week" winner. The top-ranked photo will be used to help showcase the clothing in stores, and the winner are invited to grand stores opening ceremonies. The Likes spread the brand across social networks in a natural, peer-to-peer manner, while the application has a strong e-commerce element by linking directly through to the UNIQLO online store.

Commented by Vazquez (2011), UNIQLOOKS is not only about online advertising and user-generated content, it seeks to engage fans and brand advocates by making their community both their models and their stylists. Customers can interact with each other and gain style tips and learn how to mix match with a UNIQLO product in their daily styles. This application helps to create brand awareness, enhance the brand image and maintain brand loyalty. Moreover, having an online community is essential for marketers to understand customer preference and their buying behaviors. UNIQLOOKS helps UNIQLO to observe customers' opinions of their products as well as how they use them. These insights are helpful in designing and planning future trends in manufacturing.

Figure 3. Screenshots of UNIQLOOKS application

Johnson & Johnson's Band-Aid Magic Vision

Johnson & Johnson creates the augmented-reality (AR) magic vision App for Brand-Aid's Muppet-theme bandages (Figure 4). Once the App has been downloaded to a smartphone, it can be used to scan a bandage and unlock cute animations featuring Kermitand friends.

The objective is to "turn moments of pain into moments of delight" and to create an emotional bond between parents and kids. According to Google, this application has earned more than 115 million earned media impressions, and users gave 4.5/5-star rating on iTunes store. It allows Band-Aid to have a new relationship with their audience and opens up the concept of healing in new and innovative ways.

Figure 4. Screenshots of Band-Aid application

SOLUTIONS AND RECOMMENDATIONS

This chapter illustrates marketing in mobile social networks from unique insights of concept and marketing evolution, providing both theoretical and managerial insights.

Theoretical Implications

This research aims to provide an overview of the marketing evolution with the emergence of social media and mobility. The primary theoretical contribution of our research is to propose the categorization of social networks and mobile social networks from brand and marketing perspective. The second theoretical implication lies in the marketing evolution from two phases (from traditional approach to social networks, and from web-based social networks to mobile social networks) in terms of four perspectives (communication, CRM, marketing research and product innovation). Moreover, based on a literature review approach, this research has identified social and mobile features. To our knowledge, this is the first conceptual paper to address all these perspectives.

Managerial Implications

The main managerial implication from our research is providing guidance to marketers on how to think and execute marketing strategies in the trends of mobile social networks. The mobile and social features presented in this chapter are the elements which can help marketers to define their marketing applications. The classification of general and specific mobile social networks gives ideas for companies how to choose a well established general social networks to integrate their marketing strategies (e.g., Facebook and Foursquare in our case studies), and to develop owned specific applications to engage consumers (e.g., UNIQLO and Johnson & Johnson). Furthermore, these four case studies presented in the chapters can guide the marketers to understand how to build the mobile social applications which could be positively received and accepted by customers.

FUTURE RESEARCH DIRECTIONS

Limitations and Future Work

Although this research contributes significantly to our understanding of marketing evolution, it has several limitations.

The primary concern is that though this research provides a systematic list of mobile and social features, the selection of these features for marketers is case dependent. In order to give a more precise recommendation, an empirical study should be conducted to understand the link of features and marketing effectiveness.

Another limitation lies in the case study selection. Four examples are selected in the case study section, where two examples are used to illustrate general social networks and other two examples are for specific social networks. We believe, however, more examples should be chosen for both cases, and a content analysis with mobile/social features of these examples could serve a clearer idea for marketing strategy selection.

Further Perspective

The first one is privacy. Mobile marketing constitutes new opportunities to collect information on individuals, with new data such as localization, real-time photos, consumer travels, meetings with friends. Social graph and open graph including big data allow companies to optimize product or service recommendations, but privacy and individual freedom issues remain. One future challenge for companies is therefore to respect privacy by not only opt-in procedures but also by transparently informing consumers about data collection and use. Marketing research has already shown the importance of trust in the efficiency of digital marketing strategies. Trust will be a key concept in successful mobile social networks.

The second issue, correlated to the first one, concerns data collection and analysis. As one of the biggest values of mobile social networks is the opportunity to collect new types of data, and to define marketing campaigns based on them, the techniques to collect and store data become key topics. Companies need therefore to recruit new profiles with competences in big data analysis, or to search for new providers of these specific services.

The third issue concerns mobile open innovation. Brands will probably massively develop open innovation with mobile social networks. In the future, communities built on social networks will recommend public or private products and services, will give ideas and opinions in real time on mobile. These technologies also will allow the creation of open platforms for complaints and open platforms for silent voices of unsatisfied consumers. Organizations adopting real-time answering will develop a competitive advantage.

Finally, emerging phenomena such as social shopping, social TV, social influence will become dominant in the future, introducing mobile social impact in each step of a consumer purchase process. In order to have a successful marketing strategy, companies will have to completely move to this new marketing paradigm.

CONCLUSION

Built on the foundations of Web 2.0 technologies, the evolution of social media allows users to utilize the World Wide Web in a new way. Marketing evolution with mobile social networks together with emerging mobile technologies has brought challenges and opportunities for companies to market their brands, products and services in a new channel. Companies have to move to this new culture, with new marketers' profiles and competences facing new consumer behaviors. These evolutions probably confirm the end of the consumerism era and the birth of a collaborative intelligence one, implying a new relationship between consumers and companies - more transparent, based on trust, where peer-to-peer social influence remains a key explicative factor of consumer behaviors, in a constant technological evolution.

REFERENCES

Bellman, S., Potter, R. F., Treleaven-Hassard, S., Robinson, J. A., & Varan, D. (2011). The effectiveness of branded mobile phone apps. *Journal of Interactive Marketing*, *25*(4), 191–200. doi:10.1016/j.intmar.2011.06.001

Berthon, P. R., Pitt, L. F., Plangger, K., & Shapiro, D. (2012). Marketing meets web 2.0, social media, and creative consumers: Implications for international marketing strategy. *Business Horizons*, *55*(3), 261–271. doi:10.1016/j.bushor.2012.01.007

Bijani, C., Vilrokx, M., & White, B. K. (2013). Giving voice to enterprise mobile applications. In *Proceedings of the 15th International Conference on Human-Computer Interaction with Mobile Devices and Services* (pp. 428-433). ACM Press.

Boyd, D., & Ellison, N. B. (2007). Social network sites: Definition, history, and scholarship. *Journal of Computer-Mediated Communication*, *13*(1), 210–230. doi:10.1111/j.1083-6101.2007.00393.x

Carr, A. (2010). *Foursquare's business chief on revenue plans, google adwords, and why marketers shouldn't delay on geo-location.* Retrieved July 28, 2010, from http://www.fastcompany.com/1675626/

Cho, H., & Schwarz, N. (2012). I like your product when i like my photo: Misattribution using interactive virtual mirrors. *Journal of Interactive Marketing*, *26*(4), 235–243. doi:10.1016/j.intmar.2012.03.003

Christodoulides, G., & Michaelidou, N. (2011). Shopping motives as antecedents of e-satisfaction and e-loyalty. *Journal of Marketing Management*, *27*(1/2), 181–197.

Consolvo, S. et al.. (2005). Location disclosure to social relations: Why, when, and what people want to share. In *Proceedings of the SIGCHI Conference on Human Factors in Computing Systems* (pp. 81-90). ACM Press. doi:10.1145/1054972.1054985

Craig, S. (2015). *By the numbers: 17 important foursquare stats.* Retrieved December 23, 2015, from http://expandedramblings.com/index.php/by-the-numbers-interesting-foursquare-user-stats/

De Vries, L., Gensler, S., & Leeflang, P. S. H. (2012). Popularity of brand posts on brand fan pages: An investigation of the effects of social media marketing. *Journal of Interactive Marketing*, *26*(2), 83–91. doi:10.1016/j.intmar.2012.01.003

Ellison, N. B., & Boyd, D. (2013). Sociality through Social Network Sites. In W. H. Dutton (Ed.), *The Oxford Handbook of Internet Studies*. Oxford, UK: Oxford University Press.

Heinonen, K., & Strandvik, T. (2007). Consumer responsiveness to mobile marketing. *International Journal of Mobile Communications*, *5*(6), 603–617. doi:10.1504/IJMC.2007.014177

Hinchcliffe, D. (2013). *2013 predictions for enterprise social media*. Retrieved January 18, 2013, from http://www.zdnet.com/2013-predictions-for-enterprise-social-media-7000009964/

Hinckley, K., Pierce, J., Sinclair, M., & Horvitz, E. (2000). Sensing techniques for mobile interaction. In *Proceedings of the 13th annual ACM symposium on User interface software and technology* (pp. 91-100). ACM Press. doi:10.1145/354401.354417

Ho, H. Y., & Syu, L. Y. (2010). Uses and gratifications of mobile application users. In *Proceeding of the 2010 international conference on electronics and information engineering* (pp. 315-319). IEEE Press. doi:10.1109/ICEIE.2010.5559869

JWT NEW YORK. (2012). *Johnson & Johnson Band-Aid Magic Vision*. Retrieved September, 2012, from https://www.thinkwithgoogle.com/campaigns/band-aid-brand-adhesive-bandages-johnson-johnson-band-aid-magic-vision.html

Kaplan, A. M., & Haenlein, M. (2009). The fairyland of Second Life: About virtual social worlds and how to use them. *Business Horizons*, *52*(6), 563–572. doi:10.1016/j.bushor.2009.07.002

Kaplan, A. M., & Haenlein, M. (2010). Users of the world, unite! The challenges and opportunities of social media. *Business Horizons*, *53*(1), 59–68. doi:10.1016/j.bushor.2009.09.003

Kaplan, A. M., & Haenlein, M. (2012). Social media: Back to the roots and back to the future. *Journal of Systems and Information Technology, 14*(2), 101–104. doi:10.1108/13287261211232126

Kietzman, J. H., Hermkens, K., McCarthy, I. P., & Silvestre, B. S. (2011). Social media? Get serious! Understanding the functional building blocks of social media. *Business Horizons, 54*(3), 241–251. doi:10.1016/j.bushor.2011.01.005

Kim, E., Lin, J.-S., & Sung, Y. (2013). To app or not to app: Engaging consumers via branded mobile apps. *Journal of Interactive Advertising, 13*(1), 53–65. doi:10.1080/15252019.2013.782780

Kim, S. J., Wang, R. J.-H., & Malthouse, E. C. (2015). The effects of adopting and using a brands mobile application on customers subsequent purchase behavior. *Journal of Interactive Marketing, 31*, 28–41. doi:10.1016/j.intmar.2015.05.004

Kim, Y. H., Kim, D. J., & Wachter, K. (2013). A study of mobile user engagement (MoEN): Engagement motivations, perceived value, satisfaction, and continued engagement intention. *Decision Support Systems, 56*, 361–370. doi:10.1016/j.dss.2013.07.002

Kourouthanassis, P., Georgiadis, C., Zamani, E., & Giaglis, G. (2010). Explaining the adoption of mobile Internet applications. In *Proceedings of Mobile Business and 2010 Ninth Global Mobility Roundtable* (pp. 148-153). IEEE Press. doi:10.1109/ICMB-GMR.2010.70

Lane, N. D., Miluzzo, E., Lu, H., Peebles, D., Choudhury, T., & Campbell, A. (2010). A Survey of Mobile Phone Sensing. *IEEE Communications Magazine, 48*(9), 140–150. doi:10.1109/MCOM.2010.5560598

Lindqvist, J., Cranshaw, J., Wiese, J., Hong, J., & Zimmmerman, J. (2011). I'm the mayor of my house: examining why people use foursquare: A social-driven location sharing application. In *Proceedings of the SIGCHI Conference on Human Factors in Computing Systems* (pp. 2409-2418). ACM Press. doi:10.1145/1978942.1979295

Nielsen. (2012). *Social media report 2012: Social media comes of age*. Retrieved March 12, 2012, from http://www.nielsen.com/us/en/insights/news/2012/social-media-report-2012-social-media-comes-of-age.html

Olbrich, R., & Holsing, C. (2011). Modeling consumer purchasing behavior in social shopping communities with clickstream data. *International Journal of Electronic Commerce, 16*(2), 15–40. doi:10.2753/JEC1086-4415160202

Olsson, T., & v Salo, M. (2012). Narratives of satisfying and unsatisfying experiences of current mobile augmented reality applications. In *Proceedings of the SIGCHI Conference on Human Factors in Computing Systems* (pp. 2779-2788). ACM Press. doi:10.1145/2207676.2208677

Picoto, W. N., Palma-dos-Reis, A., & Belanger, F. (2010). How does mobile business create value for firms? In *Proceedings of Mobile Business and 2010 Ninth Global Mobility Roundtable* (pp. 9-16). IEEE Press. doi:10.1109/ICMB-GMR.2010.19

Pousttchi, K., & Wiedemann, D. G. (2007). Success factors in mobile viral marketing: A multi-case study approach. In *Proceedings of the 6th International Conference on Management of Mobile Business*. IEEE Press. doi:10.1109/ICMB.2007.61

Romanov, A. (2012). The near and far of proximity marketing: The future of marketing exists at the nexus of digital signage and mobility. *IJMM Canada Issue*, *7*(1), 31–33.

Salo, M., Olsson, T., Makkonen, M., Hautamaki, A. & Frank, L. (2013). Consumer value of camera-based mobile interaction with the real world. *Journal of Pervasive and Mobile Computing*, *9*, 258-268.

Shankar, V., & Balasubramanian, S. (2009). Mobile marketing: A synthesis and prognosis. *Journal of Interactive Marketing*, *23*(2), 118–129. doi:10.1016/j.intmar.2009.02.002

Shankar, V., Venkatesh, A., Hofacker, C., & Naik, P. (2010). Mobile marketing in the retailing environment: Current insights and future research avenues. *Journal of Interactive Marketing*, *24*(2), 111–120. doi:10.1016/j.intmar.2010.02.006

Shen, G. C.-C. (2015). Users adoption of mobile applications: Product type and message framings moderating effect. *Journal of Business Research*, *68*(11), 2317–2321. doi:10.1016/j.jbusres.2015.06.018

Shin, D.-H., & Shin, Y.-J. (2011). Consumers trust in virtual mall shopping: The role of social presence and perceived security. *International Journal of Human-Computer Interaction*, *27*(5), 450–475. doi:10.1080/10447318.2011.552060

Singh, S., & Sonnenburg, S. (2012). Brand performances in social media. *Journal of Interactive Marketing*, *26*(4), 189–197. doi:10.1016/j.intmar.2012.04.001

Tang, K., Lin, J., Hong, J. I., Siewiorek, P., & Sadeh, N. (2010). Rethinking location sharing: Exploring the implications of social-driven vs. Purpose-driven location sharing. In *Proceedings of the 12th ACM international conference on Ubiquitous computing* (pp. 85-94). ACM Press. doi:10.1145/1864349.1864363

Tsai, J. Y., Kelley, P., Drielsma, P. H., Cranor, L. F., Hong, J. I., & Sadeh, N. (2009). Who's viewed you? The impact of feedback in a mobile location-sharing application. In *Proceedings of the SIGCHI Conference on Human Factors in Computing Systems* (pp. 2003-2012). ACM Press.

Vazquez, P. M. (2011). *The fashion retailer launches its latest digital creation: A social fashion community to showcase the sartorial talent of its fans and customers.* Retrieved February 24, 2011, from http://www.psfk.com/2011/02/uniqlooks-uniqlos-new-fashion-community.html

Wachter, K., Kim, Y. H., & Kim, D. J. (2012). Mobile users: Choosing to engage. *International Journal of Sales. Retailing and Marketing*, *1*(1), 3–13.

Wang, X., Yu, C., & Wei, Y. (2012). Social media peer communication and impacts on purchase intentions: A consumer socialization framework. *Journal of Interactive Marketing*, *26*(4), 198–208. doi:10.1016/j.intmar.2011.11.004

Zhao, Z., & Balagué, C. (2014). A design framework of branded mobile applications. In *Proceedings of the 16th International Conference on Human-Computer Interaction with Mobile Devices and Services* (pp. 507-512). ACM Press. doi:10.1145/2628363.2634224

Zhao, Z., & Balagué, C. (2015). Designing branded mobile apps: Fundamentals and recommendations. *Business Horizons*, *58*(3), 305–315. doi:10.1016/j.bushor.2015.01.004

KEY TERMS AND DEFINITIONS

General Social Networks: Social networks designed for the general public.

Mobile Application: Software downloadable to a mobile device.

Mobile Marketing: The two- or multi-way communication and promotion of an offer between a firm and its customers using a mobile medium, device, or technology.

Mobile Social Networks: The use of social networks on a mobile device, mobile applications with social features, or mobile applications connected to existing social networks.

Specific Social Networks: Social networks designed for specific/dedicated audience.

Social Media: Also known as consumer-generated media, is media (in the form of text, visuals and audio) created to be shared. It has changed the face of marketing by allowing collaboration and connection in a way that no other channel has been able to offer.

Social Networks: A networked communication platform in which participants (1) have uniquely identifiable profiles that consist of user-supplied content, content provided by other users, and/or system-provided data; (2) can publicly articulate connections that can be viewed and traversed by others; and (3) can consume, produce, and/or interact with streams of user-generated content provided by their connections on the site.

Chapter 3
Apps-Commerce in Emerging Markets:
Insights and Future Business Models

Sajad Rezaei
Taylor's University, Malaysia

Maryam Emmi
Universiti Teknologi Malaysia, Malaysia

ABSTRACT

The Internet and Apps related technologies are considered as information "super highway" since they are able to connect people, computers, and data to one another. Because of them, a new communication medium has risen, which provides an access to the large flow of information across various broad extensions. As a consequence, there has been a need for understanding the behaviors of online consumers, since Information Technology and its usage have had a massive impact on shopping behaviors as well as the rate of market success. This chapter's aim will be to sanitize the current understanding of Apps/online consumer behavior to shape Apps marketing strategies and implementations.

DOI: 10.4018/978-1-5225-2449-6.ch003

Copyright ©2017, IGI Global. Copying or distributing in print or electronic forms without written permission of IGI Global is prohibited.

INTRODUCTION

Managers are using consumer decision-making models in order to predict as well as to explain the consumer behaviors, that can act as a basis to make decisions in marketing (Butler & Peppard, 1998). Using the Internet and World Wide Websites (WWW) as communication and promotional tools to perform distribution functions, enabled the marketers to start finding an entirely new world of consumer purchasing behavior opportunities (Khan, 2010). Online shopping along with electronic retailing over the Internet came into existence back in 1994 (Chai Har et al., 2011; Varadarajan et al., 2010) and a revolution has been building up on marketing principals for many years. This standpoint made some dramatic alterations to the conventional ways of viewing the communication media together with advertising. The Internet and Apps related technologies are considered as information ''super highway" since they are able to connect people, computers, and data to one another. Because of them, a new communication medium has risen, which provides an access to the large flow of information across various broad extensions (Akman & Mishra, 2010). The Internet, which is a gigantic universal network, is a revolution consisting of packet-switched computer net-works that are interconnected. The Internet can be named as a trendy marketing medium with the potential to make radical transformations to the ways corporations conduct their businesses and respond to their customers (Hoffman, 1996). During the past decade, the Internet has fundamentally transformed how retailers are competing in the marketplace. According to recent reports by Akman & Mishra (2010), the number of Internet users has reached to 1412 million world-wide. In Asia, as a continent, the rapid growth of the economy has resulted in a higher Internet penetration in the past few years (Muhammad Najib et al., 2010). As an instance, A National Computer Board survey, which was conducted among 1500 citizens of Singapore, has shown that 2% of Singaporeans who are more than 18-year-old adults, actually purchased some items online and all of them were very satisfied with their purchases (Sim & Koi, 2002). From an economic perspective, many countries in Asia are well defined as emerging markets, which explain the improvement of IT infrastructure and development. In this study, Malaysia, as one of the emerging markets, will be the focus of the research.

Online Markets and E-Commerce

Previous research on electronic commerce found out that behavioral intentions in online shoppers were dissimilar to the intentions of traditional offline shoppers when it came to markets (Ganesh et al., 2010). One area, which has been receiving a growing importance, is how online consumers are interacting with marketers in a cyber environment in parallel with retailing e-commerce (O'Cass & Fenech, 2003).

The amount of the Internet retailing market expansion in every area around the world has continuously expanded by two times growth rate (Zhu et al., 2010). This implies the importance of internet marketing strategy for vendors. A new generation of Internet transactions, as a matter of fact, came into existence. This can be interpreted as a new phase of the Internet, which is a combination of high Internet penetration, mobility, speed, development, networking, usage of media, changes in communication, interaction (Web 2.0) along with innovation in business models (Heinemann & Schwarzl, 2010a). Mummalaneni (2005) found that Internet retailing is quickly emerging as an alternative mode of purchasing and is predicted to get a substantial share of the retail market in future. Great interests are being stimulated by establishing a better comprehension of how people's decisions are being influenced to either purchase or to abstain from online shopping. The fundamental growth of Internet hand in hand with its steady increase in the retailing area brings about these inspirations.

Electronic Commerce initiatives are critical to the success or even the survival of many organizations and it may be too risky not to have any e-strategies (Lao & Hu, 2005). The progress of the Internet in the entire world has pushed the popularity of online retailing and shopping activities (Lian & Lin, 2008). Even though there has been a huge exaggeration on online shopping (internet shopping) developments, and their influences on today 's society, it can be observed that since the mid-1990s, the rate of sales went through some exponential growth (Rotem-Mindali, 2010). According to Heinemann & Schwarz (2010b), there is a rapid growth of revenue when it comes to online retail (Figure 1). The main findings of the website analysis by Madlberger in (2004) indicate two key approaches in the model of online retailing business:

1. The first group is the retailers who mainly focus on just the shopping function when it comes to their online shops.
2. On the contrary, the second group is the players who improve their online shops via adding extra functions including communities, information, and some other related service.

Peterson and Balasubramanian (2002) in *Journal of Retailing* proved that retailing in the 21st century, without any doubts, will be so different from retailing in the 20th century because of the changes in an era of online retailing. O'Cass & Fenech (2003) also assert that while we are moving into the 21st century, there is a minimum of eight retail channels which are available to a consumer. As a result of this phenomenon, a variety of enormous opportunities for purchasing services and goods are presented to customers, which are located outside the conventional retail establishments. The fabulous increase of internet retailing has stimulated broad re-

Figure 1. Revenue developments in electronic commerce
Source: (Heinemann & Schwarzl, 2010b).

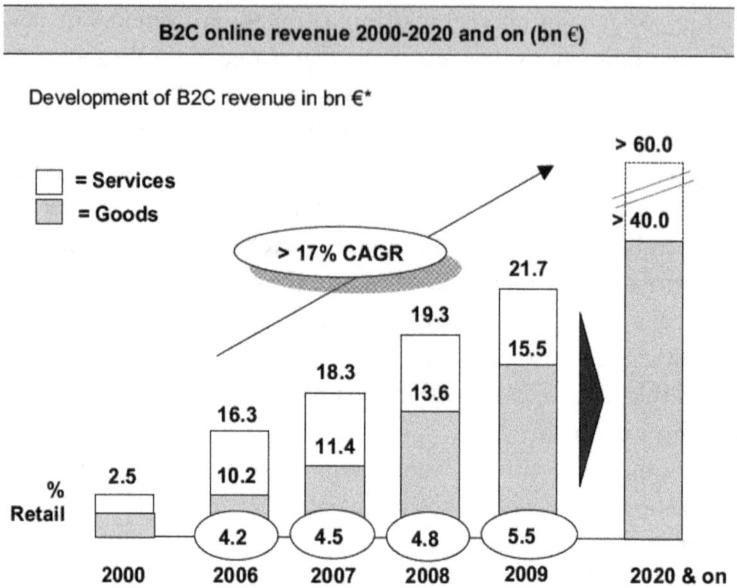

search opportunities that are aimed at comprehending consumers' drive to Internet purchase. They will pave the way for online businesses establishing themselves as the selected vendor for their loyal customers (Xiao, 2010).

Lowering the cost of shopping is a potential that is provided by the Internet since it can reduce transaction, search and needed transportation costs (Rotem-Mindali, 2010). For that reason, sustainable growth of online shopping is very much expected. Online shoppers, as well as their shopping behavior intentions, are observed as an increased interest in studies nowadays (Sim & Koi, 2002).

Impact of Web 2.0 on Internet Shopping

Novel online place, as an example of Web 2.0 activities, provided the Internet retailers with abundant new channels for reaching out to their buyers, but such online activities were not the subject of study (Hannah & Lybecker, 2010). As online shopping becomes a realistic possibility for increasingly greater proportions of the population, some studies have begun to investigate the characteristics and motivations of online shoppers (Dittmar et al., 2004). The important point is that people can communicate via their own computers, mobile, and new interactive websites.

All around the globe, the Internet is being utilized as a commercial tool to conduct some transaction activities in an environment that is computer-mediated (Armesh et al., 2010a). In the past recent years, the economy has been growing pretty rapidly and that is why the World Wide Web went through a speedy development from web 1.0 to web 2.0 and it has moved on to web 3.0. ICT or Information communication technology plays a significant part in economic growth around the world via providing some powerful tools, strategic opportunities, equity development along with the wealth redistribution (Kim et al., 2011). When it comes to buyer and sellers, new information technologies, in contrary to the older technologies, bring them true interactivity (Butler & Peppard, 1998). In addition, Web 2.0 initiatives and business applications have rocketed, outpacing even developments on the Semantic Web (that are described by some as Web 3.0) and they indeed have materially affected the business strategies (Heinemann & Schwarzl, 2010a; Khan, 2010). Yet, in the culturally fragmented and diverse global online marketplace, businesses are also facing a number of dilemmas and challenges in their effort of reaching, attracting, persuading and retaining the online customer (Efthymios et al., 2010).

Online shopping came into the picture when the Internet gained some popularities (Ng, 2003). Since modern telecommunications technology has been developing rapidly, electronic commerce (e-commerce) services are being delivered to millions of users who are labeled as ‘‘wired”, because of the efficiency and simplicity of the Internet (Lu et al., 2011). According to a previous study (Badrinarayanan et al., 2010), dozens of companies, that are purely Internet corporations, have emerged in lots of industries and the Internet was adopted by several companies that were operated conventionally. (Cai & Xu, 2006) stated that the Internet commerce has been revolutionized. As a consequence, there has been a need for understanding the behaviors of online consumers, since Information Technology and its usage have had a massive impact on shopping behaviors as well as the rate of market success (Rezaei, Ali, Amin, & Jayashree, 2016; Rezaei, Amin, et al., 2016; Rezaei, Shahijan, et al., 2016; Yeo et al., 2017). In 1995, as it was pointed out by the Business Week, the Internet was not the place for the neophyte. Since there were slow and unstable Internet connections, navigating the web needed high levels of technological knowledge and patience (Taylor & Strutton, 2010). Marketing studies, which are mainly dealing with evaluating consumer behavior within traditional markets, consistently explain the consumer behavior differences which are based on consumer ethics, nationality and culture (Lee et al., 2007). (Wan et al., 2010) assert the demographic factors which influence the Internet purchasing behaviors. Gender, age, location, and income were found to be an impact on frequency and expenditures of online purchases. As the relationship between age and Internet shopping motivations was examined by (Patricia et al., 2005), consumers who were younger considered online shopping as more pleasurable with utilitarian benefits in comparison to the older consumers.

E-Marketing and E-Commerce in Emerging Markets

A boom, which is taking place in electronic commerce, in parallel with the tremendous increase in internet technology usage are opening the doors for various business opportunities (Butler & Peppard, 1998; Guan & Cheng, 2009; Shankar et al., 2003). Multimedia Super Corridor (MSC) development has been attracting a lot of attention in Malaysia, since it helps the Internet practices to accomplish and to develop their performances in lots of industries (Armesh et al., 2010b). Heinemann & Schwarzl, (2010d) and Sherman & Topol (1996) stated that bringing marketing, retailing and information technologies together will bring about a positive synergy, which can lead to value creation for business stockholders. Mohd Safar & Ali (2010) declared that there are a lot of benefits offered by the Internet, especially to youth, which can range from providing global connectivity that is the nature of it, to various users facilities and multimedia capabilities. There have been many discussions that focus on the role of the Internet in many realms like building loyalty among customers in addition to maximizing sales when it comes to the existing customers. As it can be observed, it does not come across as a surprise that marketers are augmenting their efforts in order to get attention from the audience when it comes to their websites. It is blatant from the extensive increase of marketing budgets in online campaigns (Alavi et al., 2016; Lorenzo et al., 2007; Mohseni et al., 2016; Rezaei, Emami, et al., 2016; Valaei et al., 2017; Valaei, Rezaei, Ismail, et al., 2016; Valaei, Rezaei, & Shahijan, 2016). Worldwide enterprise spending on Web 2.0 technologies alone is expected to exceed $4.6 billion by 2013 and online retailing (e-tailing) of products and services similar to Malaysia, the bread and butter of business-to-consumer (B2C) e-commerce, is shown to be undergoing an intense growth in the coming years (Khan, 2010).

In 1990's, the public had the internet available to them in an extensive range and the "World Wide Web" received an increase in popularity, mainly because there was a boom in the number of the Internet users (Primoz et al., 2006). Mohd Safar & Ali (2010) discover that there is sustainability in internet usage among the young Malay internet users since students are certainly an attractive target market for an online retailer in different product categories (Mummalaneni, 2005). When it comes to the Malaysian consumers, purchasing products or receiving services from online retailers is feasible since the Internet technology has gone through a speedy growth. The internet is the place for them to search for product information as well (Amin et al., 2014; Amin et al., 2015; Kwek Choon et al., 2010; Moghaddam et al., 2015; Rezaei & Amin, 2013; Rezaei et al., 2014; Rezaei & Ghodsi, 2014; Rezaei & Ismail, 2014). According to an online demographic survey, a male, between the ages of 18 to 40, who attended the minimum of secondary school, is a typical Net shopper. They normally did their shopping from home and their average income was roughly about $5000 (Sim & Koi, 2002). Armesh, et al., (2010a) declare that there is a huge impact from the Internet on the Malaysian computer industry. Around 1992 in Malaysia, the Internet usage had begun (Mohd Safar & Ali, 2010). Table 1.3 shows Malaysia's total population as well as the total number of internet users between the years of 2005 to 2008. Additionally, the numbers are %47 in 2005, %50 back in 2006, %53 in 2007 and %54 back in the year 2008 (Chai Har et al., 2011).

The youth, being the leaders of tomorrow, need to master the latest available technology today; and the internet is one of such technologies (Mohd Safar & Ali, 2010). A study by Armesh, et al., (2010a) which was conducted in Malaysia, finds that youngsters are considered as the main Internet users, who are also the purchasers of online computer-related products and e-commerce services. 76.3% of purchasers, who buy all the online computer-related products, are the ones who are below the age of 30. On the other hand, the older shoppers account for only 23.7% of purchases. Hence, keeping this fact in mind, online shopping is still being developed; there is not sufficient data on customer's behaviors along with their attitudes towards online shopping in Malaysia. Factors which can influence the intention of a customer for an online purchase in an online shopping environment particularly created the gap in this realm of research (Kwek Choon et al., 2010).

Mohd Safar & Ali (2010) found that there is the sustainability of internet usage among Malay youth. A previous study (Chai Har et al., 2011) mention that when it comes to online repurchase behaviors of Malaysian internet shoppers, determining the key driving factors are significant. According to (Dwivedi et al., 2008), researches in some countries like Ireland, India, France, Finland, Malaysia and the Philippines have demonstrated a low number of publications in Adoption and Diffusion areas of IS/IT/ICT; therefore, it can be indicated from the results that additional research opportunities exist in these countries. These kinds of researches will pave the path to extend the area of knowledge in this realm. For that reason, identifying the determinants, which affect the intentions of Malaysian consumers in an online purchasing environment, is highly crucial (Kwek Choon et al., 2010). Literature (Kalantari Shahijan et al., 2014; Mohd Safar & Ali, 2010; Rezaei, 2015; Rezaei, Ali, Amin, Jayashree, et al., 2016) has shown in their studies that most Malaysians find the world wide web (WWW) and e-mail internet facilities to be the most necessary. They believe that the availability of online services is welcomed and the Internet has arrived and it will be here to stay.

DEMOGRAPHIC CHARACTERISTICS AND APPS-COMMERCE DEVELOPMENT

The different perspectives, online shopping potentials, suggest a need for a greater understanding of the association that exist between the demographic characteristics of shoppers and their online purchase behavior (Chang & Samuel, 2004). Previous studies by (Atchariyachanvanich et al., 2007; Brunelle & Lapierre, 2008; Cai & Cude, 2008; Chang & Samuel, 2004; Hong-Youl et al., 2010; Patricia et al., 2005; Wan et al., 2010) assert that online demographic characteristics are of high importance, since they play a powerful role in the duration of a revisit, which can be an indicator of possible earnings in the future. A previous study (Akman & Mishra, 2010) argue that using the Internet is not just about the technology per se, but it is about the individuals too. Youth are a distinct target for corporations, mainly because of the advanced technology and their distinct demographic group, which is aimed at researchers (Djamasbi et al., 2010; Hannah & Lybecker, 2010). According to previous researches (Brunelle & Lapierre, 2008; Wan et al., 2010), a substantial issue which was not addressed properly is: "the impact of age and shopping experience on consumers' perception of online products and services". A substantial body of research by (Cai & Cude, 2008; Efthymios et al., 2010; Hannah & Lybecker, 2010; Lee et al., 2007; Sonia San et al., 2011; Talal et al., 2011; Tan et al., 2007) found that a few studies have explored the impact of cultural differences on online shopping behavior intention. "Cross-cultural impacts on consumer behavior" was not considered in the literature of marketing/MIS online shopping in general. Most researches in this area focus on shopping experiences, that are traditional (Lee et al., 2007; Su & Adams, 2005; Talal et al., 2011). According to (Armesh et al., 2010a), ethnicity brings about unique differences, when it comes to the levels of online marketing in Malaysia.

In the context of Malaysia, while the online retailing went through an exceptional growth, there is still a need to develop a better understanding of the factors, which can facilitate customers' online purchase intention. There is a limited available research in this realm and the lack of such information in Malaysian context is blatant (Chai Har et al., 2011). Moreover, specific online shopping and its effects on the undergraduate student have seldom been the focus of studies (Dan & Xu, 2011). Indeed, looking at university alumni, who are full of curiosity and the willingness to accept new things, it can be observed that the level of knowledge and more frequent access to the Internet are at a higher level in universities (Peng et al., 2008). The argument is that students' opinions are valid, even though this age group is not earning money, but they represent a population who will earn in the near future (Chang & Chen, 2008; Dan & Xu, 2011; Hart, 2008; Talal et al., 2011). Since younger and more educated population is among the many customers of online shopping, students can be considered as the appropriate target group to be studied (Chang & Chen, 2009).

According to Patricia, et al., (2005), demographics in parallel with shopping motivations and attitudes are the relatively significant factors to foresee the online shopping trends. They are the areas in the online shopping context which need to be further discovered for the future research opportunities. Zhang Tao, et al., (2010), in their review of literature, highlighted the fact that researchers had started to pay more attention to questions like: "How a firm should design its business model and marketing strategy based on the Internet?" or "How a firm should manage the online shop and offline shop at the same time?" As Hong-Youl, et al., (2010) emphasize that behavioral intention will be the result of the attitudes which exist towards a website. What it means is that the stronger attitudes may bear more influence on other intentions that are behavioral mainly due to the associated properties of those attitudes. It is clear why firms are willing to exploit the rapid growth in online purchasing activities. The critical importance of better understanding of online consumer transaction behavior is an obvious objective in this prospect too (Khan, 2010).

CONCLUSION

From a business perspective, applications of EC can be categorized into three divisions of business-to-consumer (B2C), business-to-business (B2B) and intra-organizational (Liu et al., 2005). Previous research (Khalifa & Limayem, 2003; Su & Adams, 2005) explained that electronic commerce (business-to-business (B2B) hand in hand with business-to-consumer (B2C), as two various forms, came into the picture as an efficient way to do business with definite growth potentials in the coming years. The current research investigates the predecessors to an online purchase intention when it comes to Business to Consumer (B2C) websites. According to (Su & Adams, 2005), business-to-consumer (B2C) refers to "the e-commerce model in which business sell to individual shoppers." B2C electronic commerce creates a kind of business-customer transaction, that is different from the traditional physical purchase (Lucía Melián & Víctor Padrón, 2010).

Looking at various business models in electronic commerce, which were environed and realized both in the literature realm and practical manners, the most debated approach is the B2C online shops, which is also referred to as electronic retailing, e-tailing (Khalifa & Limayem, 2003; Madlberger, 2004; Talal et al., 2011). Nevertheless, as it is suggested by many online retailing types of research, customers who purchase their needs online, have fundamental behavioral differences with those who prefer a more traditional retail shopping approaches (Ganesh et al., 2010). According to Grewal, et al., (2004), more studied are needed to establish a better understanding of the driving factors (or the lack of them) in profitability of online retail businesses. This matter should be accentuated mainly because of the differences which exist in retailing operations and issues from the store-based businesses. Many academic journals were published on the Internet retailing in a broad scope and a few studies have examined the online retailer behavioral intention in a narrow scope. Therefore, numerous authors distinguish customer loyalty and repurchase as major research topics in the realm of the Internet, which is in need of special attention.

FUTURE RESEARCH DIRECTIONS

1. Previous researches (Butler & Peppard, 1998; Laroche, 2010a, 2010b) state that modeling the internet consumer behavior is required. Therefore, future studies should contribute to the knowledge of new insights about the consumer behavior model in the context of Apps shopping. In addition, future research can be generalized in the world, because of the convergence that exists among the youth (Chuanlan & Sandra, 2010; Taylor & Strutton, 2010).
2. Firms, in emerging markets, ought to comprehend the marketplace very well, since it will benefit their products as well as their target customers before they get involved in online retailing approaches (Chai Har et al., 2011). Entrepreneurs, hand in hand with the online retailers, should develop retail operations that are more effective and customer-focused to meet their online shopping customer's expectations and needs. This can be achieved via establishing a better understanding of their target customers.
3. Future researchers should spotlight on how to attract and to retain online customers nowadays since the Apps retail industry has been growing with a high level of competition now more than ever.
4. For a lot of organizations, having websites is the first initiator of the contact point between them and their customers. That is why the internet customer behavior has is gaining more magnitude in the research field (Jenamani et al., 2003).
5. It is declared that online shopping can have an influence on in-store shopping indeed. In fact, hybrid form of e-shopping and in-store shopping has been evolving (Farag et al., 2007). Enterprises and organizations have to restructure their own activities and work in both offline and online markets (Ieva & Gaile-Sarkane, 2009).
6. Gaining a new customer will cost about five times more than retaining an existing one; therefore, post-adoption behaviors and customer satisfaction studies are both relevant and appropriate.

7. The demographic characteristics analysis will bring about precious insights, which can assist managers in serving various customer segments in a better way.
8. Efthymios, et al., (2010) found that ignoring the cultural differences between countries or territories completely can be a mistake if it comes about too early or it is too far reaching.
9. Although in the literature of international business, the cultural differences, marketing, and their significance were highlighted, there are inadequate studies which were zoomed in the Internet sales as an emerging phenomenon. One of the promises of the current study is to fill this gap.

REFERENCES

Akman, I., & Mishra, A. (2010). Gender, age and income differences in internet usage among employees in organizations. *Computers in Human Behavior*, *26*(3), 482–490. doi:10.1016/j.chb.2009.12.007

Alavi, S. A., Rezaei, S., Valaei, N., & Wan Ismail, W. K. (2016). Examining shopping mall consumer decision-making styles, satisfaction and purchase intention. *International Review of Retail, Distribution and Consumer Research*, *26*(3), 272–303. doi:10.1080/09593969.2015.1096808

Amin, M., Rezaei, S., & Abolghasemi, M. (2014). User satisfaction with mobile websites: The impact of perceived usefulness (pu), perceived ease of use (peou) and trust. *Nankai Business Review International*, *5*(3), 258–274. doi:10.1108/NBRI-01-2014-0005

Amin, M., Rezaei, S., & Tavana, F. S. (2015). Gender differences and consumers repurchase intention: The impact of trust propensity, usefulness and ease of use for implication of innovative online retail. *International Journal of Innovation and Learning*, *17*(2), 217–233. doi:10.1504/IJIL.2015.067409

Armesh, H., Salarzehi, H., & Yaghoobi, N. M. (2010b). Impact of online/internet marketing on computer industry in malaysia in enhancing consumer experience. *International Journal of Marketing Studies*, *2*(2), 75–86. doi:10.5539/ijms.v2n2p75

Armesh, H., Salarzehi, H., Yaghoobi, N. M., Heydari, A., & Nikbin, D. (2010a). The effects of security and privacy information on trust & trustworthiness and loyalty in online marketing in malaysia. *International Journal of Marketing Studies*, *2*(2), 223–234. doi:10.5539/ijms.v2n2p223

Atchariyachanvanich, K., Okada, H., & Sonehara, N. (2007). *Theoretical model of purchase and repurchase in internet shopping: Evidence from japanese online customers*. Paper presented at the Proceedings of the ninth international conference on Electronic commerce, Minneapolis, MN. doi:10.1145/1282100.1282146

Badrinarayanan, V., Becerra, E., Kim, C.-H., & Madhavaram, S. (2010). Transference and congruence effects on purchase intentions in online stores of multi-channel retailers: Initial evidence from the u.S. And south korea. *Journal of the Academy of Marketing Science*, 1–19. doi:10.1007/s11747-010-0239-9

Brunelle, E., & Lapierre, J. (2008). *Testing media richness theory to explain consumers' intentions of buying online*. Paper presented at the 10th international conference on Electronic commerce, Innsbruck, Austria. doi:10.1145/1409540.1409582

Butler, P., & Peppard, J. (1998). Consumer purchasing on the internet: Processes and prospects. *European Management Journal, 16*(5), 600–610. doi:10.1016/S0263-2373(98)00036-X

Cai, S., & Xu, Y. (2006). Effects of outcome, process and shopping enjoyment on online consumer behaviour. *Electronic Commerce Research and Applications, 5*(4), 272–281. doi:10.1016/j.elerap.2006.04.004

Cai, Y., & Cude, B. J. (2008). Online shopping. In J. J. Xiao (Ed.), *Handbook of consumer finance research* (pp. 137–159). Springer New York. doi:10.1007/978-0-387-75734-6_9

Chai Har, L., Uchenna Cyril, E., & Nelson Oly, N. (2011). Analyzing key determinants of online repurchase intentions. *Asia Pacific Journal of Marketing and Logistics, 23*(2), 200–221. doi:10.1108/13555851111120498

Chang, H. H., & Chen, S. W. (2008). The impact of customer interface quality, satisfaction and switching costs on e-loyalty: Internet experience as a moderator. *Computers in Human Behavior, 24*(6), 2927–2944. doi:10.1016/j.chb.2008.04.014

Chang, H. H., & Chen, S. W. (2009). Consumer perception of interface quality, security, and loyalty in electronic commerce. *Information & Management, 46*(7), 411–417. doi:10.1016/j.im.2009.08.002

Chang, J., & Samuel, N. (2004). Internet shopper demographics and buying behaviour in australia. *Journal of American Academy of Business, Cambridge, 5*(1/2), 171–176.

Chuanlan, L., & Sandra, F. (2010). Post-adoption online shopping continuance. *International Journal of Retail & Distribution Management, 38*(2), 97–114. doi:10.1108/09590551011020110

Dan, S., & Xu, H. (2011). Research on online shopping intention of undergraduate consumer in china--based on the theory of planned behavior. *International Business Research*, *4*(1), 86–92.

Dittmar, H., Long, K., & Meek, R. (2004). Buying on the internet: Gender differences in on-line and conventional buying motivations. *Sex Roles*, *50*(5), 423–444. doi:10.1023/B:SERS.0000018896.35251.c7

Djamasbi, S., Siegel, M., & Tullis, T. (2010). Generation y, web design, and eye tracking. *International Journal of Human-Computer Studies*, *68*(5), 307–323. doi:10.1016/j.ijhcs.2009.12.006

Dwivedi, Y., Williams, M., & Lal, B. (2008). The diffusion of research on the adoption and diffusion of information technology. In G. León, A. Bernardos, J. Casar, K. Kautz, & J. De Gross (Eds.), Open it-based innovation: Moving towards cooperative it transfer and knowledge diffusion (Vol. 287, pp. 3-22). Springer Boston. doi:10.1007/978-0-387-87503-3_1

Efthymios, C., Carlota, L.-R., & Miguel, A. G. (2010). Effects of web experience on consumer choice: A multicultural approach. *Internet Research*, *20*(2), 188–209. doi:10.1108/10662241011032245

Farag, S., Schwanen, T., Dijst, M., & Faber, J. (2007). Shopping online and/or in-store? A structural equation model of the relationships between e-shopping and in-store shopping. *Transportation Research Part A, Policy and Practice*, *41*(2), 125–141. doi:10.1016/j.tra.2006.02.003

Ganesh, J., Reynolds, K. E., Luckett, M., & Pomirleanu, N. (2010). Online shopper motivations, and e-store attributes: An examination of online patronage behavior and shopper typologies. *Journal of Retailing*, *86*(1), 106–115. doi:10.1016/j.jretai.2010.01.003

Grewal, D., Iyer, G. R., & Levy, M. (2004). Internet retailing: Enablers, limiters and market consequences. *Journal of Business Research*, *57*(7), 703–713. doi:10.1016/S0148-2963(02)00348-X

Guan, H.-L., & Cheng, B.-D. (2009). *Analysis on the consumer's online information search behavior.* Paper presented at the E-Business and Information System Security, 2009. EBISS '09. International Conference on.

Hannah, B., & Lybecker, K. M. (2010). Determinants of recent online purchasing and the percentage of income spent online. *International Business Research*, *3*(4), 60–71. doi:10.5539/ibr.v3n4p60

Hart, M. (2008). *Do online buying behaviour and attitudes to web personalization vary by age group?* Paper presented at the 2008 annual research conference of the South African Institute of Computer Scientists and Information Technologists on IT research in developing countries: riding the wave of technology, Wilderness, South Africa. doi:10.1145/1456659.1456670

Heinemann, G., & Schwarzl, C. (2010a). *New online retailing — what does it mean? In New online retailing* (pp. 19–91). Gabler.

Heinemann, G., & Schwarzl, C. (2010b). *Online retailing in transition – revolution, not evolution. In New online retailing* (pp. 1–18). Gabler.

Hoffman, D. L. T. P. N., & Novak, T. P. (1996). Marketing in hypermedia computer-mediated environments: Conceptual foundations. *Journal of Marketing*, *60*(July), 50–68. doi:10.2307/1251841

Hong-Youl, H., Swinder, J., & Siva, K. M. (2010). A new understanding of satisfaction model in e-re-purchase situation. *European Journal of Marketing*, *44*(7), 997–1016.

Ieva, A., & Gaile-Sarkane, E. (2009). Behavioral differences in consumer purchasing behavior between online and traditional shopping: Case of latvia. *Economics & Management*, 345-352.

Jenamani, M., Mohapatra, P. K. J., & Ghose, S. (2003). A stochastic model of e-customer behavior. *Electronic Commerce Research and Applications*, *2*(1), 81–94. doi:10.1016/S1567-4223(03)00010-3

Kalantari Shahijan, M., Rezaei, S., Nigel Preece, C., & Khairuzzaman Wan Ismail, W. (2014). Examining retailers behaviour in managing critical points in halal meat handling: A pls analysis. *Journal of Islamic Marketing*, *5*(3), 446–472. doi:10.1108/JIMA-10-2013-0070

Khalifa, M., & Limayem, M. (2003). Drivers of internet shopping. *Communications of the ACM*, *46*(12), 233–239. doi:10.1145/953460.953505

Khan, O. J. (2010). Understanding consumer transaction behaviour in web retailing. *International Journal of Business and Management*, *4*(2), 17–36.

Kim, M.-J., Chung, N., & Lee, C.-K. (2011). The effect of perceived trust on electronic commerce: Shopping online for tourism products and services in south korea. *Tourism Management*, *32*(2), 256–265. doi:10.1016/j.tourman.2010.01.011

Kwek Choon, L., Lau Teck, C., & Tan Hoi, P. (2010). The effects of shopping orientations, online trust and prior online purchase experience toward customers' online purchase intention. *International Business Research*, *3*(3), 63–76.

Lao, G., & Hu, S. (2005). *Strategic enlightenment from retailing to e-tailing*. Paper presented at the 7th international conference on Electronic commerce, Xi'an, China. doi:10.1145/1089551.1089554

Laroche, M. (2010a). Advances in internet consumer behavior and marketing strategy: Introduction to the special issue. *Journal of Business Research*, *63*(9-10), 1015–1017. doi:10.1016/j.jbusres.2009.06.010

Laroche, M. (2010b). New developments in modeling internet consumer behavior: Introduction to the special issue. *Journal of Business Research*, *63*(9-10), 915–918. doi:10.1016/j.jbusres.2008.12.013

Lee, K., Joshi, K., & McIvor, R. (2007). *Understanding multicultural differences in online satisfaction*. Paper presented at the 2007 ACM SIGMIS CPR conference on Computer personnel research: The global information technology workforce, St. Louis, MO. doi:10.1145/1235000.1235048

Lian, J.-W., & Lin, T.-M. (2008). Effects of consumer characteristics on their acceptance of online shopping: Comparisons among different product types. *Computers in Human Behavior*, *24*(1), 48–65. doi:10.1016/j.chb.2007.01.002

Liu, C., Marchewka, J. T., Lu, J., & Yu, C.-S. (2005). Beyond concerna privacy-trust-behavioral intention model of electronic commerce. *Information & Management*, *42*(2), 289–304. doi:10.1016/j.im.2004.01.003

Lorenzo, C., Constantinides, E., Geurts, P., & Gómez, M. (2007). Impact of web experience on e-consumer responses. In G. Psaila & R. Wagner (Eds.), E-commerce and web technologies (Vol. 4655, pp. 191-200). Springer Berlin / Heidelberg. doi:10.1007/978-3-540-74563-1_19

Lu, Y., Cao, Y., Wang, B., & Yang, S. (2011). A study on factors that affect users behavioral intention to transfer usage from the offline to the online channel. *Computers in Human Behavior*, *27*(1), 355–364. doi:10.1016/j.chb.2010.08.013

Lucía Melián, A., & Víctor Padrón, R. (2010). The impact of pre-sale and post-sale factors on online purchasing satisfaction: A survey. *International Journal of Quality & Reliability Management*, *27*(2), 121–137. doi:10.1108/02656711011014267

Madlberger, M. (2004). *Strategies and business models in electronic retailing: Indications from the u.S. And the uk*. Paper presented at the 6th international conference on Electronic commerce, Delft, The Netherlands. doi:10.1145/1052220.1052258

Moghaddam, H. A., Rezaei, S., & Amin, M. (2015). Examining job seekers perception and behavioural intention toward online recruitment: A pls path modelling approach. *Journal for Global Business Advancement, 8*(3), 305–325. doi:10.1504/JGBA.2015.071331

Mohd Safar, H., & Ali, S. (2010). Factors affecting sustainability of internet usage among youth. *The Electronic Library, 28*(2), 300–313. doi:10.1108/02640471011033657

Mohseni, S., Jayashree, S., Rezaei, S., Kasim, A., & Okumus, F. (2016). Attracting tourists to travel companies websites: The structural relationship between website brand, personal value, shopping experience, perceived risk and purchase intention. *Current Issues in Tourism*, 1–30. doi:10.1080/13683500.2016.1200539

Muhammad Najib, R., Zaharah, M., & Azlina Mohd, Y. (2010). Internet business strategies by property companies in asia. *Property Management, 28*(4), 270–289. doi:10.1108/02637471011065692

Mummalaneni, V. (2005). An empirical investigation of web site characteristics, consumer emotional states and on-line shopping behaviors. *Journal of Business Research, 58*(4), 526–532. doi:10.1016/S0148-2963(03)00143-7

Ng, C. F. (2003). Satisfying shoppers psychological needs: From public market to cyber-mall. *Journal of Environmental Psychology, 23*(4), 439–455. doi:10.1016/S0272-4944(02)00102-0

OCass, A., & Fenech, T. (2003). Web retailing adoption: Exploring the nature of internet users web retailing behaviour. *Journal of Retailing and Consumer Services, 10*(2), 81–94. doi:10.1016/S0969-6989(02)00004-8

Patricia, S., Victor, P., & Stanley, W. (2005). Attitude and age differences in online buying. *International Journal of Retail & Distribution Management, 33*(2), 122–132. doi:10.1108/09590550510581458

Peng, H., Wang, C., & Cai, J. (2008). *An empirical investigation on the adoption of online shopping of university students in china.* Paper presented at the Business and Information Management, 2008. ISBIM '08. International Seminar on.

Peterson, R. A., & Balasubramanian, S. (2002). Retailing in the 21st century: Reflections and prologue to research. *Journal of Retailing, 78*(1), 9–16. doi:10.1016/S0022-4359(01)00062-8

Primoz, J., Maja, B., Tanja, M., Barbara, P., & Darko, M. (2006). Who says that old dogs cannot learn new tricks?: A survey of internet/web usage among seniors. *New Library World, 107*(7), 332–345.

Rezaei, S. (2015). Segmenting consumer decision-making styles (cdms) toward marketing practice: A partial least squares (pls) path modeling approach. *Journal of Retailing and Consumer Services*, *22*, 1–15. doi:10.1016/j.jretconser.2014.09.001

Rezaei, S., Ali, F., Amin, M., & Jayashree, S. (2016). Online impulse buying of tourism products: The role of web site personality, utilitarian and hedonic web browsing. *Journal of Hospitality and Tourism Technology*, *7*(1), 60–83. doi:10.1108/JHTT-03-2015-0018

Rezaei, S., Ali, F., Amin, M., Jayashree, S., & Cobanoglu, C. (2016). Online impulse buying of tourism products: The role of website personality, utilitarian and hedonic web browsing. *Journal of Hospitality and Tourism Technology*, *7*(1), 60–83. doi:10.1108/JHTT-03-2015-0018

Rezaei, S., & Amin, M. (2013). Exploring online repurchase behavioural intention of university students in malaysia. *Journal for Global Business Advancement*, *6*(2), 92–119. doi:10.1504/JGBA.2013.053561

Rezaei, S., Amin, M., & Ismail, W. K. W. (2014). Online repatronage intention: An empirical study among malaysian experienced online shoppers. *International Journal of Retail & Distribution Management*, *42*(5), 390–421. doi:10.1108/IJRDM-03-2012-0026

Rezaei, S., Amin, M., Moghaddam, M., & Mohamed, N. (2016). 3g post adoption users experience with telecommunications services. *Nankai Business Review International*, *7*(3), 361–394. doi:10.1108/NBRI-01-2016-0007

Rezaei, S., Emami, M., & Valaei, N. (2016). *The moderating impact of product classification on the relationship between online trust, satisfaction, and repurchase intention. In Encyclopedia of e-commerce development, implementation, and management* (p. 1692). IGI Global.

Rezaei, S., & Ghodsi, S. S. (2014). Does value matters in playing online game? An empirical study among massively multiplayer online role-playing games (mmorpgs). *Computers in Human Behavior*, *35*, 252–266. doi:10.1016/j.chb.2014.03.002

Rezaei, S., & Ismail, W. K. W. (2014). Examining online channel selection behaviour among social media shoppers: A pls analysis. *International Journal of Electronic Marketing and Retailing*, *6*(1), 28–51. doi:10.1504/IJEMR.2014.064876

Rezaei, S., Shahijan, M. K., Amin, M., & Ismail, W. K. W. (2016). Determinants of app stores continuance behavior: A pls path modelling approach. *Journal of Internet Commerce*, *15*(4), 408–440. doi:10.1080/15332861.2016.1256749

Rotem-Mindali, O. (2010). E-tail versus retail: The effects on shopping related travel empirical evidence from israel. *Transport Policy*, *17*(5), 312–322. doi:10.1016/j.tranpol.2010.02.005

Shankar, V., Smith, A. K., & Rangaswamy, A. (2003). Customer satisfaction and loyalty in online and offline environments. *International Journal of Research in Marketing*, *20*(2), 153–175. doi:10.1016/S0167-8116(03)00016-8

Sim, L. L., & Koi, S. M. (2002). Singapores internet shoppers and their impact on traditional shopping patterns. *Journal of Retailing and Consumer Services*, *9*(2), 115–124. doi:10.1016/S0969-6989(01)00029-7

Sonia San, M., Carmen, C., & Rebeca San, J. (2011). Dual effect of perceived risk on cross-national e-commerce. *Internet Research*, *21*(1), 46–66. doi:10.1108/10662241111104875

Su, Q.-Y., & Adams, C. (2005). *Will b2c e-commerce developed in one cultural environment be suitable for another culture: A cross-cultural study between amazon.co.uk (UK) and dangdang.com (China)*. Paper presented at the 7th international conference on Electronic commerce, Xi'an, China. doi:10.1145/1089551.1089598

Talal, A., Charles, D., & Sue Vaux, H. (2011). Antecedents of continuance intentions towards e-shopping: The case of saudi arabia. *Journal of Enterprise Information Management*, *24*(1), 85–111. doi:10.1108/17410391111097447

Tan, F. b., Yan, L., & Urquhart, C. (2007). The effect of cultural differences on attitude, peer influence, external influence, and self-efficacy in actual online shopping behavior. *Journal of Information Science & Technology*, *4*(1), 3–23.

Tao, Z., Guijun, Z., & Yuanyuan, H. (2010). A literature review on the studies of internet retailing management. *Technology & Investment*, *1*(1), 19–25. doi:10.4236/ti.2010.11003

Taylor, D. G., & Strutton, D. (2010). Has e-marketing come of age? Modeling historical influences on post-adoption era internet consumer behaviors. *Journal of Business Research*, *63*(9-10), 950–956. doi:10.1016/j.jbusres.2009.01.018

Valaei, N., Rezaei, S., & Ismail, W. K. W. (2017). Examining learning strategies, creativity, and innovation at smes using fuzzy set qualitative comparative analysis and pls path modeling. *Journal of Business Research*, *70*, 224–233. doi:10.1016/j.jbusres.2016.08.016

Valaei, N., Rezaei, S., Ismail, W. K. W., & Moi, O. Y. (2016). Cultural effect on attitude toward online advertising and online brands: Applying hofstedes cultural factors to internet marketing. *International Journal of Internet Marketing and Advertising*, *10*(4), 270. doi:10.1504/IJIMA.2016.081346

Valaei, N., Rezaei, S., & Shahijan, M. K. (2016). Couqual: Assessing overall service quality in courier service industry and the moderating impact of age, gender and ethnicity. *International Journal of Management Concepts and Philosophy*, *9*(2), 144–169. doi:10.1504/IJMCP.2016.077770

Varadarajan, R., Srinivasan, R., Vadakkepatt, G. G., Yadav, M. S., Pavlou, P. A., Krishnamurthy, S., & Krause, T. (2010). Interactive technologies and retailing strategy: A review, conceptual framework and future research directions. *Journal of Interactive Marketing*, *24*(2), 96–110. doi:10.1016/j.intmar.2010.02.004

Wan, Y., Nakayama, M., & Sutcliffe, N. (2010). The impact of age and shopping experiences on the classification of search, experience, and credence goods in online shopping. *Information Systems and E-Business Management*, 1-14. doi:10.1007/s10257-010-0156-y

Xiao, T. (2010). A cross-national investigation of an extended technology acceptance model in the online shopping context. *International Journal of Retail & Distribution Management*, *38*(10), 742–759. doi:10.1108/09590551011076524

Yeo, V. C. S., Goh, S.-K., & Rezaei, S. (2017). Consumer experiences, attitude and behavioral intention toward online food delivery (ofd) services. *Journal of Retailing and Consumer Services*, *35*, 150–162. doi:10.1016/j.jretconser.2016.12.013

Zhu, D.-S., Tsai, C.-H., & Huang, S.-S. (2010). An exploration of the intention to use online store. In R. Lee (Ed.), Computer and information science 2010 (Vol. 317, pp. 85-94). Springer Berlin / Heidelberg. doi:10.1007/978-3-642-15405-8_8

KEY TERMS AND DEFINITIONS

Apps Retailing: Sale of goods and services through the Apps and related technologies.

Business Model: The entire approach in which a firm creates value, income and makes a profit from the operations.

Emerging Markets: Developing economies by either nominal or PPP-adjusted GDP.

Web 2.0: The second generation of the Internet which is focused on the ability for consumers to collaborate and share information.

Chapter 4
Security Problems in Cloud Computing Environments:
A Deep Analysis and a Secure Framework

Mouna Jouini
Laboratoire SOIE, Institut Sup'erieur de Gestion, Tunisia

Latifa Ben Arfa Rabai
Laboratoire SOIE, Institut Sup'erieur de Gestion, Tunisia

ABSTRACT

Cloud computing technology is a relatively new concept of providing scalable and virtualized resources, software and hardware on demand to consumers. It presents a new technology to deliver computing resources as a service. It offers a variety of benefits like services on demand and provisioning and suffers from several weaknesses. In fact security presents a major obstacle in cloud computing adoption. In this chapter, we will deal with security problems in cloud computing systems and show how to solve these problems using a quantitative security risk assessment model named Multi-dimensional Mean Failure Cost (M^2FC). In fact, we present first a deep analysis of security issues related to cloud computing environments and then propose a generic framework that analysis and evaluate cloud security problems and then propose appropriate countermeasures to solve these problems.

DOI: 10.4018/978-1-5225-2449-6.ch004

Copyright ©2017, IGI Global. Copying or distributing in print or electronic forms without written permission of IGI Global is prohibited.

INTRODUCTION

Cloud Computing technology is a new concept of providing dramatically scalable and virtualized resources, software and hardware on demand to consumers. Cloud Computing offers a whole new paradigm to allow the users having high end and scalable infrastructure at an affordable cost. It is based on many new technologies like virtualization, distributed computing, utility computing, cryptography and web services. However, security concerns are terrible for these systems whose infrastructure and computational resources are owned by an outside party that sells those services to the general public. In fact, data breaches to Cloud services are also increasing every year due to hackers who are always trying to exploit the security vulnerabilities of the Cloud architecture.

In this chapter, we provide a detailed analysis of security issues of Cloud Computing systems besides the countermeasure of each one. We also present potential risks and impacts of these challenges in Cloud customers and security requirements.

The remainder of this chapter organized as follows. Section 2 presents related work. Section 3 shows security threats in Cloud Computing systems. Section 4 presents security issues in Cloud Computing environments. Section 5 illustrates a quantitative security risk model that we will use in our new approach. Section 6 presents our security framework that solves security problems in Cloud Computing environments in a quantitative way. Finally, conclusions and a direction for future work are given in section 7.

SECURITY ON CLOUD COMPUTING SYSTEM

Cloud Computing is a new way of delivering computing resources, as a public utility. Computing services such as data storage and email handling are now instantly available, and on demand. It is an on demand service model for IT provision, often based on virtualization and distributed computing technologies. It offers many benefits like highly abstracted resources, services on demand with a ''pay as you go'' billing system, immediate provisioning, shared resources (hardware, database, memory…) and programmatic management tool (Grobauer, Walloschek, & Stocker, 2011). Cloud Computing is such a type of computing environment, where business owners outsource their computing needs including application software services to a third party; and when they need to use the computing power or employees need to use the application resources like database, and emails, they access the resource via internet.

Cloud Computing can be considered a new computing paradigm as it allows the utilization of a computing infrastructure at one or more levels of abstraction, as an on-demand service made available over the Internet or other computer network. Because of the implications for greater flexibility and availability at lower cost, Cloud Computing is a subject that has been receiving a good deal of attention lately (Grobauer, Walloschek, & Stocker, 2011). It received a considerable attention from global and local IT players, national governments, and international agencies (Ben Arfa Rabai, Jouini, Ben Aissa & Mili, 2012; Jouini, Ben Arfa Rabai, Ben Aissa & Mili, 2012; Ben Arfa Rabai, Jouini, Ben Aissa & Mili, 2013). But as more and more information on individuals and companies is placed in the Cloud, concerns are beginning to grow about just how safe this environment is. The externalized aspect of outsourcing makes it harder to maintain data integrity and privacy, support data and service availability and demonstrate compliance. For example, IDC Enterprise Panel recently conducted a survey of 244 IT executives/ Chief Executive Officers (CIOs) and their line-of business (LOB) colleagues to gauge their opinions and understand their companies' use of IT Cloud services. Security ranked first as the greatest challenge or issue of Cloud Computing by 74,6%, then we find performance and availability by 63,1% (Gens, 2009). Furthermore, hackers could take advantage of the massive computing power of Clouds to fire attacks to users who are in the same or different networks. For instance, hackers rented a server through Amazon's EC2 service and carried out an attack to Sony's PlayStation Network (Amazon, 2011). Therefore, a good understanding of Cloud security problems and threats is necessary in order to provide more secure services to Cloud users.

RELATED WORK

In this section, we discuss several research works that enumerate security problems in Cloud

Computing systems and suggest some countermeasures to mitigate security risks. Gartner (2009) identified in (Gartner, 2009) seven security issues by adopting Cloud Computing environments. They are as follows: Privileged user access (information transmitted from the customer through the internet poses risks), regulatory compliance (clients are responsible for the security of their solution when it is detained by a service provider), data location (customers might never know in which country or jurisdiction their data is located), data segregation (risks posed by encrypted information by providers), recovery (every provider should have a disaster recovery mechanism to protect user data), investigative support (customer cannot pursue illegal activity committed by the provider) and long-term viability (to the ability to retract a contract and all data if the current provider is bought out by another firm).

ENISA (2010) studies the different security risks related to adopting Cloud Computing along with the affected assets, the risks likelihood, impacts, and vulnerabilities (ENISA, 2010). Balachandra et al. (2009) discussed in, (Balachandra, Ramakrishna PV & Rakshit, 2009), the security SLA's specification and objectives related to data locations, segregation and data recovery. In (Ahmed & Hossain, 2014), Ahmed et al. (2014) studied the most known security issues and threats that must be taken into account in the deployment of Cloud Computing (CC) infrastructure. The chapter addresses the following problems: Data location, trust between provider and customers and accounting and authentification. The work also discussed authentication of Cloud Computing as it forms the holistic basis to embed integrity in the context of Cloud Computing security. In (Grobauer, Walloschek, & Stocker, 2011), Grobauer et al. (2011) talk about the security vulnerabilities that threaten Cloud platform. They grouped the possible vulnerabilities into technology-related, Cloud characteristics-related and security controls related. In (Subashini & Kavitha, 2011), Subashini et al. (2011) discuss the security challenges of the Cloud service delivery model, focusing on the SaaS model. They cited mainly two problems: Multitenancy caused by hacker's intrusions or by client injection code into the SaaS system and data access problem. In (Bhadauria et al, 2011), Bhadauria et al. (2011) showed several risks related to data security in Cloud environments. In fact, data reside over a set of networked resources and are accessible through virtual machines. Indeed, they are hosted in data centers at any place of the world, which poses many security challenges like Cloud as SQL injection attacks, hidden field manipulation and distributed denial of service attacks.

A recent survey by Cloud Security Alliance (CSA) & IEEE (2009) indicates that enterprises across sectors are eager to adopt Cloud Computing but that security are needed both to accelerate cloud adoption on a wide scale and to respond to regulatory drivers (Cloud Security Alliance, 2009). It also details that Cloud Computing is shaping the future of IT but the absence of a compliance environment is having dramatic impact on CC growth. In (Kuyoro, Ibikunle, & Awodele, 2011), Kuyoro et al. (2011) considered that security plays a very important role in Cloud Computing. They presented an analysis of these challenges focusing on the Cloud Computing deployment types and the service delivery types. They cited some problems such as security of data storage on another person's hard disk, the loss of data and the problem of piracy.

Several studies in literature dealt with security concerns in Cloud Computing but we will present in this work a detailed analysis of the CC security problems and challenges, their impact on security requirements and their relative countermeasures.

SECURITY THREATS IN CLOUD COMPUTING SYSTEM

Security is one of the most challenging research works in Cloud Computing system because users secrete are by Cloud providers who try to protect the data from other outside source (Hanna, 2009; Subashini & Kavitha, 2010; Wooley, 2011; Xuan et al., 2010; Rittinghouse & Ransome, 2010). Indeed, by trusting its critical data to a service provider (externalization of service), a user (whether it be an individual or an organization) takes risks with the availability, confidentiality and integrity of this data. In addition to that, security is cited as the major issues for this environment by many surveys. For example, IDC entreprise recently conducted a survey of 244 IT executives/CIOs and their line-of business (LOB) colleagues to gauge their opinions and understand their companies' use of IT cloud services. So, Security ranked first as the greatest challenge or issue of cloud computing (Subashini & Kavitha, 2010; Xuan et al., 2010; Rittinghouse & Ransome, 2010).

We highlight in this section major security risks which can be classified into three categories. Each of these types of attacks is examined in more detail below (Cloud Security Alliance, 2010; Ibrahim et al., 2010; Subashini & Kavitha, 2010; Wayne & Timothy, 2011; Wooley, 2011):

- Security threats originating from the host (hypervisor),
- Security threats originating from the VMs,
- Security threats originating between the customer and the data center.

Security Threats Originating from the Host (Hypervisor)

Monitoring Virtual Machines from Host

Monitoring the VM from the hypervisor software is an important part of managing and controlling the VMs. Hypervisor is software that controls the layer between the hardware and the operating systems. The system administrator or other authorized user can make changes to the components of one or more virtual machines (VMs) which generates a security risk (Wooley, 2011).

Virtual Machine Modification

Hypervisor represents the next lower layer of software under the customer's operating system, applications and data. Attacks on the hypervisor layer are attractive to hackers because of the scope of control they can gain if they can install and execute their malicious software on this layer of the VM software (Ibrahim et al., 2010).

Compromising the hypervisor means that an attacker can take control of that layer and all of the hosted virtual machines that are hosted on that machine.

Threats on Communications between Virtual Machines and Host

In cloud computing system, all communications must pass through the hypervisor to all of the hosted VMs and at this point an attacker can inject malicious software in an attempt to eavesdrop or gain control over any or all of the systems. However, the worst case occurs when the hypervisor is compromised by malware, since this puts all the VMs that are being hosted on that machine at risk for security breaches (Wooley, 2011).

Placement of Malicious VM Images on Physical Systems

The attack known as cloud malware injection involves creating a malicious virtual machine image and then places that image into the hypervisor so that it is treated like a legitimate system in a collection of virtual machines. If this is successful, then the malicious virtual machine image is allowed to run the adversary's code (Ibrahim et al., 2010; Wooley, 2011).

Security Threats Originating between the Customer and the Datacenter

Flooding Attacks

Flooding attacks consist of overloading the server hosting services with an enormous number of requests for data processing (Wooley, 2011).

Denial of Service (DoS)

The denial of service attack is a critical problem for virtual machines (VMs) used on cloud components. In fact, it indicates that the hypervisor software is allowing a single VM to consume all the system resources and thus starving the remaining VMs and impairing their function (Wooley, 2011).

Data Loss or Leakage

The threat of data compromise increases because of the architectural or operational characteristics of the cloud environment (user's data is stored outside the enterprise boundary, by the service provider). Data loss may be caused operational failures, insufficient authentication or authorization, deletion or alteration of records without a backup of the original content, jurisdiction and political issues, disasters, inconsistent use of encryption and software keys. Thus, intrusion of data can be done either by hacking through the loop holes in the application or by injecting client code into the system (Subashini & Kavitha, 2010; Wayne & Timothy, 2011).

Malicious Insiders

This threat is amplified for consumers of cloud services by the convergence of information technology (IT) services combined with a general lack of transparency into provider process and procedure (Cloud Security Alliance, 2010). Such threats include fraud, sabotage and theft or loss of confidential information caused by trusted insiders. The impact that malicious insiders can have on an organization is considerable, given their level of access and ability to infiltrate organizations and assets like brand damage, financial impact and productivity losses.

Account, Service, and Traffic Hijacking

Attack methods such as phishing, fraud and exploitation of software vulnerabilities still achieve results. Cloud solutions add a new threat: If an attacker gains access to your credentials, they can eavesdrop on your activities and transaction, return falsified information and redirect your clients to illegitimate sites allowing them to compromise the confidentiality, integrity and availability of those services (Cloud Security Alliance, 2010).

Abuse and Nefarious Use of Cloud Computing

Cloud computing providers offer their customers an unlimited compute, network and storage capacity coupled with a week registration process where anyone with a valid credit card can register and immediately begin using cloud services. Cloud computing providers are so being under attack due to the weakness of their registration systems which let to spammers, malicious code authors and other criminals to perform their activities easily. We can site also as threats, zeus botnet, trojan horses (Cloud Security Alliance, 2010).

Insecure Application Programming Interfaces

Cloud computing providers expose a set of software interfaces or APIs that customers use to manage and interact with cloud services. These interfaces must be designed to protect against both accidental and malicious attempts to circumvent policy.

Reliance on a weak set of interfaces and APIs exposes organizations to a variety of security issues related to confidentiality, integrity, availability and accountability (Cloud Security Alliance, 2010). This category includes Anonymous access and/ or reusable tokens or passwords threat, clear-text authentication or transmission of content threat, inflexible access controls or improper authorizations threats, unknown service or API dependencies (Cloud Security Alliance, 2010).

Security Threats Originating from the Virtual Machines

Monitoring VMs from Other VMs

One of the security risks encountered when using virtual machines is the lack of guaranteed isolation of the application and data when a shared resource such as memory space is utilized by multiple VMs. Cloud computing servers can contain tens of VMs and these are vulnerable to attack whether they are active or not. VMs that are active are vulnerable to all of the security attacks that a conventional physical service is subject to. However, once a VM has been compromised by an attack on other VMs residing on the same physical server, they become all vulnerable to the same attack due to the fact that each machine shares memory, disk storage, driver software and hypervisor software (Ibrahim et al., 2010).

Virtual Machine Mobility

Virtual machines (VMs) which are disk images hosted in a hypervisor platform are easily copied or transferred to other locations. The ability to move and copy VMs poses a security risk because the entire system, applications and data can be stolen without physically stealing the machine (Wooley, 2011).

Threats on Communications between Virtual Machines

VMs are allowed to communicate with other VMs running on the same physical equipment using channels such as the shared clipboard functions. When sharing resources such as memory, real or virtual network connections, between VMs can introduce possible security risks for each machine because there is the possibility that one or more of the VMs has been compromised by malicious programs (Ibrahim et al., 2010; Wooley, 2011).

SECURITY PROBLEMS IN CLOUD COMPUTING APPLICATIONS

Cloud Computing system poses many new security problems due to the fact that sensitive applications and data are moved into the Cloud data centers, run on virtual computing resources in the form of virtual machine. This unique attribute poses significant vulnerabilities that should be considered when an organization is ready to move their critical applications and data to a Cloud Computing environment. We can link the vulnerabilities in CC to three main classes:

- Virtualization Vulnerability.
- Data Vulnerability.
- Software Vulnerability.

Regarding the architecture and the specific properties of Cloud systems, we identify these interrogations:

- Where is the data?
- Who has access to the data?
- What are the regulatory requirements?
- Whether the users have the right to Audit?
- What type of training does the provider offer their customers?
- What are the Service Level Agreement (SLA) terms?
- What happens if there is a security breach?
- What is the disaster recovery/Business continuity plan?

We classify security issues in Cloud Computing environments into nine sub-categories (Jouini & Ben Arfa Rabai, 2014), which include: Virtualization security issues, business services continuity, management interfaces risks, privacy issues, data location, data breaches, accountability problems, multi tenancy problem and regulation and governance problem.

Security Issues in Virtualization

Cloud Computing systems are based on many technologies like virtualization, distributed computing, cryptography and utility computing. Cloud Computing architecture is based on many virtualization components such hypervisor and virtual machine (Cloud Security Alliance, 2010; Armbrust et al. 2009). Hypervisor is a controller known also as virtual machine manager (VMM), which allows multiple operating systems to be run on a system at a time. Since multiple operating systems may be running on a single hardware platform, it is not possible to keep track of all such systems and hence maintaining the security of the operating systems is difficult. In this case, guest system can run malicious code on the machine system and bring the system down or take full control of the system and block access to other guest operating systems (Luo et al, 2009). Malicious insiders is a very serious attack hence it presents an opportunity for an adversary to harvest confidential data or gain complete control over the Cloud services with little or no risk of detection (Cloud Security Alliance, 2009).

In addition, virtual machines in Cloud Computing systems are vulnerable to many kinds of threats especially malware or malicious codes which infect machines. For example, the VM- based rootkits attack are designed to infect both client and server machines in Cloud: it abuses compromised systems by hiding files, registry keys and other operating system objects from diagnostic, antivirus and security programs. Also, VM and hypervisor are prone to other threats like communications between virtual machines and host, placement of malicious VM images on physical systems, monitoring VMs from other VM and communication between VMs and virtual machine mobility.

VM-based malware affect the confidentiality, the integrity and the availability of security requirements of Cloud Computing systems (Ramadianti, Medard, & Mganga, 2011; Wooley, 2011). In fact, confidentiality is at risk because the customers' data could be intercepted by malware. Integrity is at risk because the operation of the VM can be changed by malware which could lead to loss of integrity of the customers' data. Availability is at risk because malware can potentially erase, or obfuscate the customers' data (Wooley, 2011).

Business Services Continuity

Most organizations have some warnings of Cloud Computing use and the availability of their services. One more availability problem is distributed denial of service (DDoS) attacks. Attackers make use of large botnets (zombies) to reduce the profits of SaaS providers by DDoS by making their services unavailable (Armbrust et al, 2009; Reddy et al, 2011).

Furthermore, a major risk to services continuity in the Cloud Computing environment is loss of internet connectivity (that could occur due to some circumstances like natural disasters) as Cloud businesses are dependent on the internet access to their information. In addition, there are also concerns that the seizure of a data hosting server by law enforcement agencies may result in the unnecessary interruption or cessation of unrelated services whose data are stored on the same physical machine. This resulted in the unintended consequence of disrupting the continuity of businesses whose data and information are hosted on the seized hardware. Finally, many other threats cause unavailability of service like abuse and nefarious use of CC, authentication and authorization and service disruption (Ramadianti, Medard, & Mganga, 2011; Cloud Security Alliance, 2009).

Services availability problem poses a devastating impact on the brand and the reputation of organizations by causing unavailability of Cloud services. The security requirement related to this issue can be affected in case of availability is attacked (Cloud Security Alliance, 2009).

Management Interfaces Risks

Cloud Computing providers expose a set of software interfaces that customers use to manage and interact with Cloud services (like provisioning, management, orchestration, and monitoring). The customer management interfaces of public Cloud providers are Internet accessible and mediate access to larger sets of resources and therefore pose an increased risk especially when combined with remote access and web browser vulnerabilities (ENISA, 2010).

Unauthorized access to the management interface is therefore an especially relevant vulnerability for Cloud systems. These interfaces must be designed to protect against both accidental and malicious attempts because they allow authentication and access control to encryption and activity monitoring that depend directly on the security and availability of general Cloud ser- vices (Cloud Security Alliance, 2009). Indeed, Virtual machines must be protected against malicious attacks like Cloud malware. Therefore, Cloud providers must maintain the integrity of applications and well en- force accurate authentication checks during the transfer of data across the entire networking channels (Kuyoro, Ibikunle, & Awodele, 2011).

Moreover, Cloud interfaces are prone to many threats because they include customer interfaces which control a number of virtual machines and the operation of the overall Cloud system (ENISA, 2010). We can cite as threats: insecure interfaces and APIs threats (such as Anonymous access and/or reusable tokens or passwords, clear-text authentication or transmission of content, inflexible access controls or improper authorizations, limited monitoring and logging capabilities, unknown service or API dependencies), virtual machine modification and placement of malicious VM images on physical systems (Ben Arfa Rabai, Jouini, Ben Aissa & Mili, 2013; Ben Arfa Rabai, Jouini, Ben Aissa & Mili, 2012; Jouini, Ben Arfa Rabai, Ben Aissa & Mili, 2012; Cloud Security Alliance, 2009).

Reliance on a weak set of interfaces and APIs exposes organizations to a variety of security issues related to confidentiality, integrity, availability, authentification and authorization and accountability (Ramadianti, Medard, & Mganga, 2011; Wooley, 2011).

Data Breaches

Cloud Computing system allows the storage of customer data in different ways. In fact, data in Cloud systems travel in clusters, in virtual machines, in databases, or into third party storages; which increase the risk of information leak and data corruption. Indeed, operations in data centers might lead to information leak caused, for example, by a customer's information being mistaken by another's. Furthermore, most of the Cloud providers instead of acquiring a server try to rent a server from other service providers because they are cost affective and flexible for operation. This gives a high possibility for malicious insiders to steal customers' data can be stolen from the external server (ISO, 2009; Schechter, 2004).

Furthermore, there is the risk of rogue providers mining the data for secondary uses such as marketing and reselling the mined data to other businesses which cause data leak (Choo, 2010). In fact, Cloud services providers can provide confidential hosting and data storage services which can be abused by organized crime groups to store and distribute criminal data (like child abuse materials for commercial purposes) to avoid the scrutiny of law enforcement agencies. Moreover, certain Cloud services providers close due to financial or legal problems which lead to customers' data loss. Therefore, they will not be able to access those data because data is no longer available for them as the vendor shut down (Ben Arfa Rabai, Jouini, Ben Aissa & Mili, 2012).

Besides, Cloud computing poses several data protection risks for Cloud customers and providers. In some cases, it may be difficult for the Cloud customer (in its role as data controller) to effectively check the data handling practices of the Cloud provider and thus to be sure that the data is handled in a lawful way. This problem is exacerbated in cases of multiple data transfers, e.g., between federated Clouds (ENISA, 2010; Qaisar & Khawaja, 2012)

Many security threats can compromise data and provide losses and corruption as seen in previous works like (Ben Arfa Rabai, Jouini, Ben Aissa & Mili, 2012; Cloud Security Alliance, 2009; Grobauer, Walloschek, & Stocker, 2011):

- **Identity Theft:** Identity theft in the Cloud may lead to compromising data confidentiality and integrity of data.
- **Malware Attacks:** Cloud clients may be attacked by malware injected in the Cloud or in the network connection between Cloud customer and Cloud provider. Malware includes rootkit attack, trojan horses, cross site-scripting (XSS) attacks and viruses.
- **Lack of Data Segregation:** In multi-tenancy Cloud environment, there is a risk of one customer accessing or compromising data of other customers.
- **Data Loss:** Risks of losing data due to sharing them in the cloud.

- **Data Inconsistency:** Risks of data inconsistency due to interfacing with internal systems that are not in the cloud. Further, data inconsistency may be caused by dynamic update (inserting, deletion, modification) from multiple customers.
- **Insecure Interfaces and APIs:** Insecure API including weak authentication and access control may compromise Cloud customers' information.
- **Unauthorized Access Threats:** Rogue users and service providers' staff may access Cloud customers data due to extension of organization boundaries in the Cloud.
- **Threats Related to Virtualization Technology:** These include virtual machine mobility, monitoring virtual machines from host, communications between virtual machines and host, virtual machine modification, placement of malicious VM images on physical systems, security threats originating from the VMs Monitoring VMs from other VM, Communication between VMs and Virtual machine mobility.

Many security threats can compromise data and provide losses and corruption and it provoke a serious problems related to integrity, confidentiality and availability of data. The security requirements related to this issue and can be affect in case of attack are integrity, confidentiality and availability.

Compliance and Governance

As security in Cloud Computing systems presents a big challenge, cloud vendor has to provide some assurance in service level agreements (SLA) to convince the customer on security issues. The SLA illustrates different security levels and tries to make the customer understand the security policies that are being implemented. Customers may, also, in the SLA indicate its expectations in terms of security for these types of systems. Providers must deliver a comprehensive list of regulations that govern the system and associated services and how compliance with these items is executed (Cloud Security Alliance, 2009).

However, the SLA may not offer a promise to provide such services on the part of the Cloud provider which can create several security breaches (for example meet privacy and confidentiality needs) for many reasons. In fact, Cloud providers cannot give evidence of their own conformity with the relevant requirements and do not permit external audit by the Cloud customer and/or security certifications (Cloud Security Alliance, 2009; ENISA, 2010; Kuyoro, Ibikunle, & Awodele, 2011). In addition, a more serious problem is that there is no way to specify the policies on how sensitive data are shared, treated and located among Cloud service providers. In fact, information is routinely leaked with poor data management practices. Cloud service providers must ensure, for example, the data security in natural disasters. Indeed, there are certain legal issues entangled with Cloud security as well, because there are certain laws that Cloud service providers should comply with and these laws vary from country to country which may cause data replication across multiple sites.

Finally, many threats pose risks to SLA accomplishment (Ramadianti, Medard & Mganga, 2011). These risks give the difficulty to audit the data and verify the logs of data access (accountability breach). Attacks include (Ramadianti, Medard & Mganga, 2011):

- **Regulatory and Legal Issues:** It is difficult to enforce customers' information technology (IT) regulatory and legal issues as the data is stored outside the organizations.
- **Audit Difficulty:** It is difficult to audit a third party Cloud provider as the data may be distributed across several geographical locations.

Access Problem: Data Location

Cloud Computing environments suffer from lack of transparency since customer' data are located in Cloud provider data centers and anywhere in the world, and hence are out of the customer's control which leads to many problems (Cloud Security Alliance, 2009; Min, Shin & Bang, 2012; Dawei et al, 2011). In fact, the user space may be shared across applications that can lead to data replication, making mapping of users and their privileges a complicated task. This, also, requires the user to remember multiple accounts passwords and maintain them which may entail forgetting them in many cases. Indeed, by using the Cloud, users need to look at whom (their role and their privileges...) is managing (get access to) their data (when they release the information into the Cloud for processing) and what types of controls are applied to these individuals (Gartner, 2009; Min, Shin & Bang, 2012)

Data breaches present a crucial problem for organizations. For example: many organizations such as financial institutions, health care providers, and government agencies are legally required to protect their data from compromise due to the sensitivity of their information. Generally, these organizations are required to manage and maintain their own datacenters with stringent physical and logical protection mechanisms ensuring that their data remain protected. These organizations simply cannot utilize Cloud Computing in a generic manner due to the inherent risk of data compromise from systems they do not control.

Moreover, as the Cloud Computing users' sensitive data are stored in Cloud servers, identity management and authentication are very crucial and the verification of eligible users' credentials and protecting such credentials are part of main security issues in the Cloud because any violation in these areas could lead to undetected security breach. Indeed, many security threats menace authentification and identity managements (ID) and encryption keys. For example, disclosure of secret keys (SSL, file encryption, and customer private keys), loss or corruption of those keys, or their unauthorized use for authentication (Ramadianti, Medard & Mganga, 2011; Cloud Security Alliance, 2009; ENISA, 2010; Emam, 2013) insecure interfaces and APIs (insecure API including weak authentication and access control may compromise cloud customer's information), brute force attack that decrypts various types of passwords and then abusing cloud computing services and business (Choo, 2010), man in the middle attacks (MITM) and sniffing attack (ENISA, 2010). In addition, Insider attacks can access the cloud and easily breach the access to user's data and applications which poses a huge risk (Gartner, 2009; Min, Shin & Bang, 2012).

Similarly, loss of credentials causes access to customer data and connection as a valid user.

In fact, to connect to cloud, a client sends the request to the server by web browser which in turn has to make use of SSL to encrypt the credentials to authenticate the user. SSL support point to point communication means if there is third party, intermediary host can decrypt the data. If hacker installs sniffing packages on intermediary host, the attacker may get the credentials of the user and use them in the cloud system as a valid user.

The threat may involve fraud, theft of confidential or commercially valuable information, theft of intellectual property, or the sabotage of computer systems. Any threat has a considerable impact on organization, given its level of access and ability to infiltrate organizations and assets. It can cause as well brand damage, financial impact, and productivity losses for an operation. In fact, insider threats are harder to defend against than attacks from outsiders, since the insider already has legitimate access to the organization's information and assets. Data location problem touches confidentiality, integrity, availability (users can not access to their data), access control (identification and authorization) requirements (Ramadianti, Medard & Mganga, 2011; Cloud Security Alliance, 2009).

Privacy Issues

Privacy problems in Cloud Computing environments come from many reasons. First, Cloud

Computing customer's data and especially personal information can be breached more easily than if stored in users' machines (ENISA, 2010; Dawei et al, 2011). In fact, customer's data are stored in services provider's data centers and thus it is not guaranteed if the providers will protect their data and especially their personal information. Indeed, as most of the servers are external, the provider should make sure who is accessing the data and who is maintaining the server to protect the customer's personal information. Also, in the shared infrastructure, customers' private information risk more potential unauthorized access and exposure (ENISA, 2010; Dawei et al, 2011).

Moreover, privacy problems for organizations stems from the diversity of privacy regulations from country to country. In fact, data in Cloud system are stored anywhere and user cannot guess if you are violating privacy regulations in the countries where you operate ((ENISA, 2010; Dawei et al, 2011). Indeed, there is a need for approaches to label directly the data with security and privacy policies that would travel with sensitive data from one provider to another so that the proper technical controls can be employed by various Cloud providers to protect the data (Hamid, Bryan & Sharad, 2009).

Data are prone in this case to many attacks like: Sniffing, spoofing, man in the middle attacks, side channel and replay attacks and so in some cases the CP does not guarantee respect for the confidentiality or the non disclosure of information (ENISA, 2010).

Privacy breaches allow confidentiality problems and data leakage which leads to serious financial implications to organization and customer's trust loss (Cloud Security Alliance, 2009).

Isolation Failure (Multi Tenancy Problem)

Multi-tenancy and shared resources (computing capacity, storage, network, memory, and routing) represent main characteristics of Cloud Computing environments. There is a risk of failure of deferent mechanisms between different tenants of the shared infrastructure due to principally hypervisor vulnerability. In fact, infrastructure as a service (IaaS) Cloud layer relies on architectural designs where physical resources are shared by multiple virtual machines and therefore multiple customers. In fact, resource sharing means that malicious activities (spamming, port scanning) carried out by one tenant may affect and get access to other tenant host (ENISA, 2010).

At the same time a hypervisor vulnerability may allow an attacker to manipulate the assets inside the Cloud, provoking denial of service (which leads to shut down of running virtual machines), data leakage (for example the copying and transfer outside the Cloud of virtual machines), data compromise (such as replacement of virtual machines with modified copies), or direct financial damage (like replication and launch of many copies of the virtual machines) and other threats (Ramadianti, Medard, & Mganga, 2011; ENISA, 2010; Takabi, Joshi & Ahn, 2010).

The problem causes several threats like difficult bugs detection, difficult intruder (malicious user) detection, lack of data segregation, data inconsistency (Ramadianti, Medard, & Mganga, 2011).

As we said that, the hypervisor mediates access between guest operating systems and the physical compute resources. However, they have exhibited failings that have enabled guest operating systems to gain inappropriate levels of control or influence on the underlying platform. Disk partitions, CPU caches, GPUs, and other shared elements were never designed for strong compartmentalization. As a result, attackers focus on how to impact the operations of other Cloud customers, and how to gain unauthorized access to data (Cloud Security Alliance, 2009).

Multi tenancy problem affects the confidentiality, access control, availability, integrity and accountability of data.

Accountability Problems

Accountability has to do with keeping track of actions that are related to security actions and responsibilities (Ramadianti, Medard & Mganga, 2011). It aims to give tracking evidence on user behaviors and system status, which can also be used in system performance analysis or intrusion detection purposes.

In (Ben Arfa Rabai, Jouini, Ben Aissa & Mili, 2013; Ramadianti, Medard & Mganga, 2011), authors list security threats that affect the accountability of the system like unclear ownership and responsibility of data protection attack, loss of business, audit difficulty attack, regulatory and legal issues attack, difficult bugs detection attack and difficult intruder (malicious user) detection.

System administrators are unable to track users' activities and then Cloud users cannot be held responsible for their actions. As a solution, providers must monitor who is performing which operations on the data.

A SECURITY FRAMEWORK FOR SECURE CLOUD COMPUTING ENVIRONMENT

As we mentioned in previous works, security is the biggest challenge in Cloud Computing systems. In fact, according to recent survey by International Data Group (IDG) enterprise, the top three challenges to implementing a successful Cloud strategy in enterprises vary significantly between IT and line-of-business (LOB). For IT, concerns regarding security are (66%) and 42% of Cloud-based projects are eventually brought back in-house, with high security concerns (65%) (Sun, Chang, Sun, Li & Wang, 2012).

In this section, we will show how to solve security problems in cloud computing systems using a quantitative security risk assessment model. We aim to present a generic framework that firstly evaluates Cloud security by identifying unique security requirements, secondly to identify architectural components affected by this risk, thirdly to make out security threats that damage these components and finally to attempt to present viable solutions that eliminate these potential threats.

Related Work

Literature review has shown that there are many works that studied cloud security issues (Ukil, Jana & De Sarkar, 2013; Hu, Wu & Cheng, 2012; Sun, Chang, Sun, Li & Wang, 2012 ; Sun, Chang, Sun, Li & Wang, 2012; Zissis & Lekkas, 2012; Malik & Nazir, 2012; Wang, Wang, Ren, Lou & Li, 2011; Basescu et al., 2011). All works provide a qualitative discussion of security related issues in CC environments submitting a quick analysis and survey of security issues. In fact, they develop and deploy a qualitative security management framework on Cloud Computing environment by proposing some security strategies (countermeasures).

Arijit Ukil et al. (2013) have analyze in (Ukil, Jana & De Sarkar, 2013) security problems in cloud computing. They proposed a framework for satisfying cloud security ensuring the confidentiality, integrity and authentication of data. In fact, they provide security architecture and necessary security techniques for cloud computing infrastructure. The presented architecture incorporates different security schemes, techniques and protocols for cloud computing, particularly in Infrastructure-as-a-Service (IaaS) and Platform-as-a-Service (PaaS) systems. This would facilitate to manage the cloud system more effectively and provide the administrator to include the specific solution these security problems.

Hu et al. (2012) present in (Hu, Wu & Cheng, 2012) a Law-as-a-Service (LaaS) model for automatic enforcing of legal policies to handle queries for cloud service providers (CSPs) and their customers. The law-aware super-peer acts as a guardian providing data integration as well as protection. In fact, they provide Law-as-a-Service (LaaS) for CSPs on our law-aware semantic cloud policy infrastructure. The semantic legal policies in compliance with the laws are enforced automatically at the super-peer to enable LaaS. This allows CSPs to deploy their cloud resources and services without worrying about law violations. After that, users could query data from the law-aware super-peer within a super-peer domain. Each query is also compliant with the laws.

Sun et al. (2012) present in (Sun, Chang, Sun, Li & Wang, 2012) the pay-as you go business model of cloud infrastructure where they put forward the urge of providing high security for cloud computing as this is going over publicly accessible internet domain. The proposed model was based on the new definition of the security trust term and its properties in order to compute trust in cloud systems. In fact, they believe that we need to better define and established trust means term to better security of cloud platforms. The proposed model includes a time-variant comprehensive evaluation multi-dimensional method for expressing direct trust and a space-variant evaluation multi-dimensional method for calculating recommendation trust.

Kevin et al. (2012) present in (Sun, Chang, Sun, Li & Wang, 2012) a dynamic multidimensional trust model with time-variant comprehensive evaluation multi-dimensional method. With this backdrop, we present our proposed architecture and security model towards better protection of confidentiality, privacy in a public domain cloud infrastructural backbone.

Zissis et al. (2012) identify in (Zissis & Lekkas, 2012), firstly security requirements that can be damage when a security problem rises. Then, they present a security strategy based on encryption technique to eliminate security threats in cloud systems. The proposed solution ensures the authentication, integrity and confidentiality of involved data and communications. The solution presents a horizontal level of service available to all implicated entities and maintains a trust between customers and cloud providers.

In (Malik & Nazir, 2012), Malik et al. (2012) list the most common security threats that damages cloud computing environments and develop a methodology for cloud providers that will protect users' data and information. They provide simple countermeasures to protect users' data, messages, information against various attacks that are the major issue for anyone when they want to adopt cloud services for their work. They study the major threats arising in cloud environments, and then propose countermeasures to them. In fact, it provides security solutions to insecure application programming interfaces threat and data loss/leakage threats.

The work of Wang et al. (2011) presented in (Wang, Wang, Ren, Lou & Li, 2011), studied the integrity problem of data storage in Cloud Computing. In particular, the authors considered the task of allowing a third party auditor (TPA), to cloud client, in order to verify the integrity of the dynamic data stored in the cloud. The TPA allows eliminating the involvement of the client through the auditing of whether his data stored in the cloud are indeed intact. The work aims to ensure remote data integrity that supports public auditability and dynamic data operations. The authors constructed a verification scheme for the integration of these two salient features in their protocol design. In particular, to achieve efficient data dynamics, they improved the existing proof of storage models by manipulating the classic Merkle Hash Tree construction for block tag authentication. To support efficient handling of multiple auditing tasks, they explored the technique of bilinear aggregate signature to extend their main result into a multiuser setting, where TPA can perform multiple auditing tasks simultaneously.

In (Basescu et al., 2011), Basescu et al. (2011) proposed a generic security management framework allowing providers of cloud data management systems to define and enforce complex security policies. They designed a framework to detect and stop a large number of attacks defined through an expressive policy description language and to be easily interfaced with various data management systems. They showed that they can efficiently protect a data storage system by evaluating their security framework on top of the BlobSeer data management platform.

Several frameworks have been carried out relating to security issues in Cloud Computing in a quantitative way (Ukil, Jana & De Sarkar, 2013; Hu, Wu & Cheng, 2012; Sun, Chang, Sun, Li & Wang, 2012; Sun, Chang, Sun, Li & Wang, 2012; Zissis & Lekkas, 2012; Malik & Nazir, 2012; Wang, Wang, Ren, Lou & Li, 2011; Basescu et al., 2011). In fact, they do not propose a quantitative approach to analyze and evaluate privacy, and security in Cloud Computing environment. This section primarily aims to analyze and evaluate the most known Cloud Computing security issues using our quantitative security risk analysis model.

The M²FC Model

The Multi dimensional Mean failure cost model (M²FC) represents a quantitative security risk assessment measure that quantifies this risk in terms of financial loss per unit of operation time (for example dollars per hour ($/h)) due to security threats considering several dimensions within the threat world. The measure is called as the Multidimensional Mean Failure Cost (M²FC). The M²FC is a stakeholder based security threats assessment model. It estimates the security of a system in terms of the loss that each stakeholder incurs due to security breaches considering several dimensions within the threat world. In fact, the world of security threats is a segmentation of this world according to each of its dimensions where a dimension can be defined as an elementary aspect or extent of the threat word. The domain or world of threats can be perceived as having several dimensions like architectural components, environmental elements, time, deployment site…For example, when considering the deployment dimension; we give the mean failure cost per deployment site where a security breach occurs. The basic idea is to consider threat perspectives to estimate security failure. To better explain the usage of the proposed M²FC model, we apply on a case study to estimate the security of a system in terms of loss incurred by each stakeholder.

The M²FC model takes into account the stakeholders assessment of the cost related to their requirements with regard to the elements of two security threats dimensions. That is why, in the following model, the set H of stakeholders and the set R of their requirements are distinguished from the set of the leading dimension (where we called a leading dimension a dimension that is used to guide our decomposition of the multidimensional threat world into several slides of two dimensions each) and the set of the other considered dimension.

Model: Let S be the set of elements in the leading dimension, D be the set of elements of the other considered dimension, H be the set of stakeholders, R is a set of requirements, and T be a set of threats. For every element s ϵ S, we define the Multidimensional Mean Failure Costs M(s;D) of element s as follows:

$$M\left(s;D\right) = V_s \circ PFR_s \circ C_s \circ P_s$$

where

We denote $\circ$ by the matrix multiplication operation.

V_s is a matrix of size $\left|H\right| \times \left|R\right|$ that each entry $(i;j)$ represents the value of the stake that stakeholder Hi has in meeting requirement R_j. We denote by $\left|H\right|$ (resp. $\left|R\right|$) the size of the set H (resp. R).

PFR_s is a matrix of size $(\left|H\right|;\left|R\right|)$ that each entry $(i;j)$ represents the probability of failing requirement R_i due to a failure originating from element $d_j \in D$.

C_s is a matrix of size $(\left|D\right|;\left|T\right|)$ that each entry $(i;j)$ represents the probability that an element $d_i \in D$ fails once the threat t_j has materialized.

P_s is a column vector of size $(\left|T\right|)$ that each entry i represents the probability that threats materialize during unitary period of operation.

The M^2FC model is a formula in the form of a hierarchical linear system composed of stakeholders, security requirements (such as confidentiality, integrity, and availability), and two perspectives (architectural components, and environmental entities). In fact, an information system has its stakeholders which have its own issues in the proper functioning of the system. The proper functioning requires certain attributes of dependability which called as security requirements. If we consider the architecture of the system that has several components, a failure exhibiting a security requirement essentially is relative to a particular component. These components fail because of vulnerability due to a security threat. Finally, a threat has several dimensions like source, users and location that affect information systems.

We applied the Multi-dimensional Mean Failure Cost model (M^2FC) is a practical applications namely a Cloud Computing environment. We computed the M^2FC model for three kinds of stakeholders (bronze, silver and gold stakeholders) considering the following threats dimensions: partner application, time, components and connectors.

Methodology

After introducing security issues in cloud computing system, we need to come up with an approach that allows analyzing and linking security problems to their solutions. We notice that some investigators proposed solutions to threats but did not relate solutions to security issues. We propose, in this section, an approach that uses quantitative analysis in order to ensure that our results are more logical and efficient. We will present framework that identifies security and privacy challenges in Cloud Computing. It highlights Cloud-specific attacks and risks and clearly illustrates their mitigations and countermeasures. Our proposed architecture is modular because we consider the threats individually and seek corresponding solutions. This helps to manage the Cloud system more effectively and allows the security analysts to include the specific solution to counter the threat.

We show in this section how to use a quantitative security risk analysis model to suggest our framework for secure Cloud Computing environment. We used the Multi-dimensional Mean Failure Cost model (M^2FC) presented in previous section to propose an approach for secure CC systems.

Figure 1 shows our framework for secure Cloud Computing. It consists of four main security steps which are:

- **Associate Security Requirements to Security Problems:** For each issue, we will choose the security requirement affected by this problem.
- **Associate Security Threats Dimensions to System Requirements:** For each security requirement, we analyze the probabilities of failure threats dimension matrix (PFR_s) in order to select dimension elements with the higher probabilities where the system fails to meet this requirement if a D element dimension fails.
- **Associate Threats to the Dimensions Elements:** For each dimension element D, we analyze the probabilities of failure Dimension matrix (Cs) to choose the higher probability when a security threat is materialized given a dimension element is compromised.
- **Mitigation:** For each element of the leading dimension, propose countermeasures per security threat.

We applied in this section our framework to an illustrative example named Cloud Computing case study system. We applied the M2FC model to quantify cloud systems and estimate the financial cost for each stakeholder regarding the architectural component and deployment site dimensions. In fact, we take into account the deployment sites dimension and the architectural components dimension. Our assessment varies according to the stakes that each stakeholder has in meeting each

Figure 1. A framework for secure Cloud Computing environments

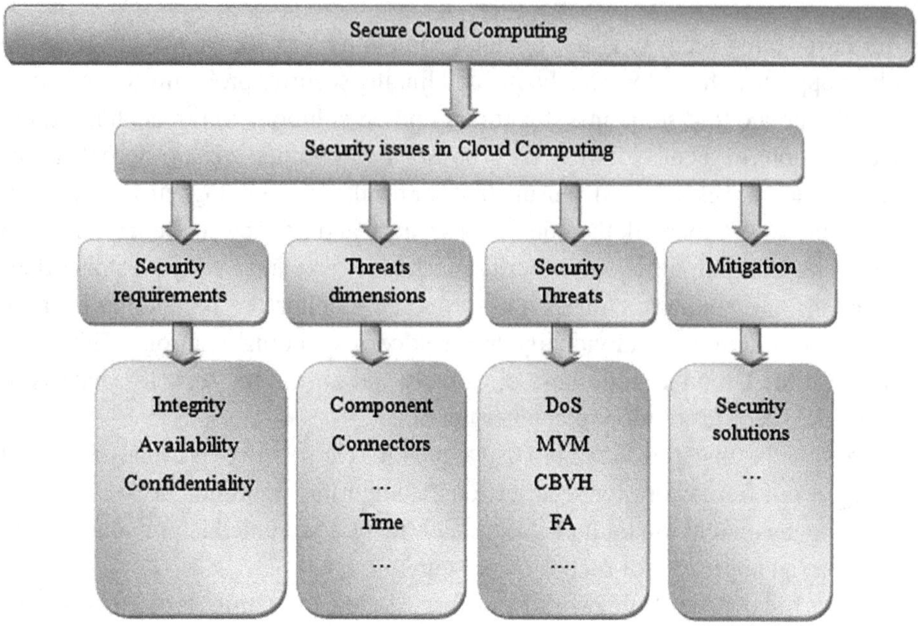

security requirement per system site (or location). We opt, as well, for using the deployment dimension (i.e., sites dimension) as the leading dimension. For each site of the considered system, we have the lists of stakeholders, security requirements, components, and security threats.

Security Requirements

This step identifies security requirements related to each Cloud Computing security problem cited above. Based on our M^2FC model and using the PFRs matrix, we identified the following security requirements:

- Availability,
- Integrity,
- Confidentiality.

Based on our study of the security problems in Cloud Computing systems shown in previous section, we summarize the security requirements associated to each security problem in the Table 1.

Table 1. Security problems and their associated security requirements

Security Problem	Security Requirements
Security issues in virtualization	Integrity, confidentiality, and availability.
Business services continuity	Integrity, confidentiality, and availability.
Management interfaces risks	Integrity, confidentiality, and availability.
Data breaches	Integrity, confidentiality, and availability.
Compliance and governance	Accountability
Access problem: data location	Integrity, confidentiality, and availability.
Privacy issues	Confidentiality
Isolation failure (multi tenancy problem)	Integrity, confidentiality, and availability.
Accountability problems	Accountability

Security Threats Dimensions

We consider in previous work in the illustrative example four threats dimensions in Cloud Computing systems which are: Components, connectors, time and partner applications. Also, we consider the deployment site dimension as a leading dimension. To illustrate our secure framework, we will consider mainly two dimensions: Components and connectors.

Architectural Components

Since the failure of security requirements depends on which component of the system architecture is operational, we will identify in this step using the probabilities of failure components for each security requirement causing this failure. We take for each security requirement the highest probability of failing this requirement Ri once the component Ck has failed. Table 2 shows the component elements per site.

We summarize the list of failed components due to security requirements failure as follow:

- In integrity case, we find the highest probabilities of impact of attack with the following components: load balancer, database server, router/ firewall, web server, browser.
- In availability case, we find the highest probabilities of impact of attack with the following components: load balancer, database server, router/ firewall, storage server.
- In confidentiality, we find the highest probabilities of impact of attack with the following components: load balancer, router/ firewall.

Table 2. Security components and their associated security requirements

	Systems Components		
	Site 1	**Site 2**	**Site 3**
Availability	Load balancer, browser	Load balancer, database server, router/ firewall, browser, proxy server	Browser, database server, web server.
Integrity	load balancer	Load balancer, router/ firewall,	Database server, Storage server.
Confidentiality	Load balancer	Load balancer, router/ firewall.	Load balancer.

Connectors Systems

Since the failure of security requirement also depends on systems connectors, we will identify in this step using the probabilities of failure connectors for each security requirement causing this failure. We take for each security requirement the highest probability of failing this requirement Ri once the connector Ck has failed. The list of failed connectors per site is given in Table 3.

We summarize the failed connectors due to requirements breakdown as follows:

- In integrity case, we find the highest probabilities of impact of attack with the following components: DIN connector (DINC), Chassis intrusion connector (CIC), BNC connector (BNCC), Edge connector (EC), XLR, VMware vCloud Connector (VMC).
- In availability case, we find the highest probabilities of impact of attack with the following components: DIN connector (DINC), BNC connector (BNCC), Edge connector (EC), XLR, Chassis intrusion connector (CIC), VMware vCloud Connector (VMC)
- In confidentiality, we find the highest probabilities of impact of attack with the following components: Chassis intrusion connector (CIC), DIN connector (DINC), Edge connector (EC)

Security Threats

Components of the architecture or system connectors may fail to operate properly as a result of security breakdowns brought about by malicious activity. Therefore, we specify, in this step, the catalog of threats that cause threats dimensions failure (components and connectors).

Table 3. Security connectors and their associated security requirements

	Systems Connectors		
	Site 1	**Site 2**	**Site 3**
Availability	DIN connector (DINC), BNC connector (BNCC)	DIN connector (DINC), Edge connector (EC), XLR	DIN connector (DINC), Chassis intrusion connector (CIC), VMware vCloud Connector (VMC)
Integrity	Chassis intrusion connector (CIC), BNC connector (BNCC)	DIN connector (DINC), Edge connector (EC), XLR	Chassis intrusion connector (CIC), XLR, VMware vCloud Connector (VMC)
Confidentiality	Chassis intrusion connector (CIC)	DIN connector (DINC), Edge connector (EC)	Chassis intrusion connector (CIC)

Components Dimension

We select for each component, the higher probabilities that in which a component Ck fails once threat Tq has materialized. We will present threats that affected components above, through an analysis of threats probabilities:

- **Denial of Service (DoS):** Browser, Proxy server, Router/ Firewall, Load balancer, Database server and Storage server.
- **Insecure Application Programming Interfaces (IAI):** Browser, Router/ Firewall, Load balancer, Database server and Storage server.
- **Communications between Virtual Machines and Host (CBVH):** Proxy server, Router/ Firewall, Load balancer and Storage server.
- **Communication Between VMs (VMC):** Proxy server, Router/ Firewall, Load balancer and Storage server.
- **Virtual Machine Mobility (VMM):** Proxy server, Router/ Firewall, Load balancer and Storage server.
- **Malicious Insiders (MI):** Browser, Proxy server, Router/ Firewall, Load balancer, Database server and Storage server.
- **Abuse and Nefarious Use of Cloud Computing (ANU):** Proxy server, Router/ Firewall, Load balancer, Database server and Storage server.
- **Monitoring Virtual Machines from Host (MVH):** Proxy server, Router/ Firewall, Load balancer, Database server and Storage server.
- **Data Loss or Leakage (DL):** Database server and Storage server.
- **Account, Service and Traffic Hijacking (ASTH):** Browser, Proxy server, Router/ Firewall, Load balancer, Database server and Storage server.
- **Monitoring VMs From Other VM (MVV):** Proxy server, Router/ Firewall, Load balancer, Database server and Storage server.

Table 4. Security connectors and their associated security requirements

Site 1	Site 2	Site 3
• DIN connector: DoS, MI, IAI • Chassis intrusion connector: FA, DoS • BNC connector: DoS, MI, IAI • Edge connector: DoS, MI, IAI	• DIN connector: DoS, FA, ASTH • Lightning Connector: • DoS, MI, ASTH, IAI • Edge connector: DoS, FA, ASTH • XLR: FA, DL, IAI	• DIN connector: DoS, MI, IAI • Chassis intrusion connector: CVH, VMC,VMM, DoS • Edge connector: MVH, MVV, FA • VMware vCloud Connector: MI, IAI

- **Flooding Attacks (FA):** Browser, Proxy server, Router/ Firewall, Load balancer, Database server and Storage server.
- **Virtual Machine Modification (VMm):** Router/ Firewall and Database server.
- **Placement of Malicious VM Images on Physical Systems (VMS):** Proxy server, Router/ Firewall, Load balancer, Database server and Storage server.

We will make synthesis of our analysis in the three steps. For example, we take "Regulatory compliance" has seven security requirements: Integrity, Confidentiality and Availability. Each security requirement related to some components. The components are: Browser (Brws), Router/Firewall (R/Fw), DB Server (DBS), Proxy Server (Prox), Load Balancer (LB) and Storage server (SS).

We conclude that each component affected by some threats and cloud computing threats risks their architectural components and hence we propose in our analysis security countermeasures by threats in cloud environment. In fact, according to the analysis, we can conclude that all threats presented by M2FC are the cause of security issues, because of the threats' distribution which is uniform for cloud computing system. We propose to focus on each threat and suggest solutions.

Connectors Dimension

We select, for each connector, the highest probabilities where a connector Ck fails once threat Tq has materialized. We will present threats that affected connectors in Table 4, through an analysis of threats probabilities.

Mitigation

In this part, we will describe threats related to security issues and we will give countermeasures to prevent them. The aim of this step is to propose solutions per threats to security problems in Cloud Computing environment. In fact, each site is characterized by its proper threats that menace Cloud Computing system and hence we will suggest security solutions per threats.

- **Denial of Service:** A DoS attack is an attempt to make the services assigned to the authorized users unavailable. In such an attack, the server providing the service is flooded by a large number of requests and hence the service becomes unavailable to the authorized user. Sometimes, when we try to access a site we see that due to overloading of the server with the requests to access the site, we are unable to access the site and hence observe an error (Qaisar, & Khawaja, 2012).

As a countermeasure for this attack, we can reduce the privileges of the user that is connected to a server. This will help to reduce the DoS attack. Furthermore, the best approach to prevent a guest consuming all the resources is to limit the resources allocated to the guests. Also, we can use intrusion detection systems (IDS) and strong anti-virus software (Qaisar, & Khawaja, 2012).

- **Insecure Application Programming Interfaces:** In order to protect organizations from several security issues such as confidentiality, integrity, availability and accountability, APIs and interfaces have to be well and strongly built. Since all customers have to go through software interfaces or APIs (Qaisar, & Khawaja, 2012) to interact with Cloud services, it is becoming a necessity to highly secure authentication, access control, encryption and activity monitoring mechanisms especially when third parties start to build on them.

(Qaisar and Khawaja, 2012) and (Priyadharshini, 2013) deal with this threat we have to analyze the security model of Cloud provider interfaces, try to ensure strong authentication, implement access controls in concert with encrypted transmission and understand the dependency chain associated with the API (Qaisar, & Khawaja, 2012; Priyadharshini, 2013).

- **Placement of Malicious VM Images on Physical Systems:** As countermeasure for Cloud malware injection attack, we can cite the use of authenticity check for received messages. Indeed, Cloud provider can store the original image file of the request by using hash function and compare it with the hash value of all upcoming service requests (Qaisar, & Khawaja, 2012).
- **Communication between VMs or between VMs and Host**: All network packets coming from a VM go through the host, thus the host is generally able to monitor network traffic of its hosted VMs. To ensure that the applications running in one VM do not have access to the applications running in another VM, the host should carefully maintain and configure the isolation in a virtual environment. Thus, the break-in into one virtual machine should

not supply access either to VMs in the same environment or to the underlying host machine (Min, Shin, & Bang, 2012) Besides, in a shared environment, customer's data are hosted in the same place. So we must provide an effective encryption mechanism to identify users.

However, encryption accidents (inconsistent use of encryption and software keys attacks) can make data totally unusable, and even normal encryption can complicate availability (Min, Shin, & Bang, 2012)

- **VM Monitoring from the Host:** As solutions, when configuring the VM environment, the host should take care and provide enough isolation which avoids the access for attacking the virtual machine (Qaisar, & Khawaja, 2012).
- **Vm Monitoring from Another Vm:** As countermeasure to this threat, we can use a process of authenticating the network traffic (Qaisar, & Khawaja, 2012; Min, Shin, & Bang, 2012).
- **Virtual Machine Mobility:** To protect migration process through the network, the host should apply a mutual authentication between source and destination VMs. Also, you can use the LoBot framework which is architecture for secure provisioning and migration of virtual machines. For Virtual Infrastructure LoBot provides many other security features, for examples environmental monitoring, secure and shutdown tampers detection (Dawoud, Takouna & Meinel, 2010).
- **Virtual Machine Modification (VMm):** There are some sensitive applications that depend on the infrastructure of the VM environment. They require a secured VM environment to execute them. As solutions to VMs modification protection, we can use the VM digitally by signing and validating the signature before execution (Min, Shin, & Bang, 2012; Dawoud, Takouna & Meinel, 2010).
- **Malicious Insiders:** To confront this threat, we should enforce strict supply chain management and conduct a comprehensive supplier assessment. Besides, we can specify human resource requirements as part of legal contracts, and require transparency into overall information security and management practices, as well as compliance reporting (Qaisar, & Khawaja, 2012).
- **Abuse and Nefarious Use of Cloud Computing:** To confront this threat, we should use a strong registration and validation processes. Besides, you can enhance credit card fraud monitoring and coordination, and comprehensive introspection of customer network traffic (Qaisar, & Khawaja, 2012).
- **Data Loss or Leak:** In (Qaisar, & Khawaja, 2012) we find these solutions to confront data loss threat:

- Implement strong key generation, storage and management, and destruction practices.
- Contractually demand providers wipe persistent media before it is released into the pool.
- Encrypt and protects integrity of data in transit, and analyze data protection at both design and run time.
- Account, service and traffic hijacking

As solution, we must prohibit the sharing of account credentials between users and services.

Then, you use strong two-factor authentication techniques where possible, and employ proactive monitoring to detect unauthorized activity (Qaisar, & Khawaja, 2012).

- **Flooding Attacks:** Flooding attacks distribute a great number of non-sense requests to a specific service. When the attacker sends a great number of requests, Cloud system will try to function against the requests by providing more resources (Qaisar, & Khawaja, 2012). We can adopt counter measures for this attack like filtering the malicious requests by intrusion detection system and installing firewalls. Sometimes intrusion detection system supplies fake alerts and Could mislead administrator (Qaisar, & Khawaja, 2012).

CONCLUSION

Security problems present a major obstacle in adopting information systems and especially in Cloud Computing environments in which sensitive applications and data are moved into the Cloud data centers and run on virtual computing resources in the form of virtual machines. Cloud computing poses many novel vulnerabilities like virtualization vulnerabilities and software vulnerabilities.

In this chapter, we primarily classify and highlight the major security problems in current existing Cloud Computing environments and help users to recognize threats associated with their uses. We also presents a review and a detailed analysis of these challenges in order to show their impacts on security requirements and thus on the full systems. In addition, we propose a quantitative approach that analyzes and evaluates security issues in Cloud Computing environment in order to suggest some countermeasures to mitigate the security risks of these problems.

REFERENCES

Ahmed, M., & Hossain, M. A. (2014). Cloud computing and security issues in the cloud. *International Journal of Network Security & Its Applications*, *6*(1), 25–36. doi:10.5121/ijnsa.2014.6103

Amazon.com. (2011). *Server Said to Have Been Used in Sony Attack.* Retrieved from http://www.bloomberg.com/news/2011-05-13/sony-network-said-to-have-been-invaded- by-hackers-using-amazon-com-server.html

Armbrust, M. (2009). *Above the clouds: A Berkeley view of cloud computing*. Technical report EECS-2009-28, UC Berkeley.

Balachandra, R. K., Ramakrishna, P. V., & Rakshit, A. (2009). Cloud security issues. *PROC'09 IEEE International Conference on Services Computing*, 517–520.

Basescu, C., Carpen-Amarie, A., Leordeanu, C., Leordeanu, C., Costan, A., & Antoniu, G. (2011). Managing Data Access on Clouds: A Generic Framework for Enforcing Security Policies. *International Conference on Advanced Information Networking and Applications (AINA).* doi:10.1109/AINA.2011.61

Bhadauria, R. (2011). A survey on security issues in cloud computing. IEEE Communications Surveys and Tutorial, 1–15.

Choo, K.K.R. (2010). Cloud computing: Challenges and future directions. *Trends & Issues in Crime and Criminal Justice, 6*, 1-6.

Cloud Security Alliance. (2010). *Security guidance for critical areas of focus in cloud computing v2.1. Technical report.* Cloud Security Alliance.

Cloud Security Alliance. (2010). *Top Threats to Cloud Computing V 1.0.* Author.

Dawei, S. (2011) Surveying and analyzing security, privacy and trust issues in cloud computing environments. CEIS, 15, 2852–2856.

Dawoud, W., Takouna, I., & Meinel, C. (2010). Infrastructure as a service security: Challenges and solutions. *The 7th International Conference on Informatics and Systems (INFOS)*, 1–8.

Emam, A. H. M. (2013). Additional authentication and authorization using registered email-id for cloud computing. *International Journal of Soft Computing and Engineering*, *3*(2), 110–113.

ENISA. (2010). *Cloud computing: benefits, risks and recommendations for information security.* Technical report, ENISA. Retrieved from http://www.enisa.europa.eu/act/rm/files/deliverables/cloud-computingrisk-assessment

Gartner, BJ. (2009). *Seven cloud-computing security risks.* Technical report.

Gens, F. (2009). *New IDC IT cloud services survey: Top benefits and challenges.* Technical report, IDC eXchange. Retrieved from http://blogs.idc.com/ie/?p=730

Grobauer, B., Walloschek, T., & Stocker, E. (2011). Understanding cloud computing vulnerabilities. *Security & Privacy*, *9*(2), 50–57. doi:10.1109/MSP.2010.115

Hamid, R. M. N., Bryan, S., & Sharad, S. (2009). Outsourcing business to cloud computing services: Opportunities and challenges. IEEE Internet Computing.

Hamlen, K., Kantarcioglu, M., Khan, L., & Thuraisingham, B. (2010). Security Issues for Cloud Computing. *International Journal of Information Security and Privacy*, *4*(2), 36–48. doi:10.4018/jisp.2010040103

Hu, Y., Wu, W., & Cheng, D. (2012). Towards law-aware semantic cloud policies with exceptions for data integration and protection. *2nd International Conference on Web Intelligence, Mining and Semantics*. doi:10.1145/2254129.2254162

Ibrahim, A. S. Hamlyn-Harris, J. & Grundy, J. (2010). Emerging security challenges of cloud virtual infrastructure. *The Asia Pacific Software Engineering Conference 2010 Cloud Workshop*.

ISO. (2009). *Information technology? security techniques information security risk management.* Technical report. ISO.

Jouini, M., & Ben Arfa Rabai, L. (2014). Surveying and Analyzing Security Problems in Cloud Computing Environments. *The 10th International Conference on Computational Intelligence and Security (CIS 2014)*, 689–493.

Jouini, M., Ben Arfa Rabai, L., & Ben Aissa, A. (2014). Classification of security threats in information systems. *ANT/SEIT 2014*, *32*, 489–496.

Jouini, M., Ben Arfa Rabai, L., & Khedri, R. (2015). A Multidimensional Approach Towards a Quantitative Assessment of Security Threats. *ANT/SEIT 2015*, *52*, 507-514.

Kuyoro, S. O., Ibikunle, F., & Awodele, O. (2011). Cloud computing security issues and challenges. *International Journal of Computer Networks*, *3*(5), 247–255.

Luo, S. (2011). Virtualization security for cloud computing services. Inter Conf on Cloud and Service Computing, 174–179. doi:10.1109/CSC.2011.6138516

Malik, A., & Nazir, M. M. (2012). Security Framework for Cloud Computing Environment: A Review. *Journal of Emerging Trends in Computing and Information Sciences*, *3*(3), 390–394.

Min, Y. G., Shin, H. J., & Bang, Y. H. (2012). Cloud computing security issues and access control solutions. SERSC. *Journal of Security Engineering*, *9*, 135–142.

Priyadharshini, A. (2013). A survey on security issues and countermeasures in cloud computing storage and a tour towards multi-clouds. *International Journal of Research in Engineering & Technology*, *1*(2), 1–10.

Qaisar, S., & Khawaja, K. F. (2012). Cloud computing: network/ security threats and countermeasures. *Interdisciplinary Journal of Contemporary Research in Business, 3*(9), 1323-1329.

Ramadianti, N., Medard, P., & Mganga, C. (2011). *Enhancing information security in cloud computing services using sla based metrics* (Master's thesis). School of Computing, Blekinge Institute of Technology SE-371 79, Karlskrona, Sweden.

Reddy, V. K. (2011). Research issues in cloud computing. *Global Journal of Computer Science and Technology*, *11*(11).

Rittinghouse, J. W., & Ransome, J. F. (2010). *Cloud computing: Implementation, management, and security*. Boca Raton, FL: CRC Press.

Schechter, S. E. (2004). *Computer Security Strength & Risk: A Quantitative Approach* (PhD thesis). Harvard University DEAS.

Subashini, S., & Kavitha, V. (2010). A survey on security issues in service delivery models of cloud computing. *Journal of Network and Computer Applications*, *34*(1), 1–11. doi:10.1016/j.jnca.2010.07.006

Subashini, S., & Kavitha, V. (2011). A survey on security issues in service delivery models of cloud computing. *Journal of Network and Computer Applications*, *34*(1), 1–11. doi:10.1016/j.jnca.2010.07.006

Sun, D., Chang, G., Sun, L., Li, F., & Wang, X. (2012). A dynamic multi-dimensional trust evaluation model to enhance security of cloud computing environments. *International Journal of Innovative Computing and Applications*, *3*(4), 200–210. doi:10.1504/IJICA.2011.044529

Takabi, H., Joshi, J. B. D., & Ahn, G. J. (2010). Security and privacy challenges in cloud computing environments. *IEEE Security and Privacy*, *8*(6), 24–31. doi:10.1109/MSP.2010.186

Ukil, A., Jana, D., & De Sarkar, A. (2013). A security framework in cloud computing infrastructure. *International Journal of Network Security & Its Applications*, *5*(5), 11–24. doi:10.5121/ijnsa.2013.5502

Wang, Q., Wang, C., Ren, K., Lou, W., & Li, J. (2011). Enabling Public Auditability and Data Dynamics for Storage Security in Cloud Computing. *IEEE Transactions on Parallel and Distributed Systems*, *22*(5), 1–13. doi:10.1109/TPDS.2010.183

Wayne, J., & Timothy, G. (2011). *Guidelines on Security and Privacy in Public Cloud Computing*. Information Technology Laboratory.

Wooley, P. S. (2011). *Identifying cloud computing security risks* (Master's thesis). University of Oregon, Eugene, OR.

Xuan, Z., Nattapong, W., Hao, L., & Xuejie, Z. (2010). Information Security Risk Management Framework for the Cloud Computing Environments.*10th IEEE International Conference on Computer and Information Technology (CIT 2010)*, 1328 – 1334.

Zissis, D., & Lekkas, D. (2012). Addressing cloud computing security issues. *Future Generation Computer Systems*, *28*(3), 583–592. doi:10.1016/j.future.2010.12.006

Chapter 5
How Cross-Platform Technology Can Facilitate Easier Creation of Business Apps

Tim A. Majchrzak
University of Agder, Norway

Jan Ernsting
University of Münster, Germany

Jan C. Dageförde
University of Münster, Germany

Christoph Rieger
University of Münster, Germany

Tobias Reischmann
University of Münster, Germany

ABSTRACT

Applications for mobile devices – apps – have seen unprecedented growth in importance. Ever better apps keep propelling the proliferation of mobile computing. App development is rather easy, particularly if it is based on Web technology. However, implementing apps that are user friendly and useful in the long-run is cumbersome. Thereby, it typically is expensive for corporate developers. Nonetheless, business apps are embraced by enterprises. To overcome the overhead of developing separately for multiple platforms and to mitigate the problems of device fragmentation, cross-platform development approaches are employed. While many such approaches exist, few have found widespread usage. In this chapter, we argue what the path towards future solutions could look like. We thereby take a rather technological look, but always keep business-orientation in mind. Our findings suggest that much effort is needed to enable the next generations of business apps. However, such apps will provide many merits and possibilities. Moreover, they provide the chance to master several of today's challenges.

DOI: 10.4018/978-1-5225-2449-6.ch005

Copyright ©2017, IGI Global. Copying or distributing in print or electronic forms without written permission of IGI Global is prohibited.

1 INTRODUCTION

Applications for mobile devices – apps – have seen an unprecedented growth in importance over the course of the last years (Rivera & van der Meulen, 2014a). An increasing number of companies embrace mobile computing (Majchrzak & Heitkötter, 2014). They employ the capabilities and versatility of apps to support business processes as well as to provide tools to connect with (existing and future) customers (McLellan, 2014). Even if technological progress was stalled in terms of device hardware, ever better apps would likely keep propelling the proliferation of mobile computing. App *development*, however, is cumbersome considering the multitude of mobile platforms that need to be supported (Heitkötter, Majchrzak, & Kuchen, 2013).

Developing apps is, in general, facilitated by rather easy to use software development kits (SDKs) released by the mobile platform vendors (such as Apple for iOS (Apple, n.d.) and Google for Android (Google, 2016a)). *Platform* in this context refers to the operation system for a mobile device along with the accompanying ecosystem of SDK, frameworks, tools, means of distribution etc. Moreover, Web-based development is widely used: Either webapps are chosen as a kind of least common denominator or, alternatively, cross-platform tools such Apache Cordova (Apache, n.d.) are employed. In addition, numerous frameworks exist that intend supporting development activities. Nonetheless, creating good apps is both complex and expensive.

It can be witnessed that app development even in companies with experience in software development differs from traditional development activities (Majchrzak & Heitkötter, 2014). Team sizes are often smaller – frequently, app development is a single-person project (Heitkötter, Majchrzak, Wolffgang, & Kuchen, 2012). While developing an app in general requires just a few steps, implementing sound concepts requires knowledge, experience, and arduous work. Unsurprisingly, there is an endless stream of complaints about low app quality in app stores (cf. e.g. Khalid, Shihab, Nagappan, & Hassan, 2015) as well as a daily emergence of security-related news, typically reporting breaches (cf. e.g. Chia, Yamamoto, & Asokan, 2012; Mansfield-Devine, 2012; Wang, Lu, Lu, Chung, & Lee, 2013). Even without serious flaws, it is hard for companies to leverage the potential of mobile computing if development is more expensive than it should be.

Despite the problems, companies virtually cannot avoid apps. Investigating the possibilities provided by modern mobile computing ought to be a task every company should pursue, almost independent of size, sector, and corporate culture (Majchrzak & Heitkötter, 2014). For many enterprises, so called *business apps* will provide benefits, or at least promise to facilitate future improvement to process management, workflows, and customer relations. Business apps are typically based on standardized GUI elements (i.e. essentially provide forms) and are data-driven (i.e. receive inputs, process them, and provide some information or request more input) (Majchrzak, Ernsting, & Kuchen, 2015). Moreover, they typically make use of a backend system (Majchrzak, Ernsting, et al., 2015; Majchrzak & Heitkötter, 2014), which contrasts many consumer apps that entirely operate on the mobile device.

Particularly business apps should provide support for multiple platforms to include a wide range of potential users. Even though Android and iOS have divided most of the market share of mobile devices platforms amongst themselves (Woods & van der Meulen, 2016), typically more platforms should be supported. This can be explained by the fact that additional platforms still have millions of users who would otherwise be excluded from a company's services (Woods & van der Meulen, 2016). In addition, future areas such as operating systems used in cars (see e.g. Google, 2016b) might shift market shares of established platforms, introduce new ones, or – possibly worse – lead to partly incompatible derivatives (or *forks*) of existing platforms. Even with the two initially mentioned platforms alone, development effort is almost doubled compared to supporting just one of them.

Moreover, it would be beneficial if existing business backend systems could be used. Ideally, established workflows should be included; the re-usage of business process models would be excellent (Evers, Ernsting, & Majchrzak, 2016). Besides that, it needs to be assessed whether business apps can partially or even fully be created by domain experts rather than by developers (Heitkötter & Majchrzak, 2013). With their relative simplicity on the one hand and business purpose on the other hand, it should be possible for people without development experience to create business apps. Here, *should* can be read in the ways of both *ought to* and *considered to be*.

The above described targets have led to numerous developments (see also Section 1). By now, many cross-platform app development frameworks exist, even though few of them have found widespread usage. Frameworks and techniques for business integration have been developed, even though again their applications are limited. Finally, methods and tools have been described that enable app development for non-developers, e.g. as learning tools. However, a cross-platform app development solution with tight business integration and accessibility for people without considerable development experience does not exist.

In this chapter, we argue what the path towards such a solution can look like. For this purpose, we assess the potential merits, what current and future obstacles look like, and which limitations are likely to remain. We will start with a look at the past, scrutinize the status quo, and provide an elaborated outlook.

The chapter will be based on our own work on a cross-platform business app framework (Heitkötter, Majchrzak, & Kuchen, 2013) but goes much beyond the technological and business process scope that existing articles have taken. Our work is structured as follows, honouring the chronological approach sketched above:

In Section 2 we first motivate the topic economically and give a brief look at the past. We then introduce existing approaches, both technology-oriented and domain-oriented. The aim of this section is particularly to meet the readers and to introduce them to the technological idiosyncrasies and ramifications that the topics of business apps and app-based commerce pose.

We then summarize related work in Section 3. This is followed by an extensive study of what cross-platform technology is already capable of in Section 4. Our synopsis is not only based on theory but also considers practical findings as well as experiences from designing a cross-platform development framework. Moreover, we will highlight existing research activities that are attractive from a business point of view, yet have failed to find wider adoption in usage by companies.

The assessment of the status quo leads to our vision of the future as laid out in Section 5. We describe required technology and the app commerce possibilities that could be provided by advanced solutions. To draw a more concrete picture, we present usage scenarios in Section 6. They illustrate the possibilities of future business app usage.

In Section 7 we then present a discussion of our findings. First, we give an outlook along with a discussion of open questions, both leading to an agenda for further research. Eventually, we name limitations of our work and sketch our own goals for the near future. Finally, we conclude in Section 8.

2 STATUS QUO OF CROSS-PLATFORM APP DEVELOPMENT

To lay out the foundation for this chapter, we introduce the basics of cross-platform app development. For this purpose, we first sketch the economic importance of business apps in particular and draw a brief history of app development in general. We then introduce a categorization of the possibilities for developing apps that will run on more than one platform. Eventually, we give a short overview of currently employed frameworks and tools in the context of cross-platform app development.

2.1 On the Economic Value of App Development

After years of immense growth (cf. e.g. Goasduff & Pettey, 2012; Rivera & van der Meulen, 2014b), the market for smartphones seems to be saturated (Woods & van der Meulen, 2016). However, there is no reason to believe that this saturation will also affect the development of apps. In fact, it is even too early to determine whether growth of the smartphone market will not resume. In the meantime, existing markets for devices that run apps will likely keep growing. This not only considers established mobile devices such as tablets but also novel fields. Examples are wearables (Chauhan, Mahanti, & Kaafar, 2014) which increasingly are customizable by the means of apps, and cars (cf. e.g. Google, 2016b).

Reasons for expecting the further proliferation of apps are manifold. Many businesses have only slowly embraced the possibilities of mobile devices and continue to explore (Majchrzak & Heitkötter, 2014). New possibilities due to hardware improvements have not been fully leveraged; particularly sensor usage is poised to gain much more momentum (Filios, Nikoletseas, & Pavlopoulou, 2015; see e.g. Ghosh & Riccardi, 2014). And there are many more ideas for sector- and domain-specific usage, e.g. in the field of healthcare (Martin, Vicente, Vicente, Ballesteros, & Maynar, 2014). With Facebook already reporting 76% of its advertising revenue being generated on mobile devices (Facebook, 2015) and mobile spam becoming *reasonable* (from a spammers point of view) (Seneviratne, Seneviratne, Kaafar, Mahanti, & Mohapatra, 2015), there are no signs of a saturation in terms of app development activities.

Unsurprisingly, *m-commerce* has been coined as a term that describes revenue creation in the mobile world. m-commerce thereby is an expansion, or rather a subcategory of the even longer discussed e-commerce. Despite the blurriness of such terms – particularly considering multi-channel approaches, which might make it hard to determine if commerce is mobile, online, or offline – they have impact. A study that set out to provide a taxonomy for m-commerce (Khansa, Zobel, & Goicochea, 2012) included an analysis of 2,300 patents related to m-commerce. It might well be the case that some countries allow filing software patents with questionably low innovation height; nonetheless, this number is a profound indicator for the topic's perceived importance by the industry.

The research dimension is limited until now. Myriads of papers exist that shed light on distinctive aspects. Very popular for analysis are for example the app stores (cf. e.g. Al-Subaihin et al., 2015; Fu et al., 2013; Kimbler, 2010). However, a comprehensive, holistic view of the importance of enterprise mobile computing as well as m-commerce is missing.

Some app store related papers provide findings concerning the economic importance of apps. For example, a study of Kang, Mun, and Johnson has affirmed a positive effect of mobile apps on shopping behaviour (Kang, Mun, & Johnson, 2015). Similarly, a study by Google (Google, 2013) found that 90% of smartphone shoppers use their phone for pre-shopping activities; 84% use their devices to help them shop while in a store. It might be suspected that this is economically objectionable, e.g. because shoppers use stores to try out product but buy them from the cheapest online vendor. The study suggests, however, that shoppers who use mobile devices more, buy more. Even though such findings have to be taken with care (in this case, an increase of the median of a shopping basket size was observed), they provide hints. Obviously, businesses cannot neglect a mobile strategy.

Existing overview articles are limited in scope but can give important hints. A Delphi study with "14 leading mobile commerce scholars" (Pousttchi, Tilson, Lyytinen, & Hufenbach, 2015) yielded several interesting observations:

- *Mobile enterprises* are expected to proliferate.
- Mobile services and applications are no new emergence but have changed in the course of time.
- m-commerce is seen as an important part of the ongoing *digitalization* of societies.
- Integration of mobility into the overall business is seen to be a driving topic of the near future.

At the same time, it was acknowledged that a theoretical foundation is missing. This finding is not only an indicator for the rapid evolvement of the field but also a motivation for work like the one provided in this chapter.

Summing up, there is still much theoretical work required to provide a better understanding of the economic importance of mobile computing. In particular, better advice for companies is required. Nevertheless, the already high and still increasing impact of m-commerce is unquestionable.

2.2 A Brief History of App Development

Mobile apps in general are not an entirely new emergence. Provisioning apps for so called *feature phones* or personal digital assistants (PDAs) turned out to be a major issue in the pre-app store era: Inconveniently, mobile apps had to be installed by their end users through desktop PCs that utilized software and hardware dedicated to installing applications on mobile devices.[1] In addition, the absence of economically viable data plans restricted mobile app use cases to a few scenarios that required little to no connectivity (West & Mace, 2010).

These devices offered a modicum of features; in fact, they often were mobile telephones with very limited computing ability. Seldom did they include localization sensors, i.e. GPS, or varied connectivity means, e.g. WiFi, Bluetooth, NFC; and if they did, these features where typically reserved to *handheld* PCs and PDAs, targeting resourceful – and typically professional – end user segments.

From an app developer's point of view, the dissemination of platforms required them to deal with vendors' proprietary development environments. As a consequence, enterprises utilizing mobile devices resorted to purchasing from specific vendors in order to reduce platform diversity. Sun Microsystems' mobile edition of Java (J2ME) (JSR 68, 2011) promised to overcome this heterogeneity, but failed to honour this. Despite its intention, concrete runtime implementations differed across device vendors, thus limiting a wider adoption by incompatibilities (Grønli, Hansen, & Ghinea, 2010).

In 2007, the mobile game changed when Apple introduced the iPhone (Macedonia, 2007). At first, the iPhone provided few substantial benefits over previous mobiles (West & Mace, 2010). In fact, its introduction lacked the concept of apps as we know it; third parties were meant to run their applications as Web sites.

The same year, Google along with the Open Handset Alliance announced the Android platform (Open Handset Alliance, 2007). It provided access to sensors such as GPS and accelerometers by default and facilitated their utilization as part of its software development kit (SDK). Consequently, hardware vendors embraced the new possibilities.

Apple followed and published its SDK for iOS along with the App Store concept in 2008 (Fletcher, 2007). Apps are exclusively exposed and centrally provisioned through the App Store, which also supports billing of apps and purchases within apps (West & Mace, 2010). For Android, the Android Market (Google, 2016c) (nowadays known as the Google Play Store) provides the same functionality (Cuadrado & Dueñas, 2012).

Other platform vendors such as Microsoft (Windows Phone) and Research in Motion (Blackberry OS) also pursue mobile ecosystems. By mid-2015, however, their cumulative sales diminished to less than five percent (IDC, 2016). To demonstrate the challenges of targeting heterogeneous platforms, it suffices to focus on iOS and Android – we do so in the following. It must nonetheless not be assumed that two platforms are the fixed goal to reach customers. In fact, the above named competitors still sell millions of devices (Woods & van der Meulen, 2016). Moreover, the already mentioned future trends with more and more devices being *app-enabled* might lead to shifts in shares.

In parallel, mobile network operators upgraded their networks (from 2G/EDGE over 3G/UMTS to 4G/LTE) enabling bandwidth-intense contents such as video streaming as well as improving their availability (Basole & Karla, 2011). They also pitched data plans making mobile data usage affordable, thus benefiting competition among operators. However, mobile bandwidth has not yet become a ubiquitous resource: Availability as well as bandwidth remain limited in rural areas and developing countries. Along with the *device fragmentation* (cf. Heitkötter, Kuchen, & Majchrzak, 2015; IDC, 2016), which especially impedes development for Android, particularly feature-rich apps need to be developed in a way that keeps them flexible.

2.3 General Approaches Towards Cross-Platform App Development

Despite Apple's and Google's efforts in making mobile app development more accessible, their respective platforms differ substantially, e.g. with regard to app development but also with regard to user experience. Consequently, developing for mobile platforms requires versatile knowledge of their particular ecosystems, such as development environment, software development kits, and human computer interaction guidelines (Joorabchi, Mesbah, & Kruchten, 2013).

In the following, we refer to native development as utilizing the platform's abstractions and SDK along with its provided programming language(s). Native development, in this context, does not necessarily mean low-level development, e.g. writing C code, using Application Binary Interfaces (ABIs), nor directly interacting with physical interfaces.

Research indicates an increasing fragmentation of mobile devices and platforms; however, app development endeavours fail to transfer their knowledge (Joorabchi et al., 2013). In addition, mobile devices' market shares entail the support of at least two platforms (IDC, 2016). Typically, projects take place per platform, i.e. employ *native, platform-specific* SDKs. Each of these projects requires capable personnel, well-versed on the respective platform, and also necessitates additional testing efforts to ensure consistent functionality across these platforms. Due to the nature of development, only requirements engineering activities partly overlap, leading to an almost linear increase in development effort with the number of supported platforms (Heitkötter, Majchrzak, & Kuchen, 2013).

Various approaches that seek to overcome this platform heterogeneity exist. So-called cross-platform development exposes varying degrees with regard to platform peculiarities it supports. Figure 1 shows a classification of approaches, based on their nativeness, i.e. how apps are developed, how they look and feel, and how they are executed.

Approaches from the broader category of *runtime environments* require a dedicated runtime that has to be available for the targeted platforms and which interprets an app's description. *Mobile webapps* feature no native elements and are displayed in a Web browser, i.e. utilize a browser engine. They are provisioned, specifically hosted, as any Web site; thus, require no app store interactions.

Hybrids are similar to webapps in that they are typically developed using Web technologies but grant access to features not available through these technologies, i.e. hybrid approaches often provide interfaces to use platform-specific features and run apps in a modified browser engine. These approaches offer mechanisms to mimic platform-specific UI elements but do not offer the same user experience

Figure 1. Classification of cross-platform development approaches
(cf. Majchrzak, Ernsting, et al., 2015).

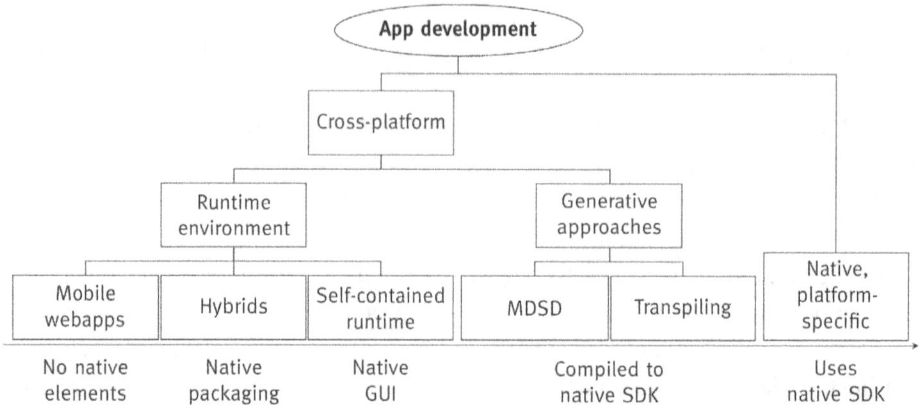

native widgets do. Bundling as a native app enables provisioning of hybrids through app stores.

Approaches that are based on a *self-contained runtime* provide their own SDKs, instead of relying on Web technologies. These SDKs often bridge gaps between platforms and grant developers access to platform features and use native UI elements. As with hybrids, self-contained runtimes have to be available per platform. These apps are natively bundled along with the runtime engine that the app runs in, which might pose a performance overhead (Heitkötter, Hanschke, & Majchrzak, 2012).

Generative approaches forgo runtime environments and utilize native SDKs and the corresponding programming language. Development is either done in the programming language of *one* of the supported platforms, or in a separate language. The latter typically is a so called domain-specific language (DSL). DSLs are tailored to a specific purpose and usually no general-purpose programming languages.

The category of generative approaches distinguishes model-driven software development (*MDSD*) and *transpilers*. The former transforms an app model into source code that executes on the targeted platforms. App modelling can be done in a textual modelling language, which might be not too different from a general programming language, or graphically. The latter translate source code for one SDK into source code for another SDK. This possibly includes the translation into a different programming language. Transpilers not necessarily need to cover all aspects of an app; it is possible to only translate certain *layers*, such as the business logic.

Thus, developers face a major decision. Either, they write native, platform-specific code using the respective SDK and accompanying tools or they leverage a cross-platform development approach. A combination of both will be a waste of resources save for particular circumstances, e.g. optimization for one platform while providing general support for many others. Even with progress in Web technology such as HTML5 (W3C, 2014) and widely popular runtime-based cross-platform approaches (see next subsection), native development is the richest and most flexible approach. However, it requires more resources (knowledgeable personnel, time (for testing), etc.) (Joorabchi et al., 2013). Moreover, it might be less suited for future developments since changes to each supported platform will need to be addressed and coordinated when developing new versions of an app.

2.4 Overview of Current Frameworks and Tools

In the following, a subset of current frameworks – one for each category – is presented. A thorough overview would be outdated swiftly and is difficult to accommodate in a single place. Nevertheless, an evaluation scheme supports decision makers in assessing frameworks' suitability for their purposes and in choosing the fittest (Heitkötter, Majchrzak, Ruland, & Weber, 2013).

Native, platform-specific development relies on the respective SDKs. For example, when developing for iPhones and iPads the iOS SDK is used in conjunction with the Objective-C and/or Swift programming language. Android development typically employs the Android SDK using the programming language Java.

The troika of HTML5, Cascading Style Sheets (CSS), and JavaScript constitute the foundation for *mobile webapps*. While HTML5 and CSS deal with the presentation of content, JavaScript enables webapps to expose interactive elements, e.g. update contents from a remote service on the fly. Apache Cordova (Apache, n.d.) (a.k.a. Adobe PhoneGap) utilizes HTML5, CSS, and JavaScript to create *hybrids* that are provisioned as native apps. In addition, Cordova fills gaps where Web standards are lacking to access platform specific features, e.g. access user's contacts.

Whereas the Appcelerator Platform's (formerly Titanium Appcelerator) (AppCelerator, n.d.) *self-contained runtime* interprets JavaScript, it utilizes native UI elements, i.e. native widgets from the respective platform SDKs, through its custom abstraction layer. If needed, developers may directly employ platform-specific UI elements or concepts from iOS, Android, or Windows. Due to its interpretative approach, loading of apps takes longer.

Applause (Applause, n.d.), in its second version, is a prototypical, *generative approach* that utilises *MDSD* techniques to generate native apps from code expressed in Applause's domain specific language (DSL). In addition, it provides facilities to express presentation-unrelated business logic in JavaScript. We will learn about another MDSD approach in Section 4. *Transpiling* as provided by J2ObjC enables sharing of non-UI code, i.e. data models and application logic. It translates Java source code to iOS compatible Objective-C code. However, even J2ObjC as the only tool with a relevant user base, is not capable of full translation. In particular, the code for the graphical user interface (GUI) *cannot* be converted. It would, however, be this code that would be most appealing for automated conversion.

3 RELATED WORK

The work presented in this chapter is literature-driven by its nature. Thus, no generic study of related work is mandated. This particularly takes in mind that on the one hand, similar articles are mentioned in Section 2.1. And, on the other hand, no articles that are very close in presentation to this chapter exist. However, in the following we will highlight articles that relate in so far as they assess the status quo of cross-platform app development or take a look at the future of app development.

Several papers have discussed general ideas of native development in comparison to other approaches (Heitkötter, Hanschke, et al., 2012; Heitkötter et al., 2015; Majchrzak & Ernsting, 2015; Ohrt & Turau, 2012). Due to the rapid progress of both hardware and platform development, these articles naturally have taken a look into the future. The status quo described is a mere snapshot and the ideas proposed a peak of what might be. It is needless to say that bold propositions have hardly been made in these scientific papers, since it would have been very hard to assess them. In general, the earlier papers faced an even more dynamic nature than we now have and thereby the authors had an even harder time to make educated predictions.

Marinho and Resende (Marinho & Resende, 2015) have taken a look at "native and multiple targeted mobile applications". They have compiled "positive and negative aspects" and explicitly target "decision-makers". Thereby, their work is complementary to ours.

There are a number of articles on cross-platform development approaches that also make proposals about the future of cross-platform app development. While typically a focus on business apps (or, actually, a domain at all) is missing, the ideas presented in such work are notable.

Mobl is a DSL for mobile Web applications (Hemel & Visser, 2011). Even though it targets Web browsers that are inherently cross-platform, the DSL is worth further consideration. In fact, by relying on browsers while still proposing the usage of a DSL, the approach brings together several existing ideas in a novel fashion. Mobl succeeds WebDSL (WebDSL, n.d.) in that it exposes a versatile approach to user interactions and extends on a library model (Hemel & Visser, 2011, p. 710f.). It dispenses the typical controller component in favour of automatic inference. Mobl's data model and view descriptions can be annotated to augment the inferred controller (Hemel & Visser, 2011, p. 696). Thereby, it positions itself as *one* integrated language (rather than using HTML5, CSS, and JavaScript as in classical webapp development). *MobiDSL* (Kejriwal, 2009) is similar to Mobl, but restricted with regard to custom controls or IDE support.

RAPPT (Barnett, Avazpour, Vasa, & Grundy, 2015; Barnett, Vasa, & Grundy, 2015) is a *bootstrapping* tool for mobile app developers. It implements ideas that are similar to frameworks for rapid Web application development, such as Twitter Bootstrap (Bootstrap, 2016). Three different views are taken in RAPPT:

- A *domain-specific visual language* (DSVL), i.e. a graphical DSL, is used.
- In addition, developers can employ an *app modelling language* (AML) as well as a *domain-specific textual language* (DSTL).
- Additionally, raw source code can be written. The three-fold approach is novel. The author "made a conscious decision not to support round trip engineering. The primary reason for this is that the generated code is the scaffolding for a new project and is intended to be heavily modified." (Barnett, Avazpour, et al., 2015, p. 1). Their approach keeps DSVL and DSTL in sync. However, RAPPT targets Android only. So far, no plans to extend support to other platforms exist. Thus, the approach can rather be seen as an attempt to ease development in general and to bridge different development philosophies. The authors' claim to produce modifiable code will need to be assessed.

The cross-platform development framework *AXIOM* (Jones & Jia, 2015) provides a multi-stage transformation (structural and with regard to style). Generators and transformations have to be specified by developers. AXIOM's authors are in the process of developing an approach to extract metamodels from AXIOM mappings. Along with other frameworks that mean to provide a more structured approach (cf. Evers et al., 2016), this could lead to a standardized way of (possibly domain-specific) cross-platform development.

Finally, the *Interaction Flow Modeling Language* (IFML) (IFML, n.d.) has to be mentioned. Its development has been driven by WebRatio (WebRatio, n.d.), even though IFML is not directly focused on mobile development. However, since it addressed GUI applications it is highly relevant for apps, which require a well thought out user interface but due to the reliance on backend systems often a relatively simple business logic. Extensions such as (Brambilla, Mauri, & Umuhoza, 2014) explicitly consider mobile specific features. This includes event processing, for example for sensor data and user interface events (such as the "long press" on the latest Apple devices).

Summing up, the rapid progress in the field of cross-platform development and related areas, in combination with the rapid proliferation of everyday mobile computing, has led to many ideas about the future course of actions. Some of them are mere proposals how *better* apps could be enabled; others are able to sketch the path more clearly, particularly if existing developments are extrapolated.

4 CURRENT CONTRIBUTIONS TO BUSINESS APP DEVELOPMENT

This chapter introduces the current status of business apps from the perspective of cross-platform development. The general outset is to illustrate what is already possible, which chances and limitations exist, and where we are currently heading. For this purpose, we start with an introduction to the topic based both on the literature and contemporary practical approaches. We continue by introducing MD^2, which is our framework aimed at cross-platform development of business apps.

4.1 Understanding the Current State of Cross-Platform Utilization

Even though the idea of cross-platform development is appealing, many companies opt for developing individual apps for every platform (Majchrzak & Heitkötter, 2014). As a result, they are faced with overhead expenditures for developing and continuously maintaining each app on its own. Also, features developed for one platform can frequently not be ported directly from one platform's app to another, but instead have to be re-implemented from scratch due to differences between the platforms (Joorabchi et al., 2013). Naturally, this leads to further unnecessary spending. Furthermore, customers changing from one platform to the other, or customers using a company's app on different devices, might be confused. This confusion might arise from two seemingly contradicting design decisions. A different look and feel of an app's version for different platforms leaves users wondering if they got the *right* app. An app looking similarly on all platforms but not being responsive to platform-specific characteristics (e.g. particular gestures) annoys users. In addition, this approach requires companies to choose their target platforms.

Needless to say, deciding against supporting certain platforms always implies that those customers who are using that platform are excluded from a company's service. Thus, intentionally leaving out platforms potentially neglects business opportunities or even disgruntles customers. Given that backdrop, it is apparent that current cross-platform approaches are unsatisfactory, so that companies perceive greater benefit from pursuing fragmented platform-specific approaches.

Mobile webapps and hybrid apps share the shortcoming that they cannot provide a truly native look-and-feel: They are always limited to the Web browser runtime in which they are executed (cf. Section 2.3), over which app developers hardly have any control. Web technology can be used to recreate visual components of native user interfaces, thus theming the Web-based app to look and act like their native counterparts. However, this requires extensive use of CSS and JavaScript, thus harming execution performance of the app (Heitkötter, Hanschke, et al., 2012). Platforms offer no standardised means to imitate their look and feel on webapps. Consequently, every company has to develop this on their own repeatedly for each supported platform, and the respective runtime environments are unable to optimise execution of the required scripts. Web development frameworks only partly mitigate this circumstance (Heitkötter, Majchrzak, Ruland, et al., 2013). Execution of Web-based apps therefore tends to be slow and battery consuming. The approach of imitating the look and feel is further harmed, as some devices do not provide a Web browser that complies with current Web technology standards (MobileHTML5, n.d.). In addition, older Android devices that are discontinued by their vendors do not receive updated Web browsers (Dobie, 2012).

Development based on self-contained runtimes results in apps that are packaged together with platform-specific runtime libraries. Platform-independent app code accesses features of all kinds of devices in a consistent way that is implemented by the runtime libraries. Consequently, these platform-specific runtimes can be optimised *per platform*, resulting in better performance than that of Web-based apps. A general downside of that approach is that the least common denominator of the targeted platforms and the chosen approach determines the expressiveness for developers, and, therefore, the capabilities (or *richness*) of developed apps. This extends to multiple aspects of apps: For UI elements and hardware-provided platform features, such as device orientation, camera, GPS, and telephony, cross-platform development approaches can only offer features that are available across all platforms. Otherwise, platform-specific development tasks would remain. Furthermore, runtime libraries – although optimised – always constitute an execution overhead, resulting in worse performance compared to truly native apps. Consequently, native apps can always leverage more features of a platform than cross-platform apps; they remain more efficient at the same time.

Generative (in particular model-driven) approaches are suited to overcome the above discussed deficiencies: They allow cross-platform development using a single code base that serves all platforms. In the context of model-driven software development this code base is referred to as a *model* of an app. From the specified model, a generator can derive one or more programs. Therefore, in the context of cross-platform development, the generator can use a single model as an input to derive one app per target platform. During this process, the generator is not required to take the model literally: Instead, if required, it can deviate from ideal implementations in order to implement the developers' *intentions*. This is necessary if the model requires certain capabilities that the target platform does not provide. Take, for example, an app that requires a user's location data. During app generation for a platform that does not provide hardware support for this, the generator can substitute the corresponding part of an app with a software emulation of that feature. Alternatively, it could add a message that informs users that their device does not provide the necessary support. For those platforms that support the feature, appropriate hardware calls would be generated. In this way not only multiple platforms are addressed but also the complexity that arises from device fragmentation is tackled.

As a result, generative approaches are not restricted to the least common denominator of all target platforms, but can mitigate this problem by providing adequate substitutions for required capabilities. Consequently, the generator's capabilities define the feature set usable for cross-platform app developers. Of course, conceiving and providing such substitutions has to be done by generator developers, which results in some development overhead. This overhead does not occur for each app, though, but only for *one* generator that will then be employed for multiple apps. In other words: the more apps are realized, the less significant is the effort for the initial generator implementation. If the generator creates purely native apps, this minimises runtime overhead. It results in *ideal* performance for end-users. With some experience and effort, the runtime performance of generated app rivals that of manually implemented native apps.

Another benefit of model-driven generative approaches is that the programming language used for specifying the model is defined by generator developers, thus enabling programming languages that abstract from platform-specific details. Rather than using a general purpose language, a domain-specific language focuses on what is important for the intended purpose. This provides two major benefits: Firstly, repetitive boilerplate code of apps can be generated automatically, thus reducing clutter from the simpler, app-specific models. This can significantly reduce the number of lines of code (LOC) that needs to be written, easily outmatching even rapid development languages that honour the convention-over-configuration paradigm. Secondly, simpler programming languages can be created that are appealing to non-programmers. In fact, the language does not even need to resemble one of the widely used imperative programming languages. Declarative programming, graphical modelling and similar approaches are feasible. Consequently, a cross-platform app development solution with tight business integration and accessibility for people with little development experience enables them to develop parts of an app or even entire apps.

4.2 MD^2 as a Contemporary Generative Approach

Aiming to provide a cross-platform development solution for business apps, the framework MD^2 has been developed (Majchrzak, Ernsting, et al., 2015). The chapter's authors combine a variety of viewpoints on MD² and, thereby, on cross-platform app development in general:

- One of the authors was a member of the original research group of 2013 (Heitkötter, Majchrzak, & Kuchen, 2013; Heitkötter & Majchrzak, 2013).
- One of the authors supervised the ongoing development (Majchrzak, Ernsting, et al., 2015; Majchrzak & Ernsting, 2015).
- Another three have recently joined the work on the approach and contribute to the revision and rejuvenation of the approach (Dageförde, Reischmann, Majchrzak, & Ernsting, 2016; Ernsting, Rieger, Wrede, & Majchrzak, 2016).

MD² follows a model-driven generative approach. It provides a consolidated programming language, MD²-DSL, which is employed to develop a business app. Following the Model-View-Controller (MVC) pattern (Buschmann, Meunier, Rohnert, Sommerlad, & Stal, 1996), a developer specifies a business app as a so-called *archetype*, which comprises multiple files in MD²-DSL.

The MD²-DSL is accompanied by software that derives actual apps from a developed archetype (cf. Figure 2). MD² contains a *preprocessor* which reads an archetype and performs platform-independent transformations on it, converting shorthand notations to more complex statements. More importantly, MD² comprises a set of generators, one per target platform. Each generator operates on the preprocessed archetype and creates platform-specific, native code for its respective target. In result, the generators create one native app per target platform, thus optimizing the generated code for execution on its target. MD² currently provides generators for iOS, Android, and the proprietary map.apps platform (Evers et al., 2016). Furthermore, a generator for a common Java EE-based backend is included which provides RESTful Web services for common data storage of all generated apps. The latter can be seen as a blueprint for access to arbitrary backend systems. This is particularly important since business apps typically rely heavily on (existing) corporate systems (Majchrzak, Ernsting, et al., 2015).

While further extensions to the set of supported platforms are desirable, this target is currently not of foremost importance. Implementing an additional generator would pose only minor challenges but be very time consuming. Moreover, if would hardly lead to additional research insights. Thus, this task ought to be reserved for the effort of a to-be-established community rather than to be a research activity.

The focus of MD² is on data-driven business apps, i.e. apps that heavily rely on display and manipulation of business data using forms (Majchrzak, Ernsting, et al., 2015). The MD²-DSL is designed such that creating, managing, and using UI elements for forms is as simple as possible for a developer. In fact, MD² should even be suited to people with some prior knowledge in textual modelling but no spe-

Figure 2. Flow from the cross-platform MD² model through the set of generators, creating multiple platform-specific native apps

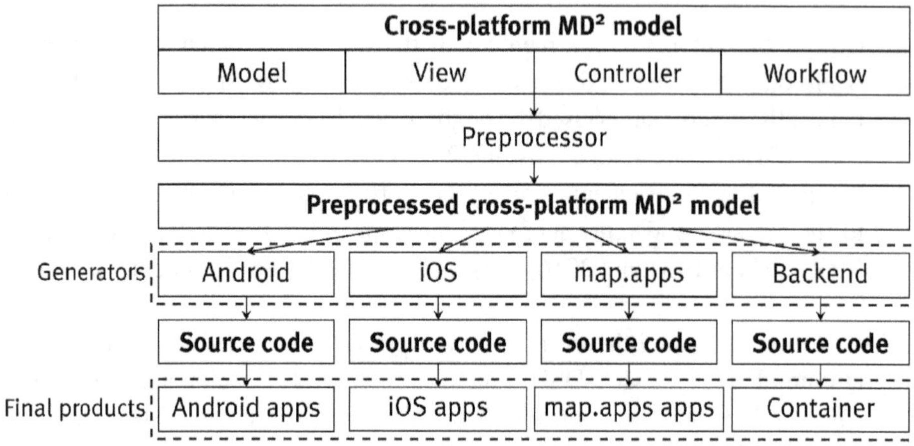

cific background as a programmer. Moreover, the developer does not have to consider peculiarities of the targeted platforms; instead, this task is delegated to the respective generators. Therefore, the amount of required boilerplate code is reduced. At the same time, the complexity is lowered since less platform-specific experience is required to realize *good* apps. The same holds true for all operations on the underlying data, as well as for connecting UI elements to data that are stored either locally or on a generated or manually developed backend: The developer only specifies the relationships between data and its display, whereas the generators will create corresponding code for the apps. An additional perk of this approach is rapid development once basic experience is gained with MD².

Exemplary, an app developer could use MD² for the development of a public sector app that lets citizens capture and describe a deficit observed in public spaces and send the report to the local authorities (Dageförde et al., 2016). Creating such a report could start with determining the citizen's location: Depending on a platform's or hardware's capabilities, this can be realised using sensor data or software emulation, but the developer does not need to consider this during development. Regarding the entire reporting workflow as a process model, several steps like this are involved (cf. Figure 3). Using MD²-DSL, each step can be developed individually as a self-contained component. Afterwards, these components can be arranged and re-arranged into a particular order, based on the final requirements of the apps. Furthermore, MD²-DSL enables to specify a set of apps that, in combination, fulfil a workflow. In this example, there would be one app targeted at citizens, which reports to another app for the public administration. The latter can also send feedback to the

Figure 3. Process model of an exemplary business app for the public sector (Dageförde et al., 2016)

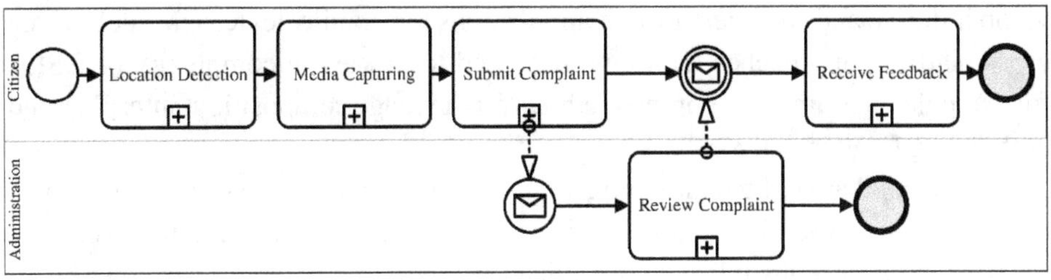

reporting citizen. The generators use the developed MD[2] archetype and generate an according set of apps, as well as a backend that coordinates the interaction and data transfer between individual apps.

Similarly, MD[2]-DSL could be used to create apps for insurance companies, integrating data-centric workflows of field staff and office staff together with a corporate backend. A further use case that could be realised is a pharmacy's inventory control system which is combined with point-of-sale data.

5 Paving the Road to Future Cross-Platform Business App Development

In this section we present our vision of cross-platform business app development. We start by sketching technological progress that we deem as a requirement. Next, we propose how a stronger domain-orientation will facilitate a wider adoption of cross-platform approaches. Based on this background, we provide our view of the future. This is detailed in the following subsections which successively discuss merits, challenges, and limitations.

5.1 Required Technological Work

From a technical perspective, some challenges arise that need to be overcome before leveraging the benefits of cross-platform approaches for mobile e-commerce apps. Firstly, reliable integration with current e-commerce back-end systems needs to be available to reuse existing business logic. Whereas in the B2B sector basic electronic data interchange standards exist for many years (Mukhopadhyay, Kekre, & Kalathur, 1995), integrations of mobile software with shop back-ends, ERP systems, mobile payment brokers, recommender software, pricing systems, and other specialized software will be required. This is necessary for the multitude of players on the market, many of them having differing proprietary interfaces. In general, managing the complexity of e-commerce systems will be essential to develop intuitive and well-performing applications for mobile devices. Model-driven cross-platform approaches therefore also need to tackle the complexity of DSLs, for example regarding developing methods for language composition, interplay, and embedding (Völter, 2013).

As a second area of technological requirements, context-sensitivity needs to be drastically improved to provide a significant benefit compared to regular Web sites (or webapps). Recent studies indicate that the mood of a potential customer influences the susceptibility for recommendations (Shi & Marini, 2016). Apps need to consider such psychological insights together with context information in order to provide an improved shopping experience for customers and higher conversion rates for merchants. As a consequence, smart notifications, geotargeted advertising, and meaningful recommendations need to rely on intelligent functionalities (Gallego, Woerndl, & Huecas, 2013; Shankar et al., 2016). In the long term, further technical innovations with regard to sensor usage and novel wireless communication mechanisms (e.g. beacons) will foster mobile e-commerce. As such technologies are usually platform-dependent, cross-platform approaches will play a major role in bridging different implementations and add to an enjoyable shopping experience. Moreover, they will be required for keeping the implementation cost-effective. Additionally, context-sensitivity also needs to be kept in mind for effectively testing the developed apps (Majchrzak & Schulte, 2015).

5.2 Improving Domain-Orientation

Mobile apps in the domain of e-commerce have not yet been researched extensively (cf. e.g. Bigné, Ruiz, & Sanz, 2007; Taylor & Levin, 2014). Apart from studies and guidelines on apps in general, which focus on user interfaces, feature fit, and functionality on mobile devices (Apple Inc., n.d.; Khalid et al., 2015), best practices and guidelines specifically for e-commerce apps are scarce. For example, the representation of shopping carts and product catalogues on mobile devices remains basically equal to traditional e-commerce Web pages. While reusing established interaction mechanisms is not a problem per se, it hinders the adoption (and probably even the *invention*) of more user-friendly possibilities. Thus, research needs to be conducted in order to uncover suitable patterns for domain-specific interactions, ultimately leading to more engaging user experiences for the app user.

Concerning MDSD as a specific approach for cross-platform development, and DSLs in particular, their appropriateness and eventual success highly depends on the apt tailoring to the targeted domain. A key element to leverage the potential gain in productivity compared to traditional programming models is the manageability of complexity though increased abstraction (Stahl & Völter, 2006). Therefore, representing domain-specific concepts of e-commerce as abstract concepts in the cross-platform approach is essential for integrating the business needs with app development. To support this development, domain experts in the field of e-commerce should be involved in the development process. This can be achieved by tightly working together with the app developers. In a model-driven context, the domain expert can even actively participate in the app creation if the language is designed to support abstract domain concepts in a declarative manner such that the intended result can be modelled rather than traditionally programmed. In the long run, an active *community* must be created. Developer communities greatly contribute to the ease-of-use of a platform (Majchrzak, Wolf, & Abbassi, 2015), and will thus be required for frameworks to become successful.

5.3 Sketching the Future

As described in Section 4, our cross-platform development framework MD² already supports the development of business apps for multiple platforms and may serve as example for a glimpse into the future of cross-platform development. There is a wide range of possibilities of how to advance the current approach, considering both technical and domain-specific aspects, while paving the road for future business app development.

From a business perspective, apps should support the existing digital ecosystem in e-commerce. Therefore, a strong focus on business processes is essential to match domain experts' knowledge and expectations. This is reflected in research on MD², where workflows have been introduced in order to group sequences of views in an app into larger, business process-oriented steps and thereby allow for interaction between interconnected apps based on user roles (Dageförde et al., 2016). In addition, there is ongoing research towards modelling use cases as self-contained archetypes and automatically inferring app structure, navigation, and data models according to user roles. In the future, manual interventions on process interfaces can be avoided, allowing fully integrated process flows towards the customer and within the organization.

Concerning technical aspects, overcoming the increase of complexity can achieve significant progress on the adoption of model-driven cross-platform approaches. While the domain-specific language has grown to a powerful tool over time, its complexity has risen, too, and may alienate new developers and modellers (Heitkötter, Majchrzak, & Kuchen, 2013). To support generator developers for new target platforms, a reference architecture for mobile business apps was developed (Ernsting et al., 2016; Evers et al., 2016). Ongoing research also deals with the development of a graphical DSL in order to ease the actual modelling of apps. Coinciding, the level of abstraction will be further increased towards a rather declarative style of creating apps in contrast to an explicit and detailed specification of user interfaces and navigation. Ideally, business users without much technical knowledge will be able to express their domain knowledge as an archetype and use them as reasonable tool for communication (Völter, 2013).

Finally, the current approach is characterised by a form-based approach using standardised view elements. In future, enhanced visualizations and new widget types can improve the apps' aesthetics. For example, new layout types such as cards and infinite scrolling (as in Twitter) are visually appealing representations of content still missing in the current version of MD^2. Although not exclusive to this domain, well-designed user interfaces with rich imagery and typography have a direct influence on user behaviour and engagement, which makes their design particularly relevant for e-commerce. Ultimately, a theming approach may be a suitable option to model the apps' appearance while taking up the challenge of balancing cross-platform abstraction and platform-specific characteristics.

5.4 Prospects of Future Business Apps

The relevance for app development in the field of m-commerce has two different facets. On the one hand, apps change the way a company can interact with its customers. On the other hand, mobile devices can be leveraged for employee usage to improve internal processes, such as order handling. However, both areas profit from advantages of model-driven software development being applied to the creation of mobile apps. Apart from the general benefits of MDSD such as higher productivity, fast development cycles, or integration of domain experts (Völter, 2013), the application of model-driven aspects on cross-platform development offers additional value. Through the native app source code generated with the MD^2 framework, these apps can deliver a native look and feel and thus increase the emphasized user experience (Heitkötter, Hanschke, et al., 2012). Additionally, they are able to integrate certain hardware features of the mobile device, such as geolocation, camera, and microphone in a way that enables new use cases for business apps.

With the aforementioned growth of the mobile computing market and the ever widening capabilities of mobile technology, it is hardly possible to predict what may be possible in ten years. However, a mid-term look is well possible. While the number of different platforms is a core issue in mobile app development, a similar issue can be observed, for instance, for the interfaces of *smart devices*. Current sharing protocols, such as Apple Airplay or UPnP, are limited in terms of collaboration among each other (Busold, Heuser, Rios, Sadeghi, & Asokan, 2015). Cross-platform development could help to overcome these limitations by generating interfaces for every possible combination of device and protocol. Enabling the interconnection of different smart devices in this way facilitates a much wider range of usage scenarios. Thus, when talking about the target platforms of cross-platform app-development, smartphones and tablets may not be the only conceivable target in the future, but new technologies for augmented reality (for instance Google Glass, Microsoft HoloLens), smart watches, or other smart entertainment devices may be considered as well. There is already research for augmented reality (AR) in the context of e-commerce (Lu & Smith, 2007). With a fully integrated software system landscape on devices through the whole supply chain, new scenarios are imaginable, which are profitable both for customers and enterprises. The customer can be given a reinvented shopping experience through in-shop information, a close contact to the company, and the possibility of testing the products while shopping by projecting them in a virtual environment using AR. Additionally, the customers have the freedom to interact with the company when and wherever they like to. Companies can profit from timely information of the customers' behaviour and needs. Further, analytical details offered by mobile technology and the innovations in combination with the Internet of Things (IoT) can improve the information needed for operational, tactical, or strategical decisions.

To embed the usage of different sorts of mobile devices into the internal workflows, a close orientation towards existing business process models can be useful. A model-to-model transformation could be leveraged to make excerpts of the company's business process models usable by model-driven approaches. Using a unified graphical modelling language, the process model excerpts could then be enriched by data necessary for app development in a way comprehensible by domain experts, which may be not IT-affine. Web services or other interfaces can help to interconnect the generated apps with the existing application landscape of the company. As a consequence, the apps can show and generate valuable information from and to the different actors of the whole supply chain in-time and thus increase the overall value generation.

5.5 Challenges, Obstacles, and Possibly Negative Ramifications

Several prerequisites from a technical and domain-oriented viewpoint have already been discussed. However, additional challenges need to be overcome when implementing and maintaining business apps using cross-platform approaches. A robust framework suffers from a chicken-and-egg problem: It will only be adopted when it proves to be useful and simultaneously profits from the application to the real world. Ultimately, the major hurdle for the initial adoption of a cross-platform approach is its usability. Therefore, improving its fit to the desired target users and usage scenarios needs to be considered permanently. Each approach needs to develop mechanisms in order to manage the complexity and to abstract from individual platform issues. For instance, model-driven approaches have to balance and reduce the complexity both on the modelling side (targeted for non-technical business users) and the generation side (targeted for individual platform generator developers). Apart from a sound technical design, proper tools and documentation are key for the initial adoption of an approach as well as the integration into the overall software development cycle including testing, build and deployment.

5.6 Remaining Issues

In the previous section, we have identified challenges that need to be overcome in order to benefit from cross-platform approaches in mobile e-commerce. In addition to these, more fundamental problems exist with regard to user acceptance and for economic reasons. Firstly, the willingness of users to install separate apps for different shops needs to be questioned. The growing number of entries in app markets leads to a competition for storage space on customers' mobile devices: If an app does not perform as expected, it is ignored in future or removed. This high competition leads to increasing challenges in the app market with regard to value proposition and user experience (Zhong & Michahelles, 2013). This observation indicates that only customers with frequent orders are likely to install a vendor-specific mobile app unless unique benefits are proposed through its usage. Webapps have lower entry barriers as no installation is required, yet customer engagement and loyalty can be expected to be comparable with traditional Web sites.

From a development perspective, cross-platform approaches offer significant benefits in terms of reusability. Yet, initial development effort for multiple platforms is high. Particularly, model-driven techniques that drastically simplify and accelerate the app creation process require substantial initial efforts for generator development. In many scenarios, no more than one application with infrequent new versions will be needed by a company, consequently incentivizing Web-based approaches. As an alternative business model, customized apps may be provided through a dedicated service provider that develops an industry-wide DSL and benefits from economies of scale. However, legal issues remain regarding the responsibility for sensitive customer information and transaction data.

Finally, mobile devices offer the possibility to track users much more comprehensively, for instance regarding customer behaviour, location profiles, or personal preferences. Potential misuse of this information leads to privacy concerns and may harm the acceptance of such applications by customers.

6 SCENARIOS

In the following, we have compiled four future usage scenarios. In parts they have already been demonstrated individually and most of them should be possible with today's technology. We believe that we will see such applications much more widely in the near future. Please note that these scenarios are for illustration, and might pose some inherent problems. In particular, privacy and security will need to be carefully considered on top of the extended functionality and comfort. The future progress regarding cross-platform business apps can also be transferred to other domains. Therefore, the fourth scenario depicts a possible application of mentioned features to crisis management.

6.1 Scenario 1: Multi-Channel Shopping Experience

Imagine Peter is looking for a new technology gadget on his tablet device while relaxing on the couch in the evening. To be well prepared, he uses an app to inform himself about different devices and their specific characteristics and capabilities. Reviews by other customers are also available within the application so that he can get a first impression based on the opinion of other customers and bookmark interesting items. To get hands-on experience, Peter decides to try out some devices in a (physical) store and therefore looks up the directions to the nearest shop location. From within the app, he can see tomorrow's opening hours and schedule an appointment with a salesperson, which is automatically added to his calendar. The next day, Peter uses the smartphone app, which synchronized the data, to show and discuss his favourite devices with the salesperson in store. While strolling through the store for a few more minutes in order to decide on a device, his phone vibrates and offers him a break with a free drink at the shopping centre lounge area. While enjoying his drink, he uses one of the tablets which are available for the customers, and is instantly redirected to a social media platform, which exchanges information about the gadgets he is about to buy. Peter raises a question to the community and after a few seconds has an answer from a former customer, who praises the quality of one device and recommends him an accessory which connects to his multimedia system at home. With intelligent app support, the multi-channel shopping experience is dramatically improved by seamlessly integrating into the customers' shopping behaviour and combining the best of the digital and physical worlds.

6.2 Scenario 2: Technology-Assisted Fashion Shopping

Claudia is visiting the close-by shopping centre, since she likes the shopping experience and is looking for a new fashionable outfit. For some inspiration she looks around through the shop's assortment. Through augmented reality (AR) glasses that she is wearing, her eye movements are tracked. After some minutes of gathering information and based on previous orders, Claudia's smartphone recommends her some additional trousers, which might suit what she is looking for. The glasses are pointing her the way to where the trousers are positioned and then towards the changing rooms. Her former purchases are saved in the cloud and the 3D models of each piece are offered through the retailers' Web interface. Claudia scrolls through her purchases using her smartphone, which are then directly projected on her body by the AR glasses. Thus, she can directly try on the new trousers in combination with the tops she bought last week in her parents' home town. Unfortunately, she is not satisfied with the colour of the tops presented in the store. Luckily, she can order unavailable items, which are then shipped to her home from the central warehouse. She does not even need to specify her size, since the combination of AR and order history allows the app to submit the proper size for the chosen apparel brand. Meanwhile, the company's purchasing department was already informed about the missing tops, including detailed information about the whole outfit Claudia is pleased with. This information is propagated through the supply chain and reaches the designer, who is now able to rethink his product line for the next season. As a result, business apps for AR devices offer novel shopping experiences to customers based on their preferences while at the same time creating the potential for cross-selling for vendors.

6.3 Scenario 3: B2B Procurement

In a B2B context, the advantage of business process integration can be highlighted. John needs to buy new consumables for his department within a large organisation. To check the current stocks in the storeroom and reorder items running short, he can use a webapp on his mobile device. In order to decide on the reorder quantity, the system provides visualisations for the consumption of the previous months. If required, a trend analysis and utilization simulation can be run. As usual in large enterprises, he has to honour existing procurement contracts. Therefore, the app acts as a marketplace in which merchants can list products that were previously negotiated in master agreements by the procurement department. After completing the activity, the order is automatically passed to the department leader who is in charge of the budget decisions for formal approval.

6.4 Scenario 4: Tunnel Fire

Judy is using her municipality's self-service app. This app provides basic e-government functionality. For example, Judy can prepare administrative formalities or report potholes. The app, however, also has an emergency functionality that only activates in case of disasters. When driving home from a visit to the mountains with her family, Judy enters a long tunnel. After hearing a loud, shaking sound, she slams the brakes as the cars in front of her come to a sudden halt. Smoke quickly fills the tunnel, making orientation impossible. The children scream. While the mobile network breaks down, the self-service app requests Judy to turn on WiFi. Within seconds, her mobile phone and the devices of other people in the tunnel form an ad hoc network. Since many devices have temperature sensors, and the devices' cameras can be used to determine the density of the smoke, in a joint effort the network can determine in which direction the fire must be located. Based on a plan of the tunnel, Judy's device displays hints on how to get to the nearest – and safest – emergency exit. When Judy and her family safely exit the tunnel, the fire fighters already arrive. They have been called automatically by the device of the first person that made it out. The fire is condemned quickly since the brigade leader can utilize the information recorded by the ad hoc network.

7 DISCUSSION

Building on the previous sections, we discuss our findings. First, we provide an outlook and name open questions for research and practice. Then, we describe limitations of the work presented in this chapter. Eventually, we sketch our own research goals, which are derived from the work presented here and which honour the limitations.

7.1 Outlook and Open Questions

Throughout the prior sections of this chapter, a need for much further research has become apparent. The observations of what is possible so far, and the study of how these possibilities have been enabled, allow for an outlook. As suggested earlier, this outlook cannot be presented in a form of looking ten (or even more years) into the future and proposing the then to-be-encountered reality.[2] Rather, it can be argued which questions will need to be answered to enable what could be a desirable future of mobile computing, specifically multi-platform business apps.

The possibly most profound question concerns technology choice: Which cross-platform app technology will prevail? While mobile platforms have become more similar than they have been a few years ago, there is no trend towards full unification in terms of a common platform, programming model or the like. Distinctive ecosystems will remain. As we have shown, no cross-platform solution has found universal acceptance, although those based on Web technology are quite widely used. At the same time, the technological superiority of generative approaches is apparent – as is the ease-of-use and development simplicity of webapps. While this makes a prediction impossible, it is not too bold to expect further unification and a strive for easier multi-platform development. We strongly believe that contributing to advanced cross-platform technology is important for pursuing this goal.

Many open questions remain when bringing together the technological and the economical dimension of business app development. Traditionally, technological progress is made by engineers, in this case particularly by computer scientists and electrical engineers. Observations are made by behaviourists, i.e. typically social scientists. Unfortunately, bringing together both worlds to provide a kind of "round-trip research" often is missing. What would be needed to pave the future are circles of observation and engineering (also cf. Majchrzak & Ernsting, 2015). How these can be designed to keep pace with the rapid proliferation of the field remains an open question, though. For rigorous research in particular, there is a very high risk that profound work is not only practically irrelevant but literally outdated once accomplished. This might be one of the reasons for the current lack of a theoretic foundation.

Considering the technological dimension of cross-platform business app development, a host of questions remains open. These typically have a high level of detail and, thus, are out of scope of discussion here. Bridging the technological dimension to the domain-oriented one remains a profound challenge, though. Our vision includes app development by people who are no seasoned programmers. How to achieve this has yet to be solved. Progress in this regard would also be beneficial for senior development staff. Nowadays, grasping the total complexity of software development is very hard. It, for example, cannot be expected that all developers have proficiency considering system security. Therefore, if next-generation tools can provide reasonable "default" security, development would become much easier. Even more, this would be highly beneficial from an economic standpoint as investment in apps would be less risky. Again, how to achieve such reasonable default provision of functionality remains an open question. Undoubtedly, integration with cross-platform frameworks would be fascinating. Of course, overcoming heterogeneity in this regard will be a challenge of its own.

While some of these questions might seem to be hard to be answered, we are very optimistic. Economic pressure and competition in searching for practicable solutions to urgent problems can lead to the rapid development of sustainable solutions. An example for this is Mobile Device Management (MDM). Desperately required only a few years ago (cf. Majchrzak & Heitkötter, 2014), it now can be regarded as pretty well conquered (Majchrzak, Wolf, et al., 2015).

7.2 Limitations

A research article should name any limitations that could diminish its accuracy or narrow its applicability. In case of this chapter, it of course has to be kept in mind that we take a rather bold look at the future. All ideas presented in this chapter are based on thorough work. However, neither of us is a prophet and, therefore, some of the developments we propose might turn out wrong. Moreover, predicting fundamental changes is notoriously hard; it is easy to sketch a future that sounds realistic but turns out to be completely different from what actually becomes reality. At the same time, it is very rewarding if you get *it* right, particularly, if the vision has been profound (cf. e.g. with Weiser's *Computer for the 21st Century* (Weiser, 1999)). Therefore, it has to be kept in mind that the further one of our proposals looks into the future, and the greater the change we propose is, the greater is the probability that *something different* will happen. We have tried to mitigate this general problem of future-oriented work by sketching alternatives and explicating uncertainties.

The second limitation of the work presented here is its non-empirical onset. This is a deliberate choice; in fact, we believe that a future-oriented article that tried to combine work from a theoretical and observational standpoint (such as ours), and empirical data is likely to become confusing. However, we deem both quantitative and qualitative studies to be necessary to tackle some of the open questions sketched above. Probably, a future article can join the non-empirical and the empirical approach to a more comprehensive vision.

7.3 Future Work

While a general need for extensive future activities in the field of cross-platform app development and many neighbouring activities has been stressed when giving an outlook, this section eventually sheds light on our own plans.

Concerning model-driven software development, our research focuses on lowering the complexity of development. In particular, the unique advantage of MDSD regarding easy-to-understand models for domain-specific purposes is further investigated. Currently, a graphical DSL with a respective modelling environment is considered. It should allow non-technical domain experts to model apps. To exploit its full potential, the language is designed to be highly declarative and rely on inference mechanisms in order to derive fully functional business apps. Furthermore, several ideas exist for the continuation of the MD^2 framework itself (see also Section 5.3), for example regarding improved business process integration as well as language modularity.

Considering app development in general, we will look at more domain-specific applications as well as on better domain-specificity. It has to be asked whether the business app as we frame it is the *perfect* constraint for domain-specific app development. Possibly, additional domains can be added, some being related, while others being widely different. An example for a related domain could by graphically intensive apps that are yet used for business purposes. For this purpose, a graphical DSL might be more suited. Another example would be a DSL that is specifically tailored to apps that are used in crisis management. This field could greatly benefit from the possibility to tailor apps in the immediate wake of a disaster. Such an app should be flexible enough to run on a multitude of devices because in disaster situations you usually have to cope with whatever might be available.

8 CONCLUSION

In this chapter we presented a vision of improved business apps that have been developed using cross-platform development approaches. Apps already have a profound economic (and societal) impact. Their importance will continue growing. However, even with only two mobile platforms that have significant market shares remaining, cross-platform development remains an important topic. Current approaches often employ Web technology, which enables quick results. However, apps often do not perform well and have user experience shortcomings. Solutions based on model-driven software development provide the benefits of cross-platform development while mitigating many current shortcomings faced when implementing apps. Based on a discussion of MD^2, being an MDSD cross-platform approach with a comparatively long development history, we have sketched the path to future business app development. To enable the next generation of apps, both technological progress and a strong domain-orientation are required. Then, however, the outlook is bright with many possibilities and merits. These also have been demonstrated in a number of scenarios. The required progress and remaining challenges and limitations hint to a number of open questions. For some of these, our own work will seek to provide answers.

Looking back at the development of mobile computing in the age of smartphones, a ludicrous pace of innovation has to be attested. While such dynamics always pose risks, the future does not look grim. In fact, the promise of future possibilities is impressive. We believe that apps will continue to enrich enterprise activities and society. As demonstrated not only in this chapter but in the whole book, the research's journey for this has by far not come to an end.

REFERENCES

Al-Subaihin, A., Finkelstein, A., Harman, M., Jia, Y., Martin, W., Sarro, F., & Zhang, Y. (2015). App Store Mining and Analysis. In *Proceedings of the 3rd International Workshop on Software Development Lifecycle for Mobile* (pp. 1–2). New York, NY: ACM. doi:10.1145/2804345.2804346

Apache. (n.d.). *Apache Cordova*. Retrieved April 28, 2016, from https://cordova.apache.org/

AppCelerator. (n.d.). *AppCelerator*. Retrieved April 30, 2016, from http://www.appcelerator.com/

Applause. (n.d.). *Applause Repository*. Retrieved April 29, 2016, from https://github.com/applause/applause

Apple Inc. (n.d.). *iOS Human Interface Guidelines*. Retrieved April 21, 2016, from https://developer.apple.com/library/ios/documentation/UserExperience/Conceptual/MobileHIG/index.html

Apple. (n.d.). *Apple iOS*. Retrieved April 30, 2016, from http://www.apple.com/de/ios/

Barnett, S., Avazpour, I., Vasa, R., & Grundy, J. (2015). A Multi-view Framework for Generating Mobile Apps. *IEEE Symposium on Visual Languages and Human-Centric Computing (VL/HCC)*, (1), 305–306. http://doi.org/ doi:10.1109/VLHCC.2015.7357239

Barnett, S., Vasa, R., & Grundy, J. (2015). Bootstrapping Mobile App Development. *Proceedings - International Conference on Software Engineering, 2*, 657–660. http://doi.org/ doi:10.1109/ICSE.2015.216

Basole, R. C., & Karla, J. (2011). On the evolution of mobile platform ecosystem structure and strategy. *Business and Information Systems Engineering*, *3*(5), 313–322. doi:10.1007/s12599-011-0174-4

Bigné, E., Ruiz, C., & Sanz, S. (2007). Key Drivers of Mobile Commerce Adoption. An Exploratory Study of Spanish Mobile Users. *Journal of Theoretical and Applied Electronic Commerce Research*, *2*(2), 48–60.

Bootstrap. (2016). *Bootstrap - The world's most popular mobile-first and responsive front-end framework*. Retrieved June 5, 2016, from http://getbootstrap.com/

Brambilla, M., Mauri, A., & Umuhoza, E. (2014). Extending the Interaction Flow Modeling Language (IFML) for Model Driven Development of Mobile Applications Front End. *MobiWIS, 2000*, 176–191. Retrieved from http://dblp.org/db/conf/mobiwis/mobiwis2014.html#BrambillaMU14

Buschmann, F., Meunier, R., Rohnert, H., Sommerlad, P., & Stal, M. (1996). *A System of Patterns: Pattern-Oriented Software Architecture*. Wiley.

Busold, C., Heuser, S., Rios, J., Sadeghi, A. R., & Asokan, N. (2015). Smart and secure cross-device Apps for the Internet of advanced things. Lecture Notes in Computer Science, 8975, 272–290. http://doi.org/ doi:10.1007/978-3-662-47854-7_17

Chauhan, J., Mahanti, A., & Kaafar, M. A. (2014). Towards the Era of Wearable Computing? In *Proceedings of the 2014 CoNEXT on Student Workshop* (pp. 24–25). New York, NY: ACM. http://doi.org/ doi:10.1145/2680821.2680833

Chia, P. H., Yamamoto, Y., & Asokan, N. (2012). Is This App Safe?: A Large Scale Study on Application Permissions and Risk Signals. In *Proceedings of the 21st International Conference on World Wide Web* (pp. 311–320). New York, NY: ACM. http://doi.org/ doi:10.1145/2187836.2187879

Cuadrado, F., & Dueñas, J. (2012). Mobile application stores: Success factors, existing approaches, and future developments. *IEEE Communications Magazine, 50*(11), 160–167. doi:10.1109/MCOM.2012.6353696

Dageförde, J. C., Reischmann, T., Majchrzak, T. A., & Ernsting, J. (2016). Generating App Product Lines in a Model-Driven Cross-Platform Development Approach. In *Proceedings of the 2016 49th Hawaii International Conference on System Sciences* (pp. 5803–5812). http://doi.org/ doi:10.1109/HICSS.2016.718

Dobie, A. (2012). *Why you'll never have the latest version of Android.* Retrieved April 30, 2016, from http://www.androidcentral.com/why-you-ll-never-have-latest-version-android

Ernsting, J., Rieger, C., Wrede, F., & Majchrzak, T. A. (2016). Refining a Reference Architecture for Model-Driven Business Apps. *WEBIST 2016 - Proceedings of the 12th International Conference on Web Information Systems and Technologies.*

Evers, S., Ernsting, J., & Majchrzak, T. A. (2016). *Towards a Reference Architecture for Model-Driven Business Apps.* http://doi.org/10.1109/HICSS.2016.708

Facebook. (2015). Facebook reports second quarter 2015 results. *Facebook Investor Relations*. Retrieved from http://investor.fb.com/releasedetail.cfm?ReleaseID=924562

Filios, G., Nikoletseas, S., & Pavlopoulou, C. (2015). Efficient Parameterized Methods for Physical Activity Detection Using Only Smartphone Sensors. In *Proceedings of the 13th ACM International Symposium on Mobility Management and Wireless Access* (pp. 97–104). New York, NY: ACM. http://doi.org/ doi:10.1145/2810362.2810372

Fletcher, N. (2007). *Apple: "we plan to have an iPhone SDK in developers' hands in February"*. Retrieved April 30, 2016, from http://www.engadget.com/2007/10/17/apple-we-plan-to-have-an-iphone-sdk-in-developers-hands-in-fe/

Fu, B., Lin, J., Li, L., Faloutsos, C., Hong, J., & Sadeh, N. (2013). Why People Hate Your App: Making Sense of User Feedback in a Mobile App Store. In *Proceedings of the 19th ACM SIGKDD International Conference on Knowledge Discovery and Data Mining* (pp. 1276–1284). New York, NY: ACM. http://doi.org/ doi:10.1145/2487575.2488202

Gallego, D., Woerndl, W., & Huecas, G. (2013). Evaluating the impact of proactivity in the user experience of a context-aware restaurant recommender for Android smartphones. *Journal of Systems Architecture*, *59*(9), 748–758. doi:10.1016/j.sysarc.2013.02.004

Ghosh, A., & Riccardi, G. (2014). Recognizing Human Activities from Smartphone Sensor Signals. In *Proceedings of the 22Nd ACM International Conference on Multimedia* (pp. 865–868). New York, NY: ACM. http://doi.org/ doi:10.1145/2647868.2655034

Goasduff, L., & Pettey, C. (2012). *Gartner Says Worldwide Smartphone Sales Soared in Fourth Quarter of 2011 With 47 Percent Growth*. Retrieved April 30, 2016, from http://www.gartner.com/newsroom/id/1924314

Google. (2013). *Mobile In-Store Research: how in-store shoppers are using mobile devices*. Google Shopper Marketing Council.

Google. (2016a). *Android*. Retrieved April 30, 2016, from https://www.android.com/

Google. (2016b). *Android Auto*. Retrieved April 28, 2016, from https://www.android.com/intl/de_de/auto/

Google. (2016c). *Google Play Store*. Retrieved April 30, 2016, from https://play.google.com/

Grønli, T.-M., Hansen, J., & Ghinea, G. (2010). Android vs Windows Mobile vs Java ME: A Comparative Study of Mobile Development Environments. In *Proceedings of the 3rd International Conference on Pervasive Technologies Related to Assistive Environments* (pp. 45:1–45:8). New York, NY: ACM. http://doi.org/ doi:10.1145/1839294.1839348

Heitkötter, H., Hanschke, S., & Majchrzak, T. A. (2012). Comparing Cross-platform Development Approaches for Mobile Applications. In *Proceedings of the 8th International Conference on Web Information Systems and Technologies (WEBIST)* (pp. 299–311). http://doi.org/ doi:10.5220/0003904502990311

Heitkötter, H., Kuchen, H., & Majchrzak, T. A. (2015). Extending a Model-Driven Cross-Platform Development Approach for Business Apps. *Science of Computer Programming*, *97*(Part 1), 31–36. doi:10.1016/j.scico.2013.11.013

Heitkötter, H., & Majchrzak, T. A. (2013). Cross-Platform Development of Business Apps with MD2. In *Proc. of the 8th Int. Conf. on Design Science at the Intersection of Physical and Virtual Design (DESRIST)* (Vol. 7939, pp. 405–411). Springer. doi:10.1007/978-3-642-38827-9_29

Heitkötter, H., Majchrzak, T. A., & Kuchen, H. (2013). Cross-Platform Model-Driven Development of Mobile Applications with MD2. In *Proc. 28th SAC* (pp. 526–533). ACM. doi:10.1145/2480362.2480464

Heitkötter, H., Majchrzak, T. A., Ruland, B., & Weber, T. (2013). Evaluating Frameworks for Creating Mobile Web Apps. In K.-H. Krempels & A. Stocker (Eds.), *WEBIST 2013 - Proceedings of the 9th International Conference on Web Information Systems and Technologies* (pp. 209–221). SciTePress.

Heitkötter, H., Majchrzak, T. A., Wolffgang, U., & Kuchen, H. (2012). *Business Apps: Grundlagen und Status quo*. Münster: Förderkreis der Angewandten Informatik an der Westfälischen Wilhelms-Universität Münster e.V.

Hemel, Z., & Visser, E. (2011). Declaratively Programming the Mobile Web with Mobl. In *Proceedings of the 2011 ACM International Conference on Object Oriented Programming Systems Languages and Applications* (pp. 695–712). New York, NY: ACM. http://doi.org/ doi:10.1145/2048066.2048121

IDC. (2016). *Smartphone OS Market Share*. Retrieved April 30, 2016, from http://www.idc.com/prodserv/smartphone-os-market-share.jsp

IFML. (n.d.). *IFML: The Interaction Flow Modeling Language*. Retrieved April 30, 2016, from http://www.ifml.org/

Jones, C., & Jia, X. (2015). Using a Domain Specific Language for Lightweight Model-Driven Development. In ENASE 2014, CCIS 551 (pp. 46–62). http://doi.org/ doi:10.1007/978-3-319-27218-4_4

Joorabchi, M. E., Mesbah, A., & Kruchten, P. (2013). Real challenges in mobile app development. In *International Symposium on Empirical Software Engineering and Measurement* (pp. 15–24). http://doi.org/ doi:10.1109/ESEM.2013.9

JSR 68. (2011). *JSR 68: J2ME Platform Specification*. Retrieved April 30, 2016, from https://www.jcp.org/en/jsr/detail?id=68

Kang, J. Y. M., Mun, J. M., & Johnson, K. K. P. (2015). In-store mobile usage: Downloading and usage intention toward mobile location-based retail apps. *Computers in Human Behavior*, *46*, 210–217. doi:10.1016/j.chb.2015.01.012

Kejriwal, A. A. (2009). MobiDSL - a Domain Specific Language for Mobile Web Applications: developing applications for mobile platform without web programming.*Proceedings of the 9th OOPSLA Workshop on Domain-Specific Modeling*.

Khalid, H., Shihab, E., Nagappan, M., & Hassan, A. E. (2015). What do mobile app users complain about? *IEEE Software*, *32*(3), 70–77. doi:10.1109/MS.2014.50

Khansa, L., Zobel, C., & Goicochea, G. (2012). Creating a Taxonomy for Mobile Commerce Innovations Using Social Network and Cluster Analyses. *International Journal ofElectronic Commerce*, *16*(4), 19–52. doi:10.2753/JEC1086-4415160402

Kim, J., Park, Y., Kim, C., & Lee, H. (2013). Mobile application service networks: Apples App Store. *Service Business*, *8*(1), 1–27. doi:10.1007/s11628-013-0184-z

Kimbler, K. (2010). App store strategies for service providers. In *Intelligence in Next Generation Networks (ICIN), 2010 14th International Conference on* (pp. 1–5). http://doi.org/ doi:10.1109/ICIN.2010.5640947

Lu, Y., & Smith, S. (2007). Augmented Reality E-Commerce Assistant System: Trying While Shopping. In J. A. Jacko (Ed.), *Human-Computer Interaction. Interaction Platforms and Techniques:12th International Conference* (pp. 643–652). Berlin: Springer Berlin Heidelberg. http://doi.org/ doi:10.1007/978-3-540-73107-8_72

Macedonia, M. (2007). iPhones Target the Tech Elite. *Computer*, *40*(6), 94–95. doi:10.1109/MC.2007.212

Majchrzak, T. A., & Ernsting, J. (2015). Reengineering an Approach to Model-Driven Development of Business Apps. In 8th SIGSAND/PLAIS EuroSymposium (pp. 15–31). http://doi.org/ doi:10.1007/978-3-319-24366-5_2

Majchrzak, T. A., Ernsting, J., & Kuchen, H. (2015). Achieving Business Practicability of Model-Driven Cross-Platform Apps. *OJIS*, *2*(2), 3–14.

Majchrzak, T. A., & Heitkötter, H. (2014). Status Quo and Best Practices of App Development in Regional Companies. In K.-H. Krempels & A. Stocker (Eds.), *Revised Selected Papers WEBIST 2013* (Vol. 189, pp. 189–206). Springer. doi:10.1007/978-3-662-44300-2_12

Majchrzak, T. A., & Schulte, M. (2015). Context-Dependent Testing of Applications for Mobile Devices. *Open Journal of Web Technologies, 2*(1), 27–39. Retrieved from http://www.ronpub.com/ojwt

Majchrzak, T. A., Wolf, S., & Abbassi, P. (2015). Comparing the Capabilities of Mobile Platforms for Business App Development. In S. Wrycza (Ed.), *Information Systems: Development, Applications, Education: 8th SIGSAND/PLAIS EuroSymposium 2015* (pp. 70–88). Cham: Springer International Publishing; doi:10.1007/978-3-319-24366-5_6

Mansfield-Devine, S. (2012). Paranoid Android: Just how insecure is the most popular mobile platform? *Network Security*, (9): 5–10. doi:10.1016/S1353-4858(12)70081-8

Marinho, E. H., & Resende, R. F. (2015). Native and Multiple Targeted Mobile Applications. In O. Gervasi, B. Murgante, S. Misra, L. M. Gavrilova, C. A. M. A. Rocha, C. Torre, … O. B. Apduhan (Eds.), *Computational Science and Its ApplicationsICCSA 2015: 15th International Conference* (pp. 544–558). Springer International Publishing. http://doi.org/ doi:10.1007/978-3-319-21410-8_42

Martin, D., Vicente, O., Vicente, S., Ballesteros, J., & Maynar, M. (2014). I Will Prescribe You an App. In *Proceedings of the 2014 Summer Simulation Multiconference* (pp. 58:1–58:8). San Diego, CA: Society for Computer Simulation International. Retrieved from http://dl.acm.org/citation.cfm?id=2685617.2685675

McLellan, C. (2014). *Enterprise mobility in 2014: App-ocalypse Now?* Retrieved April 30, 2016, from http://www.zdnet.com/article/enterprise-mobility-in-2014-app-ocalypse-now

MobileHTML5. (n.d.). *Mobile HTML5 compatibility*. Retrieved April 29, 2016, from http://mobilehtml5.org/

Mukhopadhyay, T., Kekre, S., & Kalathur, S. (1995). Business Value of Information Technology: A Study of Electronic Data Interchange. *Management Information Systems Quarterly, 19*(2), 137–156. doi:10.2307/249685

Ohrt, J., & Turau, V. (2012). Cross-Platform Development Tools for Smartphone Applications. *IEEE Computer, 45*(9), 72–79. doi:10.1109/MC.2012.121

Open Handset Alliance. (2007). Industry Leaders Announce Open Platform for Mobile Devices. *Open Handset Alliance*. Retrieved from http://www.openhandsetalliance.com/press_110507.html

Pousttchi, K., Tilson, D., Lyytinen, K., & Hufenbach, Y. (2015). Introduction to the Special Issue on Mobile Commerce: Mobile Commerce Research Yesterday, Today, Tomorrow - What Remains to Be Done? *International Journal of Electronic Commerce, 19*(4), 1–20. doi:10.1080/10864415.2015.1029351

Rivera, J., & van der Meulen, R. (2014a). *Gartner Says Annual Smartphone Sales Surpassed Sales of Feature Phones for the First Time in 2013.* Retrieved April 30, 2016, from http://www.gartner.com/newsroom/id/2665715

Rivera, J., & van der Meulen, R. (2014b). *Gartner Says Sales of Smartphones Grew 20 Percent in Third Quarter of 2014.* Retrieved April 30, 2016, from http://www.gartner.com/newsroom/id/2944819

Seneviratne, S., Seneviratne, A., Kaafar, M. A., Mahanti, A., & Mohapatra, P. (2015). Early Detection of Spam Mobile Apps. In *Proceedings of the 24th International Conference on World Wide Web* (pp. 949–959). New York, NY: ACM. http://doi.org/ doi:10.1145/2736277.2741084

Shankar, V., Kleijnen, M., Ramanathan, S., Rizley, R., Holland, S., & Morrissey, S. (2016). Mobile Shopper Marketing: Key Issues, Current Insights, and Future Research Avenues. *Journal of Interactive Marketing, 34*, 37–48. doi:10.1016/j.intmar.2016.03.002

Shi, F., & Marini, J. (2016). Can e-Commerce Recommender Systems be More Popular with Online Shoppers if they are Mood-aware? *WEBIST, 2*, 173–180.

Stahl, T., & Völter, M. (2006). *Model-Driven Software Development.* Chichester, UK: John Wiley & Sons.

Taylor, D. G., & Levin, M. (2014). Predicting Mobile App Usage for Purchasing and Information-Sharing. *International Journal of Retail & Distribution Management, 42*(8), 759–774. doi:10.1108/IJRDM-11-2012-0108

Völter, M. (2013). *DSL engineering: Designing, implementing and using domain-specific languages.* Lexington, KY: CreateSpace Independent Publishing Platform.

W3C. (2014). *HTML5: A vocabulary and associated APIs for HTML and XHTML, 28. October 2014.* Retrieved from https://www.w3.org/TR/html5/single-page.html

Walker, M., Turnbull, R., & Sim, N. (2007). Future Mobile Devices: An Overview of Emerging Device Trends, and the Impact on Future Converged Services. *BT Technology Journal, 25*(2), 120–125. doi:10.1007/s10550-007-0035-3

Wang, T., Lu, K., Lu, L., Chung, S., & Lee, W. (2013). Jekyll on iOS: When Benign Apps Become Evil. In *22nd USENIX Security Symposium (USENIX Security 13)* (pp. 559–572). Washington, D.C.: USENIX. Retrieved from https://www.usenix.org/conference/usenixsecurity13/technical-sessions/presentation/wang_tielei

WebDSL. (n.d.). *WebDSL Repository*. Retrieved January 1, 2016, from https://github.com/webdsl/webdsl

WebRatio. (n.d.). *WebRatio*. Retrieved April 30, 2016, from http://www.webratio.com/

Weiser, M. (1999). The Computer for the 21st Century. *SIGMOBILE Mob. Comput. Commun. Rev.*, *3*(3), 3–11. doi:10.1145/329124.329126

West, J., & Mace, M. (2010). Browsing as the killer app: Explaining the rapid success of Apples iPhone. *Telecommunications Policy*, *34*(5–6), 270–286. doi:10.1016/j.telpol.2009.12.002

Woods, V., & van der Meulen, R. (2016). *Gartner Says Worldwide Smartphone Sales Grew 9.7 Percent in Fourth Quarter of 2015*. Retrieved April 30, 2016, from http://www.gartner.com/newsroom/id/3215217

Zhong, N., & Michahelles, F. (2013). Google play is not a long tail market: an empirical analysis of app adoption on the Google play app market.*Proceedings of the 28th Annual ACM*, 499–504. doi:10.1145/2480362.2480460

ENDNOTES

1. Actually, some distribution alternatives existed quite early, but their usage was inconvenient (Kim, Park, Kim, & Lee, 2013).
2. Even forecasts that are less than 10 years old need to be considered outdated by now (Walker, Turnbull, & Sim, 2007).

Chapter 6
Essential of Apps Marketing Implementation and E-Commerce Strategies:
Apps Users' Decision-Making Process

Sajad Rezaei
Taylor's University–Lakeside, Malaysia

Chew Hong Wee
Taylor's University–Lakeside, Malaysia

Naser Valaei
Sunway University, Malaysia

ABSTRACT

Consumer behaviors and attitudes represent a continuously evolving field, thus, by understanding consumer behavior towards Apps from marketing strategy standpoint, managers can benefit from acquiring much information from applying and translating new insights into strategies and tactics that could be helpful for retailer's decision makers. Furthermore, the buying behavior of online shoppers is substantial in the prosperity of Apps marketing strategies and by identifying and understanding the factors that influence the consumer's buying decision, Apps retailers can design their online marketing strategy accordingly to maximize customer satisfaction and ultimately increase the sales volume. This chapter mainly proposed an integration of Internet consumer attitudes, behavior and Apps marketing strategy. This chapter is twofold in terms of having implications both in theory and practice. Indeed, this study helps in understanding consumer decision-making process in Apps environment and

DOI: 10.4018/978-1-5225-2449-6.ch006

Copyright ©2017, IGI Global. Copying or distributing in print or electronic forms without written permission of IGI Global is prohibited.

produce new knowledge to online and Apps retailers, marketing managers as well as marketing and IT scholars. The Apps related technologies have developed as an important medium for marketing in various areas, including expanded geographic scope, novel opportunities for appreciating customers and offering cost efficiencies.

INTRODUCTION

The area of online marketing is diverse. In recent years, marketing has transformed drastically in the areas of academic and industry (Heinemann & Schwarzl, 2010a). Dwayne et al. (2004) state that the adoption of marketing as firms' guideline is evolving, to some extent due to the customer databases that enable personalized service at cheaper cost, computer-mediated communication, and partly because of intensive competition and globalization. The notable growth of IT, information system and the capacity to store and process great amounts of personal information has reflected the increased use of the Internet in marketing activities (Dinev & Hart, 2005). Consequently, a new marketing phenomenon is emerging which is Apps marketing. According to Slater, Hult, & Olson (2010), it is fair to state that the firm's performance is optimized when they develop a creative marketing strategy and ensure the effectiveness of marketing strategy implementation in today's intensive business world. In fact, a stockholder of all businesses is thinking about how to use Apps related technology in their company performance and practice especially in their marketing strategy.

The remarkable of increasing growth in numbers of Internet users and the promising potential of electronic commerce have pushed firms to conduct business online (Chang & Chen, 2008). Since the early 1990s, the gaining importance of Internet has driven many manufacturers and retailers to invest a significant amount of capital to build the Apps channel (Chu et al., 2010). The scale of the electronic commerce in the global market grows since then. Consequently, the marketing strategies of the firms could be perceived from the layout of their web-page (Tang, 2011), but the Apps related activities replacing Webpage scenarios. The gaining importance of the Apps as an effective marketing channel and the commercial tool has driven businesses to improvise their online venture. Currently various types of organizations from for commercial to non-profit organizations are struggling to implement Apps in their marketing efforts to target their market globally to gain more market share. This makes the understanding that Apps marketing is critical for business survival. Therefore, a growing number of firms and organizations in the various industry are exploiting and creating business opportunities on Apps (Liao & Cheung, 2001) as a new medium of communication.

Combination of Apps Consumer Behavior and Marketing Strategy

The recent slowdown of electronic commerce raised the need to understand online consumer behavior. Close & Kukar-Kinney (2010) quote that "since e-commerce is becoming a critical and important aspect of marketing strategy and customer relationship, there is a growing need for developing new knowledge, models, and theories on Internet customer behavior". The best reason to make this combination rational is the work of Grewal & Levy (2007), which conducted a meta-analysis of all studies published between "2002" and "2007" (a total of 130 articles in *journal of Retailing*), indicating that, due to the advancement in the retail strategy implementation, more researches should accept the finding derived from consumer behavior. Therefore, ignoring attitudes and behaviors of people towards Apps is a mistake. Various consumer activities on the web and speedy adoption of information technologies stress the indispensability to conduct more in-depth studies on alterations in consumer buying behavior because it is evident that buying and consumer behavior is evolving ordinary (Cai & Xu, 2006; Hong-Youl et al., 2010; Ieva & Gaile-Sarkane, 2009; Khalifa & Limayem, 2003). In addition, Internet marketing research is thriving and the hottest topical area in future study and it will be about traditional consumer behavior topics with an internet strategy concept. Previous studies (Butler & Peppard, 1998; Grewal & Levy, 2007; Khalifa & Limayem, 2003) declared that consumer behaviors and attitudes represent a continuously evolving field, thus, by understanding consumer behavior towards Apps from marketing strategy standpoint, managers can benefit from acquiring much information from applying and translating new insights into strategies and tactics that could be helpful for retailer's decision makers.

Definition of Apps Marketing

Apps marketing refer to a firm's process of developing and maintaining the relationships between the firm and its customer. It includes the Apps activities to facilitate the communication regarding products and services. As discussed, without doubt, Apps marketing is an exciting, emerging and growing in marketing strategy that runs the spectrum from email, to electronic brochures, to electronic commerce. The level of satisfaction towards Apps marketing strategy has a great impact on the improvement of the product value to consumers. This is not just about making a profit for the company but this makes the transaction easier for the customer who needed a product or services. On the other hand, as all marketing activities are about creating superior value for the customer in the market space. It is rational to say that Apps is one of the best tools to make economic profit and value of a targeted market. It is no surprising that predictions on the growth of Apps transactions around the globe remain implausible.

The purpose of Apps marketing and Apps-Commerce is to generate profit and income through the online channel by appreciating customer demands and wants to require knowledge of how online customer evolve from recognition of products to purchase commitment. According to Cai & Cude (2008), the emergence and implementation of the online environment to buying behavior is a remarkable turnaround in the way sellers and buyers communicate with each other. Therefore, by the development of Apps-Commerce, the marketing effort becomes more and more important and critical in the new competitive environment landscape. Additionally, the Apps bring together the marketers and producers with a new medium which is more effective, efficient, capable, and coherent than traditional channels. The prospect of changing technology has changed everything even the way of behavior and attitudes of people in the whole world. Many believe the revolution of the Apps that is happening in the 21st centuries and this is obvious for everybody. In fact, the Apps which started with providing a simple feature that allows browsing and e-mail has now turned into an application to creatively circulate information around the world. The Apps is a tool that uses for various reasons by individuals, public services, academic institutions, and businesses. Thus, the impact of Internet revolution has been on marketing research as well.

Internet marketing literature is experiencing an important trend in providing an in-depth outlook of the research problems/gaps and expecting current topical areas of interest. In fact, the relationship between Internet application like Apps and market performance is a common debatable topic in the studies and reports conducted during the past years. This is a portion of IT revolution as we can witness over the years, thus, Apps marketing could create a great economic value for stakeholders and therefore be beneficial to an entire society.

Apps Consumer Attitudes and Behaviors

The Apps related technologies have developed as an important medium for marketing in various areas, including expanded geographic scope, novel opportunities for appreciating customers and offering cost efficiencies. Comprehending why, how or when consumers decide to select and use online channel is vital (Taylor & Strutton, 2010). He & Chai (2009) in his work mentioned the future growth of e-commerce depends heavily on how customers view the new online retail tools. In fact, individual and firms are trying to make money by using online mediums; that is the reason why the online transaction is growing dramatically. In retail property, for example, although there is a perception that the Internet will reduce the demand for physical location; but the fact is it could still attract shareholders to keep investing in retail property for potential investment gain (Mummalaneni, 2005). Motives for purchasing in retail property have long been a focus of consumer research (Patricia et al., 2005). It is pivotal for companies to understand and maintain prolonged business relationship with their customers in order to achieve superior growth (Liu et al., 2005) because consumers adopted digital technology tools to acquire product and services are in the process of changing the way they purchase their want and need (McKinsey Quarterly, 2010). Sherman & Topol (1996) predicted that the changes in consumer behavior will strongly impact on the structure and advancement of the online commercial dealings. Therefore, compared to conventional shoppers, Apps retailing consumers have their distinct attitudes, behavior, and characteristics.

Apps Consumer Attitude Definition

According to Shih (2004) "attitudes are defined as the positive or negative feelings of an individual toward a specific event, and these are influenced by individual beliefs". Consumer motives of online purchasing are different from the conventional market (Ieva & Gaile-Sarkane, 2009) and there are many evidence and well-documented article that testify the existence of e-behavior and e-attitudes. Web usage mining techniques became more popular. They help to understand e-customers' behavior better. Analysis of e-customer behavior can help in improving the design and content of a website, improve customer service and customer relationship, and enhance communication with the existing and potential customer (Jenamani et al., 2003). In the Apps shopping environment, consumers form an idea of the value their shopping experiences by taking into account their degree of awareness and recognition of product delivery, information, risk, terms of settling the payment, entertainment, security and privacy, service offered, navigation, and enjoyment. Wan et al. (2010) declare that there exists a positive association between age and web shopping experience. Sherman & Topol (1996) anticipated that buyers will possess the capability to search and find relevant product information being saved in available databases for those who are 'non-techies', who would use online bulletin boards where other peers post their ideas/viewpoints/knowledge and openly provide their shopping experiences with their traditional retailers. In fact, related to attitude and behavior, majority of the organizations collect customer information through their websites, and by using ''cookies'' and tracking software to understand a customer's online interests and preferences to formulate company strategy (Daliri et al., 2014; Kalantari Shahijan et al., 2014; Liu et al., 2005; Rezaei, 2015; Rezaei, Ali, et al., 2016; Rezaei et al., 2014; Rezaei & Ghodsi, 2014; Rezaei, Shahijan, Valaei, et al., 2016). Taylor and Strutton (2010) claim that electronic marketing developed gradually

Figure 1. Apps users' decision-making process
Source: *Adopted from Kotler and Armstrong (2015)*

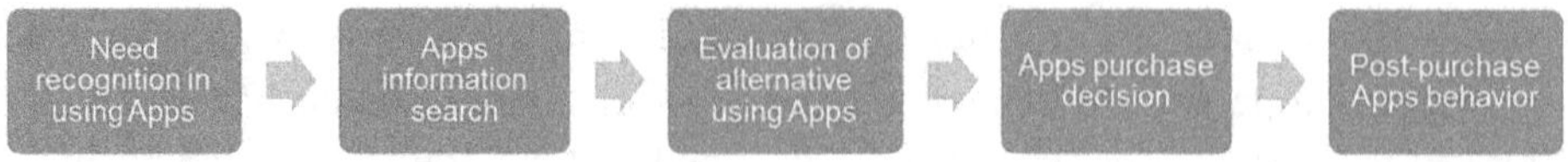

from a relatively exceptional category of "dot-com" companies to a conventional marketing channel activities. This progression has impacted on the customers and their "e-behavior" in all stages of the Apps usage, adoption and behavior as well.

Apps Consumer Behavior: Definition and Its Process

As highlighted in the prior section, e-commerce is transforming many aspects of the business transaction between customers and businesses. This transformation has resulted in a need to understand online consumer behavior because of the significant impact from the use of IT and its consequential impact on market success and failure. Consumer behavior is dynamic interaction with other customer or toward businesses and their activities throughout the entire shopping/searching process. Figure 1 shows the stages of buying decision-making process (Kotler & Armstrong, 2015) which is applicable in market space as well. These stages include needing recognition in using Apps, information search via Apps, evaluation of alternative using Apps, Apps purchase decision, and Apps Post-purchase behavior. The American Marketing Association (2016) describes consumer behavior as "the vigorous reciprocal action of cognition, behavior, environment, and affect by which individuals direct and manage the exchange aspect of their daily lives". According to Ieva and Gaile-Sarkane (2009), the buying activity of the consumers is comprised of several interrelated factors: understanding the need/problem, seeking related information, assessing other options/possibilities, buying decision, and post-purchase evaluation. However, potential customer delays their purchases for different reasons, including short of stock, lack of product information, and limited product selection.

Comprehending Apps consumer behavior in a better way enable the marketers to improvise marketing mix strategies prosperously due to the fact that the Internet gives marketers all the related information about customers which can't be accessed in a traditional/offline shopping environment. E-commerce is inevitable for businesses to survive and grow in the Internet era in which the competitive advantage of a business depends on its capability to attract and retain customers (Wang & Feng, 2010). Nowadays, consumers have slowly moved from transacting in offline markets through traditional channels to online markets through digital channels and unlike traditional information systems, e-commerce systems contain features of information system and marketing communication channel, thus incorporating both machine and human elements (Hausman & Siekpe, 2009). Vijayasarathy (2004) state that the challenges for on-line retailers are identifying, acquiring, and retaining customers. According to Gefen, Karahanna, & Straub (2003) acquiring new customers and subsequently retaining them is critical for the success of e-commerce and there is a noticeable effect on consumer behavior intention (Ieva & Gaile-Sarkane, 2009).

E-tailing has gained significant attention both in literature and business (To, 2004). Understanding consumer's desire to stay on an Apps site contributes to the likelihood to purchase on the net. The customers are a primary "stakeholder" in the online shopping process because it is he who ultimately making the purchase decision (Alavi et al., 2016; Amin et al., 2014; Amin et al., 2015; McCole et al., 2010; Moghaddam et al., 2015; Rezaei & Amin, 2013; Rezaei, Emami, et al., 2016; Rezaei & Ismail, 2014; Shahijan et al., 2016). Web shopper behaviors are influenced by several keys such as years of experience in using the Web, age, and gender that perceive purchase risk differently, thus leading to different shopping behaviors. Therefore, Apps marketing research is thriving and the hottest topical area in future study and it will be about traditional consumer behavior topics with Apps strategy which usually includes the policies and allocation of marketing resource and decision on marketing mix.

Moreover, Apps shopping has become an emerging market in recent years. "E-retail, e-tail, and e-commerce are all terms use for Internet-based transactions". According to Baker (2006) shopping defined as a "social action, interaction and experience which increasingly structures the everyday practices of urban people". E-commerce refers to business activities conducted via electronic networks but online retailing is referring to selling and buying goods via the Internet. Sherman & Topo (1996) stated that the key concerns in future of online retailing are the advancement of technologies that have a direct impact on the infrastructure that enables the retailers to easily approach the consumers and having a new communication means to interact with, communicate, promote and sell their services and products. Apps retailing has transformed from a trendy emerging purchasing channel into the norm and Apps shopping also is determined in general by a process consisting of several steps such as thoroughly scrutinizing the online retailers, searching for products, related information about products, share and exchange information with other retailers and consumers, choosing payment methods, and last but not the least purchasing services or products (Cai & Cude, 2008; Rezaei, Shahijan, Amin, et al., 2016; Valaei & Rezaei, 2016). Therefore, buying through Apps is a form of exchange in which the potential customers spends time browsing for information, and perform the transaction.

Retailing strategy is entire activities of creating, interconnecting and delivering value to target customers. Tao, Guijun, & Yuanyuan (2010) declare that online retailing is the retailing business conducted via the Internet which means providers sell products or services on their website; on the other side, consumers buy products or services by accessing such website. Apps shopping is the transfer process of product or service from a seller to a buyer by means of the network and in the whole process. Apps retailing can be referred to the act of trading money, effort, and time for acquiring services or products that are the general evaluation of the exchange in terms of what is acquired and what is handed over that forms individuals' satisfaction with the retailing experiences. An example of Apps retailing of the intangible product is an online vendor that is selling their product like software, music or movie and so on. Even traditional retailers like Tesco and Jusco have integrated the Apps and the Web into their businesses and benefited from the usage. Successful examples of online commerce are highly varied, depending on the strategy formulation and implementation and its type of doing business.

Therefore, many of the largest manufacturers (such as Unilever and Procter and Gamble) retailers (for instance, Target, Tesco, and Wal-Mart) have successfully combined their existing operations with online retailing to gain more market share (Grewal et al., 2004). According to O'Cass & Fenech (2003) it is critical to recall that the Internet is not the earliest online market to be exploited for retailing exchanges and there are several non-store retailing marketplaces that extends over the distribution channels of interactive cable television, vending machines, door-to-door selling, catalogue showrooms, telephone selling, and mail order selling.

Adoption vs. Post-Adoption of Apps Shopping

According to Brent (2011), Internet shopping continues to increase rapidly. Apps shopping becoming a viable alternative to shopping at stores and shopping malls due to changing consumer lifestyle (Chang & Samuel, 2004). The fast-pace changing of Apps marketplace has made a competitive business environment that gives challenges, threats, and opportunities for different types of firms, and one of the opportunities that Apps environment provides is directing and organizing businesses online (Chai Har et al., 2011). Customer retention is important to all companies and especially to those with an established customer base (Blery et al., 2009) as consumers currently have several choices either offline and online to choose from, and the online environment has enabled them to select one retailer over another without a convincing reason, they continuously test, evaluate, and switch among numerous firms. The building blocks of the supply chain in the retailing industry also have altered extensively in previous years because new IT and digital technologies have provided novel ways of exchange between consumers and retailers.

Users perception towards business and customer loyalty become a vital component in marketing field (Dwayne et al., 2004; Valaei, Rezaei, & Shahijan, 2016) despite the fact that it is important for businesses to sell their product, but what is probably more important is to retain customers for repeated purchases. Koo (2006) founds that retaining customers for repeat purchase has been the primary aim for marketers for decades because retaining existing customers require less marketing resources than acquiring new ones, therefore, it can be stated that the new advancements in the digital marketing environment should facilitate the detailed examination of online shoppers (experienced buyers) whose behavior is different from other shoppers (Blanca et al., 2011; Rezaei, Rezaei, et al., 2016). Furthermore, customers repurchase intention or behavior is noteworthy to the digital environment and researches indicate that repurchase intentions are intimately related to the extent to which customers turn being loyal (Chai Har et al., 2011). It appears to be of sound reasoning to presume that the more positive attitude is shaped over the online buying (Rezaei, Rezaei, et al., 2016), the higher will be the frequency of shopping and the higher will be the inclination to carry on with purchasing through online channel in the future (Hernandez et al., 2009).

Wang & Chiang (2009) defines continuance intention (post-adoption) "as user plans to continue using already adopted online auction systems so, continuance intention to usage is a conceptually distinct construct from initial adoption". We can categorize an IT adoption as a favorable outcome when the post-adoption usage of the IT or information system can be confirmed (Thong et al., 2006). Other studies in the field of marketing mix strategies, for instance, advertising, has pondered on determining other factors associating with online buyers' future intention and behavior (Jones & Reynolds, 2006). In contrast, in examining post-adoption behavior, many studies show that normative forces impacted on the adopters, whereas post-adopters are affected by attitudes as well. Besides, the digital marketplace empowers the customers to come out with their suggestions base on their experiences that may impact on other prospective consumers (Lee et al., 2008; Mohseni et al., 2016; Valaei, Rezaei, Ismail, et al., 2016; Valaei, Rezaei, & Shahijan, 2016). Therefore, the global reach of the Internet and Apps related technologies opens new windows of opportunity to many corporations worldwide.

Studies were mainly conducted on the selection and acceptance of online buying or on post-adoption of online retailing and the related facilitating technologies (Hernandez et al., 2009; Taylor & Strutton, 2010). Post-adoption of the online retailing is characterized by constant change and involves several aspects Chuanlan and Sandra (2010). Continued usage (continuance) of an Internet technology in customer relationship management to continue the possession of valued customers is going to be a critical factor as well as becoming a key research issue (Blery et al., 2009; Dwayne et al., 2004). Accordingly, it is noteworthy to conduct further research on the elements that impact on customers' post-adoption attitude and behavior, considering the fact that the prolonged usage will be an advantage for the long-run financial gain and viability of an IT company like Apps retailers. Indeed, the degree of the prosperity of the Apps retailing channel is contingent upon the post-adoption use of the online channel for buying purposes than on the preliminary decision to apply digital channel for shopping.

CONCLUSION

This chapter mainly proposed an integration of Internet consumer attitudes, behavior and Apps marketing strategy. Understanding of consumer's behavior in cyberspace cannot be achieved without a good appreciation of the factors affecting the motivation and decision. Classifying and identifying new and repeated Apps buyer's behavior and finding the differences is critical for enterprises that sell goods online to formulate market strategies. Therefore, marketers and Apps retailers have to pay attention to the Apps user's attitudes and behavior in the digital environment as a powerful procedure to entice online users for retail purchase. This is an important factor for Apps retailers to take into consideration in formulating their marketing strategies. Shopping is an essential societal activity hence it is essential to examine consumers attitude and behavior in the electronic world (Grewal et al., 2004). Apps marketers are suggested to examine the participating factors in online buying intention between the online shoppers. More precisely a recent study by Dennis, Morgan, Wright, & Jayawardhena (2010) raise the awareness that all firms mainly in the saturated retailing marketplace are required to deal with the issues that may increase due to neglecting to satisfy the needs of generation Y consumers who have been either disregarded and refused to be acknowledged or circumvented by the offline/traditional marketing channels. Therefore, managers of e-retailers should note the importance of enticing the consumers to apply online stores as well as boosting the financial gains of online stores is a critical matter that requires full attention.

According to Grewal et al. (2004), online retailing fulfills numbers of consumer demands and wants more efficiently and in an effective manner than traditional retailing method. Understanding purchasing behavior of online buyers is one of the main characteristics of successful retailers in the current marketplace that is overwhelmed with digital technologies (Reynolds et al., 2002). There is a high rivalry and intense competition due to the emergence and uninterrupted grow of online buying as well as the unparalleled growth rate in the quantity of Apps shops (Hsin Hsin et al., 2009). All these increases the acquisition value of the purchase for consumers and it seems to attract people to go online. According to a previous study (Cai & Cude, 2008), the digital technologies and its effects maintain its growing pace and the consumers have the opportunity to take advantage of e-commerce through controlling business transactions in the digital environment. Previous studies (Heinemann & Schwarzl, 2010b; Mummalaneni, 2005; Tao et al., 2010) stated that retail businesses need an Internet strategy more than ever. Firms need to adjust their marketing strategies based on attentive of consumer's online behavior (Chu et al., 2010). According to previous research (Reynolds et al., 2002), it is imperative for managers to recognize what retail characteristics matter most and to which buyers with the result that the relevant retail strategy can be implemented. Online marketers are required to initiate a thorough comprehension of consumer behavior in profit-oriented digital environments (Lorenzo et al., 2007).

Therefore, the buying behavior of online shoppers is substantial in the prosperity of Apps marketing strategies and by identifying and understanding the factors that influence the consumer's buying decision, Apps retailers can design their online marketing strategy accordingly to maximize customer satisfaction and ultimately increase the sales volume. This research is twofold in terms of having implications both in theory and practice. Indeed, this study helps in understanding consumer decision-making process in Apps environment and produce new knowledge to online and Apps retailers, marketing managers as well as marketing and IT scholars.

REFERENCES

Alavi, S. A., Rezaei, S., Valaei, N., & Wan Ismail, W. K. (2016). Examining shopping mall consumer decision-making styles, satisfaction and purchase intention. *International Review of Retail, Distribution and Consumer Research*, *26*(3), 272–303. doi:10.1080/09593969.2015.1096808

Amin, M., Rezaei, S., & Abolghasemi, M. (2014). User satisfaction with mobile websites: The impact of perceived usefulness (pu), perceived ease of use (peou) and trust. *Nankai Business Review International*, *5*(3), 258–274. doi:10.1108/NBRI-01-2014-0005

Amin, M., Rezaei, S., & Tavana, F. S. (2015). Gender differences and consumers repurchase intention: The impact of trust propensity, usefulness and ease of use for implication of innovative online retail. *International Journal of Innovation and Learning*, *17*(2), 217–233. doi:10.1504/IJIL.2015.067409

Baker, S. M. (2006). Consumer normalcy: Understanding the value of shopping through narratives of consumers with visual impairments. *Journal of Retailing*, *82*(1), 37–50. doi:10.1016/j.jretai.2005.11.003

Blanca, H., Julio, J., & Martín, M. J. (2011). Age, gender and income: Do they really moderate online shopping behaviour? *Online Information Review*, *35*(1), 113–133. doi:10.1108/14684521111113614

Blery, E. K., Andreas, D., Anna, B., Anna, E., Efi, K., Nertilda, T., & Ioanna, R. (2009). Customer retention in the greek internet market. *International Journal of Business and Management*, *3*(1), 35–48.

Butler, P., & Peppard, J. (1998). Consumer purchasing on the internet: Processes and prospects. *European Management Journal*, *16*(5), 600–610. doi:10.1016/S0263-2373(98)00036-X

Cai, S., & Xu, Y. (2006). Effects of outcome, process and shopping enjoyment on online consumer behaviour. *Electronic Commerce Research and Applications*, *5*(4), 272–281. doi:10.1016/j.elerap.2006.04.004

Cai, Y., & Cude, B. J. (2008). Online shopping. In J. J. Xiao (Ed.), *Handbook of consumer finance research* (pp. 137–159). Springer New York. doi:10.1007/978-0-387-75734-6_9

Chai Har, L., Uchenna Cyril, E., & Nelson Oly, N. (2011). Analyzing key determinants of online repurchase intentions. *Asia Pacific Journal of Marketing and Logistics*, *23*(2), 200–221. doi:10.1108/13555851111120498

Chang, H. H., & Chen, S. W. (2008). The impact of customer interface quality, satisfaction and switching costs on e-loyalty: Internet experience as a moderator. *Computers in Human Behavior*, *24*(6), 2927–2944. doi:10.1016/j.chb.2008.04.014

Chang, J., & Samuel, N. (2004). Internet shopper demographics and buying behaviour in australia. *Journal of American Academy of Business, Cambridge*, *5*(1/2), 171–176.

Chu, J., Arce-Urriza, M., Cebollada-Calvo, J.-J., & Chintagunta, P. K. (2010). An empirical analysis of shopping behavior across online and offline channels for grocery products: The moderating effects of household and product characteristics. *Journal of Interactive Marketing*, *24*(4), 251–268. doi:10.1016/j.intmar.2010.07.004

Chuanlan, L., & Sandra, F. (2010). Post-adoption online shopping continuance. *International Journal of Retail & Distribution Management*, *38*(2), 97–114. doi:10.1108/09590551011020110

Close, A. G., & Kukar-Kinney, M. (2010). Beyond buying: Motivations behind consumers online shopping cart use. *Journal of Business Research*, *63*(9-10), 986–992. doi:10.1016/j.jbusres.2009.01.022

Daliri, E., Rezaei, S., & Ismail, W. K. W. (2014). Online social shopping: The impact of attitude, customer information quality, effectiveness of information content and perceived social presence. *International Journal of Business Environment*, *6*(4), 426–450. doi:10.1504/IJBE.2014.064995

Dennis, C., Morgan, A., Wright, L. T., & Jayawardhena, C. (2010). The influences of social e-shopping in enhancing young womens online shopping behaviour. *Journal of Customer Behaviour*, *9*(2), 151–174. doi:10.1362/147539210X511353

Dinev, T., & Hart, P. (2005). Internet privacy concerns and social awareness as determinants of intention to transact. *International Journal of Electronic Commerce*, *10*(2), 7–29. doi:10.2753/JEC1086-4415100201

Dr. Brent Lynn Selby, C., Dr. Nicholas Jeremy, A., & Dr. Beverley, H. (2011). Measuring internet product purchase risk. *European Journal of Marketing*, *45*(7), 6–6.

Dwayne, B., Pedro Simões, C., & Alexandra, M. (2004). The role of communication and trust in explaining customer loyalty: An extension to the ecsi model. *European Journal of Marketing*, *38*(9), 1272–1293.

Gefen, D., Karahanna, E., & Straub, D. W. (2003). Inexperience and experience with online stores: The importance of tam and trust. *Engineering Management. IEEE Transactions on*, *50*(3), 307–321.

Grewal, D., Iyer, G. R., & Levy, M. (2004). Internet retailing: Enablers, limiters and market consequences. *Journal of Business Research*, *57*(7), 703–713. doi:10.1016/S0148-2963(02)00348-X

Grewal, D., & Levy, M. (2007). Retailing research: Past, present, and future. *Journal of Retailing*, *83*(4), 447–464. doi:10.1016/j.jretai.2007.09.003

Hausman, A. V., & Siekpe, J. S. (2009). The effect of web interface features on consumer online purchase intentions. *Journal of Business Research*, *62*(1), 5–13. doi:10.1016/j.jbusres.2008.01.018

He, W., & Chai, J. (2009). *Study on mechanism and models of customer segmentation of c2c shopping*. Paper presented at the Information Science and Engineering (ICISE), 2009 1st International Conference on.

Heinemann, G., & Schwarzl, C. (2010a). *New online retailing — what does it mean?. In New online retailing* (pp. 19–91). Gabler.

Heinemann, G., & Schwarzl, C. (2010b). *Online retailing in transition – revolution, not evolution. In New online retailing* (pp. 1–18). Gabler.

Hernandez, B., Jimenez, J., & Jose Martin, M. (2009). The impact of self-efficacy, ease of use and usefulness on e-purchasing: An analysis of experienced e-shoppers. *Interacting with Computers*, *21*(1-2), 146–156. doi:10.1016/j.intcom.2008.11.001

Hong-Youl, H., Swinder, J., & Siva, K. M. (2010). A new understanding of satisfaction model in e-re-purchase situation. *European Journal of Marketing*, *44*(7), 997–1016.

Hsin Hsin, C., Yao-Hua, W., & Wen-Ying, Y. (2009). The impact of e-service quality, customer satisfaction and loyalty on e-marketing: Moderating effect of perceived value. *Total Quality Management & Business Excellence*, *20*(4), 423–443. doi:10.1080/14783360902781923

Ieva, A., & Gaile-Sarkane, E. (2009). Behavioral differences in consumer purchasing behavior between online and traditional shopping: Case of Latvia. *Economics & Management*, 345-352.

Jenamani, M., Mohapatra, P. K. J., & Ghose, S. (2003). A stochastic model of e-customer behavior. *Electronic Commerce Research and Applications*, *2*(1), 81–94. doi:10.1016/S1567-4223(03)00010-3

Jones, M. A., & Reynolds, K. E. (2006). The role of retailer interest on shopping behavior. *Journal of Retailing*, *82*(2), 115–126. doi:10.1016/j.jretai.2005.05.001

Kalantari Shahijan, M., Rezaei, S., Nigel Preece, C., & Khairuzzaman Wan Ismail, W. (2014). Examining retailers behaviour in managing critical points in halal meat handling: A pls analysis. *Journal of Islamic Marketing*, *5*(3), 446–472. doi:10.1108/JIMA-10-2013-0070

Khalifa, M., & Limayem, M. (2003). Drivers of internet shopping. *Communications of the ACM*, *46*(12), 233–239. doi:10.1145/953460.953505

Koo, D.-M. (2006). The fundamental reasons of e-consumers loyalty to an online store. *Electronic Commerce Research and Applications*, *5*(2), 117–130. doi:10.1016/j.elerap.2005.10.003

Kotler, P., & Armstrong, G. (2015). *Principles of marketing*. Pearson.

Lee, J., Park, D.-H., & Han, I. (2008). The effect of negative online consumer reviews on product attitude: An information processing view. *Electronic Commerce Research and Applications*, *7*(3), 341–352. doi:10.1016/j.elerap.2007.05.004

Liao, Z., & Cheung, M. T. (2001). Internet-based e-shopping and consumer attitudes: An empirical study. *Information & Management*, *38*(5), 299–306. doi:10.1016/S0378-7206(00)00072-0

Liu, C., Marchewka, J. T., Lu, J., & Yu, C.-S. (2005). Beyond concerna privacy-trust-behavioral intention model of electronic commerce. *Information & Management*, *42*(2), 289–304. doi:10.1016/j.im.2004.01.003

Lorenzo, C., Constantinides, E., Geurts, P., & Gómez, M. (2007). Impact of web experience on e-consumer responses. In G. Psaila & R. Wagner (Eds.), E-commerce and web technologies (Vol. 4655, pp. 191-200). Springer Berlin / Heidelberg. doi:10.1007/978-3-540-74563-1_19

McCole, P., Ramsey, E., & Williams, J. (2010). Trust considerations on attitudes towards online purchasing: The moderating effect of privacy and security concerns. *Journal of Business Research*, *63*(9-10), 1018–1024. doi:10.1016/j.jbusres.2009.02.025

Moghaddam, H. A., Rezaei, S., & Amin, M. (2015). Examining job seekers perception and behavioural intention toward online recruitment: A pls path modelling approach. *Journal for Global Business Advancement*, *8*(3), 305–325. doi:10.1504/JGBA.2015.071331

Mohseni, S., Jayashree, S., Rezaei, S., Kasim, A., & Okumus, F. (2016). Attracting tourists to travel companies websites: The structural relationship between website brand, personal value, shopping experience, perceived risk and purchase intention. *Current Issues in Tourism*, 1–30. doi:10.1080/13683500.2016.1200539

Mummalaneni, V. (2005). An empirical investigation of web site characteristics, consumer emotional states and on-line shopping behaviors. *Journal of Business Research*, *58*(4), 526–532. doi:10.1016/S0148-2963(03)00143-7

OCass, A., & Fenech, T. (2003). Web retailing adoption: Exploring the nature of internet users web retailing behaviour. *Journal of Retailing and Consumer Services*, *10*(2), 81–94. doi:10.1016/S0969-6989(02)00004-8

Patricia, S., Victor, P., & Stanley, W. (2005). Attitude and age differences in online buying. *International Journal of Retail & Distribution Management*, *33*(2), 122–132. doi:10.1108/09590550510581458

Reynolds, K. E., Ganesh, J., & Luckett, M. (2002). Traditional malls vs. Factory outlets: Comparing shopper typologies and implications for retail strategy. *Journal of Business Research*, *55*(9), 687–696. doi:10.1016/S0148-2963(00)00213-7

Rezaei, S. (2015). Segmenting consumer decision-making styles (cdms) toward marketing practice: A partial least squares (pls) path modeling approach. *Journal of Retailing and Consumer Services*, *22*, 1–15. doi:10.1016/j.jretconser.2014.09.001

Rezaei, S., Ali, F., Amin, M., Jayashree, S., & Cobanoglu, C. (2016). Online impulse buying of tourism products: The role of website personality, utilitarian and hedonic web browsing. *Journal of Hospitality and Tourism Technology*, *7*(1), 60–83. doi:10.1108/JHTT-03-2015-0018

Rezaei, S., & Amin, M. (2013). Exploring online repurchase behavioural intention of university students in malaysia. *Journal for Global Business Advancement*, *6*(2), 92–119. doi:10.1504/JGBA.2013.053561

Rezaei, S., Amin, M., & Ismail, W. K. W. (2014). Online repatronage intention: An empirical study among malaysian experienced online shoppers. *International Journal of Retail & Distribution Management*, *42*(5), 390–421. doi:10.1108/IJRDM-03-2012-0026

Rezaei, S., Emami, M., & Valaei, N. (2016). *The moderating impact of product classification on the relationship between online trust, satisfaction, and repurchase intention. In Encyclopedia of e-commerce development, implementation, and management* (p. 1692). IGI Global.

Rezaei, S., & Ghodsi, S. S. (2014). Does value matters in playing online game? An empirical study among massively multiplayer online role-playing games (mmorpgs). *Computers in Human Behavior*, *35*, 252–266. doi:10.1016/j.chb.2014.03.002

Rezaei, S., & Ismail, W. K. W. (2014). Examining online channel selection behaviour among social media shoppers: A pls analysis. *International Journal of Electronic Marketing and Retailing*, *6*(1), 28–51. doi:10.1504/IJEMR.2014.064876

Rezaei, S., Rezaei, S., Amin, M., Amin, M., Moghaddam, M., Moghaddam, M., & Mohamed, N. et al. (2016). 3g post adoption users experience with telecommunications services: A partial least squares (pls) path modelling approach. *Nankai Business Review International*, *7*(3), 361–394. doi:10.1108/NBRI-01-2016-0007

Rezaei, S., Shahijan, M. K., Amin, M., & Ismail, W. K. W. (2016). Determinants of app stores continuance behavior: A pls path modelling approach. *Journal of Internet Commerce*, *15*(4), 408–440. doi:10.1080/15332861.2016.1256749

Rezaei, S., Shahijan, M. K., Valaei, N., Rahimi, R., & Ismail, W. K. W. (2016). Experienced international business traveller's behaviour in Iran: A partial least squares path modelling analysis. *Tourism and Hospitality Research*.

Shahijan, M. K., Rezaei, S., & Amin, M. (2016). International students course satisfaction and continuance behavioral intention in higher education setting: An empirical assessment in malaysia. *Asia Pacific Education Review*, *17*(1), 41–62. doi:10.1007/s12564-015-9410-9

Sherman, E., & Topol, M. T. (1996). Anticipating the impact of new technologies on retailing. *Journal of Retailing and Consumer Services*, *3*(2), 107–111. doi:10.1016/0969-6989(95)00070-4

Shih, H.-P. (2004). An empirical study on predicting user acceptance of e-shopping on the web. *Information & Management*, *41*(3), 351–368. doi:10.1016/S0378-7206(03)00079-X

Slater, S. F., Hult, G. T. M., & Olson, E. M. (2010). Factors influencing the relative importance of marketing strategy creativity and marketing strategy implementation effectiveness. *Industrial Marketing Management*, *39*(4), 551–559. doi:10.1016/j.indmarman.2008.03.007

Tang, J. (2011). A locality analysis on purchasing helper at e-commerce webpage - the example in tw, cn, mo and hk. *Expert Systems with Applications*, *38*(1), 371–378. doi:10.1016/j.eswa.2010.06.074

Tao, Z., Guijun, Z., & Yuanyuan, H. (2010). A literature review on the studies of internet retailing management. *Technology & Investment*, *1*(1), 19–25. doi:10.4236/ti.2010.11003

Taylor, D. G., & Strutton, D. (2010). Has e-marketing come of age? Modeling historical influences on post-adoption era internet consumer behaviors. *Journal of Business Research*, *63*(9-10), 950–956. doi:10.1016/j.jbusres.2009.01.018

Thong, J. Y. L., Hong, S.-J., & Tam, K. Y. (2006). The effects of post-adoption beliefs on the expectation-confirmation model for information technology continuance. *International Journal of Human-Computer Studies*, *64*(9), 799–810. doi:10.1016/j.ijhcs.2006.05.001

To, L. M. (2004). *Determinants affecting organizations' intent to adopt e-tailing: A study based on innovation theories*. Paper presented at the 9th annual SIGCSE conference on Innovation and technology in computer science education, Leeds, UK. doi:10.1145/1007996.1008074

Valaei, N., & Rezaei, S. (2016). Does web 2.0 utilisation lead to knowledge quality, improvisational creativity, compositional creativity, and innovation in small and medium-sized enterprises? A sense-making perspective. *Technology Analysis and Strategic Management*, 1–14. doi:10.1080/09537325.2016.1213806

Valaei, N., Rezaei, S., Ismail, W. K. W., & Moi, O. Y. (2016). Cultural effect on attitude toward online advertising and online brands: Applying hofstedes cultural factors to internet marketing. *International Journal of Internet Marketing and Advertising*, *10*(4), 270. doi:10.1504/IJIMA.2016.081346

Valaei, N., Rezaei, S., & Shahijan, M. K. (2016). Couqual: Assessing overall service quality in courier service industry and the moderating impact of age, gender and ethnicity. *International Journal of Management Concepts and Philosophy*, *9*(2), 144–169. doi:10.1504/IJMCP.2016.077770

Vijayasarathy, L. R. (2004). Predicting consumer intentions to use on-line shopping: The case for an augmented technology acceptance model. *Information & Management*, *41*(6), 747–762. doi:10.1016/j.im.2003.08.011

Wan, Y., Nakayama, M., & Sutcliffe, N. (2010). The impact of age and shopping experiences on the classification of search, experience, and credence goods in online shopping. *Information Systems and E-Business Management*, 1-14. doi:10.1007/s10257-010-0156-y

Wang, J.-C., & Chiang, M.-J. (2009). Social interaction and continuance intention in online auctions: A social capital perspective. *Decision Support Systems*, *47*(4), 466–476. doi:10.1016/j.dss.2009.04.013

Wang, S.-j., & Feng, C. (2010). *Ways to maximize customer perceived value in e-commerce age*. Paper presented at the Networking and Digital Society (ICNDS), 2010 2nd International Conference on.

KEY TERMS AND DEFINITIONS

Apps Marketing: Refer to a firm's process of developing and maintaining the relationships between firm and its customer.

Apps Shopping: A social action, interaction and experience which increasingly structures the everyday practices of urban people.

Apps-Commerce: Refers to business activities conducted via Apps networks and selling and buying goods via Apps.

Attitudes Towards Apps: Attitudes are defined as the positive or negative feelings of an individual toward Apps that are influenced by individual beliefs.

Chapter 7
Mobile Social Commerce

Christine Balague
Institut Mines Telecom, France

Zhenzhen Zhao
ISC Paris Business School, France

ABSTRACT

S-commerce and M-commerce become buzz word recent years. The social and mobile elements have brought new ways of thinking as well as challenging opportunities in e-commerce. In this chapter, we firstly introduce the concepts of online social commerce, its classifications and social shopping behaviors. Secondly, we analyze the evolution from online social commerce to mobile social commerce. Different case studies are given to demonstrate the concept of mobile social commerce, to precisely define how mobile and social feathers add value to traditional e-commerce.

INTRODUCTION

According to Criteo State of Mobile Commerce report on Q4 2015, percentage of transactions occurring on a mobile device in US, increased from 35% to 44% between Q4 2014 and Q4 2015. Japan, UK and South Korea make up the top three countries ranked by mobile share of transactions, globally. In parallel to this phenomenon, GlobalWebIndex research shows that "digital consumers are comfortable using social networks to find new brands and research products they are interested in buying. Messaging apps like Line and WeChat have pushed beyond simple chat apps to integrate a broad range of commerce options and opportunities for monetization, forming the clear inspiration for Facebook's recent development of Messenger

DOI: 10.4018/978-1-5225-2449-6.ch007

Copyright ©2017, IGI Global. Copying or distributing in print or electronic forms without written permission of IGI Global is prohibited.

Platform. All these developments mean that social commerce has a bright future". Mobile accounts for 40% of time spent on social media. This context underlines the growing behavior of mobile social shopping and the new topic of interest that represent mobile social commerce applications for companies. Social commerce has begun to be studied in research literature and by companies' experiments; however, few literature exists on the analysis of this new concept of mobile social commerce.

The objective of this chapter is to present an overview of e-commerce with the changing trend of social media and mobility. Towards this new trend, several questions are raised.

- What is social commerce? What is the classification of social commerce?
- How social shopping behaviors affect on e-commerce?
- What is the evolution from traditional e-commerce to online social commerce?
- How mobile features affect on social commerce?

We will focus first on the recent evolution from e-commerce to one line social commerce. Then we will present mobile specificities for social commerce before analyzing different existing social mobile commerce applications. We conclude this chapter with some prospective on mobile social commerce.

BACKGROUND

In the digital era, customer's empowerment increased through four main phases (Labrecque et al., 2013): demand-based at the beginning of 90's, information-based during the contribution economy period, network-based at the end of 2000's with the launch of Facebook, Twitter and You Tube, and finally crowd- based through recent sharing economy. According to these authors, social networks provide a network-based power to customers through network actions and distribution, remixing and enhancement of digital content. This value derives from activities such as content dissemination (e.g., sharing and organizing content through networks), content completion (e.g., comments on a blog post that contribute to previous content, tagging), or content modifications (e.g., repurposing content, such as a video or image meme) in social networks. Social commerce emerged in this context, and social networks platforms tried to monetize their enormous audience by implementing social commerce functionalities (F-stores or Gifts for Facebook, buy button for Twitter). Stephen & Toubia (2010) show the value derived by social commerce networks.

Social Commerce on the Internet is characterized by the convergence between e-commerce and social networks. This phenomenon emerged in the 2000's, with the creation of forums, virtual communities, comments and recommendation tools, and price comparators on the web. Used initially in 2005 by David Beach, Yahoo! Shopping manager, the term "social commerce" is a set of collaborative tools dedicated to e-commerce (products lists, clients' comments, notations, and recommendation systems). A new form of social e-commerce appears in 2008 with Groupon, a successful website during the years following his creation, where individuals can buy at lower prices products and services by grouping their purchases. However, nowadays, Groupon's model has become a source of controversies due to its highly decreasing audience during the last year. In parallel to these new models, social networks and their highly increasing audience provide new opportunities for e-commerce. According to Addshopers, Facebook and Pinterest combine for over 56% of social generated e-commerce at the moment. In this context, social commerce focuses on developing on line sales by using social networks or virtual communities' platforms. From a consumer point of view, social commerce gathers a set of social and participative technologies and capitalize on collaborative web 2.0 usages such as information sharing between web users. Therefore, individuals' purchase is not any more private but becomes a social activity with his/her own community of friends or web users' networks.

Historically, shopping activity is the focus of numerous published papers in marketing literature. From a long time, shopping in real world has been considered as a social experience relying on communications with other persons presenting same centers of interests (Tauber, 1972). In current e-commerce, web consumers are both utilitarian and hedonist, searching for experience (Holbrook & Hirschman, 1982; Wolfinbarger & Gilly, 2001). Utilitarian web users aim to quickly find a product on a web site and purchase it easily. Hedonist consumers search for pleasure during web surfing and purchase process. Contrary to traditional shopping, online shopping in often considered as a mediated environment characterized by a low social dimension, based on anonymity and automatism (Hassanein & head, 2007). Answering these issues, social commerce is therefore an increasing phenomenon, and mobile applications allow to largely develop these usages everywhere and every time.

In the next section we will further investigate the concepts from e-commerce to online social commerce, and from online social commerce to mobile social commerce, respectively. Case studies are given to demonstrate the concepts.

MAIN FOCUS OF THE CHAPTER

Issues, Controversies, Problems

As mentioned in the previous section, s-commerce is at the convergence of social networks and e-commerce, topics largely studied in numerous researches. However, social commerce is considered as emerging by practitioners, and research is still needed on this new phenomenon. This section presents two marketing evolutions: (1) from e-commerce to on line social commerce, and (2) from one line social commerce to mobile social commerce. Applications of social mobile commerce are presented afterwards to illustrate this new trend through real cases.

Marketing Evolution

From E-Commerce to Online Social Commerce

Social Commerce Different Models

In this section we present a classification of different social commerce models. According to Marsden (2010), two main interaction modes exist in social commerce: social networks integrated to e-commerce web sites (web users connect with others on the platforms where they buy) or e-commerce integrated in social networks (web users can buy on the platforms they connect with others). However, nowadays, social commerce models classification has become more complex. Therefore we identify four categories.

The first model is social commerce models with collective buying on specific communities of information and recommendation sharing on products and services. One well known example in this category is Groupon, based on a simple process: each day, Groupon web site sends promotional offers to his members (with 50% to 90% of price decrease) on restaurants, shops, spas or other services. This offer is only available when a minimum number of individuals buy it. The social characteristic of this web site is first due to this collective buying process, and second linked to viral marketing tools inviting web users to recommend the offer to their friends' community. Bazando and Tribway constitute also typical examples of this first model. These websites are communities of web users sharing information and recommendations on products which can be bought with cash back (money retribution to the clients of this website). Therefore, more numerous people buy on this web site, more they benefit of cashback. Web users increase their utility by developing the community of buyers on this type of e-commerce site.

The second model of social commerce is characterized by an individual purchase on a traditional e-commerce website, with information and recommendation sharing on specific communities. In this case, web users select products during surfing on the web and create a personalised area on the social commerce community, in which they comment and recommend (or not) the products. On this type of collective platforms, people discover new products by different members, inform themselves on the basis of peer to peer communication and evaluation of product. One example of this social commerce model is Kaboodle, a community of 5 million monthly users around fashion and beauty products. On Kaboodle, users can generate content by using specific tools (drag-and-drop functionality to create styleboards). However, products are bought directly on the traditional e-commerce web site. ProductWiki is another example. Content is completely user generated on this community of consumers commenting and giving reviews on products and services, with links to the e-commerce web sites to buy them.

The third model of social commerce relies on individual online purchase with information and recommendation sharing on social networks. It includes, first, social plugins ("like", "share", "comment") used on e-commerce sites connecting web users to their friends on Facebook, Twitter, Google+, or Foursquare. These social plugins are largely used nowadays in earned media. In this social commerce model, web users share comments or recommendations of products with their friends on social networks, either before or after the purchasing act. Another mechanism is "Facebook connect" to subscribe on a web site services, which is more intrusive (even in opt-in case) on account of the Facebook personal data collected by the e-commerce site. This socla commerce mechanism is frequently used by e-commerce sites as Amazon for instance. A final case is Twitter Dell page @DellOutlet, social network page used as a distribution channel and providing to Dell an amount of sales of more than 7 millions of dollars (in 2010).

The fourth and last category of social commerce model is both collective buying and information and recommendation sharing on social networks. We find in this category F-commerce, including Tab store, Page store and Wallstore on Facebook, or specific area on e-commerce site such as "My social shopping" created in 2012 on C-Discount website, with specific plugins ("I want" and not only "I like") and numerous information sharing and recommendations with friends on social networks.

Social Shopping Behaviour

On a theoretical point of view, several key concepts contribute to a better understanding of social shopping behaviour. First one is buying motivations, largely studied in marketing literature. Tauber (1972) distinguishes personal motivation (such as individual role or entertainment regardless to daily life) and social motivations (such as social experience outside home, communication with persons having same center of interest, pleasure of negotiating). Christodoulides and Michaelidou (2011) have shown that social interaction positively impacts e-satisfaction and e-loyalty and is a key variable of e-commerce. Other trend of research has shown that social commerce is an answer to the lack of social dimension in human-machine interaction on traditional e-commerce web sites. To compensate this fact, web buyers connect with others on virtual communities or social networks to share information ad recommendation on products and services. The sense of community explains this infatuation for community behavior. This psychological construct represents one of the key contributions of sociology research (Tartaglia, 2006). McMillan and Chavis (1986) distinguish the following dimensions: (1) *Membership feeling*: users have a feeling of membership and identification to the community, a personal commitment maintained over time in relation to the community. Users also share a symbolic and common system with other members of the community, translated into behaviors aiming at "singing the praises" and defining the community limits; (2) *The influence feeling:* the individual feels that his place is recognized inside the community, and his presence makes a difference; (3) *The integration and meeting needs feeling*: members consider that the available resources inside the community correspond to their expectations and needs; (4) *the feeling of a shared emotional link*: users feel this emotional link by frequent and high quality interactions, by organizing common events with the community. It also has been showed by Olbrich and Holsing (2011) that social functionalities positively impacts shopping behaviour. Social presence is also a key concept of online social commerce. Another concept is social presence relying on how individuals interacting through a technology, feel they are together (Shen and Khalifa, 2008). Shin and Shin (2011) show that social presence is a key element of buying on online web sites, reinforcing security and confidence. Different vectors of social presence exist, either anthropomorphic (virtual agent, voices, photos or videos) or non-anthropomorphic (text, emailing, consumers' reviews and recommendation search). Information research and peer to peer influence impact on consumers' behavior have been shown by different authors (Chevalier et Mayzlin, 2006 ; Aral et Walker, 2011). Gender impact has also been underlined: for women, shopping is a social activity with implication (Bakewell and Mitchell, 2004), and young women consider socialization and entertainment as important factor of their buying behaviour (Haytko et Baker, 2004). Finally, social psychology theories, and more particularly Cialdini's dimensions (1984) provide a theoretical framework to better understanding social shopping. This author emphasize on six particular dimensions explaining online social shopping. The first one is reciprocity: humans generally aim to return favors or pay back debts and treat others as they treat them. An application in social commerce is a recommendation I will provide on a product because I have previously receive a valuable one from one individual. The second dimension is commitment: we have a deep desire to be consistent. For this reason, once we have committed to something, we are then more inclined to go through with it. In terms of social commerce, we will be more confident toward brands or companies sharing the same values. The third dimension is social proof: we are even more likely to be influenced by people similar to us. Application in social commerce is friends' recommendation. The fourth dimension is "liking": we tend to be more influence by people we like. In social commerce, recommendation or comments from friends (or web users with closed affinity) will influence me. The fifth dimension is authority: we feel a sense of duty or obligation to people in positions of authority, such as experts for instance on social commerce communities. The last Cialdini's dimension is scarcity: things are more attractive when their availability is limited. In terms of social commerce, companies for instance often offer limited edition products on Facebook.

From Online Social Commerce to Mobile Social Commerce

Mobile social commerce (M-commerce) is a type of social commerce conducted over mobile or wireless networks. Mobile commerce services are accessible with fundamentally different presentation, processing, and interaction modalities compared to a desktop computer, such services enable a whole new set of unprecedented service capabilities, including location awareness, context sensing, and push delivery (Kourouthanassis and Giaglis, 2012). It's important to understand how mobile features add values to social commerce and e-commerce in general.

Kourouthanassis and Giaglis (2012) distinguish three main periods of M-commerce. The first one concerns M-portals, between 1997 and 2000, dominated by mobile network operators and m-commerce services bundled into mobile portals. The second period, between 2000 and 2006, focuses on m-internet with e-commerce providers and users enjoying direct internet access through their mobile devices. The third period, from 2000 until now, is characterized by m-applications creating a new m-commerce system. More recently, a new trend emerges in this historical evolution of m-commerce: SoLoMo. Today, location awareness and mobility have added context to even the most ordinary actions. SoLoMo, which stands for Social-Local-Mobile, is a new buzzword being thrown around by marketing teams these years. Social Local Mobile applications open new developments of location-based and context aware services, allowing companies to increase on the market their added value for consumers. For instance, SMS push localized promotions on mobile on customers closed to a shop allow retailers to improve sales. Social features allowing links on social networks or communities allow customer to be in 2.0 social shopping usage.

One challenge for companies is to capture users' attention: a difference between mobile and web services is the usage context (Oinas-Kukkonen and Kurkela, 2003), people often using mobile in a noisy and distracting environments. However, real time contextual information including peer o peer information and recommendation is source of new consumer behaviors on markets. Marketing techniques and teams need to be adapted to this new world. Hui et al. (2013) have shown that mobile promotions aimed at increasing in-store path length can increase unplanned spending.

Another interesting characteristic of social m-commerce relies on QR-code. Abbreviated from Quick Response Code, QR Code is the trademark for a type of matrix barcode (or two-dimensional barcode). A barcode is an optically machine-readable label that is attached to an item and that records information related to that item. Most recently, Starbucks turned to QR codes to create a unique opportunity for engagement with their customers. The company added QR codes to marketing materials for some of their recent products to allow customers to learn more about them. As part of the recent campaign, baristas passed out handy bookmarks with the scannable codes to customers who came in for a cup of coffee. When scanned, the codes directed users to a mobile website with a video and information about Starbucks products. Several Iphone applications include smart shopping lists with integrated access to manufacturers' coupons and support for QR code scanning. In social m-commerce era, these applications add social link and connection with friends of close persons, either on existing social networks (By Facebook connect and Facebook plugins) or on specific users' communities of information and recommendation of products and services. @Walmart Labs develop social mobile applications dedicated to m-commerce and to improve retailer's sales.

Mobile scan possibilities also provide a new way to sell products. For instance, price-comparison applications let users scan the barcode or snap a photo of a physical product (or type or speak a search for one) and then look up the price on the spot and purchase it from the online retailer or directly on mobile, or see its availability and prices at nearby stores with geo-localization maps. One can store the credit card info and pay with the Application. Some applications also include social features such as friends' reviews to help users to make decisions. Aside from price comparisons, some applications can even watch price changes: one can set up an alert for when an item reaches the price you're willing to pay for it.

Social m-commerce relies on mobile payment to pay in real time. For instance, Starbucks uses mobile to improve the customer experience by making it easier for guests to pay for their morning coffee. The company developed Square Wallet, a mobile payment app that was launched in November 2012. The convenience factor of Square Wallet is undeniable. To date, mobile payments have been implemented in over 7,000 Starbucks stores nationwide.

APPLICATION CASE STUDIES OF MOBILE SOCIAL COMMERCE

In this last section we present and comment different user cases and mobile social commerce applications.

Asos: Buy on Facebook Page

ASOS.com is a global online fashion and beauty retailer and offers over 50,000 branded and own label product lines, which is one of the UK's largest online-only fashion and beauty stores. In January 2011, Asos became the world's first fully integrated Facebook Store in Europe, extend the same e-commerce experience to their Facebook Page. The Facebook page offers approximately 1,300 new product lines each week. On their site you can view items, "like" them, share items and comments on certain items on your Facebook profile, see which items your friends have also liked within the store and complete a purchase without ever leaving the ASOS Facebook page.

Said by ASOS community manager: "Millions of our users already interact with ASOS through Facebook, commenting on, sharing and discovering new items. Many of those go on to buy something on one of our sites. Our Facebook Store will allow them to do this directly through Facebook."

While a little slower than shopping on their site, it's a move that will definitely broaden its user base and position it as a brand that is both social media savvy and technologically hip.

Figure 1 shows the screenshots of ASOS Facebook page, by clicking the shopping link within the description of the photo within a post, you will be redirected to ASOS e-commerce boutique to shop directly.

Figure 1. Screenshots of ASOS e-commerce shop on Facebook

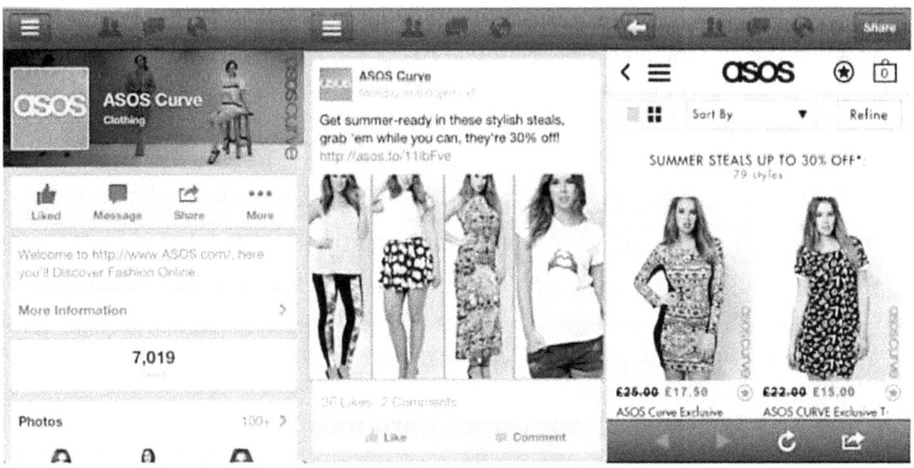

Table 1. Evaluation of the ASOS Facebook Page

Social Features	
Social annotation	Like, Comment
Share aspect	Facebook
View friends' choice	
E-Commerce Features	
Online purchase	
Similar Social Commerce	
Topshop	Facebook commerce

LISTIA: ONLINE SOCIAL MARKETPLACE TO EXCHANGE THINGS

Listia is a fun & free online marketplace where users can get rid of things they don't need anymore and get stuff they want in return for free. On Listia, you use credits to bid on auctions instead of cash. You receive credits when you sign up and anytime you give something away, and you use those credits to get free stuff you really want from other users. The more stuff you give away, the more free things you can get.

The guideline is simple:

1. A user lists something they don't want anymore (like an old cell phone).
2. Other users bid on the cell phone using credits they received for signing up and listing their own stuff.
3. When the auction ends, the user who bid the highest amount of credits wins!
4. The winner gets the cell phone, and the lister gets credits to use for something else on Listia.

Concerning the mobile elements in Listia, you can take a photo with your device, enter a few brief details and post it to Listia instantly. You can also use the phone to see what people are giving away nearby through the geo location feature, bid on other items and receive instant notifications any time you are outbid or an item you are watching is ending soon. Figure 2. shows the screenshots of usage of Listia.

LivingSocial: Share Shopping Experience

LivingSocial is a deal-of-the-day website that features discounted gift certificates usable at local or national companies. Like Groupon, deals are pushed to mobile device every day, one can click to view the deal and buy directly on your phone.

Figure 2. Screenshots of Listia application

Table 2. Evaluation of the Listia application

Social Features	
User generated business	Items with image and text
Social annotation	Comment
Share aspect	Facebook, Email
Follow/Unfollow a seller	
Mobile Features	
Camera	Take a snap
Location awareness	Geo-localization of items
Instant notifications	
E-commerce Features	
Credits	
Auction	

Concerning other mobile feathers, deals map is designed to check a deal nearby. You'll also be able to browse tons of on-demand, real-time offers on dining experiences, spa treatments, fitness classes, and other nearby deals—ready for immediate use. After one purchase, a QR code is generated to be shown to the merchant. No printing any more.

Concerning the social feathers, each deal can be shared to friends by email, message, Twitter AND Facebook by one click. As a reward, if three of your friends buy the deal, you'll get yours for free.

Figure 3 shows the screenshots of usage of LivingSocial application.

Figure 3. Screenshots of LivingSocial application

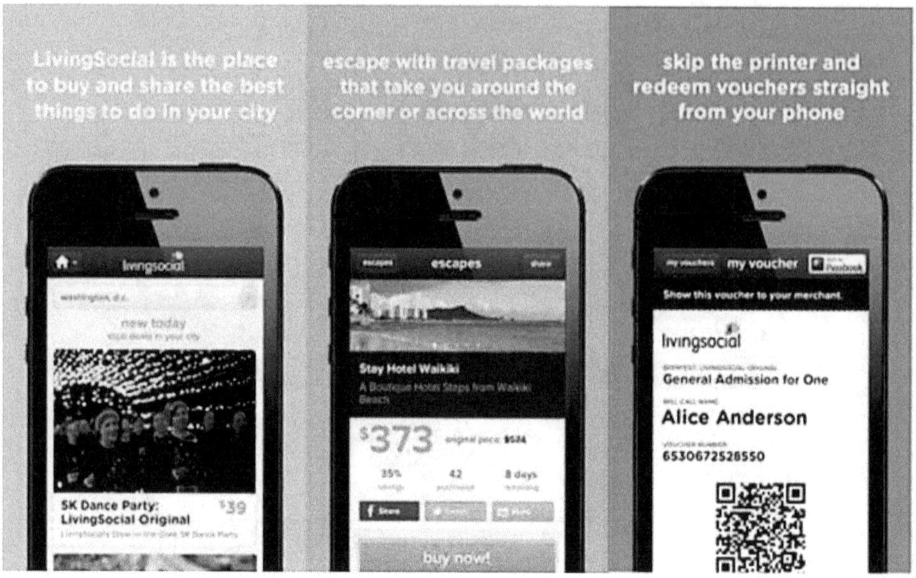

Table 3. Evaluation of the LivingSocial application

Social Features	
Share aspect	Facebook, Twitter, Email, Message
Mobile Features	
Location awareness	Instant notifications
QR code	Geo-localization of deals
E-Commerce Features	
Online purchase	
Similar Social Commerce	
Groupon	

You Loot: User Generated Business

With the slogan “Sell the world around you”, You Loot is the world’s first ever social commerce marketing app for both consumers and business owners alike. You Loot makes it easy for users to take pictures of the things they want then add their own artistic touch to it before adding the price, the link, and sharing it with friends via email, facebook, twitter, or instagram.

Figure 4. Screenshots of You Loot application

Table 4. Evaluation of the You Loot application

Social Features	
User generated business	Items with image, text, business-related logo
Share aspect	Facebook, Twitter, Instagram, Email
Mobile Features	
Camera	Take a snap

Figure 4 shows the screenshots of usage of You Loot application.

Trace: From Online to Offline – Discover the Cool Things People Buy

With Trace application, one can share the cool things you buy. Make a purchase and after it you can share it with your friends and followers. Just connect your credit or

Figure 5. Screenshots of Trace application

Table 5. Evaluation of the Trace application

Social Features	
User generated content	Items with image, text and location
Social annotation	Like, Comment
Share aspect	Facebook, Twitter, Foursquare
View friends' choice	
Follow/Unfollow people	
Mobile Features	
Camera	Take a snap
Location awareness	Geo-localization of interests
Instant notifications	

debit card to trace for easy sharing. Users can discover the cool things your friends are buying and the most popular trending purchases. When you see something you want to try, add it to your wish list and Trace will keep you noticed when you are near it. Share all of the cool things you buy with your friends on your favorite social networks including facebook, twitter, and foursquare.

Figure 5 shows the screenshots of usage of Trace application.

SOLUTIONS AND RECOMMENDATIONS

Social Mobile Social commerce presents several theoretical and managerial implications. Theories on consumer behavior in e-commerce or social networks are mobilized to explain this new emerging trend. On a managerial point of view, the examples show the importance and the specificities of mobile features such as location, QR code, notifications, camera, allowing new interactions between companies and customers. Mobile functionalities constitute interaction tools for direct marketing which has to integrate human-computer interfaces design and user experience design for social mobile commerce.

FUTURE RESEARCH DIRECTIONS

Social M-commerce applications constitute an emerging trend source of numerous future researches direction. The first one concerns ergonomics and user experience in order to develop easy to use and usefulness Human-machine interfaces. Linked to this topic, future research is needed to better understand and measure fluent navigation and flow concept, that Oinas-Kukkonen and Kurkela (2003) has shown as a key variable impacting in mobile applications a positive mobile user experience. Social M-commerce is also a rich area of future research in marketing: how to measure ROI ? Is it more efficient than other distribution channels? How better understanding Social m-shopping behavior? What is the new marketing paradigm of social m-commerce? What about social m-commerce communities and their impact on markets and innovation? Future researches in the sociology field will also lighten on the societal implications of these new technologies, behaviors and form of commerce.

CONCLUSION

Social m-commerce constitutes a new area of opportunities for companies. Based on emerging trend of social networks and peer influence, and existing on line shopping behavior, social m-commerce provides new technological features increasing consumer value on markets and allowing innovation on new services or products. It also opens a new area for future research in different fields such as computer science, technology, sociology and marketing. In 2013, this phenomenon is just at his beginning. However, his potential development in the future years and his consequences in terms of consumer behavior changes and marketing paradigm may be a particular source of attention for both worldwide and very local companies.

REFERENCES

Aral, S., & Walker, D. (2011). Creating social contagion through viral product design: A randomized trial of peer influence in networks. *Management Science*, *57*(9), 1623–1639. doi:10.1287/mnsc.1110.1421

Chevalier, J. A., & Mayzlin, D. (2006). The effect of word of mouth on sales: Online book reviews. *JMR, Journal of Marketing Research*, *43*(3), 345–354. doi:10.1509/jmkr.43.3.345

Christodoulides, G., & Michaelidou, N. (2011). Shopping motives as antecedents of e-satisfaction and e-loyalty. *Journal of Marketing Management*, *27*(1-2), 181–197. doi:10.1080/0267257X.2010.489815

Cialdini, R. (1984). *Influence, the psychology of Persuasion*. Collins Business Essentials.

Curty, R. G., & Zhang, P. (2011). Social commerce: looking back and forward. *Proceedings of the American Society for Information Science and Technology (ASIST) Annual Conference*, *48*(1), 1-10.

Haytko, D. L., & Baker, J. (2004). Its all at the mall: Exploring adolescent girls experiences. *Journal of Retailing*, *80*(1), 67–83. doi:10.1016/j.jretai.2004.01.005

Holbrook, M. B., & Hirschman, E. C. (1982). The experimental aspects of consumption: Consumer fantasies, feelings, and fun. *The Journal of Consumer Research*, *9*(2), 132–140. doi:10.1086/208906

Hui, S.K., Inman, J., Huang, Y., & Suher, J. (2013). The effect of in-store travel distance on unplanned spending: applications to mobile promotion strategies. *Journal of Marketing*, *77*, 1-16.

Kourouthanassis, P. E., & Giaglis, G. M. (2012). Introduction to the Special Issue Mobile Commerce: The Past, Present, and Future of Mobile Commerce Research. *International Journal of Electronic Commerce*, *16*(4), 5–18. doi:10.2753/JEC1086-4415160401

Labrecque, L. I., vor dem Esche, J., Mathwick, C., Novak, T. P., & Hofacker, C. F. (2013). Consumer Power: Evolution in the Digital Age. *Journal of Interactive Marketing*, *27*(4), 257–269. doi:10.1016/j.intmar.2013.09.002

Mardsen, P. (2010). *Social Commerce: monetizing social media*. Hamburg, Germany: Syzygy Deutschland Gmbh.

McGuire, W. (1974). Psychological motives and communication gratification. In J. F. Blumler & J. Katz (Eds.), *The uses of mass communications: Current perspectives on gratification research* (pp. 106–167). Beverly Hills, CA: Sage.

McMillan, D. W., & Chavis, D. M. (1986). Sense of community: A definition and theory. *Journal of Community Psychology*, *14*(1), 6–23. doi:10.1002/1520-6629(198601)14:1<6::AID-JCOP2290140103>3.0.CO;2-I

Oinas-Kukkonen, H., & Kurkela, V. (2003). Developing successful mobile applications. *Proceedings of Computer Science and Technology*, 19–21.

Olbrich, R., & Holsing, C. (2011). Modeling Consumer Purchasing Behavior in Social Shopping Communities with Clickstream Data. *International Journal of Electronic Commerce*, *16*(2), 15–40. doi:10.2753/JEC1086-4415160202

Shen, K. N., & Khalifa, M. (2008). Exploring multidimensional conceptualization of social presence in the context of online communities. *International Journal of Human-Computer Interaction*, *24*(7), 722–774. doi:10.1080/10447310802335789

Shin, D. H., & Shin, Y. J. (2011). Consumers trust in virtual mall shopping: The role of social presence and perceived security. *International Journal of Human-Computer Interaction*, *27*(5), 450–475. doi:10.1080/10447318.2011.552060

Stephen, A. T., & Toubia, O. (2010). Deriving value from social commerce networks. *JMR, Journal of Marketing Research*, *47*(2), 215–228.

Tartaglia, S. (2006). A Preliminary Study for a New Model of Sense of Community. *Journal of Community Psychology*, *34*(1), 25–36. doi:10.1002/jcop.20081

Tauber, E. M. (1972). Why do people shop. *Journal of Marketing*, *36*(4), 46–59. doi:10.2307/1250426

The New York Times. (2006). *Like shopping? Social networking? Try social shopping*. Retrieved June 2013, from www.nytimes.com/2006/09/11/technology/11ecom.html?_r1/41&adxnnl1/41& oref1/4 slogin&partner1/4rssnyt&emc1/4rss&adxnnlx1/41210267372-1HIJXtBN3gaeie1G/0HTcg

Chapter 8
Brand Personality, Social Status, and Physical Vanity in Building Luxury Fashion Branded Apps

Shanthi Bavani V. Raja Mohan
Taylor's University, Malaysia

Sajad Rezaei
Taylor's University, Malaysia

ABSTRACT

While there have been an increasing number of researches done on branding and consumer behavior especially on brand personality, social status and vanity and its influence on purchase intention, there are little researches that focus on the influence of all these factors collectively on Apps purchase intention. In addition, the fact that the influence of some factors will vary from country to country could not be ignored. This chapter conceptually argues that brand personality, social status, and physical vanity are important in building luxury fashion branded Apps. While brand personality and luxury fashion branded Apps as an internal factor plays an important role in deciphering if it has an influence on an individual's Apps purchase intention for luxury fashion brands; therefore, it is important to look into how external factors have an influence on an individual. The theoretical and future research directions are discussed.

DOI: 10.4018/978-1-5225-2449-6.ch008

Copyright ©2017, IGI Global. Copying or distributing in print or electronic forms without written permission of IGI Global is prohibited.

INTRODUCTION

In this global business world, companies are emphasizing more on creating global brands through effective marketing in order to create powerful brands that are able to sustain in the competitive environment. Regardless of technology related advancement such as Apps, managers spend millions on developing or maintaining a strong brand image consequently their brand is perceived to be distinctive and most unique in the eyes of the customers (O' Cass &Lim, 2001). As consumers are increasingly attracted towards brands that appeal to their specific personality; marketers are increasingly facing the challenge to create a marketing strategy that attracts the consumers. Hence, a detailed research on this topic will further equip luxury marketers with the relevant information required to understand the market for luxury fashion brands (Rezaei, Shahijan, Valaei, Rahimi, & Ismail, 2016; Sajad, Muslim, Minoo, & Norshidah, 2016; Valaei, Rezaei, Ismail, & Moi, 2016). Furthermore, this research will help identify what kind of people who buy these products this, in turn, will aid in an effective execution of marketing strategies for luxury fashion branded Apps.

According to Euromonitor (2015), the number of luxury consumer's goods globally intend to purchase, have more than tripled increased to around 330 million people and in the past two decades with each year more than 10 million new customers entering the market. In a multinational country, fashion brands have laid a reputation for young shoppers. In today's culture, it has become a social trend among youngsters' using luxury fashion brands to represent their image and reputation. These consumers have become concerned on the preferred brands for their daily usage. Fashion brand industries have also grown widely and had a lead pathway for luxury fashion market, and modern shoppers. Brand personality is increasingly becoming essential to marketers as it helps them to develop and cultivate the bond between the consumer and the brands. The stronger is the congruence between the brand personality and the consumer's self-image, the stronger is the customer's relationship with the brand (O' Cass & Lim, 2001). Similarly, the influence of Social Status on consumers purchase behavior has also seen to be strong. The focus of this study is specifically on the luxury fashion goods category. This research has inspected the influencing factors on the young Malaysian consumer's purchase intentions of luxury fashion branded Apps by looking into three major factors that are brand personality, social status, and physical vanity. This research intended to find out how these symbolic values influence consumers Apps purchase intention among consumers.

While there have been an increasing number of researches ended on branding and consumer behavior especially on brand personality, social status and vanity (Mulyanegara, 2009; Hung et al., 2011; Park, Rabolt & Sook Jeon, 2008) and its influence on purchase intention, there are little researches that focus on the influence of all these factors's collectively on purchase Intention. Also, the fact that the influence of some factors will vary from country to country cannot be denied; thus, this research will be focusing particularly on the conceptualization of branded Apps. This research will aid greater understanding in the field of branding as the influence of brand personality, social status and vanity will be studied collectively on Apps purchase intention of the luxury consumer.

BACKGROUND

Statistics report that in Malaysia alone, approximately RM 1,457.4 Million and 832.7 Million was spent on luxury apparels and luxury accessories respectively which indicate that the consumption of luxury fashion brands is high in Malaysia. International luxury fashion brands like Louis Vuitton, Prada, Coach, Gucci, Dior and others have a physical presence in various shopping malls and are recording strong sales (Alavi, Rezaei, Valaei, & Wan Ismail, 2016; Mohseni, Jayashree, Rezaei, Kasim, & Okumus, 2016; Rezaei, Emami, & Valaei, 2016). As the culture of carrying luxury fashion brands is sharply increasing throughout Asia, carrying a research in terms of luxury fashion branded Apps will be meaningful (Euromonitor, 2015). Goody (2006) defines the concept of luxury as "refined enjoyment, of elegance, of things desirable but not essential" and shoppers these days are increasingly attracted towards such luxury brands. Modern shoppers define themselves through shopping; by showing how they shop, where they shop and what kind of products and brands they buy. Increasingly, brands these days are seen as essential in shaping an individual's identity, sense of achievement and individuality amongst customers (O' Cass & Frost, 2002).

According to Murphy, 1990, the brands that the costumer's carry tells people around them what kind of lifestyle they live, how their personality is and also provides the consumers with the sense of belonging to a particular group. This encourages and has a positive influence on the consumer's purchase intention towards luxury fashion branded Apps. Luxury fashion branded Apps are often consumed to indicate status and are displayed noticeably (O' Cass and McEwen 2004) which implies that consumers are motivated by a desire to make an impression on people around them in luxury fashion perception of branded Apps. Factor that is essential to explain the influence on Apps purchase intention and luxury fashion branded Apps is the role of vanity. Though numerous research has been conducted in the past (Hung et al., 2011) suggest that the role of Vanity has become even more prominent than previously stated (Amin, Rezaei, & Tavana, 2015; Rezaei, 2015; Valaei et al., 2016).

Brand personality and signaling of Social Status and Vanity are all related to having a symbolic value such as luxury fashion branded Apps.

MAIN FOCUS OF THE CHAPTER

This research mainly focuses on Apps purchase intention of luxury fashion branded Apps as it has a greater implication and will often have a positive impact on a person's action and has been supported by researchers who have conducted many studies on significance of Apps purchase intention the context of brand consumption (Hung et al., 2011). Apps purchase intention is an individual's predisposition to buy a certain luxury fashion branded Apps. Apps purchase intention is when the purchase motive matches with the brand attribute. Once the consumer does decide which brands they want to purchase they must still go ahead and make the actual purchase (Moghaddam, Rezaei, & Amin, 2015; Rezaei & Ghodsi, 2014; Rezaei & Ismail, 2014; Shahijan, Rezaei, & Preece, 2016). In addition, the consumer also might need to consider how to purchase, when to purchase and how much money to spend on a particular product such as luxury fashion branded Apps. It has been seen many times that there is a slight delay between the Apps purchase intention and the time where the consumer actually purchases the product (Dzisah & Ocloo, 2013).

In line with the past researches findings, conducting a research on the Apps purchase intention of luxury fashion brands will not only contribute to the existing knowledge in this field but will also provide the marketers with information on how

Figure 1. Conceptualization of Apps purchase intention toward luxury fashion branded apps

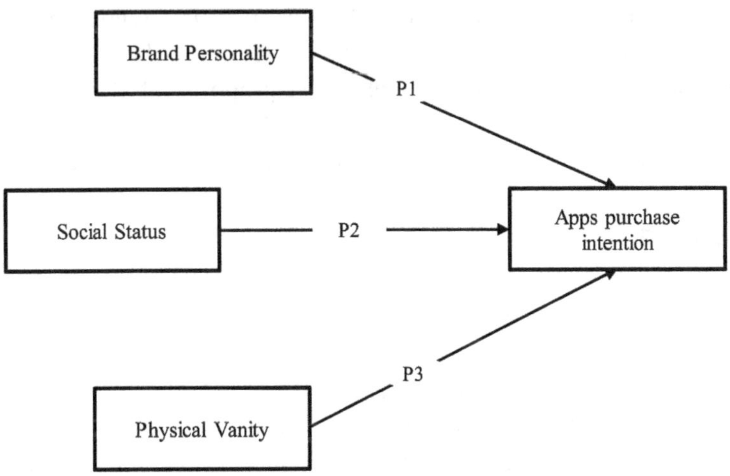

they can make their brands more appealing to the customers using these three factors. Since there are very little studies that focus on the influence of all the three personal and interpersonal factors which are brand personality, social status, and physical vanity; a conceptual framework was developed and used in this paper (See Figure 1).

Brand Personality

Related to luxury fashion branded Apps, brand personality has been described as the set of human characteristics associated with a brand. According to APA, brand personality is "the psychological nature of a particular brand as intended by its sellers, though persons in the marketplace may realize the luxury fashion branded Apps otherwise and these two standpoints compare to the behaviors of individual humans include what we intend or desire, and what others see or believe". Previous researches have shown that brand personality and social status and vanity have a significant influence on the Apps purchase intention of luxury fashion brands. Using previous research findings (Mulyanegara, 2009; Hung et al., 2011; Park, Rabolt & Sook Jeon, 2008), the three variables which are the brand personality, social status and vanity and one variable which is the Apps purchase intention this study was proposed to study the influence of these three factors on purchase intention towards luxury fashion branded Apps (Amin et al., 2015; Julian, Rezaei, & Amin, 2014; Kalantari Shahijan, Rezaei, Nigel Preece, & Khairuzzaman Wan Ismail, 2014; Rezaei, Amin, & Ismail, 2014). As discussed, luxury fashion branded Apps as one of the essential factors in determining the Apps purchase intention is the brand personality. A positive brand personality which matches with the ideal self is likely to influence the purchase intention (Amatulli & Guido, 2011). Similarly, it has been found that the greater the congruity between the brand and the human characteristics the greater is the preference for the brand (O' Cass & Lim, 2001). However, there are some studies that have shown that the brand personality does not influence the consumers to brand purchase intention of luxury fashion brands (Mulyanegara & Tsarenko, 2009). Therefore, we propose as follow:

P1: Brand personality influence Apps purchase intention of luxury fashion brands.

Social Status

Social status is a position in the society or the social system employed by designated performers (i.e., individuals or social organizations) towards luxury fashion branded Apps. Statuses are ranked hierarchically in terms of prestige, unequal distribution of relatively scarce social resources and unsatisfactory opportunity for procurement them, and power, that is the ability to persuade others to accomplish one's goals in the direction of luxury fashion branded Apps. Furthermore, social status is another factor that has a large influence on Apps purchase intention of luxury fashion branded Apps. According to a previous study (Hung et al., 2011) social status influence of the society had a significant impact on the Apps purchase intention of a luxury fashion brand. Similarly, in the findings of previous research (Zhang & Hwan Kim, 2013) it was confirmed that consumers compare themselves with people around them which motivate them to purchase more luxury fashion brands. The influence of social status was further proved by studies that emphasized that it, in fact, does have an impact on the purchase intention of luxury fashion brand (Park, Rabolt & Sook Jeon, 2008). Thus, we propose:

P2: Social status influence Apps purchase intention of luxury fashion brands.

Physical Vanity

Vanity refers to a person's concern with and the awareness and total perception of social attainments and physical appearances (Durvasula & Lysonski, 2008). Netemeyer, Burton and Lichtenstein, (1995) defined Vanity as having four different characteristic traits where it consists of an extreme concern for physical appearance and/or a positive and perhaps overstated view of one's physical appearance. For the purpose of this study focus on the physical vanity taken related to luxury fashion branded Apps. Physical vanity has an important influence on Apps purchase intention of luxury fashion brands. While there are many studies that show that Physical Vanity has an influence on Apps purchase intention (Din & Sahn, 2013). There have been studies that show that Physical Vanity does not have a significant influence on Apps purchase intention (Hung et al., 2011). Since, there is a dearth of researches that have shown the influence of brand personality, social status and physical vanity on Apps purchase intention of luxury fashion brand particularly focusing on university students (Daliri, Rezaei, & Ismail, 2014; Rezaei, 2015; Rezaei & Amin, 2013; Rezaei, Shahijan, et al., 2016). Based on this, the following was derived:

P3: Physical Vanity influence Apps purchase intention of luxury fashion brands.

SOLUTIONS AND RECOMMENDATION

The literature provided an overview of what online purchase intention are related to luxury fashion branded Apps. This research gives a clearer understanding of the factors that was investigated in this research which was brand personality, status consumption and physical vanity in terms of purchase intention in examining luxury fashion branded Apps. The past findings of other researchers have also been highlighted. According to (Ramaeseshan and Tsao, 2007) brand personality is the soul of the brand that is created by the brand's attributes and the marketing techniques. They state that brand personality can positively increase the preference and the usage which ends up forming an emotional bonding and loyalty towards the particular brand. According to stated researchers, it has been established in the past that there are significant benefits of having favorable brand personality on luxury fashion branded Apps. As cited in by Freling & Forbes, 2005, According to Sirgy, 1982, a positive brand personality leads to a liking for the brand and increased usage of the products. Moreover, it is said to increase the level of emotions towards the brand (Biel, 1993). Also, Fournier, 1998 found that it has a positive impact on the level of loyalty; and promotes product differentiation (Aker, 1996). Empirical evidence, however, resulted that brand personality does have a positive influence on the brand image. Similarly, a research was carried out by Mehele and Shenor (2010) on a variety of industries which included branded apparels, furniture and supermarkets. The findings indicate that overall consumers prefer brands with personalities matching to their own. Likewise, findings reported that consumers express their identity through the clothes they wear might be related to luxury fashion branded product. In addition, a research conducted by Goldsmith & Goldsmith, 2012 focusing on the association between brand personality and brand engagement on North face clothing brand the research confirmed that brand personality is in fact related to brand engagement and provided empirical evidence on how consumers become attached to some brands.

While brand personality and luxury fashion branded Apps; as an internal factor plays an important role in deciphering if it has an influence on an individual's Apps purchase intention for luxury fashion brands; it is important to look into how external factors have an influence on an individual. Previous researches (Ahuvia, 2005; Belk, 1988; Coulter et al., 2003; Jenkins, 2004; Truong et al., 2010) have found that external factors moreover to luxury fashion branded Apps can influence a product perceived value. This is also because of the society's' influence, as no brand can operate outside of the community (Wilcox et al., 2009). Charles, Hurst, and Roussanov (2007) argue that consumers who purchase certain brands to signal status are usually products that are very expensive as it signals higher income and is visible to people around them such as luxury cars, luxury fashion brands or jewelry. In a research conducted by Zhang & Hwan Kim (2013) data was collected from 161 respondents through online questionnaires from three most populated cities in China. The survey measured variables such as brand consciousness, materialism, social comparison, fashion innovativeness and involvement as influencing factors on Apps purchase intention of luxury fashion brands. It was found that there is a positive purchase attitude towards luxury fashion brands among Chinese consumers.

People may not only compare themselves with their friends, family, and celebrities but also compare themselves with the people they admire the most such as the rich people in the perception of luxury fashion branded Apps.

An individual perception of how others would distinguish them if they showed off their expensive luxury brands plays an important role in their purchase of luxury fashion branded Apps. The above findings relate with the results that have been obtained in a similar research conducted in Korea which aimed to identify the determinants of Apps purchase intention in terms of materialism, ethnocentrism, conformity, need for uniqueness, purchasing frequency, social recognition, and vanity. The data was gathered by surveying university students from four different universities in the metropolitan area of Seoul where 319 responses were generated. The result showed that social recognition had the second most significant correlation with the purchase intention of purchasing frequency (Alavi et al., 2016; Amin, Rezaei, & Abolghasemi, 2014; Daliri et al., 2014; Rezaei, 2015). Furthermore, it was found that social recognition had a significant positive effect on Apps purchase intention of global luxury brands among Koreans (Park, Rabolt & Sook Jeon, 2008).

Similarly, in a study conducted in Taiwan where 1380 responses were generated; it was found that social influence does, in fact, have a correlation with purchase intention. Researchers also found that influence of social relationship with the Apps purchase intention of the luxury fashion brands was strongly positive. Furthermore, it was found that luxury brands place a high emphasis on experiential and symbolic values (Hung et al., 2011). Hence, the focus of managerial efforts would be on influences of status consumption on the Apps purchase intention of luxury fashion brands. Eastman and Goldsmith, 1999 argue that consumers possess certain products to put them into the display to people around them. This, in turn, helps them to enhance their self-concept, show the world who they are, what they feel and what kind of social bonds expect to have. Another research conducted by (O'Cass & Siahtiri, 2014) administered to 580 students studying at two universities in the city of Shanghai revealed similar results. The research aimed to examine the fashion consumption in relation to status consumption along with the perception of fashion clothing. The findings revealed that the Chinese student population were highly status conscious and believed that using specific brands will help them differentiate from others. They mostly identified it as a sign of prestige, wealth, and success. Therefore, luxury fashion branded Apps has an important implication.

In addition, in a research conducted by Tsai (2005) also aligns with the findings shown that consumers who were more socially oriented were more likely to be motivated to purchase and own luxury brands. By liability this strategy they are able to demonstrate to the society their status as well as their successes. This would specifically be true for international luxury brands. Likewise, a cross-cultural study was conducted on Japanese and Canadian consumers which resulted in a conclusion that the for the Japanese consumer's upward social comparison is positively related to the greater desire for branded luxury products and also indicated a higher Apps purchase intention for such luxury brands (Ogden and Venkat,2001). Consumer desire for possession of luxury goods because they want to make an impression on the people around them by using the luxury product. With reference to the studies that have been discussed above it can be derived that social status does have a positive impact on the Apps purchase intention of luxury fashion brands. It has been seen so far that consumers place a high importance to social consumption so that they can show the society where they stand. A person concerned with status would be worried about their standing in the society and hence will purchase things that will give them the sense of belonging in the society.

Vanity is an essential influencing factor on the Apps purchase intention of luxury fashion products because there is a relationship between a person's self-concept and their desire for external and materialistic things through symbolic fulfillment (Wang and Waller, 2006; Watchravesringkan, 2008) in the perception of luxury fashion branded Apps. As discussed, vanity consists of two (2) main aspects; the physical appearance aspect which is concerned with one's physical appearance and the achievement aspect are concerned for achievements. A person concern for physical appearance means that the person is bothered about their personal appearance and has a rather positive and at times exaggerated view of themselves (Durvasula & Lysonski, 2008). Thus, luxury fashion branded Apps are highly related to individual's self-concept and their craving for external and materialistic belongings.

Studies have further emphasized on how an individual's physical appearance plays a vital role in forming a positive self-concept about themselves. Studies by (Durvasula & Lysonski, 2008) stresses buying behavior is in fact motivated totally or in part by physical appearance. Similar findings were generated by (Din & Sahn, 2013) where it was proved that physical vanity has a significant influence on consumers purchase intent. The data was collected from upscale shopping malls in Cairo and Alexandria where 385 responses were generated. The research aimed to find the effects of personal values, materialism, consumer ethnocentrism, conformity, vanity, social recognition, need for uniqueness on Apps purchase intention of consumers. The result concluded that after social recognition, vanity had the strongest correlation with purchase intention. Moreover, analysis (Durvasula & Lysonski, 2001) showed a significant effect of vanity on purchase intention towards person's self-concept and their desire for external and materialistic things.

Similarly, a study was conducted in Pakistan which aimed to find the influence of Conformity, Materialism, Ethnocentrism, Need for Uniqueness and Vanity. The data collected from 138 respondents revealed that vanity had quite an influence on the consumer's Apps purchase intention (Ahmad et al., 2013). A research conducted by Durvasula and Lysonski (2001) has further established the consumption of luxury fashion brands are positively linked to Vanity. As luxury fashion products are crafted to enhance an individual's physical appearance, this variable will provide the research with an in-depth knowledge of how physical vanity influences a consumer's purchase intention. On the contrary, a study done on Taiwanese consumers have proved with empirical evidence that vanity does not have a positive relation with Apps purchase intention of luxury fashion goods. The participant's responses generated a result signaling insignificant or negative effect of physical vanity on Apps purchase intention (Hung et al., 2011). Similarly, the findings of the study done by (Park, Rabolt & Jeon, 2008) clearly reveal that vanity is not a strong enough variable to have an influence on consumers purchasing intentions of fashion brands. Hung, et al., (2011) suggested that that though a large body of research has been dedicated to this area of research, thus, luxury fashion branded Apps and the importance of Vanity in consumers purchase intention has increased even more in the past few years.

CONCLUSION

With the growing global market of luxury fashion brands, this study aimed to find the influencing factors on Apps purchase intention of luxury fashion brands among luxury fashion branded Apps oriented consumers. The objective was to conceptualize the notion of Brand Personality, Social Status, and Physical Vanity had an influence on purchase intention of luxury fashion brands. Research implications show how managers or the fashion industries can further improve the marketing of the luxury fashion brands to attract more consumers in enhancing luxury fashion branded Apps. However, the limitation of the current study should be considered and further recommendations for future researches should be considered.

The aim of this study was to conceptualize the link between consumer personality and brand personality beyond the big five personality dimensions which are neuroticism, extroversion, openness, agreeableness and conscientiousness. It still found some significant and essential relationship between some of the big five personality dimensions and the brand preference type. For example, people chose brands that are similar to their own personalities; people who are conscientious prefer trusted brand which in turn reflects their personal reliable characteristic and people who are extroverts prefer sociable brands more which supports their outgoing nature. Other findings of this research included brand value having a higher influence on a consumer purchasing behavior. In relation to the studies that have been conducted by researchers in the past, it can be said that the brand personality does to some extent have a significant influence on brand preference and purchase intention in the perception of luxury fashion branded Apps. It has been seen that a positive brand personality leads to a better liking for the brand, a positive brand image along with the preference for the brand which in turn leads to a positive influence on the purchase intention. Therefore, it is also observed that effect of brand personality dimensions is more visible among young consider segment in the perception of luxury fashion branded Apps.

To summarize, this study proposed that the influence of Brand Personality, Social Status and Physical Vanity on Apps purchase intention of luxury branded fashion products are related to luxury fashion branded Apps. This study can provide information to marketers as to how they can change their marketing strategy to reach out to consumers. In the past few years, the consumption of luxury goods has increased tremendously. Even in developed context, it has been seen that there is a growing demand for luxury fashion brands in the recent years (Euromonitor, 2015). Increasing number of companies is involved in cultivating new and enhancing their existing marketing strategy to attract more consumers. As very little research has been conducted on the topic of the influence of the three factors Brand Personality, Social Status and Physical Vanity on Apps purchase intention of luxury fashion brands; this paper has fruitfully filled this notion.

This study aimed to give the marketing managers some in depth and useful insights on the strategies which they can use to enhance consumers purchase intention towards luxury fashion branded Apps. From the findings discussed above in the previous chapters, it can be established that the Apps purchase intention of consumers is influenced significantly by brand personality, social status, and physical vanity. Firstly, it would be useful if marketers could focus on developing a brand personality for their target segment. This means that the marketers should try and design promotional strategies that are relevant to the personality and values of the segment of people they are targeting. They should try and focus and try and match the self-image of the population with the personality of the brand. For example, the manager can construct a fashion brand personality and style that portrays down to earth or practical characteristics for the people in the target segment who value the brand personality dimension sincerity.

Similarly, in terms of social status in the future marketers should first determine if their target segments Apps purchase intention is influenced by the social status or not. The importance of social status is an important piece of information for luxury fashion brand marketers. They should come up with marketing strategies that would be consistent with the values of people who put an emphasis on Social status. The brand managers can focus on image building where they can integrate and focus on enhancing the "prestigious" image of the brand. This will increasingly gather the attention of consumers who give value to status consumption. Furthermore, it has been seen that many consumers give importance to what kind of people use particular brands and increasingly compare themselves to celebrities and wealthy people hence it might be helpful to get the brand advertised by celebrities and influential people to build luxury fashion branded Apps.

Marketers can come up with advertisements by emphasizing and tapping into an individual's concern for their physical appearance. As for a person who is preoccupied with their appearance, it is always important for them to look good in front of others therefore, an advertisement which focuses on and emphasizes on this trait of vanity marketers will be able to gather the attention of many consumers who rate high on the physical vanity. Lastly, as this study focuses on both personal and interpersonal factors; where brand personality being a personal factor and social status and physical vanity being interpersonal factors it would be favorable if marketers could use such a strategy which strikes a balance between providing both personal and interpersonal functions. This way the marketer is able to synthesize different values, meanings and emotional responses of consumers which would also enable them to take care of both personally oriented and socially oriented consumers towards luxury fashion branded Apps.

FUTURE RESEARCH DIRECTION

This study futile to take into account other key factors that make the consumers buy a particular brand and luxury fashion branded Apps. For example, system quality could be one of the important factors that consumers consider before buying a product such as luxury fashion branded Apps. Therefore, any research conducted in this area of study in the future should essentially widen the study area and analyze several different factors that have an influence on consumers purchase intention specially branded Apps. This research ignored the different fashion brands that the consumers prefer and purchase the most. Hence, future researchers are recommended to include different options the respondents can choose from as these two recommendations will improve the study findings and will also further provide marketers with the accurate findings that will enable them to come up with the correct and suitable strategies. Lastly, as a conceptual proposition, this research only focused on the terms of luxury products. Any future research should acknowledge this difference (Figure 1) and should select the proper age sample in the proper location that will enable them to generate accurate and meaningful findings towards luxury fashion branded Apps.

REFERENCES

Aaker, J. (1997). Dimensions of Brand Personality. *JMR, Journal of Marketing Research*, *34*(3), 347–356. doi:10.2307/3151897

Ahmad, W., Arshad, H., Sabir, R., & Ashraf, R. (2013). Antecedents of Purchase Intention for Foreign Apparel Products among Pakistani University Students: Implications for Market Entry Strategy. *Middle-East Journal of Scientific Research*, *16*(9), 1255–1263.

Alavi, S. A., Rezaei, S., Valaei, N., & Wan Ismail, W. K. (2016). Examining shopping mall consumer decision-making styles, satisfaction and purchase intention. *International Review of Retail, Distribution and Consumer Research*, *26*(3), 272–303. doi:10.1080/09593969.2015.1096808

Ama.org. (2015). *Dictionary*. Available from: https://www.ama.org/resources/pages/dictionary.aspx?dLetter=B

Amatulli, C., & Guido, G. (2011). Determinants of purchasing intention for fashion luxury goods in the Italian market. *Journal of Fashion Marketing and Management: An International Journal*, *15*(1), 123–136. doi:10.1108/13612021111112386

Amin, M., Rezaei, S., & Abolghasemi, M. (2014). User satisfaction with mobile websites: The impact of perceived usefulness (PU), perceived ease of use (PEOU) and trust. *Nankai Business Review International*, *5*(3), 258–274. doi:10.1108/NBRI-01-2014-0005

Amin, M., Rezaei, S., & Tavana, F. S. (2015). Gender differences and consumers repurchase intention: The impact of trust propensity, usefulness and ease of use for implication of innovative online retail. *International Journal of Innovation and Learning*, *17*(2), 217–233. doi:10.1504/IJIL.2015.067409

Brown, M., Pope, N., & Voges, K. (2003). Buying or browsing? *European Journal of Marketing*, *37*(11/12), 1666–1684. doi:10.1108/03090560310495401

Charles, K., Hurst, E., & Roussanov, N. (2009). Conspicuous Consumption and Race. *The Quarterly Journal of Economics*, *124*(2), 425–467. doi:10.1162/qjec.2009.124.2.425

Daliri, E., Rezaei, S., & Ismail, W. K. W. (2014). Online social shopping: The impact of attitude, customer information quality, effectiveness of information content and perceived social presence. *International Journal of Business Environment*, *6*(4), 426–450. doi:10.1504/IJBE.2014.064995

Din, D., & Sahn, F. (2013). Measuring the factors affecting Egyptian consumers` intentions to purchase global luxury fashion brands. *The Business and Management Review*, *3*(4), 44–59.

Durvasula, S., & Lysonski, S. (2008). A double edged sword: Understanding vanity across cultures. *Journal of Consumer Marketing*, *25*(4), 230–244. doi:10.1108/07363760810882425

Durvasula, S., Lysonski, S., & Watson, J. (2001). Does Vanity Describe Other Cultures? A Cross-Cultural Examination of the Vanity Scale. *The Journal of Consumer Affairs*, *35*(1), 180–199. doi:10.1111/j.1745-6606.2001.tb00108.x

Dzisah, W., & Ocloo, C. (2013). Celebrity Endorsement and Consumer Buying Behaviour; Enhancing the Promotion Function of Marketing in the Central Business Area of Accra, Ghana. *European Journal of Business and Management*, *5*(25), 197–209.

Eastman, J., Goldsmith, R., & Flynn, L. R. (1999). Status Consumption in Consumer Behavior: Scale Development and Validation. *Journal of Marketing Theory and Practice*, *7*(3), 41–51. doi:10.1080/10696679.1999.11501839

Euromonitor. (2015). Luxury Goods in Malaysia. *Euromonitor International.*

Freling, T., & Forbes, L. (2005). An empirical analysis of the brand personality effect. *Journal of Product and Brand Management*, *14*(7), 404–413. doi:10.1108/10610420510633350

Goldsmith, R., & Goldsmith, E. (2012). Brand Personality and Brand Engagement. *American Journal of Management*, *12*(1), 11–20.

Goody, J. (2006). From Misery to Luxury. *Social Sciences Information. Information Sur les Sciences Sociales*, *45*(3), 341–348. doi:10.1177/0539018406066526

Hung, K., Huiling Chen, A., Peng, N., Hackley, C., Amy Tiwsakul, R., & Chou, C. (2011). Antecedents of luxury brand purchase intention. *Journal of Product and Brand Management*, *20*(6), 457–467. doi:10.1108/10610421111166603

Indexmundi.com. (2015). *Malaysia Demographics Profile 2014.* Available from: http://www.indexmundi.com/malaysia/demographics_profile.html

Jamal, A., & Goode, M. (2001). Consumers and Brands: A study of the impact of self congruence on brand preferance and satisfaction. *Marketing Intelligence & Planning*, *19*(7), 482–492. doi:10.1108/02634500110408286

Joseph, P. (2000). How Personality Makes a Difference. *Journal of Advertising Research*, *40*(6), 79–83. doi:10.2501/JAR-40-6-79-83

Julian, C. C., Rezaei, S., & Amin, M. (2014). *14 The impact of knowledge management, brand orientation and global marketing strategy on performance. In Research Handbook on Export Marketing* (pp. 305–333). Edward Elgar Publishing.

Kalantari Shahijan, M., Rezaei, S., Nigel Preece, C., & Khairuzzaman Wan Ismail, W. (2014). Examining retailers behaviour in managing critical points in Halal meat handling: A PLS analysis. *Journal of Islamic Marketing*, *5*(3), 446–472. doi:10.1108/JIMA-10-2013-0070

Li, N. (2014). *The antecedents and consequences of brand commitment towards luxury brand buying behaviour: A study of mainland China* (Doctoral Thesis). University of Northumbria.

Maehle, N., & Shneor, R. (2010). On congruence between brand and human personalities. *Journal of Product and Brand Management*, *19*(1), 44–53.

Moghaddam, H. A., Rezaei, S., & Amin, M. (2015). Examining job seekers perception and behavioural intention toward online recruitment: A PLS path modelling approach. *Journal for Global Business Advancement*, *8*(3), 305–325. doi:10.1504/JGBA.2015.071331

Mohseni, S., Jayashree, S., Rezaei, S., Kasim, A., & Okumus, F. (2016). Attracting tourists to travel companies websites: The structural relationship between website brand, personal value, shopping experience, perceived risk and purchase intention. *Current Issues in Tourism*, 1–30. doi:10.1080/13683500.2016.1200539

Mulyanegara, R., & Tsarenko, Y. (2009). Predicting brand preferences. *Journal of Fashion Marketing and Management: An International Journal*, *13*(3), 358–371. doi:10.1108/13612020910974492

Mulyanegara, R., Tsarenko, Y., & Anderson, A. (2007). The Big Five and brand personality: Investigating the impact of consumer personality on preferences towards particular brand personality. *Journal of Brand Management*, *16*(4), 234–247. doi:10.1057/palgrave.bm.2550093

Murphy, J. (1990). Assessing the Value of Brands. *Long Range Planning*, *23*(3), 23–29. doi:10.1016/0024-6301(90)90049-A

Netemeyer, R., Burton, S., & Lichtenstein, D. (1995). Trait Aspects of Vanity: Measurement and Relevance to Consumer Behavior. *The Journal of Consumer Research*, *25*(4), 612–626.

O'Cass, A., & Frost, H. (2002). Status brands: Examining the effects of non product related brand associations on status and conspicuous consumption. *Journal of Product and Brand Management*, *11*(2), 67–88.

O'Cass, A., & Lim, K. (2001). The influence of Brand Associations on Brand Preference and Purchase Intention: An Asian Perspective on Brand Associations. *Journal of International Consumer Marketing*, *14*(2/3), 1–10.

O'Cass, A., & McEwen, H. (2004). Exploring Consumer Status and Conspicuous Consumption. *Journal of Consumer Behaviour*, *4*(1), 25–39. doi:10.1002/cb.155

O'Cass, A., & Siahtiri, V. (2014). Are young adult Chinese status and fashion clothing brand conscious? *Journal of Fashion Marketing and Management: An International Journal*, *18*(3), 284–300. doi:10.1108/JFMM-03-2012-0013

Ogden, H., & Venkat, R. (2001). Social comparison and possessions: Japan vs Canada. *Asia Pacific Journal of Marketing and Logistics*, *13*(2), 72–84. doi:10.1108/13555850110764775

Park, H., Rabolt, N., & Sook Jeon, K. (2008). Purchasing global luxury brands among young Korean consumers. *Journal of Fashion Marketing and Management: An International Journal*, *12*(2), 244–259. doi:10.1108/13612020810874917

Rageh Ismail, A., & Spinelli, G. (2012). Effects of brand love, personality and image on word of mouth. *Journal of Fashion Marketing and Management: An International Journal*, *16*(4), 386–398. doi:10.1108/13612021211265791

Ramaseshan, B., & Tsao, H. (2007). Moderating effects of the brand concept on the relationship between brand personality and perceived quality. *Journal Of Brand Management*, *14*(6), 458–456. doi:10.1057/palgrave.bm.2550090

Rezaei, S. (2015). Segmenting consumer decision-making styles (CDMS) toward marketing practice: A partial least squares (PLS) path modeling approach. *Journal of Retailing and Consumer Services*, *22*, 1–15. doi:10.1016/j.jretconser.2014.09.001

Rezaei, S., & Amin, M. (2013). Exploring online repurchase behavioural intention of university students in Malaysia. *Journal for Global Business Advancement*, *6*(2), 92–119. doi:10.1504/JGBA.2013.053561

Rezaei, S., Amin, M., & Ismail, W. K. W. (2014). Online repatronage intention: An empirical study among Malaysian experienced online shoppers. *International Journal of Retail & Distribution Management*, *42*(5), 390–421. doi:10.1108/IJRDM-03-2012-0026

Rezaei, S., Emami, M., & Valaei, N. (2016). *The moderating impact of product classification on the relationship between online trust, satisfaction, and repurchase intention. In Encyclopedia of E-Commerce Development, Implementation, and Management* (p. 1692). IGI Global.

Rezaei, S., & Ghodsi, S. S. (2014). Does value matters in playing online game? An empirical study among massively multiplayer online role-playing games (MMORPGs). *Computers in Human Behavior, 35*, 252–266. doi:10.1016/j.chb.2014.03.002

Rezaei, S., & Ismail, W. K. W. (2014). Examining online channel selection behaviour among social media shoppers: A PLS analysis. *International Journal of Electronic Marketing and Retailing, 6*(1), 28–51. doi:10.1504/IJEMR.2014.064876

Rezaei, S., Shahijan, M. K., Valaei, N., Rahimi, R., & Ismail, W. K. W. (2016). Experienced international business traveller's behaviour in Iran: A partial least squares path modelling analysis. *Tourism and Hospitality Research.*

Sajad, R., Muslim, A., Minoo, M., & Norshidah, M. (2016). *3G post adoption users experience with telecommunications services: a partial least squares (PLS) path modelling approach.* Nankai Business Review International. doi:10.1108/NBRI-01-2016-0007

Schooler, C. (2013). *Social Class and Social Status.* Oxford Bibliographies. doi:10.1093/OBO_dataset_home

Shahijan, M. K., Rezaei, S., & Preece, C. N. (2016). Developing a framework of internationalisation for higher education institutions in Malaysia: A SWOT analysis. *International Journal of Management in Education, 10*(2), 145–173. doi:10.1504/IJMIE.2016.075556

The Economist. (2014). *Disillusioned hedonist shoppers.* Available from: http://www.economist.com/blogs/schumpeter/2014/02/luxury-goods-market

Tsai, S. (2005). Impact of personal orientation on luxury-brand purchase value An international investigation. *International Journal of Market Research, 47*(4), 429–453.

Valaei, N., Rezaei, S., Ismail, W. K. W., & Moi, O. Y. (2016). Cultural effect on attitude toward online advertising and online brands: Applying Hofstedes cultural factors to Internet marketing. *International Journal of Internet Marketing and Advertising, 10*(4), 270. doi:10.1504/IJIMA.2016.081346

Zhang, B., & Hwan Kim, J. (2013). Luxury fashion consumption in China: Factors affecting attitude and purchase intent. *Journal of Retailing and Consumer Services, 20*(1), 68–79. doi:10.1016/j.jretconser.2012.10.007

KEY TERMS AND DEFINITIONS

Brand Personality: A set of human characteristics related to brands attributes that relate to consumer segment enjoyments.

Luxury Fashion Branded Apps: A prestige branded Apps in which a majority of its retail products are a high price or high quality.

Physical Vanity: Pride or admiration of a consumer own or achievements and appearance.

Social Status: The position or possible rank of an individual or group from the entire society.

Chapter 9
Post-Purchase Apps Usage Attitudes:
Revisiting Trust, Customer Satisfaction, and Loyalty of Apps Usage

Sajad Rezaei
Taylor's University, Malaysia

Srikaanth Sivasubramaniam
Taylor's University, Malaysia

Ree C. Ho
Taylor's University, Malaysia

ABSTRACT

The importance of relationship between customer and retailer has become prevalent in the ever-increasing competitive online market. The customers buying process often begin with the downloading of the required Apps in relation to the products they intended to purchase. Hence, customer satisfaction depends on customers' post-purchase evaluation on their experience with the use of the Apps. The aim of this chapter is to conceptualize the apps usage for online shopping, by examining the role of trust and satisfaction gained from the market interaction between the customers and retailers. Customers rely heavily on the information as well as the experiences encountered from the use of the apps. The retailers need to gain insights from the customer's perspective on the apps usage in order to improve customer relationship. This has impact on retailers' marketing efforts for winning the customers' loyalty.

DOI: 10.4018/978-1-5225-2449-6.ch009

Copyright ©2017, IGI Global. Copying or distributing in print or electronic forms without written permission of IGI Global is prohibited.

INTRODUCTION

Due to increasing competition, retailers need to attract more satisfied customers and transform them to be loyal to products and brands (Ye, Zhang, & Zan, 2009). The investments in both technology and human capital which include the development and management of the online apps are part of the operating cost of the online commerce. These costs are often huge financial commitment to many firms and are directly link to maintaining and improving customer satisfaction (Arnold, Reynolds, Ponder, & Lueg, 2005). Customer satisfaction undoubtedly remains as the main performance indicator to measure the customers' purchase intention. However, it is often noticed that even satisfied customers have the tendency to switch brands and retailers, especially within online shopping platform (Jones & Reynolds, 2006; Rezaei, Ali, Amin, & Jayashree, 2016; Rezaei, Amin, Moghaddam, & Mohamed, 2016; Rezaei, Shahijan, Amin, & Ismail, 2016; Yeo, Goh, & Rezaei, 2017). In their efforts in extending the European Customer Satisfaction Index (ECSI) model, Dwayne, et al., (2004) found that customer satisfaction, trust and communication are precursors to customer loyalty. Furthermore, customer satisfaction is affected greatly by the following factors: reliability, navigation, information responsiveness, site design, customer support, ease of use and security (Finn, Wang, & Frank, 2009). These factors apply to apps and the web, as apps inherit the similar characteristic from the user interface of the web.

Enormous efforts are devoted to researching and increasing the customer satisfaction in both online and offline businesses. Dwayne, et al., (2004) argue that customer satisfaction is crucial in leading to customer retention and loyalty. Previous studies (Alavi, Rezaei, Valaei, & Wan Ismail, 2016; Rezaei & Amin, 2013; Rezaei, Amin, et al., 2016; Rezaei, Emami, & Valaei, 2016) have been conducted in describing the mechanism and process of satisfaction. There is limited research attempt to investigate the concept of satisfaction from its root (Ye et al., 2009). Nevertheless, research stream focus on examining the customer satisfaction and loyalty have gradually progressed from offline environment to online environment, especially marketing journals in past few years (Jaiswal, Niraj, & Venugopal, 2010). This is envisaged to be the similar case with the deployment of apps in a mobile setting. Customer satisfaction is the key factor in leading to subsequent loyalty, and resulting in increasing company profits (Finn et al., 2009).

Therefore, marketers have attempted to discover the major factors leading to customer loyalty which customer satisfaction is noticeably one of the major driving force behind (Chang & Chen, 2009). Loyal customers derived from app usage are vital as they are the contributors for the profitability by reducing the cost to serve the customer and benefit from the positive worth of mouth (Armesh, Salarzehi, Yaghoobi, Heydari, & Nikbin, 2010a).

Customer Satisfaction and Loyalty Towards Apps Usage

Customer satisfaction is defined as the degree of the perceived product performance and expectations in satisfying customer needs (Jingdong & Xiaoqian, 2010). However, businesses treat customer satisfaction as the precursor in providing the monetary return for maintaining the profits necessary for their survival in the competitive market (Finn et al., 2009).

Customer loyalty and satisfaction are two distinctive concepts albeit their interdependency. It is obvious that a customer who is loyal may not essentially satisfied with the products and services, but not a highly satisfied customer is often loyal to the product or firm (Chang & Chen, 2008). Jones & Reynolds (2006) described loyalty as "a deeply held commitment to repurchase a particular brand or to re-patronize a particular retailer or service provider". This contradicts to customer satisfaction which is considered as an attitude (Tao, 2008).

Customer satisfaction has a significant effect on the following desired business dimensions (Arnold et al., 2005). Larger market share, higher profit, customer repurchase intentions, greater customer retention and positive word-of-mouth effects. It is important to note that loyalty is regarded as an on-going process, instead of an outcome (Dwayne, et al., (2004). This explains why the main strategic outcome of many marketing campaigns is to retain a customer by increasing customer loyalty (Wallace, Giese, & Johnson, 2004). Therefore, firms' profitability is highly correlated with customer repeat purchase with aid of the similar apps required as the transactional tool (Ye et al., 2009).

Customer satisfaction is critical for loyalty development in order for the customer to purchase from the be it online or offline retailers (M.-J. Kim, Chung, & Lee, 2011). In a normal situation, the return purchase would always be satisfied customers and often spread good words about the products (Chiou & Pan, 2009). The direct relationship between customer satisfaction and repeat patronage could generate positive feedback as established in many types of research (Jaiswal et al., 2010; Ye et al., 2009). Gefen, Karahanna and Straub (2003) found that perceived ease of use and familiarity of the web interface were important in driving re-purchase intention by satisfied customers in online retailing. Similarly, Chang and Burke (2007) gathered that the entire purchase and decision-making process can be critical in increasing customer satisfaction. In addition, good experiences from previous interaction with the retailers coupled with post-adoption expectations are vital in developing satisfied customers (Talai et. al. 2011). Previous studies (Zhang, Wang, Chen, & Rong, 2007) hailed that customers who are satisfied with the purchase process of one retailer from online transactions are not likely to purchase from another retailer. As for the app usage within online retailing, ease of use, information quality, and friendly interface are essentially needed in molding satisfied the customer (Armesh, Salarzehi, Yaghoobi, heydari, & Nikbin, 2010b).

Trust and Customer Satisfaction

In general, trust is defined as "willingness to rely on another based on expectations of ability, benevolence, and integrity" (Mary Ann & Sherry, 2011). Trust is a major determinant in online business (Jumin, Do-Hyung, & Ingoo, 2011). In the same vein, Wu & Chang (2006) describe online trust as "a dynamic process; trust can only be built over a certain period of time, and it usually contributes to customer satisfaction over and beyond the effects of the economic outcomes of the relationships.'' Trust leads to customer satisfaction and subsequently cultivates customer loyalty in the electronic channel (Jaiswal et al., 2010).

However, trust can be challenging to handle as it can be an individual belief about another's intention Andaleeb, (1995). According to (Ji-Seok, Jae-Nam, & Hoffmann, 2008), trust complicates the online buying process due to the specific features of electronic channel such as customer not being able to physically try out and touch the product, the waiting time for the product arrival after order made can be troubling and the anonymity of Internet leads to possibility of fraudulent shopping scams (Amin, Rezaei, & Abolghasemi, 2014; Amin, Rezaei, & Tavana, 2015; Rezaei & Ghodsi, 2014; Rezaei & Ismail, 2014). As for mobile shopping, trust on the apps required to perform the shopping tasks is necessary. With reference to TAM (Technology Acceptance Model), Gefen et. al. (2003) found that customer's trust on online retailers enables the acceptance of the online shopping channel.

Trust and Customer Loyalty

Chiou and Pan (2009) found that trust has a direct impact on retaining customers and developing customer loyalty in the electronic retailing environment. A Higher level of trust can be cultivated from the target segmentation resulting in greater sales volumes. The long list of studies in theorizing trust as the determinant in building customer relationship is one major research stream in marketing (Chiou & Pan, 2009; Dwayne et al., 2004).

It can be backdated to twenty years of rigorous works, especially in the perspective of trust as exchange agent (Andaleeb, 1995). Therefore, it is no surprise that the studies of perceived trust have been prevalent and extensively carried out in electronic commerce spectrum (Wu & Chang, 2006). However, many electronic commerce models developed tended to examine the role of trust in deciding the acceptance of web pages in general usage. This leads to the call of Wang and Chiang (2009) to call for more works in extending the more in depth of web as an online sales tool.

For instance, research work by M.-J. Kim, et al., (2011) which confirms the online trust has contributed to greater customer satisfaction, and improve customer retention and loyalty subsequently. Hence, online trust can be conceptualized in increasing the customer satisfaction when apps are used as the sales transaction tool.

In general, the existing literature on online trust is extensive but little effort has been placed on its impact on long-term development for enhancing the customer loyalty (Ji-Seok et al., 2008). The majority of the studies are devoted to examining the level of trust in web acceptance, especially the intention from the behavior perspective. However, customer trust toward the online sales tool is vital in developing a long-term profitable relationship (Chai Har, Uchenna Cyril, & Nelson Oly, 2011; Chiou & Pan, 2009).

The greater trust customer places on the online tool, the longer the relationship between the retailer and the customer (Liu, Marchewka, Lu, & Yu, 2005). Hence, it is critical for the firm to improve it for the development of customer loyalty. The lack of trust can often result in negative business consequences (Andaleeb, 1995). Trust appears to be prevalence in our day to day life. It is how one expresses his or her expected behavior as a result of his or her earlier experiential encounters (Juan Carlos, Juan José, & Juan José de la, 2009).

The direct relationship between trust and the electronic shopping acceptance were examined in the extant literature. Trust is regarded as the key determinant in influencing the positive attitudes in adopting the online shopping (Wahab & Elias, 2010). Alternatively, lack of trust and minimum protection over online customer confidentiality encumbers the business growth (Liu et al., 2005). Therefore, Rotem-Mindali (2010) propagated that trust was the main reason for many customers' rejection on accepting the electronic sales tools. Comparatively, customers often were rather a confidence and placed higher perceived trust in traditional brick and mortar sales environment (Mary Ann & Sherry, 2011).

It is important to regard trust over represents one direct effect on improving customer loyalty and customer retention (Dwayne et al., 2004). Consumers are expected to use apps for sales transaction rapidly and trust over its function as sales transaction tool is the key to its wide adoption. Therefore, online retailers have to cultivate the trust needed to increase the purchase intention by using it (Chen & Lee, 2008).

Trust and Attitude

The research stream which examines the direct influence of trust over the attitude toward purchase intention was prevalence in the electronic commerce (Dinev & Hart, 2005; Juan Carlos et al., 2009). It becomes noticeable when the transactions were conducted online due to its risky nature (J.-C. Wang & Chiang, 2009). A customer would be less likely to stick to the product or brand if he or she does not believe the online retailer is trustworthy (Dwayne et al., 2004). Online trust is about belief and customer would not buy by depending solely on the web interface (Tao, 2008). Trust is even more critical within online space over the traditional offline shopping (Liu et al., 2005).

According to Andaleeb, (1995) the effect of trust was directly related to the attitude of the respondents who were students instead of other users such as managers and executive. Trust often linked to the costs involved in completing the sales when viewed it from an economic perspective. For instance, a customer engaging in the online transaction may be swayed by crafty retailers who are seeking opportunities (Ji-Seok et al., 2008). One of the major objectives for the online vendors is to cultivate the customers' trust in them (Talal, Charles, & Sue Vaux, 2011). Comparatively, online shops have been viewed by customers as more unsafe than the offline brick and mortar setting (Chiou & Pan, 2009). Harris & Goode (2004) maintained that "establishing online customer loyalty is dependent on first generating consumer trust in the procedural rigor and operational abilities of the supplier and generating loyal customers online is both more difficult and more important than in offline retailing".

Customers were presented and provided with a variety of web interfaces, with non-uniform features, and run by millions of vendors ranging from small traders to large international corporations (Wu & Chang, 2006). (Mary Ann & Sherry, 2011) reasoned that customers' attitude and trust change from their first encounter with the vendors, and ultimately forming their institutional trust over the online purchase process. Furthermore, (Kim et al., 2011) suggested that trust building is a long-term ongoing process that builds the desired customer satisfaction required to produce the necessary monetary return for the online retailers. The entire process would cause the changes in social, psychology and management dimensions for both customers and vendors (Liu et al., 2005).

In a cross-cultural perspective, online customers in Asia tended to be more anxious and feel unsafe as compared to North American customers who are more accustomed to the online environment (Chiou & Pan, 2009). The degree of trust is a logical process cross over a period of time and often gained from a series of related interaction and experiences in both web and app interface (Mary Ann & Sherry, 2011). Therefore, the online purchase could not be carried if there is no trust between the parties involved (Wu & Chang, 2006). Rotem-Mindali (2010) believed that attitude is molded by the level of trust placed on the transacting medium over a substantial amount of time spent on it. There is a need to investigate what are the role of trust in determining the attitude of the customer towards the online shopping mechanism (J.-C. Wang & Chiang, 2009). Hence, it is proposed that trust exerts influence on the attitude of the customer on apps usage.

Attitude and Customer Satisfaction

Jones and Reynods (2006) proposed that customer loyalty towards the online vendors was caused by the residual amount of positive word of mouth and related hedonic feelings gained, such as excitement and enjoyment. With the increase of five percent of loyal customers can yield a surge of thirty to eighty percent of revenue depends on the nature of the business involved (Talal et al., 2011). Loyalty and satisfaction are closely associated and yet they are both two different concepts (Dwayne et al., 2004). Loyalty can be considered as both attitudinal and behavioral aspects. It is the return buying behavior demonstrated caused by desirable attitude over a lapse of time (Chang & Chen, 2008). Taylor & Strutton (2010) theorized that the ability of customers to assess the product quality largely depends on the following variables; perceived quality, ease of use and expected product performance. In general, the affective reactions would contribute to the subsequent attitude of the customers. There are two noticeable attitudes influencing the level of satisfied customer (Chang & Chen, 2009). The first being the transaction-specific approach which is caused by the emotions and feelings of customers derived from their recent involvements with the sellers and the cumulative satisfaction is solely determined by the total experience gained while transacting with an individual seller.

Customer satisfaction is often an outcome derived from an after-sale assessment of the customer over their experience with the vendors (Taylor & Strutton, 2010). Customers would perform the act of re-purchase the product from the same retailers only after they are satisfied with the quality of the products and experiences encountered. It is the same scenario with the online commerce (W. G. Kim, Ma, & Kim, 2006).

Chang & Chen (2008) further exposed that customer satisfaction is the precursor to cultivate customer loyalty in electronic commerce. Online loyalty is augmented by the improved customer satisfaction. In addition, Shankar, et al., (2003) found that customer loyalty and satisfaction mutually depend on each other. This kind of relationship evidently exists in electronic commerce environment. Delving further, the direct impact of customer satisfaction has a direct impact on the intention of return purchase (Taylor & Strutton, 2010). (M.-J. Kim et al., 2011) also conceived that the importance of customer loyalty in synthesizing the attitude to purchase, in addition to trust and customer satisfaction while customers are shopping online.

Attitude and Loyalty

Loyalty can be viewed from both attitude and behavior perspectives (Dwayne et al., 2004). Most of the works were devoted to examining loyalty based on the behavioral term, such as the frequency of purchase and re-purchase. There is a lack of studies focuses on attitude perspective. Customer satisfaction is the sole contributor to customer loyalty as presented in the in recent marketing literature (Ji-Seok et al., 2008). Many studies focus on examining their inter-dependency relationship, especially in B2B and B2C online shopping environment (Dwayne et al., 2004). The importance of customer satisfaction in gaining customer loyalty is highly needed but it is not the sole contributor. For instance, highly satisfied customers would be attracted to buy from another seller due to low switching costs, and dissatisfied customers may have to buy again if it is constrained by high switching costs (Chang & Chen, 2008).

Customers prefer resellers who are willing to reduce and solve product-related issues, such as firm whom they perceived as "zero defect". However, online retailers must place more efforts to attract and retain the customers in the long run (Baker, 2006). Customer satisfaction consists of the ultimate product assessment gained from both the product experience and usage, which subsequently mold the attitude of customers to re-purchase for increased revenue (Diehl & Poynor, 2010).

For instance, there a few stages involved in the purchase of a car, ranging from the initial search for information, the act of evaluating different options or models, and also the experiences with the employees of the car company. Andreas, Lan, Kent, & Frank (2007) posited that customer satisfaction gained from any one stage of the purchase process relates and influences other stages of the entire process. Retaining customer loyalty is getting more and more difficult for online retailers in the highly competitive online market. Especially as the switching costs involved by moving from one seller to another is rather low (Wallace et al., 2004).

Previous researches (Daliri, Rezaei, & Ismail, 2014; Rezaei, 2015; Rezaei, Amin, & Ismail, 2014; Rezaei & Ghodsi, 2014) recommended that the retailers provide customer oriented buying process in order to assist the customers and improve their customer experience. The customer would have higher satisfaction in using the retailers' web if they were pleased with the entire shopping process, which includes information searching, product evaluation, logistics in product delivery and return, as well as the customer support (Jaiswal et al., 2010).

The need to further understand the inter-dependency relationship of customer satisfaction and loyalty is pushing the firms to improvise and re-evaluate their overall marketing strategy, i.e. the deployment of customer-centered loyalty programs (Shankar et al., 2003). Online shopping experience provides the avenue to grasp a better understanding of consumer behavior and attitude (Chang & Chen, 2008). In addition, the online shopping experience was considered as a moderator in improving the web interface of the retailers. Positive and influential word of mouth produced by the satisfied customers has strong impacts on their circle of friends and family members (Finn et al., 2009).

With reference to the B2C online platform, Y. J. Wang, Hernandez, & Minor (2010) concluded that the attractiveness and usability of the web were critical in achieving greater customer satisfaction. The online customer satisfaction was an ongoing process affected by social, contextual and emotional factors (Taylor & Strutton, 2010). Customer loyalty and even complaints can be directly influenced by it (Dwayne et al., 2004). Conclusively, online customer loyalty was the extension of consumer behavior from the traditional offline shopping setting (Chang & Chen, 2008)

Trust is the foundation for developing effective and permanent profitable customer relationship and influences the future attitude for forming the customer loyalty envisage by the retailers (Wahab & Elias, 2010). The critical role of customer loyalty has draws the attentions of both academia and marketing practitioners. The Loyal customer would visit the online shopping sites repeatedly and purchase more. They are unlikely to sway by competitors' promotions and more likely to spread the good word of mouth about the product and retailers (Chai Har et al., 2011). The attitudinal loyalty and behavioral loyalty are substantially different:

1. **Behavioral Loyalty:** Shown by repeat purchase and can be measured with observational techniques.
2. **Attitudinal Loyalty:** Considered as positive and commitment in maintaining relationship and can be measured by questionnaire.

However, there is a dearth of work devoted to determining the precursors of online shopping's loyalty and customer retention (Chang & Chen, 2008). Furthermore, marketing practitioners are likely to emphasize on cultivating the relationship between customer satisfaction and loyalty (Shankar et al., 2003). Jaiswal, et al., (2010) stressed that customer satisfaction is the basis for successful sales transacted and it is the foundation for loyalty and purchase intention. Caruana & Ewing (2010) suggested that good grasp of the concept of loyalty would provide the avenue to plan for effective ways to retain the customers. Conversely, customer loyalty must be complement by return purchase, customer retention and purchase intention from the customer perspective (Finn et al., 2009).

CONCLUSION

Online trust is one of the key determinants in influencing the adoption of online business by customers (Ji-Seok et al., 2008). Laroche (2010) suggested that more research works should be carried out to investigate the role of trust in online retailers, as well as the determinants and outcome values of trust for further understanding the behavior of the online customers. Trust is what others would expect one's attitude and behavior not to behave opportunistically (Talal et al., 2011).

Harris & Goode (2004) concluded that the importance of trust to yield the customer loyalty for online retailers. This is because the development and continuance of loyalty are sophisticated which is built upon customer trust (Chen & Lee, 2008). Lack of trust could lead customers' refusal to purchase from these unworthy retailers whom they could not rely on (Chai Har et al., 2011; Mary Ann & Sherry, 2011). Lack of trust is pervasive in Apps business and contributes to the weak and volatile relationship between customers and retailers (Andaleeb, 1995). Therefore, it is important for online retailers to understand the three major dimensions of trust. as suggested by (Tao, 2008). First, the retailer's ability, this is when the customers consider retailers' expertise and know-how. Second is integrity, this is when customers have faith in the retailers to keep their promise. Third is benevolence, this is when customers have confidence that the retailers are protecting customers' interest

Gefen, et al., (2003) further elaborated that customers return to buy again because they were convinced by the trust mechanism proposed by the retailers. Trust was more important than the web features and functions provided by the online mechanism. Obviously, customers would expect the online sales channel to maintain high degree trust and guarantee their purchases. Hence, substantial of research studies and marketing initiatives have been devoted to examining trust in facilitating the online business (Juan Carlos et al., 2009). The position of trust in providing reliable sales medium was equally critical (M.-J. Kim et al., 2011).

Andaleeb (1995) theorized that the attitude derived from the behavioral intention of the involved parties in electronic commerce was moderated by high level of perceived trust. The success of online shopping mall often determined by how well the customers viewed it as a trustworthy transactional channel (Jumin et al., 2011). Customers would not want to purchase from the online retailers who could not deliver the sense of trustworthiness (Talal et al., 2011). Conclusively, trust building process has to be developed between the transacting parties once they were satisfied with the experiences gained (Mary Ann & Sherry, 2011).

REFERENCES

Alavi, S. A., Rezaei, S., Valaei, N., & Wan Ismail, W. K. (2016). Examining shopping mall consumer decision-making styles, satisfaction and purchase intention. *International Review of Retail, Distribution and Consumer Research*, *26*(3), 272–303. doi:10.1080/09593969.2015.1096808

Amin, M., Rezaei, S., & Abolghasemi, M. (2014). User satisfaction with mobile websites: The impact of perceived usefulness (PU), perceived ease of use (PEOU) and trust. *Nankai Business Review International*, *5*(3), 258–274. doi:10.1108/NBRI-01-2014-0005

Amin, M., Rezaei, S., & Tavana, F. S. (2015). Gender differences and consumers repurchase intention: The impact of trust propensity, usefulness and ease of use for implication of innovative online retail. *International Journal of Innovation and Learning*, *17*(2), 217–233. doi:10.1504/IJIL.2015.067409

Andaleeb, S. S. (1995). Dependence relations and the moderating role of trust: Implications for behavioral intentions in marketing channels. *International Journal of Research in Marketing*, *12*(2), 157–172. doi:10.1016/0167-8116(94)00020-O

Andreas, H., Lan, X., Kent, B. M., & Frank, H. (2007). The influence of price fairness on customer satisfaction: An empirical test in the context of automobile purchases. *Journal of Product and Brand Management*, *16*(1), 49–58. doi:10.1108/10610420710731151

Armesh, H., Salarzehi, H., & Yaghoobi, N. M. (2010b). Impact of Online/Internet Marketing on Computer Industry in Malaysia in Enhancing Consumer Experience. *International Journal of Marketing Studies*, *2*(2), 75–86. doi:10.5539/ijms.v2n2p75

Armesh, H., Salarzehi, H., Yaghoobi, N. M., Heydari, A., & Nikbin, D. (2010a). The Effects of Security and Privacy Information on Trust & Trustworthiness and Loyalty in Online Marketing in Malaysia. *International Journal of Marketing Studies*, *2*(2), 223–234. doi:10.5539/ijms.v2n2p223

Arnold, M. J., Reynolds, K. E., Ponder, N., & Lueg, J. E. (2005). Customer delight in a retail context: Investigating delightful and terrible shopping experiences. *Journal of Business Research*, *58*(8), 1132–1145. doi:10.1016/j.jbusres.2004.01.006

Baker, S. M. (2006). Consumer normalcy: Understanding the value of shopping through narratives of consumers with visual impairments. *Journal of Retailing*, *82*(1), 37–50. doi:10.1016/j.jretai.2005.11.003

Caruana, A., & Ewing, M. T. (2010). How corporate reputation, quality, and value influence online loyalty. *Journal of Business Research*, *63*(9-10), 1103–1110. doi:10.1016/j.jbusres.2009.04.030

Chai Har, L., Uchenna Cyril, E., & Nelson Oly, N. (2011). Analyzing key determinants of online repurchase intentions. *Asia Pacific Journal of Marketing and Logistics*, *23*(2), 200–221. doi:10.1108/13555851111120498

Chang, H. H., & Chen, S. W. (2008). The impact of customer interface quality, satisfaction and switching costs on e-loyalty: Internet experience as a moderator. *Computers in Human Behavior*, *24*(6), 2927–2944. doi:10.1016/j.chb.2008.04.014

Chang, H. H., & Chen, S. W. (2009). Consumer perception of interface quality, security, and loyalty in electronic commerce. *Information & Management*, *46*(7), 411–417. doi:10.1016/j.im.2009.08.002

Chen, S.-H., & Lee, K.-P. (2008). The Role Of Personality Traits And Perceived Values In Persuasion: An Elaboration Likelihood Model Perspective On Online Shopping. *Social Behavior & Personality: An International Journal*, *36*(10), 1379–1400. doi:10.2224/sbp.2008.36.10.1379

Chiou, J.-S., & Pan, L.-Y. (2009). Antecedents of Internet Retailing Loyalty: Differences Between Heavy Versus Light Shoppers. *Journal of Business and Psychology*, *24*(3), 327–339. doi:10.1007/s10869-009-9111-7

Daliri, E., Rezaei, S., & Ismail, W. K. W. (2014). Online social shopping: The impact of attitude, customer information quality, effectiveness of information content and perceived social presence. *International Journal of Business Environment*, *6*(4), 426–450. doi:10.1504/IJBE.2014.064995

Diehl, K., & Poynor, C. (2010). Great Expectations?! Assortment Size, Expectations, and Satisfaction. *JMR, Journal of Marketing Research*, *47*(2), 312–322. doi:10.1509/jmkr.47.2.312

Dinev, T., & Hart, P. (2005). Internet Privacy Concerns and Social Awareness as Determinants of Intention to Transact. *International Journal of Electronic Commerce*, *10*(2), 7–29. doi:10.2753/JEC1086-4415100201

Dwayne, B., Pedro Simões, C., & Alexandra, M. (2004). The role of communication and trust in explaining customer loyalty: An extension to the ECSI model. *European Journal of Marketing*, *38*(9), 1272–1293.

Finn, A., Wang, L., & Frank, T. (2009). Attribute Perceptions, Customer Satisfaction and Intention to Recommend E-Services. *Journal of Interactive Marketing*, *23*(3), 209–220. doi:10.1016/j.intmar.2009.04.006

Gefen, D., Karahanna, E., & Straub, D. W. (2003). Inexperience and experience with online stores: The importance of TAM and trust. *Engineering Management. IEEE Transactions on*, *50*(3), 307–321.

Harris, L. C., & Goode, M. M. H. (2004). The four levels of loyalty and the pivotal role of trust: A study of online service dynamics. *Journal of Retailing*, *80*(2), 139–158. doi:10.1016/j.jretai.2004.04.002

Jaiswal, A. K., Niraj, R., & Venugopal, P. (2010). Context-general and Context-specific Determinants of Online Satisfaction and Loyalty for Commerce and Content Sites. *Journal of Interactive Marketing*, *24*(3), 222–238. doi:10.1016/j.intmar.2010.04.003

Ji-Seok, Y., Jae-Nam, L., & Hoffmann, J. (2008). *Trust in Online Shopping: The Korean Student Experience.* Paper presented at the Hawaii International Conference on System Sciences.

Jingdong, C., & Xiaoqian, G. (2010). *The Theory and Empirical Research of Network Profit Based on the Perceived Value.* Paper presented at the Computer Modeling and Simulation, 2010. ICCMS '10. Second International Conference on.

Jones, M. A., & Reynolds, K. E. (2006). The role of retailer interest on shopping behavior. *Journal of Retailing*, *82*(2), 115–126. doi:10.1016/j.jretai.2005.05.001

Juan Carlos, R., & Juan José, G. (2009). The importance of perceived trust, security and privacy in online trading systems. *Information Management & Computer Security*, *17*(2), 96–113. doi:10.1108/09685220910963983

Jumin, L., Do-Hyung, P., & Ingoo, H. (2011). The different effects of online consumer reviews on consumers purchase intentions depending on trust in online shopping malls: An advertising perspective. *Internet Research*, *21*(2), 187–206. doi:10.1108/10662241111123766

Kim, M.-J., Chung, N., & Lee, C.-K. (2011). The effect of perceived trust on electronic commerce: Shopping online for tourism products and services in South Korea. *Tourism Management*, *32*(2), 256–265. doi:10.1016/j.tourman.2010.01.011

Kim, W. G., Ma, X., & Kim, D. J. (2006). Determinants of Chinese hotel customers e-satisfaction and purchase intentions. *Tourism Management*, *27*(5), 890–900. doi:10.1016/j.tourman.2005.05.010

Laroche, M. (2010). Advances in internet consumer behavior and marketing strategy: Introduction to the special issue. *Journal of Business Research*, *63*(9-10), 1015–1017. doi:10.1016/j.jbusres.2009.06.010

Liu, C., Marchewka, J. T., Lu, J., & Yu, C.-S. (2005). Beyond concern a privacy-trust-behavioral intention model of electronic commerce. *Information & Management*, *42*(2), 289–304. doi:10.1016/j.im.2004.01.003

Mary Ann, E., & Sherry, L. (2011). Cognitive and institutional predictors of initial trust toward an online retailer. *International Journal of Retail & Distribution Management, 39*(4), 234–255. doi:10.1108/09590551111117527

Rezaei, S. (2015). Segmenting consumer decision-making styles (CDMS) toward marketing practice: A partial least squares (PLS) path modeling approach. *Journal of Retailing and Consumer Services, 22*, 1–15. doi:10.1016/j.jretconser.2014.09.001

Rezaei, S., Ali, F., Amin, M., & Jayashree, S. (2016). Online impulse buying of tourism products: The role of web site personality, utilitarian and hedonic web browsing. *Journal of Hospitality and Tourism Technology, 7*(1), 60–83. doi:10.1108/JHTT-03-2015-0018

Rezaei, S., & Amin, M. (2013). Exploring online repurchase behavioural intention of university students in Malaysia. *Journal for Global Business Advancement, 6*(2), 92–119. doi:10.1504/JGBA.2013.053561

Rezaei, S., Amin, M., & Ismail, W. K. W. (2014). Online repatronage intention: An empirical study among Malaysian experienced online shoppers. *International Journal of Retail & Distribution Management, 42*(5), 390–421. doi:10.1108/IJRDM-03-2012-0026

Rezaei, S., Amin, M., Moghaddam, M., & Mohamed, N. (2016). 3G post adoption users experience with telecommunications services. *Nankai Business Review International, 7*(3), 361–394. doi:10.1108/NBRI-01-2016-0007

Rezaei, S., Emami, M., & Valaei, N. (2016). *The moderating impact of product classification on the relationship between online trust, satisfaction, and repurchase intention. In Encyclopedia of E-Commerce Development, Implementation, and Management* (p. 1692). IGI Global.

Rezaei, S., & Ghodsi, S. S. (2014). Does value matters in playing online game? An empirical study among massively multiplayer online role-playing games (MMORPGs). *Computers in Human Behavior, 35*, 252–266. doi:10.1016/j.chb.2014.03.002

Rezaei, S., & Ismail, W. K. W. (2014). Examining online channel selection behaviour among social media shoppers: A PLS analysis. *International Journal of Electronic Marketing and Retailing, 6*(1), 28–51. doi:10.1504/IJEMR.2014.064876

Rezaei, S., Shahijan, M. K., Amin, M., & Ismail, W. K. W. (2016). Determinants of App Stores Continuance Behavior: A PLS Path Modelling Approach. *Journal of Internet Commerce, 15*(4), 408–440. doi:10.1080/15332861.2016.1256749

Rotem-Mindali, O. (2010). E-tail versus retail: The effects on shopping related travel empirical evidence from Israel. *Transport Policy*, *17*(5), 312–322. doi:10.1016/j.tranpol.2010.02.005

Shankar, V., Smith, A. K., & Rangaswamy, A. (2003). Customer satisfaction and loyalty in online and offline environments. *International Journal of Research in Marketing*, *20*(2), 153–175. doi:10.1016/S0167-8116(03)00016-8

Talal, A., Charles, D., & Sue Vaux, H. (2011). Antecedents of continuance intentions towards e-shopping: The case of Saudi Arabia. *Journal of Enterprise Information Management*, *24*(1), 85–111. doi:10.1108/17410391111097447

Tao, Z. (2008). *The Impact of Perceived Value on User Acceptance of Mobile Commerce*. Paper presented at the Electronic Commerce and Security, 2008 International Symposium on.

Taylor, D. G., & Strutton, D. (2010). Has e-marketing come of age? Modeling historical influences on post-adoption era Internet consumer behaviors. *Journal of Business Research*, *63*(9-10), 950–956. doi:10.1016/j.jbusres.2009.01.018

Wahab, S., & Elias, J. (2010). *The influence of trust on electronic banking adoption: Views of Malaysian university lecturers*. Paper presented at the Advanced Management Science (ICAMS), 2010 IEEE International Conference on.

Wallace, D. W., Giese, J. L., & Johnson, J. L. (2004). Customer retailer loyalty in the context of multiple channel strategies. *Journal of Retailing*, *80*(4), 249–263. doi:10.1016/j.jretai.2004.10.002

Wang, J.-C., & Chiang, M.-J. (2009). Social interaction and continuance intention in online auctions: A social capital perspective. *Decision Support Systems*, *47*(4), 466–476. doi:10.1016/j.dss.2009.04.013

Wang, Y. J., Hernandez, M. D., & Minor, M. S. (2010). Web aesthetics effects on perceived online service quality and satisfaction in an e-tail environment: The moderating role of purchase task. *Journal of Business Research*, *63*(9-10), 935–942. doi:10.1016/j.jbusres.2009.01.016

Wu, J.-J., & Chang, Y.-S. (2006). Effect of transaction trust on e-commerce relationships between travel agencies. *Tourism Management*, *27*(6), 1253–1261. doi:10.1016/j.tourman.2005.06.009

Ye, J.-h., Zhang, M.-l., & Zan, J.-Y. (2009). *Study on Customer Satisfaction in Benefit/Sacrifice Hierarchy*. Paper presented at the Fuzzy Systems and Knowledge Discovery, 2009. FSKD '09. Sixth International Conference on.

Yeo, V. C. S., Goh, S.-K., & Rezaei, S. (2017). Consumer experiences, attitude and behavioral intention toward online food delivery (OFD) services. *Journal of Retailing and Consumer Services*, *35*, 150–162. doi:10.1016/j.jretconser.2016.12.013

Zhang, R., Wang, K., Chen, K., & Rong, R. (2007). *Customer Switching Intention in Service Industries and the Effect of Customer Perceived Value.* Paper presented at the Service Operations and Logistics, and Informatics, 2007. SOLI 2007. IEEE International Conference on.

KEY TERMS AND DEFINITIONS

Apps Trust: A consumer's intention to rely on as honest or truthful Apps retail.

Attitudinal Loyalty: The positive and commitment in maintaining relationship and can be measured by questionnaire.

Behavioral Loyalty: Shown by repeat purchase and can be measured with observational techniques.

Trust: Willingness to rely on another based on expectations of ability, benevolence, and integrity.

Chapter 10
Apps in Hospitality and Tourism:
Conceptualization of Branded Apps in Building Traveler Satisfaction and Loyalty

Sajad Rezaei
Taylor's University, Malaysia

Milad Kalantari Shahijan
Universiti Teknologi, Malaysia

ABSTRACT

The development of Apps usage in the tourism industry is along with the rise of relevant technologies that has affected the tourism industry all around the world. In order to build a competitive brand, firms are forced to implement the information technology related functions in their core business model. This chapter mainly focuses on the impact of Apps implementation in hospitality and tourism sector and conceptually propose that how branded Apps could yield tourist satisfaction and loyalty. Apps awareness, Apps quality and Apps image are proposed as several indicators of traveler's satisfaction and loyalty. The chapter argue that branding makes a business advantage; the brand follows indication of quality and assurance to the buyer and also special characteristics that could inspire consumers to buy products or services that are branded.

DOI: 10.4018/978-1-5225-2449-6.ch010

Copyright ©2017, IGI Global. Copying or distributing in print or electronic forms without written permission of IGI Global is prohibited.

INTRODUCTION

One of the key research topics is considered to be brand equity for customer-based view in marketing management context in the late 1990's and early 2000's; therefore, it has been identified as a significant element build a competitive advantage and marketing approaches for distinction (Ferns & Walls, 2012; Kim, Kim, et al., 2008). Brand equity is a valuable, yet fragile, firm asset (Buil et al., 2013; Seo & Jang, 2013). The relationship between satisfaction and brand equity is very vague (Wong, 2013). The literature regarding brand equity, specifically about hospitality and tourism, commonly lacks in research (Oh & Hsu, 2014). Furthermore, equity of a brand is the main index for brand achievement. Realizing this and developing equity of a brand is definitely crucial for operators (Buil et al., 2013).

Branding makes a business advantage; the brand follows the indication of quality and assurance to the buyer and also special characteristics that could inspire consumers to buy products or services that are branded (Lee & Back, 2010). Previous studies have investigated about the correlation among variables, for instance, consumer satisfaction as well as consumer loyalty, and found that there is a shortage of analysis regarding equity of brand and brand loyalty, which are influenced by customer satisfaction (Nam et al., 2011). Thus, by using the hospitality notion in service delivery businesses can easily motivate the interplay among receivers and suppliers, where provisions affect an intricate blend of food, beverage and also accommodation (Teng, 2011).

Branding has existed for many centuries as a method of differentiating the goods of one producer from another (Sheng & Teo, 2012). The topic of customer loyalty has received attention since the 1990s when relationship marketing became popular; perhaps, businesses are attempting to find out different methods in order to improve the effectiveness of loyalty marketing (Yoo & Bai, 2013). It is very difficult and expensive to gain a new customer due to advertising, and promotion and as such, it is better to retain and serve the current customers (Power et al., 2001). Customer loyalty is described as an individual's repeated purchase or visitation behavior while including the emotional pledge (Yoo & Bai, 2013). The focus on brand equity is on the advantages of powerful brand equity, which is called the buffering point of view (Seo & Jang, 2013). The hospitality organizations have admitted that the scope of marketing is to collect as many new customers as it is feasible (Ajzen et al., 1980).

Therefore, to build a competitive brand, firms are forced to implement the information technology related functions in their core business model. This chapter mainly focuses on the impact of Apps implementation in hospitality and tourism sector and conceptually propose that how branded Apps could yield tourist satisfaction and loyalty. Apps awareness, Apps quality, and Apps image are proposed as several indicators of traveler's satisfaction and loyalty.

APPS IN TOURISM AND HOSPITALITY SECTOR

The fast development of information communication technologies and the expansion of the internet have changed industry structures around the world (Ma et al., 2003). Perhaps, impacts even more on the tourism industry than on any other (Amin et al., 2014; Bhat & Shah, 2014; Daliri et al., 2014; Rezaei & Amin, 2013). Similarly, the internet has played a fundamental role in reshaping the means through which information related to tourism is transmitted as well as the plans people draw in preparation for travel and how they consume it (Buhalis & Law, 2008).

Today, the tourism industry is one of the major users of internet technology (Yuan et al., 2003). In order to provide reliable and accurate information, for example, travel agencies, use IT for reservation, accounting, and inventory management functions (Alavi et al., 2016; Rezaei et al., 2014; Shahijan et al., 2015; Standing et al., 2014). Likewise, the internet has been the major source of information for tourists around the world (Anwar et al., 2014). According to McCabe et al. (2012) tourists are expecting to know what is available to a destination, book travel, accommodation and visitor attractions, find relevant information before and during the trip, capture and share experiences. Therefore, the apps tourism help facilitate those interactions and most importantly will free up the precious time as well as save the tourists from frustration.

Apps tourism refer to mobile apps that are specifically targeted at tourists such as Airbnb, Tripadvisor, Skyscanner as well as those used in a typical travel context, for example Google map, Money, Instagram (Lu, Mao, et al., 2015). The rapid uptake of mobile technology has enabled people to negotiate their day-to-day mobility with increasing fluidity and providing scope for decision-making on the go, based on networked connectivity between people (Dickinson et al., 2014). Likewise, smartphones are becoming a primary platform for information access and a primary application area for mobile applications is tourism (Alavi et al., 2016; Pesonen & Horster, 2012; Rezaei et al., 2014; Shahijan et al., 2015). In particular, it is possible to access a broad variety of tourism and hospitality related mobile applications (Adukaite et al., 2013). Moreover, the smartphone offers a wide range of possibilities to support tourists in their use of information and communications home and away (Wang et al., 2015). The link between tourism and information communication technology, whilst always strong, changes with every new generation of technologies, as well as with people, location, and culture (O'Regan & Chang, 2015).

Building Competitive Brand Strategy

Indeed, brand equity is a significant notion in management practice and also in academic research, because brand achievement can let the dealer and the marketer obtain a competitive advantage such as expansion of opportunity and the ability to make some limit for rivalry entry (Kim, Kim, et al., 2008). Despite the significance of branding, the restaurant sector needs more studies in terms of brand research (Hyun, 2009). Brands will improve the trust of customers especially for an intangible purchase, and also the risk perception will reduce as well by helping the customers to conceive and understand the intangible form of service products (Lee & Back, 2008). The methods of branding have become such a powerful mechanism for destinations where tourists are visiting because the brand is able to make a positive brand image and identity that particular destination (Esper & Rateike, 2010). The hospitality industries can expand their share of the market by raising the number of their loyal customers; perhaps, this is an appropriate approach compared to other marketing activities, for example: discounting or promotional agenda (Power et al., 2001) and indicates that managers and the employees of the hotel should strive as much as possible to impact quality, brand loyalty and brand image as well as brand awareness in their hotels and also they need to design a procedure to deliver services based on the relations among customer brand equity constructs (Mohseni et al., 2016; Rezaei, Ali, et al., 2016; Rezaei, Amin, et al., 2016; Shahijan et al., 2016; Yeo et al., 2017).

Brand achievement does not only assist in developing a powerful identity for the products of the organization but it can also impact the preferences that assist the brands as a competitive advantage (Toufaily et al., 2013). Via communication of brand, the brand works as a tool in order to involve both seller and buyer in the long term consumer brand relationship (Hair et al., 2013). Brand commitment implies on commitment or binding of the individual self-behavior, which shows an association between internal attitude and public behavior (Brady et al., 2008). The research result has attributed to the hotel as an organization which should literally take quality perception, brand image, and loyalty into consideration when attempting to describe brand equity from customer's viewpoint (Goswami et al., 2012).

Brand Equity Dimensions

"Hospitality implies on the hosting behavior that impacts hospitality or hospitable nature of the hotel services" (Ariffin & Maghzi, 2012, p. 192). A brand is defined as an indication for a collection of products decided for sale by the same organizational entity (Randall et al., 1998). Brand equity is applied as a pressure indicator of brand stability via the use of its name, logo, and symbol (Lee & Back, 2008). Additionally, a brand is considered as a legal material, company, logo, image, personality, and identity system and relationship or adding value. "Brand Equity is a set of brand assets and liabilities linked to a brand, its name, and symbol that add to or subtract from the value provided by a product or service to a firm and/

Table 1. Brand equity dimensions

Dimension	Definition
1. Awareness	It demonstrates the presence of the brand in the memory which can influence perception and attitudes
2. Loyalty	The connection of the customers towards a brand, and his or her intention to purchase again or recommend it to others
3. Perceived Value	Consumers overall assessment of the brand based on the perception that they have regarding other kinds of brands
4. Perceived Quality	The consumer's belief and opinion on the priority or excellence of the brand.
5. Image	According to numerous studies, the personality of a brand can make a unique group and desirable affiliation in the mind of the consumers.

Source: Alahuhta et al., (2005)

or to that firm's customers" (Oh & Hsu, 2014). Customers brand equity can be the different effects of consumer response by brand knowledge in order to market the brand (Keller, 1993). From a product perspective, brand equity implies on the brand name value which it brings to a particular product (Liao & Cheng, 2014). Table 1 shows the brand equity dimensions.

A previous research has proposed that building brand equity can improve the rivalry advantage (Nyadzayo et al., 2011). A final direction within planning, management and the literature of strategy is the fact and essence of the branding study (Line & Runyan, 2012). Brand equity is very significant therefore it can create certain brand associates in the customers' minds and show a common market about the reliability of that brand (Hyun, 2009). Brand equity has different definition terms such as desirable impressions attitudinal disposition and behavioral forecasting (Sheng & Teo, 2012). Brand equity follows consumers' desirable, powerful, and unique attitudes which are related to a branded product (Liao & Cheng, 2014). From the consumer point of view, brand equity will take place when the individual customer is familiar with the desirable association of any brand which is already in his or her mind (Wong, 2013). Interestingly the brand, which is well-known globally, will remain in numerous markets, such as financial services or telecom or even those from the fast moving consumer commodity market.

Brand equity is actually wider in terms of a concept which embraces the image of the brand; for example, service quality perception and brand familiarity (Nam et al., 2011). Brand equity is a customer's emotion about the intangible measurement of the particular brand as well as the value (Kim & Ko, 2012). There are four most broadly recognized and cited variables by scholars such as perceived quality, brand awareness, brand image, and brand loyalty in the customer based notion of brand equity (Namkung & Jang, 2013). One of the significant factors in business to business market and business to consumer is brand building which can separate the organization away from its rivals and perhaps improve the market share (Amin et al., 2014; Daliri et al., 2014; Nyadzayo et al., 2011; Rezaei & Amin, 2013). Basically, the brand equity concept is established in the business to customer market and it is well-known and recognized; the equity of brand and brand management are critical for achievement in this particular context (Biedenbach et al., 2011). In fact, brand equity could appear as the added value to any particular product or the one which is already in the minds of consumers (Kim, Kim, et al., 2008).

Conceptual Model and Propositions

A summarized paper about brand equity literature shows that there are three types of basic frameworks in order to realize and assess brand equity such as (1) Aaker's (1991) model, which is a commanding vision of brand equity; (2) Keller's (Zhou, 2011) Psychological or memory vision of brand equity, and (3) (Kautonen et al., 2007). The brand equity model has based on economic data as well as the theory of signaling (Haverila, 2011). Progressively, the brand is very significant to the organizations and managers; similarly, academics have indicated that they have a keen interest in order to measure the brands' value (Voleti & Ghosh, 2013). The brand is defined as a single and specific name or a symbol that comprises of trademark, logo or even package design in order to identify and distinguish the products or services of a particular organization (Aaker, 1991). To be specific, it can be any name, symbol, design, sign, and term or even a combination of these in order to identify products or services of an individual or group of sellers to differentiate them from other competitors (Kotler 1991, 442). Branding is able to differentiate two products from each other by making different brand factors such as name, logo, package design, and symbol, as it gets some value for the particular organization not only in terms of economic benefit but also creates reputation awareness as well as prominence in the market (Esper & Rateike, 2010).

Apps Awareness

"Brand awareness includes consumer recognition, top-of-mind awareness, knowledge dominance, and recall performance of brands, as well as brand attitude" (Kim, Kim, et al., 2008, p. 77). "Loyalty is defined as a profoundly held pledge to buy again or encourage a preferable product or service continually in the future" (Callarisa et al., 2012, p. 75). "Brand loyalty has traditionally been conceived as a behavioral construct relating to intentions towards repeat purchase" (Nam et al., 2011, p. 1011). Service industry's quality can be illustrated based on three important unique attributes of services such as intangibility, heterogeneity, and inseparability of production and consumption (Bastič & Gojčič, 2012). The notion of quality of service is broadly acknowledged as being multi-dimensional; besides, the amount and figure of its characteristics could still be disputed (Nam et al., 2011).

Positive reputation associated with the brand could create trust, which is generated by products and services offered in the past (Kim, Ferrin, et al., 2008). Consumer awareness influences their satisfaction and trust; therefore, a well-known website has greater capability to fulfill customer needs than other brands (Chang & Chen, 2008). The physical quality projects images by using such aspects like facilities, tools, design as well as hotel industry materials whereas the behavior of staff are just an illustration which is planned by qualification, friendliness, helpfulness of the hotel/restaurant employees and workers (Nam et al., 2011, p. 113). Consumers perceive that controlling or using the service can draw out a positive sensation (Cronin Jr et al., 2000). The overall satisfaction is an assessment of the last purchase moment and according to all confrontations with the service provider (Nam et al., 2011, p. 114). Basically, satisfaction is considered as dealing with a specific assessment of the moment of truth which promptly decays, at the post-purchasing point, among the consumers' overall attitude to the service firm (Ekinci et al., 2008). However, the study was done by Lee and Back (2010) regarding the differential effects of brand knowledge and shown that brand awareness is negatively associated with brand satisfaction.

Awareness is considered as the central element of the effects of the brand in the tourists' behavior (Callarisa et al., 2012). Similarly, awareness can help in building loyalty (Rana et al., 2015). A study was explored how online promotion and its influence on awareness and loyalty in the tourism industry and found that there is a strong, significant relationship among awareness and loyalty (Lai & Vinh, 2013). Moreover, awareness is recognized as a prerequisite for loyalty as consumers tend to trust a high-awareness brand and purchase products and services of that brand more frequently (Hyun & Kim, 2011; Lu, Gursoy, et al., 2015). According to Hsu et al. (2011) loyalty results partially from strong awareness; hence, awareness is positively related to loyalty. Conversely, Makanyeza (2015) stated that consumer awareness does not influence consumer loyalty and revealed that as consumers become aware of their rights and responsibilities in the marketplace, they can make informed purchase decisions. Thus:

P1: Apps awareness influences traveler satisfaction.
P2: Apps awareness influences traveler loyalty.

Apps Quality

Brand quality refers to "consumers' global assessments and judgments of the superiority or excellence of a product or services" (Dens & Pelsmacker, 2016, p. 466). Quality is one of the most important elements frequently used by tourism researchers (Im et al., 2012; Liu et al., 2014). Similarly, quality is considered to be an important management tool for being competitive, as positive quality affects customer satisfaction (Benitez et al., 2007). Quality in general acts as a significant predictor of satisfaction; and this relationship is fundamental in generating behavioral intentions (Han & Hyun, 2015). According to Dortyol et al. (2014) quality is a conceptual reaction, customer satisfaction consists of both conceptual and affective reactions. Sigurðardóttir and Helgadóttir (2015) pointed out that, customer satisfaction may be a broader concept than quality, but a low level of quality is likely to reduce the total satisfaction of customers. In the same vein, Thaichon and Quach (2015) stated that consumers will evaluate quality to determine satisfaction. Su et al. (2016) stated that quality has a significant effect on satisfaction. Likewise, quality is an important factor influencing satisfaction which should receive special attention in the tourism management context (Allameh et al., 2015). Moreover, the study investigated the determinants of current visitors' festival revisit intentions and stated that festival quality has been used as a precursor to festival satisfaction (Choo et al., 2016).

Tran et al. (2013) asserted that quality can be critical to predicting loyalty. The increasing recognition of perceived quality has been attributed to its positive effects on loyalty (Debata et al., 2015). Quality is connected with the loyalty of the customer, his / her propensity to recommend or his / her complaint behavior (Moliner et al., 2007). According to Wong et al. (2015) quality has been considered as the key driver of loyalty. In the same vein, Yoon et al. (2010) asserted that the linkages between quality and loyalty are recognized as an important area of research. A case study examined how destination image, perceived value, and service quality affect destination loyalty and found that quality is an immediate antecedent of satisfaction and affects destination loyalty both directly and indirectly through satisfaction (Kim et al., 2013).

P3: Apps quality influences traveler satisfaction.
P4: Apps quality influences traveler loyalty.

Apps Image

"Brand image refers to consumers' brand perceptions in their minds" (Horng et al., 2012, p. 2609). The image is commonly accepted as an important aspect in successful tourism development due to its impact on both supply- and demand-side aspects of marketing (Tasci & Gartner, 2007). Likewise, tourism image has been a focal area of conceptual and empirical tourism research over the last 30 years (Kaur et al., 2016; Tasci et al., 2007). Therefore, the image is so significant because it is presumed to have direct consequences for variables such as the satisfaction felt by the tourist (Hernández-Lobato et al., 2006). It has been acknowledged that the image perceived by tourists of an app has an important role in their decision-making, app choice, and future behaviors (Cheng & Lu, 2013; Liu, 2014; Zhang et al., 2014). Furthermore, deciding which app to use might depend heavily on the image of that particular app (Chen et al., 2013). According to Veasna et al. (2013) apps image is a key determinant influencing tourists' attitudes toward the app. A positive app image should be magical, unique and pleasing, among others (Pan et al., 2014). In the same vein, the positive image may help the tourists in order to select the best app (Hallmann et al., 2013).

Several scholars confirmed that image has a positive influence on satisfaction (Assaker et al., 2011; Castro et al., 2007; Chi & Qu, 2008). Similarly, Prayag and Ryan (2012) pointed out that the positive relationship between image and satisfaction is well established in the tourism literature. A study examined the role of travel experience in the structural relationships among tourists' perceived image, satisfaction, and behavioral intentions. Therefore, this study found that perceived destination image has a significant impact on satisfaction level (Liu et al., 2015). Prayag et al. (2015) asserted that favorable assessment of a destination's overall image positively influences tourist satisfaction. Study examined the moderating effect on the relations between satisfaction, behavioral intentions, as well as destination image and revealed that destination image seems to have a more significant impact on visitor satisfaction, meaning that visitors will be more likely to be comprehensively satisfied if their cognitive image of a destination is more positive (Li & Yang, 2015; Rezaei, Ali, et al., 2016; Rezaei, Emami, et al., 2016; Rezaei & Ismail, 2014; Shahijan et al., 2016).

Chen and Phou (2013) stated that image plays an important role in creating tourist loyalty. Liat et al. (2014) reported that image influences customer loyalty in the hotel industry. Similarly, Song et al. (2013) stated that destination image has direct and/or indirect influences on destination loyalty in terms of tourists' behavioral intentions. A study regarding the importance of quality, satisfaction, trust, and image in relation to rural tourist loyalty indicates that rural tourism lodging image has a direct positive effect on loyalty (Loureiro & González, 2008). On the other hand, the study was done in a hotel setting and found that hotel image had a lesser impact on loyalty (Jani & Han, 2014).

P5: Apps image influences traveler satisfaction.
P6: Apps image influences traveler loyalty.

Traveler Satisfaction

The expectation-confirmation model has been developed by Oliver (1977) and Oliver (1980) in order to profoundly investigating consumers satisfaction (Pantano & Viassone, 2014). The topic of satisfaction has held a significant position in the marketing literature over the decades since satisfied customers can generate long-term benefits for companies (Liu & Jang, 2009). Similarly, tourism satisfaction has received considerable attention from tourism scholars (Chen et al., 2016). Satisfaction can be defined as tourist's judgment about product or service fulfillment (Jang & Feng, 2007). According to Nash et al. (2006), a tourist is considered satisfied when his/her total of experiences shows a feeling of gratification when compared with his/her expectations. However, if it does not meet his/her expectations, then tourists are normally unsatisfied (Li et al., 2013).

Customer satisfaction and loyalty are an integral part of doing a business (Yuksel et al., 2010). Therefore, Lee et al. (2009) stated that increased customer satisfaction also increases loyalty. Similarly, Eid (2015) argued that customer satisfaction is a direct determinant of customer loyalty. A study was aimed at investigating the relationship among customer satisfaction, and customer loyalty in the restaurant industry and the findings revealed that customer satisfaction has high effect on customer loyalty (Amin et al., 2014; Han & Ryu, 2009; Kalantari Shahijan et al., 2014; Mohseni et al., 2016; Rezaei, 2015; Rezaei & Ghodsi, 2014; Valaei, Rezaei, Ismail, et al., 2016; Valaei, Rezaei, & Shahijan, 2016). Another study regarding the impact of tour quality and tourist satisfaction on tourist loyalty in South Korea and the results shown that a positive relationship exists between satisfaction and loyalty (Lee et al., 2011). On the other hand, the study examined the value, satisfaction, and loyalty of TV travel product shopping and found that satisfaction has a negative relationship with loyalty (Chen & Tsai, 2008). Therefore, customer satisfaction is a direct determining of customer loyalty, which:

P7: Traveler satisfaction influences traveler loyalty.

Traveler Loyalty

According to Moore et al. (2015) loyalty has been proposed and studied as a complex, sequenced construct. Thus, loyalty is defined as a traveler's deep and consistent commitment to a product, service, or brand (Kandampully et al., 2011). For many years, loyalty has been considered a significant indicator of marketing success of firms in many industries, including tourism and hospitality (So et al., 2014). Therefore, Velázquez et al. (2011) stated that creating consumer loyalty has become a strategic goal for companies in these types of services as it helps them to grow.

Figure 1. Conceptual research framework

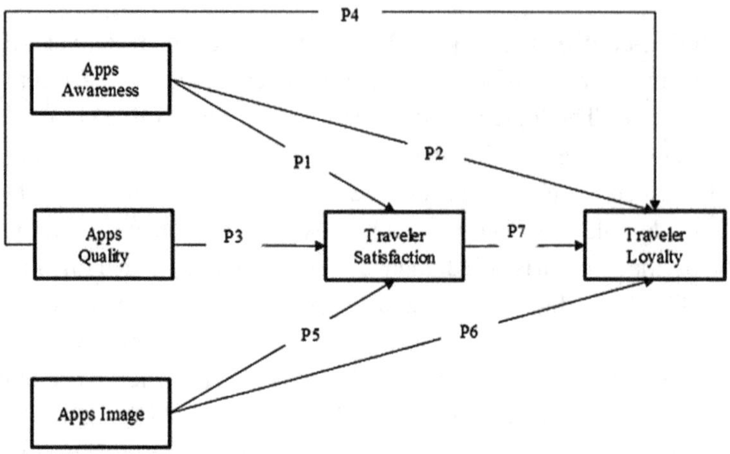

Loyalty is important because loyal customers buy more products or services, they are less price sensitive and pay less attention to competitors' advertising, and they help recruit other customers by word of mouth (Murray & Kline, 2015). Similarly, customer loyalty is worth 10 times the price of a single purchase, and, if customers like the service, they will tell three people. If they do not, they will tell 11 people (Cheng et al., 2015).

CONCLUSION

The development of internet usage in the tourism industry went along with the rise of relevant technologies that has affected the tourism industry all around the world. The internet provides great opportunities for the marketers to sell their products and services through online channels. Apps, as a face of the company in an online environment, offers a great environment for the customers to get relevant information and purchase products and services by a simple click. On the other hand, companies could reach tourists more effectively and create a strong relationship with them.

Individual awareness impacts on satisfaction, thus, a well-known website has greater capability to fulfill consumer needs and wants than other brands. Many scholars confirmed that awareness has a significant effect on satisfaction and also claimed that the linkages between awareness and satisfaction are considered as a significant area of research. Moreover, awareness is recognized as a prerequisite for loyalty; hence awareness is positively related to loyalty. Quality is an important factor frequently used by tourism scholars. Likewise, researchers and practitioners asserted that quality has a significant effect on satisfaction.

A study (Rezaei, Shahijan, et al., 2016) pointed out that quality is an antecedent of satisfaction and impacts loyalty both directly and indirectly via satisfaction. Tourism image has been a central focus of conceptual and empirical tourism research over the last three decades. It has been acknowledged that the image perceived by tourists of an app has a crucial role in their decision-making and also app choice. Studies in tourism context claimed that the positive relationship between image and satisfaction is well established. In the same vein, image has direct and/or indirect effects on loyalty in terms of travelers' behavioral intentions.

Travelers' satisfaction has received considerable attention from tourism researchers. A traveler is considered satisfied when his/her total of experiences indicates a feeling of gratification when compared with his/her expectations. However, if it does not meet his/her expectations, then travelers are normally unsatisfied. Scholars stated that travelers' satisfaction is a direct determinant of travelers' loyalty (Rezaei, Shahijan, et al., 2016; Valaei & Rezaei, 2016). Furthermore, the study pointed out that creating traveler loyalty has become a strategic goal for the tourism industry.

FUTURE RESEARCH DIRECTIONS FOR EMPIRICAL ASSESSMENT

The quantitative method should be used for this research in order to examine the relationship among proposed variables. The secondary data should be collected from several journals and publications from previous related studies. Moreover, primary data should be collected via paper and pencil questionnaires among tourists. A pilot test of 30 respondents should be conducted before the actual study. Before distributing the questionnaires, the researcher tested the questionnaire to identify whether the questionnaire is able to capture the required data as expected. Once all the data have been collected, it will be keyed into the Package of Statistic for social Sciences software version 17.0 (SPSS-Version 17.0). SPSS software will be used in order to analyze data. This study should further deploy structural equation modeling (SEM) to assess measurement and the structural model. To evaluate the reflectively measured models, the outer loadings, composite reliability, average variance extracted (AVE = convergent validity), and discriminant validity should be performed in this research. Moreover, structural model relationships (the path coefficients), which represent the hypothesized relationships between the constructs are analyzed.

REFERENCES

Adukaite, A., Reimann, A. M., Marchiori, E., & Cantoni, L. (2013). *Hotel mobile apps. The case of 4 and 5 star hotels in european german-speaking countries. In Information and communication technologies in tourism 2014* (pp. 45–57). Springer.

Ajzen, I., Heilbroner, R. L., Fishbein, M., & Thurow, L. C. (1980). *Understanding attitudes and predicting social behaviour*. Prentice Hall PTR.

Alahuhta, P., Löthman, H., Helaakoski, H., Koskela, A., & Röning, J. (2005). *Apricot agent platform for user-friendly mobile service development. In Systems aspects in organic and pervasive computing-arcs 2005* (pp. 65–78). Springer. doi:10.1007/978-3-540-31967-2_5

Alavi, S. A., Rezaei, S., Valaei, N., & Wan Ismail, W. K. (2016). Examining shopping mall consumer decision-making styles, satisfaction and purchase intention. *International Review of Retail, Distribution and Consumer Research*, *26*(3), 272–303. doi:10.1080/09593969.2015.1096808

Allameh, S. M., Khazaei Pool, J., Jaberi, A., Salehzadeh, R., & Asadi, H. (2015). Factors influencing sport tourists revisit intentions: The role and effect of destination image, perceived quality, perceived value and satisfaction. *Asia Pacific Journal of Marketing and Logistics*, *27*(2), 191–207. doi:10.1108/APJML-12-2013-0159

Amin, M., Rezaei, S., & Abolghasemi, M. (2014). User satisfaction with mobile websites: The impact of perceived usefulness (pu), perceived ease of use (peou) and trust. *Nankai Business Review International*, *5*(3), 258–274. doi:10.1108/NBRI-01-2014-0005

Anwar, M. A., Carmody, P., Surborg, B., & Corcoran, A. (2014). *The diffusion and impacts of information and communication technology on tourism in the western cape, south africa*. Paper presented at the Urban Forum. doi:10.1007/s12132-013-9210-4

Ariffin, A. A. M., & Maghzi, A. (2012). A preliminary study on customer expectations of hotel hospitality: Influences of personal and hotel factors. *International Journal of Hospitality Management*, *31*(1), 191–198. doi:10.1016/j.ijhm.2011.04.012

Assaker, G., Vinzi, V. E., & OConnor, P. (2011). Examining the effect of novelty seeking, satisfaction, and destination image on tourists return pattern: A two factor, non-linear latent growth model. *Tourism Management*, *32*(4), 890–901. doi:10.1016/j.tourman.2010.08.004

Bastič, M., & Gojčič, S. (2012). Measurement scale for eco-component of hotel service quality. *International Journal of Hospitality Management*, *31*(3), 1012–1020. doi:10.1016/j.ijhm.2011.12.007

Benitez, J. M., Martín, J. C., & Román, C. (2007). Using fuzzy number for measuring quality of service in the hotel industry. *Tourism Management*, *28*(2), 544–555. doi:10.1016/j.tourman.2006.04.018

Bhat, S. A., & Shah, M. A. (2014). Diffusion of internet technology in the tourism sector: An empirical study. *Journal of Transnational Management*, *19*(2), 152–164. doi:10.1080/15475778.2014.904674

Biedenbach, G., Bengtsson, M., & Wincent, J. (2011). Brand equity in the professional service context: Analyzing the impact of employee role behavior and customer–employee rapport. *Industrial Marketing Management*, *40*(7), 1093–1102. doi:10.1016/j.indmarman.2011.09.007

Brady, M. K., Cronin, J. J. Jr, Fox, G. L., & Roehm, M. L. (2008). Strategies to offset performance failures: The role of brand equity. *Journal of Retailing*, *84*(2), 151–164. doi:10.1016/j.jretai.2008.04.002

Buhalis, D., & Law, R. (2008). Progress in information technology and tourism management: 20 years on and 10 years after the internet—the state of etourism research. *Tourism Management*, *29*(4), 609–623. doi:10.1016/j.tourman.2008.01.005

Buil, I., de Chernatony, L., & Martínez, E. (2013). Examining the role of advertising and sales promotions in brand equity creation. *Journal of Business Research*, *66*(1), 115–122. doi:10.1016/j.jbusres.2011.07.030

Callarisa, L., García, J. S., Cardiff, J., & Roshchina, A. (2012). Harnessing social media platforms to measure customer-based hotel brand equity. *Tourism Management Perspectives*, *4*, 73–79. doi:10.1016/j.tmp.2012.04.005

Castro, C. B., Martín Armario, E., & Martín Ruiz, D. (2007). The influence of market heterogeneity on the relationship between a destinations image and tourists future behaviour. *Tourism Management*, *28*(1), 175–187. doi:10.1016/j.tourman.2005.11.013

Chang, H. H., & Chen, S. W. (2008). The impact of online store environment cues on purchase intention trust and perceived risk as a mediator. *Online Information Review*, *32*(6), 818–841. doi:10.1108/14684520810923953

Chen, C.-C., Huang, W.-J., & Petrick, J. F. (2016). Holiday recovery experiences, tourism satisfaction and life satisfaction–is there a relationship? *Tourism Management*, *53*, 140–147. doi:10.1016/j.tourman.2015.09.016

Chen, C.-F., & Phou, S. (2013). A closer look at destination: Image, personality, relationship and loyalty. *Tourism Management*, *36*, 269–278. doi:10.1016/j.tourman.2012.11.015

Chen, C.-F., & Tsai, M.-H. (2008). Perceived value, satisfaction, and loyalty of tv travel product shopping: Involvement as a moderator. *Tourism Management*, *29*(6), 1166–1171. doi:10.1016/j.tourman.2008.02.019

Chen, H.-J., Chen, P.-J., & Okumus, F. (2013). The relationship between travel constraints and destination image: A case study of brunei. *Tourism Management*, *35*, 198–208. doi:10.1016/j.tourman.2012.07.004

Cheng, Q., Fang, L., & Chen, H. (2015). Visitors' brand loyalty to a historical and cultural theme park: A case study of hangzhou songcheng, china. *Current Issues in Tourism*, 1–8.

Cheng, T.-M., & Lu, C.-C. (2013). Destination image, novelty, hedonics, perceived value, and revisiting behavioral intention for island tourism. *Asia Pacific Journal of Tourism Research*, *18*(7), 766–783. doi:10.1080/10941665.2012.697906

Chi, C. G.-Q., & Qu, H. (2008). Examining the structural relationships of destination image, tourist satisfaction and destination loyalty: An integrated approach. *Tourism Management*, *29*(4), 624–636. doi:10.1016/j.tourman.2007.06.007

Choo, H., Ahn, K., & Petrick, F., J. (. (2016). An integrated model of festival revisit intentions: Theory of planned behavior and festival quality/satisfaction. *International Journal of Contemporary Hospitality Management*, *28*(4), 818–838. doi:10.1108/IJCHM-09-2014-0448

Cronin, J. J. Jr, Brady, M. K., & Hult, G. T. M. (2000). Assessing the effects of quality, value, and customer satisfaction on consumer behavioral intentions in service environments. *Journal of Retailing*, *76*(2), 193–218. doi:10.1016/S0022-4359(00)00028-2

Daliri, E., Rezaei, S., & Ismail, W. K. W. (2014). Online social shopping: The impact of attitude, customer information quality, effectiveness of information content and perceived social presence. *International Journal of Business Environment*, *6*(4), 426–450. doi:10.1504/IJBE.2014.064995

Debata, B. R., Patnaik, B., Mahapatra, S. S., & Sree, K. (2015). Interrelations of service quality and service loyalty dimensions in medical tourism: A structural equation modelling approach. *Benchmarking: An International Journal*, *22*(1), 18–55. doi:10.1108/BIJ-04-2013-0036

Dens, N., & Pelsmacker, D. P. (2016). Does poor fit always lead to negative evaluations? Extension advertising and perceived brand quality. *International Journal of Advertising*, *35*(3), 465–485.

Dickinson, J. E., Ghali, K., Cherrett, T., Speed, C., Davies, N., & Norgate, S. (2014). Tourism and the smartphone app: Capabilities, emerging practice and scope in the travel domain. *Current Issues in Tourism*, *17*(1), 84–101. doi:10.1080/13683500.2012.718323

Dortyol, I. T., Varinli, I., & Kitapci, O. (2014). How do international tourists perceive hotel quality? An exploratory study of service quality in antalya tourism region. *International Journal of Contemporary Hospitality Management*, *26*(3), 470–495. doi:10.1108/IJCHM-11-2012-0211

Eid, R. (2015). Integrating muslim customer perceived value, satisfaction, loyalty and retention in the tourism industry: An empirical study. *International Journal of Tourism Research*, *17*(3), 249–260. doi:10.1002/jtr.1982

Ekinci, Y., Dawes, P. L., & Massey, G. R. (2008). An extended model of the antecedents and consequences of consumer satisfaction for hospitality services. *European Journal of Marketing*, *42*(1/2), 35–68. doi:10.1108/03090560810840907

Esper, F. S., & Rateike, J. Á. (2010). Tourism destination image and motivations: The spanish perspective of mexico. *Journal of Travel & Tourism Marketing*, *27*(4), 349 360. doi:10.1080/10548408.2010.481567

Ferns, B. H., & Walls, A. (2012). Enduring travel involvement, destination brand equity, and travelers visit intentions: A structural model analysis. *Journal of Destination Marketing & Management*, *1*(1–2), 27–35. doi:10.1016/j.jdmm.2012.07.002

Goswami, A., Chung, S. H., Chittar, N., & Islam, A. (2012). *Assessing product image quality for online shopping*. Paper presented at the IS&T/SPIE Electronic Imaging. doi:10.1117/12.906982

Hair, J. F., Hult, G. T. M., Ringle, C., & Sarstedt, M. (2013). *A primer on partial least squares structural equation modeling (pls-sem)*. SAGE Publications.

Hallmann, K., Zehrer, A., & Müller, S. (2013). Perceived destination image: An image model for a winter sports destination and its effect on intention to revisit. *Journal of Travel Research*, *54*(1), 94–106. doi:10.1177/0047287513513161

Han, H., & Hyun, S. S. (2015). Customer retention in the medical tourism industry: Impact of quality, satisfaction, trust, and price reasonableness. *Tourism Management*, *46*, 20–29. doi:10.1016/j.tourman.2014.06.003

Han, H., & Ryu, K. (2009). The roles of the physical environment, price perception, and customer satisfaction in determining customer loyalty in the restaurant industry. *Journal of Hospitality & Tourism Research (Washington, D.C.)*, *33*(4), 487–510. doi:10.1177/1096348009344212

Haverila, M. (2011). Mobile phone feature preferences, customer satisfaction and repurchase intent among male users. *Australasian Marketing Journal*, *19*(4), 238–246. doi:10.1016/j.ausmj.2011.05.009

Hernández-Lobato, L., Solis-Radilla, M. M., Moliner-Tena, M. A., & Sánchez-García, J. (2006). Tourism destination image, satisfaction and loyalty: A study in ixtapa-zihuatanejo, mexico. *Tourism Geographies*, *8*(4), 343–358. doi:10.1080/14616680600922039

Horng, J.-S., Liu, C.-H., Chiu, H.-Y., & Tsai, C.-Y. (2012). The role of international tourist perceptions of brand equity and travel intention in culinary tourism. *Service Industries Journal*, *32*(16), 2607–2621. doi:10.1080/02642069.2011.594879

Hsu, C. H., Oh, H., & Assaf, A. G. (2011). A customer-based brand equity model for upscale hotels. *Journal of Travel Research*.

Hyun, S. S. (2009). Creating a model of customer equity for chain restaurant brand formation. *International Journal of Hospitality Management*, *28*(4), 529–539. doi:10.1016/j.ijhm.2009.02.006

Hyun, S. S., & Kim, W. (2011). Dimensions of brand equity in the chain restaurant industry. *Cornell Hospitality Quarterly*, *52*(4), 429–437. doi:10.1177/1938965510397533

Im, H. H., Kim, S. S., Elliot, S., & Han, H. (2012). Conceptualizing destination brand equity dimensions from a consumer-based brand equity perspective. *Journal of Travel & Tourism Marketing*, *29*(4), 385–403. doi:10.1080/10548408.2012.674884

Jang, S. S., & Feng, R. (2007). Temporal destination revisit intention: The effects of novelty seeking and satisfaction. *Tourism Management*, *28*(2), 580–590. doi:10.1016/j.tourman.2006.04.024

Jani, D., & Han, H. (2014). Personality, satisfaction, image, ambience, and loyalty: Testing their relationships in the hotel industry. *International Journal of Hospitality Management*, *37*, 11–20. doi:10.1016/j.ijhm.2013.10.007

Kalantari Shahijan, M., Rezaei, S., Nigel Preece, C., & Khairuzzaman Wan Ismail, W. (2014). Examining retailers behaviour in managing critical points in halal meat handling: A pls analysis. *Journal of Islamic Marketing*, *5*(3), 446–472. doi:10.1108/JIMA-10-2013-0070

Kandampully, J., Juwaheer, T. D., & Hu, H.-H. (2011). The influence of a hotel firms quality of service and image and its effect on tourism customer loyalty. *International Journal of Hospitality & Tourism Administration*, *12*(1), 21–42. doi:10.1080/15256480.2011.540976

Kaur, A., Chauhan, A., & Medury, Y. (2016). Destination image of indian tourism destinations: An evaluation using correspondence analysis. *Asia Pacific Journal of Marketing and Logistics*, *28*(3), 499–524. doi:10.1108/APJML-05-2015-0074

Kautonen, T., Karjaluoto, H., Jayawardhena, C., & Kuckertz, A. (2007). Permission-based mobile marketing and sources of trust in selected european markets. *Journal of Systems and Information Technology*, *9*(2), 104–123. doi:10.1108/13287260710839201

Keller, K. L. (1993). Conceptualizing, measuring, and managing customer-based brand equity. *Journal of Marketing*, *57*(1), 1. doi:10.2307/1252054

Kim, A. J., & Ko, E. (2012). Do social media marketing activities enhance customer equity? An empirical study of luxury fashion brand. *Journal of Business Research*, *65*(10), 1480–1486. doi:10.1016/j.jbusres.2011.10.014

Kim, D. J., Ferrin, D. L., & Rao, H. R. (2008). A trust-based consumer decision-making model in electronic commerce: The role of trust, perceived risk, and their antecedents. *Decision Support Systems*, *44*(2), 544–564. doi:10.1016/j.dss.2007.07.001

Kim, K. H., Kim, K. S., Kim, D. Y., Kim, J. H., & Kang, S. H. (2008). Brand equity in hospital marketing. *Journal of Business Research*, *61*(1), 75–82. doi:10.1016/j.jbusres.2006.05.010

Kim, S. H., Holland, S., & Han, H. S. (2013). A structural model for examining how destination image, perceived value, and service quality affect destination loyalty: A case study of orlando. *International Journal of Tourism Research*, *15*(4), 313–328. doi:10.1002/jtr.1877

Lai, W.-H., & Vinh, N. Q. (2013). Online promotion and its influence on destination awareness and loyalty in the tourism industry. *Advances in Management and Applied Economics*, *3*(3), 15.

Lee, J.-S., & Back, K.-J. (2008). Attendee-based brand equity. *Tourism Management*, *29*(2), 331–344. doi:10.1016/j.tourman.2007.03.002

Lee, J.-S., & Back, K.-J. (2010). Reexamination of attendee-based brand equity. *Tourism Management*, *31*(3), 395–401. doi:10.1016/j.tourman.2009.04.006

Lee, S., Jeon, S., & Kim, D. (2011). The impact of tour quality and tourist satisfaction on tourist loyalty: The case of chinese tourists in korea. *Tourism Management*, *32*(5), 1115–1124. doi:10.1016/j.tourman.2010.09.016

Lee, Y.-K., Back, K.-J., & Kim, J.-Y. (2009). Family restaurant brand personality and its impact on customers emotion, satisfaction, and brand loyalty. *Journal of Hospitality & Tourism Research (Washington, D.C.)*, *33*(3), 305–328. doi:10.1177/1096348009338511

Li, H., Ye, Q., & Law, R. (2013). Determinants of customer satisfaction in the hotel industry: An application of online review analysis. *Asia Pacific Journal of Tourism Research*, *18*(7), 784–802. doi:10.1080/10941665.2012.708351

Li, J., & Yang, Y. (2015). Describing and testing gender as moderator: Illustrated substantively with a hypothesized relation between image, satisfaction, and behavioural intentions. *Anatolia*, *26*(2), 258–268. doi:10.1080/13032917.2014.939203

Liao, S., & Cheng, C. C. J. (2014). Brand equity and the exacerbating factors of product innovation failure evaluations: A communication effect perspective. *Journal of Business Research*, *67*(1), 2919–2925. doi:10.1016/j.jbusres.2012.10.001

Liat, C. B., Mansori, S., & Huei, C. T. (2014). The associations between service quality, corporate image, customer satisfaction, and loyalty: Evidence from the malaysian hotel industry. *Journal of Hospitality Marketing & Management*, *23*(3), 314–326. doi:10.1080/19368623.2013.796867

Line, N. D., & Runyan, R. C. (2012). Hospitality marketing research: Recent trends and future directions. *International Journal of Hospitality Management*, *31*(2), 477–488. doi:10.1016/j.ijhm.2011.07.006

Liu, M. T., Wong, I. A., Shi, G., Chu, R., & Brock, J. L. (2014). The impact of corporate social responsibility (csr) performance and perceived brand quality on customer-based brand preference. *Journal of Services Marketing*, *28*(3), 181–194. doi:10.1108/JSM-09-2012-0171

Liu, X., Li, J. J., & Kim, W. G. (2015). The role of travel experience in the structural relationships among tourists' perceived image, satisfaction, and behavioral intentions. *Tourism and Hospitality Research*.

Liu, Y., & Jang, S. S. (2009). Perceptions of chinese restaurants in the us: What affects customer satisfaction and behavioral intentions? *International Journal of Hospitality Management*, *28*(3), 338–348. doi:10.1016/j.ijhm.2008.10.008

Liu, Y.-D. (2014). Image-based segmentation of cultural tourism market: The perceptions of taiwans inbound visitors. *Asia Pacific Journal of Tourism Research, 19*(8), 971–987. doi:10.1080/10941665.2013.833124

Loureiro, S. M. C., & Gonzâlez, F. J. M. (2008). The importance of quality, satisfaction, trust, and image in relation to rural tourist loyalty. *Journal of Travel & Tourism Marketing, 25*(2), 117–136. doi:10.1080/10548400802402321

Lu, A. C. C., Gursoy, D., & Lu, C. Y. (2015). Authenticity perceptions, brand equity and brand choice intention: The case of ethnic restaurants. *International Journal of Hospitality Management, 50*, 36–45. doi:10.1016/j.ijhm.2015.07.008

Lu, J., Mao, Z., Wang, M., & Hu, L. (2015). Goodbye maps, hello apps? Exploring the influential determinants of travel app adoption. *Current Issues in Tourism*, 1-21.

Ma, J. X., Buhalis, D., & Song, H. (2003). Icts and internet adoption in chinas tourism industry. *International Journal of Information Management, 23*(6), 451–467. doi:10.1016/j.ijinfomgt.2003.09.002

Makanyeza, C. (2015). Consumer awareness, ethnocentrism and loyalty: An integrative model. *Journal of International Consumer Marketing, 27*(2), 167–183. do i:10.1080/08961530.2014.980927

McCabe, S., Sharples, M., & Foster, C. (2012). Stakeholder engagement in the design of scenarios of technology-enhanced tourism services. *Tourism Management Perspectives, 4*, 36–44. doi:10.1016/j.tmp.2012.04.007

Mohseni, S., Jayashree, S., Rezaei, S., Kasim, A., & Okumus, F. (2016). Attracting tourists to travel companies websites: The structural relationship between website brand, personal value, shopping experience, perceived risk and purchase intention. *Current Issues in Tourism*, 1–30. doi:10.1080/13683500.2016.1200539

Moliner, M. A., Sánchez, J., Rodríguez, R. M., & Callarisa, L. (2007). Relationship quality with a travel agency: The influence of the postpurchase perceived value of a tourism package. *Tourism and Hospitality Research, 7*(3-4), 194–211. doi:10.1057/palgrave.thr.6050052

Moore, S. A., Rodger, K., & Taplin, R. (2015). Moving beyond visitor satisfaction to loyalty in nature-based tourism: A review and research agenda. *Current Issues in Tourism, 18*(7), 667–683. doi:10.1080/13683500.2013.790346

Murray, A., & Kline, C. (2015). Rural tourism and the craft beer experience: Factors influencing brand loyalty in rural north carolina, USA. *Journal of Sustainable Tourism, 23*(8-9), 1198–1216. doi:10.1080/09669582.2014.987146

Nam, J., Ekinci, Y., & Whyatt, G. (2011). Brand equity, brand loyalty and consumer satisfaction. *Annals of Tourism Research, 38*(3), 1009–1030. doi:10.1016/j.annals.2011.01.015

Namkung, Y., & Jang, S. (2013). Effects of restaurant green practices on brand equity formation: Do green practices really matter? *International Journal of Hospitality Management, 33*(0), 85–95. doi:10.1016/j.ijhm.2012.06.006

Nash, R., Thyne, M., & Davies, S. (2006). An investigation into customer satisfaction levels in the budget accommodation sector in scotland: A case study of backpacker tourists and the scottish youth hostels association. *Tourism Management, 27*(3), 525–532. doi:10.1016/j.tourman.2005.01.001

Nyadzayo, M. W., Matanda, M. J., & Ewing, M. T. (2011). Brand relationships and brand equity in franchising. *Industrial Marketing Management, 40*(7), 1103–1115. doi:10.1016/j.indmarman.2011.09.004

Oh, H., & Hsu, C. H. C. (2014). Assessing equivalence of hotel brand equity measures in cross-cultural contexts. *International Journal of Hospitality Management, 36*(0), 156–166. doi:10.1016/j.ijhm.2013.09.002

Oliver, R. L. (1977). Effect of expectation and disconfirmation on postexposure product evaluations: An alternative interpretation. *The Journal of Applied Psychology, 62*(4), 480–486. doi:10.1037/0021-9010.62.4.480

Oliver, R. L. (1980). A cognitive model of the antecedents and consequences of satisfaction decisions. *JMR, Journal of Marketing Research, 17*(4), 460–469. doi:10.2307/3150499

ORegan, M., & Chang, H. (2015). Smartphone adoption amongst chinese youth during leisure-based tourism: Challenges and opportunities. *Journal of China Tourism Research, 11*(3), 238–254. doi:10.1080/19388160.2015.1077181

Pan, S., Lee, J., & Tsai, H. (2014). Travel photos: Motivations, image dimensions, and affective qualities of places. *Tourism Management, 40*, 59–69. doi:10.1016/j.tourman.2013.05.007

Pantano, E., & Viassone, M. (2014). Demand pull and technology push perspective in technology-based innovations for the points of sale: The retailers evaluation. *Journal of Retailing and Consumer Services, 21*(1), 43–47. doi:10.1016/j.jretconser.2013.06.007

Pesonen, J., & Horster, E. (2012). Near field communication technology in tourism. *Tourism Management Perspectives, 4*, 11–18. doi:10.1016/j.tmp.2012.04.001

Power, D. J., Sohal, A. S., & Rahman, S.-U. (2001). Critical success factors in agile supply chain management-an empirical study. *International Journal of Physical Distribution & Logistics Management*, *31*(4), 247–265. doi:10.1108/09600030110394923

Prayag, G., Hosany, S., Muskat, B., & Del Chiappa, G. (2015). Understanding the relationships between tourists' emotional experiences, perceived overall image, satisfaction, and intention to recommend. *Journal of Travel Research*.

Prayag, G., & Ryan, C. (2012). Antecedents of tourists loyalty to mauritius the role and influence of destination image, place attachment, personal involvement, and satisfaction. *Journal of Travel Research*, *51*(3), 342–356. doi:10.1177/0047287511410321

Rana, A., Bhat, A., & Rani, L. (2015). A classificatory scheme for antecedents of the sources of online brand equity. *Journal of Research in Interactive Marketing*, *9*(4), 262–298. doi:10.1108/JRIM-02-2014-0008

Randall, T., Ulrich, K., & Reibstein, D. (1998). Brand equity and vertical product line extent. *Marketing Science*, *17*(4), 356–379. doi:10.1287/mksc.17.4.356

Rezaei, S. (2015). Segmenting consumer decision-making styles (cdms) toward marketing practice: A partial least squares (pls) path modeling approach. *Journal of Retailing and Consumer Services*, *22*, 1–15. doi:10.1016/j.jretconser.2014.09.001

Rezaei, S., Ali, F., Amin, M., & Jayashree, S. (2016). Online impulse buying of tourism products: The role of web site personality, utilitarian and hedonic web browsing. *Journal of Hospitality and Tourism Technology*, *7*(1), 60–83. doi:10.1108/JHTT-03-2015-0018

Rezaei, S., & Amin, M. (2013). Exploring online repurchase behavioural intention of university students in malaysia. *Journal for Global Business Advancement*, *6*(2), 92–119. doi:10.1504/JGBA.2013.053561

Rezaei, S., Amin, M., & Ismail, W. K. W. (2014). Online repatronage intention: An empirical study among malaysian experienced online shoppers. *International Journal of Retail & Distribution Management*, *42*(5), 390–421. doi:10.1108/IJRDM-03-2012-0026

Rezaei, S., Amin, M., Moghaddam, M., & Mohamed, N. (2016). 3g post adoption users experience with telecommunications services. *Nankai Business Review International*, *7*(3), 361–394. doi:10.1108/NBRI-01-2016-0007

Rezaei, S., Emami, M., & Valaei, N. (2016). *The moderating impact of product classification on the relationship between online trust, satisfaction, and repurchase intention. In Encyclopedia of e-commerce development, implementation, and management* (p. 1692). IGI Global.

Rezaei, S., & Ghodsi, S. S. (2014). Does value matters in playing online game? An empirical study among massively multiplayer online role-playing games (mmorpgs). *Computers in Human Behavior, 35*, 252–266. doi:10.1016/j.chb.2014.03.002

Rezaei, S., & Ismail, W. K. W. (2014). Examining online channel selection behaviour among social media shoppers: A pls analysis. *International Journal of Electronic Marketing and Retailing, 6*(1), 28–51. doi:10.1504/IJEMR.2014.064876

Rezaei, S., Shahijan, M. K., Amin, M., & Ismail, W. K. W. (2016). Determinants of app stores continuance behavior: A pls path modelling approach. *Journal of Internet Commerce, 15*(4), 408–440. doi:10.1080/15332861.2016.1256749

Seo, S., & Jang, S. (2013). The roles of brand equity and branding strategy: A study of restaurant food crises. *International Journal of Hospitality Management, 34*(0), 192–201. doi:10.1016/j.ijhm.2013.02.014

Shahijan, M. K., Rezaei, S., & Amin, M. (2016). International students course satisfaction and continuance behavioral intention in higher education setting: An empirical assessment in malaysia. *Asia Pacific Education Review, 17*(1), 41–62. doi:10.1007/s12564-015-9410-9

Shahijan, M. K., Rezaei, S., Preece, C. N., & Ismail, W. K. W. (2015). International medical travelers behavioral intention: An empirical study in iran. *Journal of Travel & Tourism Marketing, 32*(5), 475–502. doi:10.1080/10548408.2014.916248

Sheng, M. L., & Teo, T. S. H. (2012). Product attributes and brand equity in the mobile domain: The mediating role of customer experience. *International Journal of Information Management, 32*(2), 139–146. doi:10.1016/j.ijinfomgt.2011.11.017

Sigurðardóttir, I., & Helgadóttir, G. (2015). Riding high: Quality and customer satisfaction in equestrian tourism in iceland. *Scandinavian Journal of Hospitality and Tourism, 15*(1-2), 105–121. doi:10.1080/15022250.2015.1015765

So, K. K. F., King, C., Sparks, B. A., & Wang, Y. (2014). The role of customer engagement in building consumer loyalty to tourism brands. *Journal of Travel Research, 55*(1), 64–78. doi:10.1177/0047287514541008

Song, Z., Su, X., & Liaoning, L. (2013). The indirect effects of destination image on destination loyalty intention through tourist satisfaction and perceived value: The bootstrap approach. *Journal of Travel & Tourism Marketing*, *30*(4), 386–409. doi:10.1080/10548408.2013.784157

Standing, C., Tang-Taye, J.-P., & Boyer, M. (2014). The impact of the internet in travel and tourism: A research review 2001–2010. *Journal of Travel & Tourism Marketing*, *31*(1), 82–113. doi:10.1080/10548408.2014.861724

Su, L., Swanson, S. R., & Chen, X. (2016). The effects of perceived service quality on repurchase intentions and subjective well-being of chinese tourists: The mediating role of relationship quality. *Tourism Management*, *52*, 82–95. doi:10.1016/j.tourman.2015.06.012

Tasci, A. D. A., & Gartner, W. C. (2007). Destination image and its functional relationships. *Journal of Travel Research*, *45*(4), 413–425. doi:10.1177/0047287507299569

Tasci, A. D. A., Gartner, W. C., & Tamer Cavusgil, S. (2007). Conceptualization and operationalization of destination image. *Journal of Hospitality & Tourism Research (Washington, D.C.)*, *31*(2), 194–223. doi:10.1177/1096348006297290

Teng, C.-C. (2011). Commercial hospitality in restaurants and tourist accommodation: Perspectives from international consumer experience in scotland. *International Journal of Hospitality Management*, *30*(4), 866–874. doi:10.1016/j.ijhm.2011.01.007

Thaichon, P., & Quach, T. N. (2015). From marketing communications to brand management: Factors influencing relationship quality and customer retention. *Journal of Relationship Marketing*, *14*(3), 197–219. doi:10.1080/15332667.2015.1069523

Toufaily, E., Ricard, L., & Perrien, J. (2013). Customer loyalty to a commercial website: Descriptive meta-analysis of the empirical literature and proposal of an integrative model. *Journal of Business Research*, *66*(9), 1436–1447. doi:10.1016/j.jbusres.2012.05.011

Tran, X., Dauchez, C., & Szemik, A.-M. (2013). Hotel brand personality and brand quality. *Journal of Vacation Marketing*, *19*(4), 329–341. doi:10.1177/1356766713481218

Valaei, N., & Rezaei, S. (2016). Does web 2.0 utilisation lead to knowledge quality, improvisational creativity, compositional creativity, and innovation in small and medium-sized enterprises? A sense-making perspective. *Technology Analysis and Strategic Management*, 1–14. doi:10.1080/09537325.2016.1213806

Valaei, N., Rezaei, S., Ismail, W. K. W., & Moi, O. Y. (2016). Cultural effect on attitude toward online advertising and online brands: Applying hofstedes cultural factors to internet marketing. *International Journal of Internet Marketing and Advertising*, *10*(4), 270. doi:10.1504/IJIMA.2016.081346

Valaei, N., Rezaei, S., & Shahijan, M. K. (2016). Couqual: Assessing overall service quality in courier service industry and the moderating impact of age, gender and ethnicity. *International Journal of Management Concepts and Philosophy*, *9*(2), 144–169. doi:10.1504/IJMCP.2016.077770

Veasna, S., Wu, W.-Y., & Huang, C.-H. (2013). The impact of destination source credibility on destination satisfaction: The mediating effects of destination attachment and destination image. *Tourism Management*, *36*, 511–526. doi:10.1016/j.tourman.2012.09.007

Velázquez, B. M., Saura, I. G., & Molina, M. E. R. (2011). Conceptualizing and measuring loyalty: Towards a conceptual model of tourist loyalty antecedents. *Journal of Vacation Marketing*, *17*(1), 65–81. doi:10.1177/1356766710391450

Voleti, S., & Ghosh, P. (2013). A non-parametric model of residual brand equity in hierarchical branding structures with application to us beer data. *Journal of the Royal Statistical Society: Series A (Statistics in Society)*. doi:10.1111/rssa.12004

Wang, D., Xiang, Z., Law, R., & Ki, T. P. (2015). Assessing hotel-related smartphone apps using online reviews. *Journal of Hospitality Marketing & Management*.

Wong, I. A. (2013). Exploring customer equity and the role of service experience in the casino service encounter. *International Journal of Hospitality Management*, *32*, 91–101. doi:10.1016/j.ijhm.2012.04.007

Wong, J., Wu, H. C., & Cheng, C. C. (2015). An empirical analysis of synthesizing the effects of festival quality, emotion, festival image and festival satisfaction on festival loyalty: A case study of macau food festival. *International Journal of Tourism Research*, *17*(6), 521–536. doi:10.1002/jtr.2011

Yeo, V. C. S., Goh, S.-K., & Rezaei, S. (2017). Consumer experiences, attitude and behavioral intention toward online food delivery (ofd) services. *Journal of Retailing and Consumer Services*, *35*, 150–162. doi:10.1016/j.jretconser.2016.12.013

Yoo, M., & Bai, B. (2013). Customer loyalty marketing research: A comparative approach between hospitality and business journals. *International Journal of Hospitality Management*, *33*(0), 166–177. doi:10.1016/j.ijhm.2012.07.009

Yoon, Y.-S., Lee, J.-S., & Lee, C.-K. (2010). Measuring festival quality and value affecting visitors satisfaction and loyalty using a structural approach. *International Journal of Hospitality Management, 29*(2), 335–342. doi:10.1016/j.ijhm.2009.10.002

Yuan, Y.-L., Gretzel, U., & Fesenmaier, D. R. (2003). Internet technology use by american convention and visitors bureaus. *Journal of Travel Research, 41*(3), 240–255. doi:10.1177/0047287502239032

Yuksel, A., Yuksel, F., & Bilim, Y. (2010). Destination attachment: Effects on customer satisfaction and cognitive, affective and conative loyalty. *Tourism Management, 31*(2), 274–284. doi:10.1016/j.tourman.2009.03.007

Zhang, H., Fu, X., Cai, L. A., & Lu, L. (2014). Destination image and tourist loyalty: A meta-analysis. *Tourism Management, 40*, 213–223. doi:10.1016/j.tourman.2013.06.006

Zhou, T. (2011). An empirical examination of initial trust in mobile banking. *Internet Research, 21*(5), 527–540. doi:10.1108/10662241111176353

KEY TERMS AND DEFINITIONS

Apps Tourism: Mobile apps that are specifically targeted at tourists as well as those used in a typical travel context.

Brand Equity: "Brand Equity is a set of brand assets and liabilities linked to a brand, its name and symbol that add to or subtract from the value provided by a product or service to a firm and/or to that firm's customers" (Oh & Hsu, 2014).

Brand Image: "Brand image refers to consumers' brand perceptions in their minds" (Horng et al., 2012, p. 2609).

Branded Apps: A branded Apps is defined as an indication for a collection of products decided for sale by the same organizational entity.

Hospitality: "Implies on the hosting behavior that impacts hospitality or hospitable nature of the hotel services" (Ariffin & Maghzi, 2012, p. 192).

Chapter 11
Augmented Reality Apps for Tourism Destination Promotion

Roya Rahimi
University of Wolverhampton, UK

Azizul Hassan
Cardiff Metropolitan University, UK

Ozlem Tekin
Necmettin Erbakan University, Turkey

ABSTRACT

Current chapter focuses on the effectiveness of Augmented Reality (AR) supported applications for mobile and wearable devices during the visitation of tourist destinations. AR as an innovative technology tool becomes inseparable part of destinations' marketing in different countries across the world. However, the use of AR for marketing purpose in tourism destinations is fully dependent on access and resource availabilities. Hence the effective of AR application in tourism destination marketing remains a subject to detailed and accurate information availability of a particular destination or a region. This chapter draws particular reference to the AR supported 'Mobile guides' that replaced conventional human tourist guides. The chapter is indebted to AR literature written in the Turkish. Results demonstrate that AR as an innovative technology can be applied for tourism destination promotion.

DOI: 10.4018/978-1-5225-2449-6.ch011

Copyright ©2017, IGI Global. Copying or distributing in print or electronic forms without written permission of IGI Global is prohibited.

1. INTRODUCTION

Marketing of tourist destinations evidently interacts with innovative technologies. The unprecedented accessibility of the Internet acts as the facilitator and the most reliable powerful avenue for this interaction. The interfaces sway the conventional patterns of tourism destination marketing creating more spaces for interactive technology application. Development of wireless and mobile technologies in the last couple of decades made human lives easier and more enjoyable than ever before (Azim and Hassan, 2013). This chapter aims to investigate the effectiveness of Augmented Reality (AR) supported applications in handheld mobile and wearable devices for promoting tourist destinations. AR supported applications are also use in implementing interactive analysis system applications for trip management. Layered hologram applications, archaeological excavations and matching games, land information system, interactive surface system, e-catalogue, virtual assistants and objects, transparent LCD showcases applications, video mapping are some relevant applications that are supported by AR and can be used for tourism destination promotion. As mentioned earlier current chapter critically analyses the effectiveness of these applications in marketing of tourist destinations. The chapter will also focus on the reduction of tourists' mobility when they can roam to destinations that are mostly virtualized with the help of Augmented Reality. The chapter explores that in practice, tourists can go to wherever they want with the handheld mobile or wearable devices that connect servers of web-based information on GPS (Global Positioning System location). In the conclusion we reveal that the recent development and expansion of mobile phone applications is the key reason for tourism development in some destinations.

2. TOURIST DESTINATION

Destinations can be featured as a tourism product consisting of a variety of components. On this feature, destinations can be of many different types. From the theoretical understanding owed to Page (1995:1), tourism destinations can be classified as below:

- Capitals (i.e. London, Paris, New York) and cultural capital (i.e. Roman, Istanbul);
- Metropolitan Centers (i.e. cities that are built with walls) and small castle cities;
- Big historical cities (i.e. Venice, Oxford);
- Enlivened seaside areas (i.e. Sydney, Darling Harbour);

- Industrial cities;
- Coast resorts and winter sports resorts;
- Tourist resorts that are specially created;
- Tourist entertainment centers (i.e. Disneyland, Las Vegas);
- Cultural Art Cities (i.e. Florence).

In the recent decades tourism industry has experienced different changes. These changes forced destinations to promote their potential correctly to be able to get sufficient share from the competitive world tourism market, where intense competition reaches an international level. To achieve a successful market strategy and get monophony, cooperative marketing communication should be enabled in destinations. Industrial products are produced firstly and they are delivered to the nearest retailer businesses with consumers and consumers purchases the products from retailers. However, unlike industrial products, tourism products are consumed where they are produced (Olalı, 1982; Olalı ve Timur, 1988). Considering key feature of touristic product, in order to be successful in destination marketing, all the organizations working in tourism industry must act together. Destination marketing organization needs support of public and private industry stakeholders for effective branding and positioning (Williams et al., 2004: 8).

Tourist destination is a part of tourism product or service provision. Hence, marketing and searching for more business opportunities become essential for them (Hassan, 2012a; Hassan, 2012b). However, a sort of conceptual confusion persists in featuring industry-led and theory-led tourism products and services. In principle, touristic products are attraction like that is more or less involved with activities. However, a touristic product is more expandable than tourism services. The meaning of touristic product is very often influenced by the tourism industry itself. Tourism industry differentiates itself from the others by accommodating six influential components that are related to present day realities. The six logically related components form the tourism product or service range that leads to define a tourism destination. These six components of a tourism product or service related to a tourism destination are:

1. Attraction is accommodated in all tourism products or services and do not necessarily require deeper clarifications.
2. Access is meant as accessing capacities of a tourism product or service. However in the perspective of a tourism destination, access refers to the arrival capacities of visitors in a specific destination. Access becomes critical in many cases and thus requires proper attention, while relating it to tourism product or service development for a tourist destination. Very rarely, access means the opposite in relation to tourist destination. A tourist destination can be very attractive,

because the access to visit is controlled. Such examples can be wilderness and adventure tourist destinations that commonly have less access than general tourist destinations. In principle, access is very much required for exploiting the attractive of a tourist destination.

3. Activity is related to experience generation. This is very normal that, all visitors experience an attraction, but the way of experience generation relies directly on activity in a tourist destination. In a highly technology induced age, visitors do not always necessarily need to travel, while they can enjoy virtually. Still, the authentic feeling will be always missed in a virtual environment. Different tourist destination offers different type experience and this is one of the reasons, visitors need to be engaged in activities that are related to a tourist destination. Real experiences always rely on engagement with activities.
4. Services sense that activity is required in a tourist destination. In the simplest meaning services are such functions that visitors in a tourist destination may require for themselves. However, these functions are not chosen by themselves, rather somebody else performs for them. Services make actual activity to happen like the granted access to a tourist destination. In this case, officials or personnel of that particular tourist destination offer visitors accommodation, fooding, transportation, communication or souvenirs provisions that grossly make services. When a special activity does not necessarily require services, this cannot be termed as a tourism product.
5. Qualified personnel are the other element of a tourism product or service as offered by a tourism destination. Service provision in a tourist destination requires qualified and well-trained people that can perform and act for visitors. Chefs, guides, drivers, security staffs or other service providers are these qualified personnel. These personnel are responsible for offering quality services or a particular product in a tourist destination. In recent years due to technological advancements, robots are gradually replacing the position of human personnel. According to Hassan and Rahimi (in press), business enterprises in tourism are becoming profit oriented in their way to survive in a fiercely competitive market setting that however, shows the necessity of expert and qualified personnel.
6. Promotion is concerned with tourism product or service design for a tourist destination. This is important as promotion allows visitors know about the existence of specific tourism product or service. A particular tourism product or service obviously require promotion and can rely on technology in the form of electronic word-of-mouth. Promotion of a tourist destination thus, obviously influenced by updated technology Apps as AR.

3. TOURISM DESTINATION PROMOTION

Tourists taking into account different features in order to prefer a destination for example beauty of natural environment, cultural values, and quality of accommodation, variety of food and beverage or climate. Destination management includes evaluating interests of people, visitors, and suppliers together and deal with economic and cultural development of a destination (Pearce and Schänzel, 137). According to TDMSZ (2015), there are many actively public and private stakeholders need to be considered in managing a destination such as national and regional authorities; economic development organizations; local governments; city centre management organizations; national park authorities; transportation providers; attractiveness, events and cultural organizations; accommodation providers; restaurant, leisure and retail operators; intermediaries (i.e. for tour operators and conference organizers); destination representing organizations; media; local tourism consortium and stakeholders; business support organizations and skill development organizations. Destination resources are city's tourist attractiveness, tourism businesses and infrastructure. The important thing is not that there is too much of destination resources, but it is important how they should be assessed (Hsu et al., 2004). In this context, successful destination developments start with a market strategy and the promotion phase frequently demands a market context beyond the boundary of the site, or indeed of the area. The city strategy is the next logical step, which in turn begins to raise issues about competing interests as to what sort of city need.

3.1 Impacts of Technology on Tourism Destination Promotion

The advancement of technologies such as mobile devices with wireless connections to the Internet opens up new prospects for mobile commerce (m-commerce) (Schwinger, et al., 2005). Location-based services are widely spread both the entertainment and business applications, comprising tourist-oriented information services (Koren et al., 2011). In recent years Smart phones got in favour in many international markets more precisely EU5 (i.e. United Kingdom, France, Germany, Spain and Italy) and Canada (comScore, 2013). With the increasing popularisation of travel apps, it is very important for the tourism industry and technology developers to have a solid understanding and landscape of mobile applications in the market to offer new products (Kennedy-Eden and Gretzel, 2012). Destination Marketing Organisations (DMO) worldwide is increasingly investing into their online promotion. Via implementing of some technologies and applications in e-destination marketing, they make efforts to become strong and competitive destinations (Buhalis and Wagner, 2013) as the result mobile marketing has received a great amount of investment.

The Mobile Marketing Association (MMA) defines mobile marketing *"as a set of practices that enables organisations to communicate and engage with their audience in an interactive and relevant manner through any mobile device or network*' (PR Newswire, 2009: 1). This definition covers two aspects of mobile marketing: i. the application methods include all marketing activities of social marketing, industry players, promotions, relationship management, customer services and loyalty. ii. To '*engage*' means to stimulate social interaction with organisation and community members, and be present at time of consumers expressed need. To be successful in mobile marketing, DMO must develop marketing strategies to cover all perspectives present in the complex definition created by the MMA (Emmanouilidis et al., 2011).

3.2 Wearable Device Application for Tourism Activities

Information age brought a lot of advances in communication and transportation. A differentiated space perception of tourism industry was established after the 20th century. One of the most obvious indicators of this situation was interactive applications in museums (Donmezoglu, 2013). The concept of 'interactive' is a form of communication based on mutual interaction. With new applications being used in museums, visitors can get information about museums or archaeological sites with the help of these devices (Eralp, 2009). Portable devices are increasingly used in a wide range of mobile guidance applications. Most commonly examples are guides in urban areas, museum guides, and exhibition environment tools. Appropriate technology forms have been used with touristic attraction's infrastructure and audience for effective exhibition or informing. For example,

Strasbourg Historical Museum adopts the display style of high- resolution screens, projectors, kiosks and holograms for exhibition. Often benefiting from technology in display systems, museum host to military equipment, oil painting works, coins of the money, many of city mockups. The most important feature of using holograms in museum is preferred forms expression depending on the target audience. When promoting the historical events for the city, sometimes a fictional character or sometimes a voice - over (story-teller) is used for children. Interactive applications are also used for exhibition of cultural, historical or artistic work of arts in order to effective promotion, via Kiosks visitors can also get more information about museum exhibition (Boyraz, 2013: 10).

The techniques on interactive museum applications are continuously advance. Some of the systems used in archeological sites and museums within the scope of promotion are listed below (Donmezoglu, 2013):

1. **Interactive Analysis System Applications**: All the pieces of inspection system are modeled in accordance with reality and deployed in their orijinal positions according to the layout of the ancient sites. Placing the soil and vegetation appropriate to the air of the area, the feeling of being a city living whole domesticated animals, vegetation and locals is given (Reo-tek, 2015).
2. **E-Catalog:** E-Catalog is defined as tools that nonconsumable and imposible to become old. They are budget friendly because don't need printing and paper, prepared in an electronic environment. This electronic product can be released on CD or internet environment, in addition to this, they are valuable as actual printed product. E-book Apps can be used on wep sites, tablets, iPhones, iPads and other mobile devices. And this system can be used via changing the pages with hand movements on a digital image in museums (Ekatalog, 2015).
3. **Virtual Assistant:** It is possible with virtual assistant system to create a human-shaped virtual characters and interact with visitors (Donmezoglu, 2013).
4. **Transparent LCD Showcases Application:** This Apps can be applied to surfaced like glass or acrylic. It is a projection screen technology can be obtained high resolution and excellent imaje quality (avart, 2015).
5. **Virtual Objects:** It is a system created in order to be examined the virtual objects by touching easily in every aspect. System is used via scanning the virtual objects with 3-D scanner and transfering them into digital environment. Similarly, transplantation process is performed and information points are places on system (Reo-tek, 2015).
6. **Layered Hologram Applications:** Layered Hologram Apps is a system that can provide real imaje detection with 3D animation and it is possible to create holographic images that can be seen from all angles (Donmezoglu, 2013). Illustrations and story vocalization founded in theatre stage size that appear as if standing in the air via layered hologram technique create an impressive presentation with a mystical air. In this context, this applications are used for strengthening the expressions.
7. **Archaeological Excavations and Matching Games:** This Apps is located on a touch panel and it is used as excavating a archaeological site with fingers. Users try to find all archaeological monuments (Reo-tek, 2015).
8. **Video Mapping:** Video Projection Mapping is an exciting new projection techique that can turn almost any surface into a dynamic video display. Specialized software is used to warp and mask the projected image to make it fit perfectly on irregularly shaped screens. When done right, the last results is a dynamic projection installation that transcends ordinary video projection (tumblr, 2016).

9. **Interactive Surface System:** Applied as to interact with images projected onto the walls of human motion, it is a system defined converting a wall to a touch screen (Esdorlion, 2015).
10. **Land Information System:** System is aimed to give detailed information about importance of archaeological site for region. With projection images on three dimensional topographical map mockup displaying the border of region, imagery of region is realistically colourised. And changes in vegetation is presented with the help of map animations and explanatory texts (Reo-tek, 2015).

3.3 Augmented Reality Supported Applications in Promoting Destinations

3.3.1. The Concept of Augmented Reality

AR is amalgamation of digital information with the user's environment or live video in real time. AR gets a current picture combining with newer information into it. Over the years, the sequence of AR spectrum has evolved within SMS/QR Codes based simple experimentations, Webcam/3D based gimmicks, unnatural location based satellite navigation towards more natural and effective point-of-sale (POS), then most developed useful and natural real-world Apps as AR glass (Dadwal and Hassan, 2015). The very early commercial Apps of AR technology was in the televised football games naming the '*yellow first down line*'. The very generic element of AR is its operating software because, AR programmes are written in special ways. Specialised 3D augmented reality programmes as D'Fusion, FLARToolKit or Unifye Viewer are used for the purpose (Henderson and Feiner, 2007). Such specialised programmes offer the developers unifying contextual digital information or animation in computer programmes to an AR marker in a real environment. The end user needs to download specific software Apps or app or has to plug in browser to get AR experience. Most of the AR applications are built in Shockwave or Flash requiring a web camera programme for delivering the information either in the marker or in the computer. The marker can either be a simple geometric shape series or a barcode. The marker is very often called a target. As soon as browser plug-in or AR app in the computer receives the digitalised information containing the marker, this starts executing the code for AR programme. The Global Positioning System (GPS) is included in AR applications for Smartphones for pinpointing the user's location followed by using its compass for detecting the device orientation. Updated AR programmes as used by the military for training purposes can include gesture recognition, object recognition or machine vision technologies (Virtual Reality Site, 2016).

AR is one part of the general area of mixed reality. Both virtual environments (or virtual reality) and augmented virtuality, in which real objects are added to virtual ones, replace the surrounding environment by a virtual one. In contrast, AR provides local virtuality. AR system (Krevelen and Poelman, 2010: 1):

- Combines real and virtual objects in a real environment;
- Registers (aligns) real and virtual objects with each other; and
- Runs interactively, in three dimensions, and in real time.

According to Virtual Reality Site (2016), the history of AR dates back to the decade of the 90s, when Professor Tom Caudell was associated with a neural of Boeing. This project was aiming to find new ways for helping the company's engineering process by involving VR. Professor Caudell developed software that could display the cables during the construction of an airplane (Virtual Reality Site, 2016). This software supported a lot by replacing the requirement of using the complex manuals. This is seen as the very first example AR. Later, Professor Caudell explored more opportunities to use AR related projects. Following this trend, a user guided system for the US Air Force was undertaken by L. B. Rosenberg. For using printer, an AR enabled manual was also invented. This manual helped the users loading papers to the printer while, performing other tasks without using the manual. This manual was designed to be used by different operating systems and a handset. Many operating systems as Mac, Linux, Windows etc. were used allowing the displays of 3D images onto the real world (Virtual Reality Site, 2016). The most elaborate and comprehensive use of AR appeared in the gaming industry. The scope and application of AR is gradually expanding in diverse areas: tourism marketing (Hassan and Rahimi, in press); in education (Hassan and Jung, 2015); in museum visitor experience generation (Hassan and Ramkissoon, in press); in tourism destination image formation (Hassan, in press) at the present time outlining huge potentials in coming years.

AR is a type of technology in which computers generate images which are superimposed into any surface to enhance the issue of concern. It can be defined as a technology that provides more enriched environment via including objects like 3D model in real time, animation, film, audio on a real image in current environment. Created image can be displayed as if they were almost in real world with the augmented reality applications. Mobile Applications are one of the main tools for AR. The essential characteristics of mobile applications are largely defined by their functional and non-functional requirements. Functional requirements may vary significantly, as they are application specific. On the other hand, key non-functional requirements are shared across the applications domain, to the extent that they are imposed by technology usage and its associated restrictions. The characteristics promoting the business of mobile marketing which tie in specifically with the marketing needs of the tourist industry are the following (Emmanouilidis et al., 2013):

- **Mobility:** Which relates to the capacity of users to utilise specific services in any place and at any time.
- **Localisation:** Which enables companies to offer products and services to potential customers depending on their location.
- **Convenience:** Size and user-friendliness are attributes making mobile devices a highly suitable tool in comparison with a desktop PC.
- **Personalisation:** Which when applied to mobile devices is a unique characteristic that differs from traditional home PCs or computers in public venues which could be used by numerous people.

All these particular features of mobile marketing should be adapting to the companies' requirements.

The popularity of mobile apps has attracted new entrants to the travel landscape as providers of maps (Google) and GPS (Global Positioning System) navigation services. Navigation resources give the user the opportunity to interact with the app by changing location information based on individual preferences, as personal taste, purchase, and several activities (Kennedy-Eden and Gretzel, 2012). Mobile devices have lots of features to make our lives easier. Recently, the usage of mobile devices is becoming widespread as a result of rapidly established 3G technology which can provide broadband and speed internet. Tourists want to reach the required information from any where in any time as simple as possible. It is an excelent solution to get some information about the place of interest during walking around historical and touristic places or in a new city or a campus. Mobile guides began to replace of tourist guides that tourists take advantage in order to receive detailed and accurate information about the destination and knowing the region closely. Tourists can go wherever they want by themselves with the devices that connect servers of web-based information on GPS (global positioning system location) with expansion of smart phones. There is a comprehensive literature about mobile guide features (Emmanouilidis et al., 2013). Some of these has been mentioned as below:

System Technologies and Characteristics:

- Localization techniques (i.e. how user location and/or orientation are inferred);
- Environment type (i.e. indoors/outdoors);
- Data retrieval (i.e. means of data delivery to the device);
- Context aware implementations, according to a comprehensive context classification scheme and context support level.

Client-Side Devices and Components:

- The mobile guide device type;
- The Apps type (i.e. native, browser-based or Virtual Machine-based applications);
- The offered functionalities that enhance user experience, like navigation, bookmarking, games and support for con- tent types (i.e. textual, multimedia, history).

3.3.2 AR Technology in Tourism Industry

The emergence of AR applications has changed the way tourist's experience in a destination, leading to more interactive and diversified experiences (Fritz et al., 2005; Kourouthanassis et al., 2015). AR applications provide tourists with the opportunity to get to know unknown surroundings in an enjoyable and interactive manner (tom Dieck and Jung, 2015). The increased situational awareness for tourists gained from linkages of information and real world elements has been utilized in many fields. The possibility to provide three-dimensional content through AR makes information about cultural heritage accessible and understandable for non-expert tourists (tom Dieck and Jung, 2015; Garau, 2014). Furthermore, AR provides tourists with a dynamic and interactive experience of culture and heritage with the potential to bring history to life (Höllerer and Feiner, 2004; Fritz et al., 2005). Researchers claim that AR will be one of the main reasons to visit cultural heritages because of experience a new and innovative technology. AR will be used by the mass market (Jung et al., 2015).

3.2.3 Augmented Reality in Tourism: Some Drawbacks

There are many experimental and exploratory research studies on the use of mobile guides. Current chapter concludes that, within the scope of transferring cultural heritage, ccomparing mobile guide applications and professional tour guides, AR supported mobile guides should be use as a presentation tool for professional tour guides. However on the other side as a drawback, mobile guides may not be possible to give detailed information about touristic destinations as well as professional tour guides. Within the mediatory mission of tour guiding, guides can broker visitors' physical access (i.e. to places and spaces), visitor encounters (i.e. interactions with host communities and environments), visitor understanding (i.e. cognitive access) and visitor empathy (i.e. affective or emotional access) (Tekin et.al., 2015).

4. MANAGERIAL IMPLICATION, FUTURE RESEARCH, AND CONCLUSION

This chapter is expected to benefit tour guides in relation to widen their knowledge about innovative technology application as AR. Tour guides and the entire tourism industry in particular are also expected to learn both ongoing and potential changes that AR brings. Future research can possibly discover the unexplored areas of AR supported Tour Guide that is made available in both handheld mobile and wearable devices. The aim of this chapter is to outline the effectiveness and use of AR as a solid technology for tourism destination promotion. In order to reach this a set of theoretical explanations are offered to establish the understanding AR is supporting destinations' promotion. Tourism industry is overwhelmingly influenced by the recent technological developments in particular with mobile and wearable devices and replaced the conventional human being. This chapter particularly stresses on making AR as an inseparable tool for tourism marketing destination, because tourism destination promotion commonly depends on detailed and elaborated information availability. The wider popularity of technology supported applications can significantly reduce tourist mobility. On the contrary, this is also important to learn that AR technology supported Tour Guides increases scopes to know more of a tourist destination than ever before. The chapter thus concludes by stating that AR is both theoretically and practically a helpful technology for the well-being of tourism industry. The basic limitation of this chapter is not to attach empirical evidences while making critical explanations. A combination of both theoretical and empirical evidences could possibly deepen the arguments.

REFERENCES

avart. (2015). *How Augmented Reality Works*. Retrieved from: http://www.avart.com.tr/medya/interaktifvitrin.aspx (in Turkish)

Azim, R., & Hassan, A. (2013). Impact Analysis of Wireless and Mobile Technology on Business Management Strategies. *Journal of Information and Knowledge Management*, *2*(2), 141–150.

Boyraz, B. (2013). Museum Technologies and Exhibition Differences. *Journal of Academic View, 39*. (in Turkish)

Buhalis, D., & Wagner, R. (2013). eDestination: International best practices of tourism technologies and application. *Tourism Tribune*, *28*(1), 3–6.

Dadwal, S., & Hassan, A. (2105). The Augmented Reality Marketing: A Merger of Marketing and Technology in Tourism. In N. Ray (Ed.), *Emerging innovative marketing strategies in the tourism industry* (pp. 78–96). IGI Global.

Donmezoglu, D. (2013). *Exhibition Technical with Support of Virtual Technology in our Present Day's Museology and Application Examples* (Unpublished Thesis). Turkish Republic Ministry of Culture and Tourism Genereal Directorate of Cultural Assets and Museums, Ankara, Turkey. (in Turkish)

Ekatalog. (2015). *Who we are?* Retrieved from: http://www.ekatalog.com.tr/ (in Turkish)

Emmanaouilidis, C., Koutsiamanis, R. A., & Tasidou, A. (2013). Mobile Guides: Taxonomy of Architectures, Context Awareness, Technologies and Applications. *Journal of Network and Computer Applications*, *36*(1), 103–125. doi:10.1016/j.jnca.2012.04.007

Eralp, E. E. (2009). *Mobile Tour Guidance* (Unpublished Master Thesis). Ege University Institute of Science Department of Computer Engineering, Izmır, Turkey. (in Turkish)

Esdorlion. (2015). *Digital Course*. Retrieved from: www.esdorlion.com (in Turkish)

Fritz, F., Susperregui, A., & Linaza, M. T. (2005). Enhancing Cultural Tourism Experiences with Augmented Reality Technologies. *The 6th International Symposium on Virtual Reality, Archaeology and Cultural Heritage (VAST).*

Garau, C. (2014). From Territory to Smartphone: Smart Fruition of Cultural Heritage for Dynamic Tourism Development. *Planning Practice and Research*, *29*(3), 238–255. doi:10.1080/02697459.2014.929837

Hassan, A. (2012). bc). Rationalization of Business Planning Through the Current Dynamics of Tourism. *International Journal of Management and Development Studies*, *2*(1), 61–63.

Hassan, A. (2012a). Key Components for an Effective Marketing Planning: A Conceptual Analysis. *International Journal of Management and Development Studies*, *2*(1), 68–70.

Hassan, A. (in press). Destination Image Formation: The Function Analysis of Augmented Reality Application. In M. Khosrow-Pour (Ed.), *The Encyclopaedia of Information Science and Technology*. IGI Global.

Hassan, A., & Jung, T. (2016). Augmented Reality as an Emerging Application in Tourism Education. In D. H. Choi, A. Dailey-Hebert, & J. S. Estes (Eds.), *Emerging Tools and Applications of Virtual Reality in Education* (pp. 168–185). IGI Global. doi:10.4018/978-1-4666-9837-6.ch008

Hassan, A., & Rahimi, R. (in press). Consuming 'Innovation': Augmented Reality as an Innovation Tool in Digital Tourism Marketing. In P. Nikolaos & I. Bregoli (Eds.), *Global Dynamics in Travel, Tourism, and Hospitality*. IGI Global. doi:10.4018/978-1-5225-0201-2.ch008

Hassan, A., & Rahimi, R. (in press). Insights and Rumination in Human Resource Management Practices of SMEs: Case of a Family Run Tour Operator in London. In P. O. de Pablos & R. D. Tennyson (Eds.), *Handbook of Research on Human Resources Strategies for the New Millennial Workforce*. IGI Global. doi:10.4018/978-1-5225-0948-6.ch012

Henderson, S. J., & Feiner, S. K. (2007). *Augmented Reality for Maintenance and Repair (ARMAR)*. Retrieved from: http://graphics.cs.columbia.edu/projects/armar/pubs/henderson_feiner_AFRL_RH-WP-TR-2007-0112.pdf

Hollerer, T. H., & Feiner, S. K. (2004). Mobile Augmented Reality. In H. Karinzi & A. Hammand (Eds.), Telegeoformatics: Location-based computing services. Taylor and Francis Books Ltd.

Hsu, C. H. C., Wolfe, K., & Kang, S. K. (2004). Image Assessment for a Destination with Limited Comparative Advantages. *Tourism Management*, *25*(1), 121–126. doi:10.1016/S0261-5177(03)00062-1

Jung, T., Chung, N., & Leue, M. C. (2015). The Determinants of Recommendations to Use Augmented Reality Technologies: The Case of a Korean Theme Park. *Tourism Management*, *49*, 75–86. doi:10.1016/j.tourman.2015.02.013

Kennedy-Eden, H., & Gretzel, U. (2012). A Taxonomy of Mobile Applications in Tourism. *eReview of Tourism Research*, *10*(2), 47-50.

Koren, A., Stash, N., & Andreev, A. (2011). A Proposal for Semantic Recommender for Outdoor Audio Tour Guides.*Workshop on Personalization in Mobile Applications at the 5th ACM Conference on Recommender Systems.*

Kourouthanassis, P., Boletsis, C., Bardaki, C., & Chasanidou, D. (2015). Tourists Responses to Mobile Augmented Reality Travel Guides: The Role of Emotions on Adoption Behavior. *Pervasive and Mobile Computing*, *18*, 71–87. doi:10.1016/j.pmcj.2014.08.009

Krevelen, D. W. F., & Poelman, R. (2010). A Survey of Augmented Reality Technologies, Applications and Limitations. *The International Journal of Virtual Reality*, *9*(2), 1–20.

Olalı, H. (1982). *Turizm Politikası ve Planlaması*. Izmir: Ege Üniversitesi Matbaası. (in Turkish)

Olalı, H., & Timur. (1988). *Turizm Ekonomisi*. Izmir: Ofis Ticaret Matbaacılık. (in Turkish)

Page, S. (1995). Urban Tourism. Oxon, UK: Academic Press.

Pearce, D. G., & Schänzel, H. A. (2013). Destination management: The tourists perspective. *Journal of Destination Marketing and Management*, *2*(3), 137–145. doi:10.1016/j.jdmm.2013.06.001

PR Newswire. (2009). *MMA Updates Definition of Mobile Marketing*. Retrieved from: http://www.mmaglobal.com/news/mma-updates-definition-mobile-marketing

Reo-tek. (2015). *Ana Sayfa*. Retrieved from: http://www.Reo-Tek.Com/Tr/Hakkimizda/ (in Turkish)

Schwinger, W., Grün, Ch., Pröll, B., Retschitzegger, W., & Schauerhuber, A. (2005). *Context-awareness in Mobile Tourism Guides - A Comprehensive Survey*. Retrieved from: http://publik.tuwien.ac.at/files/PubDat_177481.pdf

TDMSZ. (2016). *keededves látogatóink!* Retrieved from: http://www.tdmszovetseg.e (in Turkish)

Tekin, Ö., Bideci, M., & Aydın, A. (2015). Kültürel Mirasın Aktarımında Mobil Rehber Uygulamaları ile Turist rehberlerinin Yetkinliğinin Karşılaştırması (Konya Mevlana Müzesi Örneği). *Uluslararası Avrasya Turizm Kongresi*. (in Turkish)

tom Dieck, M. C., & Jung, T. (2015). A Theoretical Model of Mobile Augmented RealityAcceptance in Urban Heritage Tourism. *Current Issues in Tourism*, 1–21. doi:10.1080/13683500.2015.1070801

tumblr. (2016). *Video Projection Mapping*. Retrieved from: http://videomapping.tumblr.com/

Virtual Reality Site. (2016). *How Augmented Reality Works*. Retrieved from: http://www.vrs.org.uk/augmented-reality/invention.html

Williams, H., Williams, R. L., & Omar, M. (2014). Gastro-Tourism as Destination Branding in Emerging Markets. *International Journal of Leisure and Tourism Marketing*, *4*(1), 1–17. doi:10.1504/IJLTM.2014.059257

KEY TERMS AND DEFINITIONS

Augmented Reality: AR is amalgamation of digital information with the user's environment or live video in real time.

Mobile Application: Technology application placed in mobile and wearable devices for customer use.

Tourist Destination: Tourist destination is a destination attached to tourism activities and a part of tourism product or service provision.

Chapter 12
Antecedents of Apps Channel Selection:
A Research Proposal

Mark Arjun Muthukumaran
Taylor's University, Malaysia

Yoke Moi Oh
Taylor's University, Malaysia

Sajad Rezaei
Taylor's University, Malaysia

Gu Manli
Taylor's University, Malaysia

ABSTRACT

Apps on mobile devices like smartphones have become the core of the digital life of consumers. Apps are used for shopping or communicating in social networks and are gaining more and more attention in enterprises as an enabler for agile process optimization. The increase in the number of mobile Apps has greatly contributed to social capital and e-commerce worldwide. However, there is a lack of evidence in examining the impact of privacy, fulfillment, perceived Apps channel service quality and relative benefits of Apps channel selection. Hence, this chapter aims to propose a research proposal in the determinants and the factors influencing App channel selection. It is essential to build an understanding of concepts of social enterprise regarding the Apps marketing and to design an empirical based research to cultivate an understanding in terms of the perceptions and practices of Apps enterprises within the context of marketing. The significance of this research is to provide undergraduate researcher a guideline in proposing a research and forming strategic marketing and tactical decision-making when defining the roles of Apps channel.

DOI: 10.4018/978-1-5225-2449-6.ch012

Copyright ©2017, IGI Global. Copying or distributing in print or electronic forms without written permission of IGI Global is prohibited.

INTRODUCTION

Background of Research

The Internet is a powerful platform for Apps regarding distribution of goods and services (Mohseni et al., 2016). Reports from Digital Marketing Ramblings stated that there were 600 million WhatsApp users in August 2014 since its start-up in 2009 (Aharony, 2015). In 2012, annual worldwide downloads from mobile App store grasped $64 billion and generated $18 billion revenue (Peng, Chen and Wen, 2014). By 2017, the revenue of mobile App stores is forecasted to reach $268.7 billion (Peng, Chen and Wen, 2014). Mobile banking tends to be the most promising App of mobile commerce in terms of outstanding flexibility and mobility in completing financial transaction (Tran and Corner, 2016). In addition, App for mobile-assisted language learning has transformed largely and have become increasingly popular due to the availability of free App for language learning (Böhm and Constantine, 2016).

According to a study conducted by Carter and Yeo (2016) in Malaysia, undergraduates aged between 18-24 use Apps mainly for social networking, videos, photos and texting, while postgraduates aged between 35-54 use Apps for emails, news, information and maps. Effective Measure and the Malaysian Digital Association states that Facebook Apps is ranked among the top Applications used in the country. Approximately 90% of Malaysians use Facebook as their primary choice of social media network (Mustaffa et al., 2011). Malaysians Communication and Multimedia Commission (MCMC) reported that 34.6% of Malaysians download 10 to 20 App, 16.3% download 20 to 30 App, 7.4% download 30 to 40 App, 4.2% download 40 to 50 App and 1.5% download 50 to 60 (Rezaei and Amin, 2013). Furthermore, it is evidently proven that 21.2% of Malaysian use mobile App on a daily basis and 14.9% on a weekly basis.

One of the most important elements of any value chain is marketing channels due to a nation's manufacturing outflow passes through them in bulk (Krafft et al., 2015). The past fifty years have shown that the scope of research regarding international marketing channels has drastically evolved (Hoppner and Griffith, 2015). A study by Anderl, Schumann and Kunz (2016) provides the retailers with a taxonomy-based approach to aid retailers to engage in relatively better understanding in usage of channels. A wide variety of dominant channel format is a unique characteristic of emerging economies (Venkatesan et al., 2015). The dominance of the Internet imposes an empathetic of e-service quality and by adopting means-ends-chain theory (Amin et al., 2015; Rezaei, 2015; Rezaei and Ghodsi, 2014), thus, a conceptual framework can be generated to understand the numerous models and related measures that have been industrialized to observe this construct (Blut et al., 2015). According to a multi-wave field study, suppliers tend to invest heavily in channel partner programs that motivate learning and selling from gratitude and indebtedness that help in transforming such investments into profitable returns (Pelser et al., 2015).

Research Gap and Problem Statement

As of January 2015, there were 80,000 educational Apps on the Apple's Apps Store that are largely unregulated and untested (Hirsh-Pasek et al., 2015). Reports by an industry watcher evidently display that every smartphone user will ultimately embrace "Apps culture" (Taylor and Levin, 2014). The emergence of Apps commerce provides a context to study about the consumer's preferences and behaviors towards Apps channel (Rezaei et al., 2016a; Rezaei et al., 2016b; Rezaei et al., 2016c; Yeo et al., 2017). In addition, it provides some useful insights for Apps channel research (Taylor and Levin, 2014). With the development of security, consumers can use online channels as an informational medium (Yee-Loong Chong et al., 2010). Due to immense increase in marketing channels research published in the past decade, minor on-going reviews synthesize the domain (Watson et al., 2015).

Moreover, social media has been growing rapidly becoming an integral part of organizations' marketing communications and strategy due to its interactive environment that highlights collaboration of efficient and steady information collection (Valos et al., 2016). A study by Cluley (2016) evidently shows that there is an image problem when it comes to marketing as they noted other professionals group, consumers and wider public do not trust marketing practices. This addresses a significant gap within the existing literature platform and provides perceptions for social marketers that seek to practice social change initiatives through social enterprise (Mitchell, Madill & Chreim, 2015). Statistics show that the popularity of location-based Apps and news is growing among the young adults (Schmitz Weiss, 2013). Attributes such as cognitive load tends to be overlooked in usability models that are most conspicuous despite their impact on failure or success of the Application (Harrison, Flood & Duce, 2013). Study by Han Rebekah Wong (2012) revealed evidence and trend resulting in the increase use of Apps compared to websites. However, there are fewer empirical researches have been conducted on the dynamics of mobile Apps despite growth in the Apps market (Chung, 2014). Therefore, problem statement, research questions and research objectives are as follows:

Problem Statement

Apps on mobile devices like smartphones have become the core of the digital life of consumers and this study is among few attempts to put forward a research proposal in understanding consumers' Apps channel selection behavior (Watson et al., 2015; Mitchell, Madill and Chreim, 2015; Chong et al., 2010; Taylor and Levin,

2014; Harrison, Flood and Duce, 2013). Apps and related 3G applications are used for shopping or communicating in social networks and are gaining more and more attention in enterprises as an enabler for agile process optimization (Amin et al., 2014; Rezaei et al., 2016b; Rezaei et al., 2016c; Yeo et al., 2017). Thus, the problem statement in this study is as follows. "There is a lack of evidence in examining the impact of privacy, fulfilment, perceived App channel service quality, relative benefits of Apps channel on Apps channel selection".

Research Objectives (RO)

This research is an explanatory in nature that attempts to establish causal relationship between variables for exploring the cause and effect (Saunders, Lewis & Thronhill, 2015). Based on explanatory research, research question begin with "Why" and/or "How" (Fisher, 2010; Saunders, Lewis & Thronhill, 2015). In addition, explanatory research aims to establish casual relationships between variables (Malhotra & Singh, 2007). According to the research gap with relevance to the problem statement, the research objectives are the following:

RO1: To investigate factors that influence Apps channel selection.
RO2: To examine the impact of Privacy and Fulfillment on Apps channel selection.
RO3: To determine the impact of perceived apps channel quality and relative benefits of apps channel on apps channel selection.

Research Questions (RQ)

RQ1: What factors influence online channel selection in Malaysia?
RQ2: How is the impact of privacy and fulfillment on apps channel selection?
RQ3: How is the impact of perceived apps channel quality and relative benefits of apps channel on apps channel selection?

Research Rationale

As proposed by previous study (Mitchell, Madill & Chreim, 2015), it is essential to build an understanding of concepts of social enterprise regarding the social marketing community and to design an empirical based research to cultivate an understanding in terms of the perceptions and practices social enterprises within the context of marketing. Hence, this research aims to investigate the factors influencing Apps channel selection in Malaysia. The challenges stipulated by mobile Apps enable the youth to acquire wide knowledge regarding the latest progression in mobile commerce in Malaysia (Carter and Yeo, 2016). Therefore, this enables individuals to enhance decision-making process through App in order to utilize the prospects from mobile commerce (Li, Dong & Chen, 2012). Furthermore, this research will be able to contribute to the success of young adults this research enables them to gain a better understanding towards the most influencing factors that affect App channel selection in Malaysia (Ding & Chai, 2015). According to Tanusondjaja et al., (2015), international brands are increasingly intensifying by emerging into markets seeking potential consumers and multiple research showcase that consumer segments vary from developed and emerging markets.

Furthermore, according to Kotler and Kotler, (2010), marketing research can be defined as the function that links the consumer, customer and public to generate, refine and evaluate marketing actions of the marketing process. The significance of this research is to provide marketers with empirically based answers regarding the research questions mentioned above, which can aid them in forming their strategic and tactical decision-making and when defining the roles of Apps channel. Marketers tend to understand the relationship between Apps channel selection and privacy, perceived Apps channel service quality, relative benefits of Apps channel and fulfillment. Subsequently, the linkage between recent usage of Apps for acquiring services would impose strong implication not for the segment alone, but also support of Apps and promotions. Hence, this study is important as it will test the boundaries of theories of consumers attitude and Apps channel, as well as imposing Application of such theories to the context on Apps channel selection (Taylor & Levin, 2014).

LITERATURE REVIEW

Strategic online Apps channel selection has been broadly used worldwide as it is not only being used for the purpose of Apps but also being used in sectors such as banking, shopping, learning, etc. Through online channels, selection takes place depending completely on the preference of the user where the key perception is the price charged through the online channel on one side as it is inversely related to the price-elasticity, which is accustomed by the strength of network externality. On the other hand, it creates some platforms to stipulate free services to one side and still be able to earn revenues from the opposite party, such an example can eBay as it is practiced by them, which in fact is also a method of online channel selection (Zhang and Chung, 2016). Just like online banking and e-commerce, online auction is another unique realm of e-commerce and has now become a standout in business innovations on the web (Yen and Lu, 2008). Consumers shopping and purchasing behavior has widened since the quantity of vendors available through the Internet has increased drastically (Ahmed and Akhlaq, 2015). The Internet now offers first-hand customer-retention possibilities through accurate management of professional relationship between consumers and marketers due to consumer's access to various channels to more Apps and service information and an extensive range of products. Various organizations have encountered highly competitive business environment by executing e-business to their strategies for business (Al-Debei, Akroush and Ashouri, 2015).

Due to development of Internet, it is unavoidable that even banks start moving towards online banking (Tan and Leby Lau, 2016). Although branch based retail banking is still the most used method for directing transactions, Internet has really changed the landscape of banking by providing personal services to customers through online Apps channel selection (Susanto, Chang and Ha, 2016). Top managers including the CME's, with the right mindset can critically analyze and reflect on their ideas about essential marketing processes and proficiencies function with regard to initializing change processes (Tollin & Schmidt, 2015). Marketing channels meet the customers' needs and wants by consisting of intermediaries that function in an interconnected approach while fulfilling the intermediaries goals (Paswan, Blankson & Guzman, 2011). Many firms have responded to competitive environment developments by restructuring their marketing channel system by counterfeiting coalitions and partnerships across nations (Picot-Coupey, Huré & Piveteau, 2016). The rapidly evolving nature of social media indicates that senior service marketers have to ensure that organizational stakeholders regarding implementation issues are educated (Valos et al., 2016). Due to unyielding competition within nations, many firms discover that more prospects are available to them in foreign markets (Picot-Coupey, Huré & Piveteau, 2016).

Theoretical Background and Hypotheses Development

Apps Channel Selection

According to Rezaei & Ismail (2014), the skill and knowledge of internet users of might have a strong influence on usage regarding considerations of channel and retail selection and therefore. This is because using online social media enables users to share their experiences about retail experience and future purchase. Technology Acceptance Model (TAM), a theory originated from Theory of Reasoned Action (TRA) is a very influential and commonly used theory for the understanding of electronic commerce and adoption of online Apps channel selection (Rezaei, Amin and Ismail, 2014). Theory of Reasoned Action and planned behavior theories suggest that the attitude of consumers is directly correlated with the intention to perform an action. For example, if a consumer has positive attitudes towards a particular channel, he or she will be more likely to considering using that channel.

Research has shown that consumer attitude towards channels tends to positively influence their information-search at those channels (Seock and Norton, 2007). Fishbein and Ajzen have proposed Theory of reasoned action model (TRA) and this model can accurately predict behavioral nature that is usually very straightforward under cognitive control (Pookulangara, Hawley & Xiao, 2011). Fishbein and Ajzen introduced a framework describing a relationship between behavior intention and attitude in 1967 (Zhikun & Fungfai, 2009). TRA proposed that a person's intention is a purpose of two essential causes, i.e. both social and personal in nature (Lada, Harvey Tanakinjal and Amin, 2009). This means that individuals with the intention to engage themselves into a behavior that can directly influence their decisions will engage in a particular behavior (Lorenzo-Blanco et al., 2016). The estimated inconsistency that existed between attitude and behavior led to the formation of TRA (The Theory of Reasoned Action) (Otieno et al., 2016). TRA can be used as the building block of hypothesizing security and safety performance (Hinsz and Nickell, 2015). Under TRA, there are two categories of explanatory variables in relation to intention: subjective norm and behavioral attitude (Zarzuela and Antón, 2015). Figure 1 depicts the proposed research model.

Figure 1. Theoretical research model

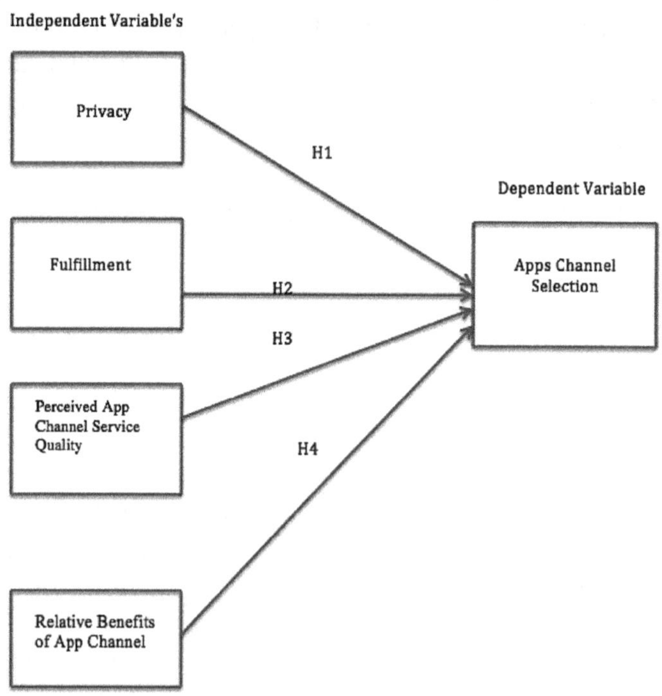

Privacy

According to previous research (Chiu et al., 2009) privacy refers to the extent to which online shopping website/channel is secure in safeguarding customers' personal information. As mentioned by previous study (Chiu et al., 2009) the primary reason for consumers to be reluctant to give out their personal details via online shopping channels is due to the lack of trust. This takes place when consumers fear that their information will be misused by vendors for their own personal gains. This may very well include distribution of personal information to unwanted third parties or unwelcomed communication from retailers. Hence, privacy is one of the major concerns of an individual when it comes to their personal information (Lu, Chang and Yu, 2013). Privacy is the condition where consumers acquire the ability to either reveal or control information that occur during market transactions (Chang et al., 2016). There are growing concerns since early 1990's regarding consumer's privacy linked to marketing activities (Page and Luding, 2003).

Consumers are more likely to trust the protection mechanism of information when the requirements of privacy are met while initiating the transaction (Hsu, Chuang and Hsu, 2014). Internet banking customers face possible risks of financial loss due to perceived privacy threats (Giovanis, Binioris and Polychronopoulos, 2012). Due to radical complex technological expansion and increasing reliance of the internet, privacy has become an important issue for online consumers (Casaló, Flavián and Guinalíu, 2007). Disclosure of personal information has led to perceived fear and feeling of insecurity resulting in negative influence on Apps channel usage (Aldás-Manzano et al., 2009). The evolution of standard phones to smartphones has similarly undergone catastrophic ultimatum by the threats that pinpoint personal devices and extract personal information (Atkinson et al., 2016). Therefore, this study hypothesis as follows.

H1: There is a significant relationship between privacy and Apps channel selection.

Fulfillment

According to Vos et al (2014), fulfilment is the accurate display, description and delivery of the product along with the promised time. It is defined as the degree to which a consumer assumes that they will be able to place an order through online Apps channel selection (Lu, Chang and Yu, 2013). As mentioned by Chiu et al., (2009), fulfillment takes place when an online vendor promises to deliver orders, and they are subsequently fulfilled. This is one of the most crucial factors related to verdicts regarding quality of service in online Apps channel selection. Fulfilment is also linked to human needs as the degree and assortment of such needs defines the possibility of fulfilment. Apps marketers should understand that successful social exchange indicates that fulfilment is achieved and insights on fulfilment are essential as it represents how good the app are at managing customers' needs. Therefore, this study hypothesis as follows.

H2: There is a significant relationship between fulfilment and Apps channel selection.

Perceived Apps Channel Service Quality

Perceived online service quality can be defined as the difference between customers' expectations for service performance prior to the service encounter and their perceptions of the service received (Rezaei et al., 2016b). The key factor in developing consumer retention strategy is service quality as it has been recognized as the crucial value-added contributor. There have been many empirical studies which examine the relationship between perceived service quality and perceived value of consumers. It is found that there is a positive influence of service quality on the selection of both offline and online channels (Yang, Lu and Chau, 2013). Service quality research over the past two decades indicated that consumption decisions are directly influenced by service quality (Lee and Lin, 2005). As mentioned by Honore Petnji Yaya, Marimon and Casadesus (2011), perceived service quality can be used to view consumers' overall evaluation of delivery service in the cybernetic marketplace. Therefore, this study hypothesis as follows.

H3: There is a significant relationship between perceived service quality of Apps Channel and Apps channel selection.

Relative Benefits of Apps Channel

According to previous research (Yang, Lu and Chau, 2013) it could be concluded that consumers are more likely to adopt online channels if they become aware of the relative benefits of the channels such as efficiency of suitability and collaboration over old-fashioned channels. Relative benefits of Apps channels are consumer's overall view regarding the positive effect or behavioural response towards a specific threat (Tingchi Liu *et al.*, 2013). Therefore, an in-depth understanding of relative benefits is essential as it can help Apps developers to invent unique activities and services that match the needs of the customers (Casidy and Tsarenko, 2014). Relative benefits can also be depicted as the accumulation of advantages that balance consumers need with satisfaction (Al-Debei, Akroush, and Ashouri, 2015). The relative benefit is obtained when consumers gather information to extract satisfaction from searching apps itself (Jeng, 2013). Apps channels may include a variety of benefits such as Apps download cash reward, points for loyalty, discounts etc. (Madan and Yadav, 2016). Previous studies suggest that the main elements that affect the adoption decisions are traditional website surfing in relation to perceived benefits of apps (Riviere, 2014). Therefore, to enhance optimistic and favorable customer attitude towards apps, perceived benefits of apps would be a relevant motive for consumers (Chien, 2006). Therefore, it can hypothesize that:

H4: There is a significant relationship between the relative benefits of Apps channel and Apps channel. selection.

RESEARCH METHODOLOGY

According to Lee and Lings (2008), methodology is most discussed concept in most research following ontology, epistemology and axiology. Methodology is the approach through which the research is conducted. There are two types of research methodology, namely quantitative and qualitative research. Qualitative research tends to confront everyday constraints of life while quantitative research tends to abstract them from the world and hence they rarely conduct a study on it. Quantitative research can be defined as a research where large samples are drawn from the population of interest, behaviors are then measured and an attempt is made to construct overviews concerning the entire population (Wilson, 2010).

Research Design

Research Philosophy

Research philosophy is a certainty about a particular method through which data is collected, analyzed and used regarding a phenomenon. There have been two major research philosophies identified in the western tradition of science, specifically positivism and interpretivist (Mkansi and Acheampong, 2016). In western philosophy, positivism generally is a system that limits itself towards the data of experience and excludes hypothetical theory. This term more narrowly entitles the thought of the French philosopher Auguste Comte (1798–1857) (Feigi, 2016). According to previous research (Jakobsen, 2013), the purpose to use positivism is because its principle depends on quantifiable observations that itself leads to statistical analysis and in agreement with empiricist view that from human experience knowledge can be derived and it possesses an atomistic and ontological global view embracing evident and distinct fundamentals engages in an observable manner. Therefore, a positivist approach is used when one studies quantifiable observations as in the case of natural science and prominent theory is used as an anchor to develop hypotheses, which would be tested using the observable quantitative data.

Research Approach

There are two approaches in conducting research, which are inductive and deductive approaches. Deductive Approach is defined as a deduction or reasoning that starts with a hypothesis or general statement and assesses the probability to reach a conclusion (Walliman, Buckler and Walliman, 2008). This study adopts the deductive approach as one or more sources are used and a single conclusion is deduced from it.

Research Strategy

Research strategy is the methodology where research issues are investigated by the researchers. There several kinds of research strategy that exist i.e., survey, case study etc. The strategy applied here would be survey. Survey is defined as "a popular and common strategy in business and management research and is most frequently used to answer 'what', 'who', 'where', 'how much' and 'how many' questions" (Saunders, Lewis and Thornhill, 2016). Typically, semi-structured questionnaires are distributed to respondents where data are collected on standardized questions.

Data Analysis Strategy

The research presented here has embraced multiple regression analysis (MRA) that are used to compute the significance level of each of the independent variable. The p value of the coefficient tells whether the independent variable is significant or helpful in predicting the dependent variable. Furthermore, descriptive analysis is also used to run frequency tests of key demographic variables such as gender, ethnic group, income, age, and highest education level attained. The respondents of the questionnaire tends to have an almost equal participation from male and female in this study. Majority of the respondents are students as the social group targeted is frequent apps users and the questionnaires are only distributed among universities.

Sampling Type, Technique, and Size

There are two types of sampling, probability and non-probability. The major difference between the two is that probability sampling offers the respondents equal chance to be selected while non-probability only selects a small sample size, which is the case in this research. Non-probability sampling is defined as "A case study research design that tend to focus on small samples and are intended to examine real-life phenomenon, not to make statistical inferences in relation to the wider population" (Wilson, 2010). There are several types of non-probability sampling mentioned by (Wilson, 2010) and technique Applied in this research is purposive sampling as it is focused on selecting a very small sample size. Purposive sampling is defined as "A strategy in which particular settings, person or events are selected deliberately in order to provide important information that cannot be obtained from other choices" (Wilson, 2010). The minimum sampling size required to conduct this explanatory research is 384 with 5% margin of error and 95% confidence level due to the fact the actual population cannot be determined (Saunders, Lewis and Thornhill, 2016).

Data Collection Approach

Research data collection is the gathering and measuring of information of variables in a systematic way, which allows one to interpret relevant question and weigh outcomes (Walliman, Buckler and Walliman, 2008). The questionnaire was self-adjusted, validated and pre-tested. The self-administered questionnaire was used as a tool for data collection because it is quicker in getting data from the respondents.

Measurement of Variables and Survey Design

As a methodological norm (Rezaei, 2015; Valaei et al., 2017), researcher should use the scales from previous studies to measure the variables (See Appendix 1). Privacy was measured basing on a 7-item scale developed according to previous studies (Honore Petnji Yaya, Marimom and Casadesus, 2011; Liu et al., 2008). Fulfillment was measured basing on a 5-item scale developed by Honore Petnji Yaya, Marimom and Casadesus, (2011) and Lu, Chang and Yu (2013). Furthermore, Relative Benefits of App Channel was measured basing on a 7-item scale developed by Al-Debei, Akroush and Ashouri (2015). Perceived App Channel Service Quality was measured basing on a 5-item scale developed by Yang, Lu and Chau (2013) and App Channel Selection was measured basing on a 6-item scale developed by Razaei and Ismail (2014).

Validity and Reliability Test

Researcher has used Content Validity Index (CVI) to test the validity of the instrument, ensure that the scale items are meaningful to the sample; used Cronbach's coefficient alpha to ascertain reliability of the instruments and to test the internal consistency of the scales used to measure the variables. Alpha coefficient value of above 0.5 has confirmed the instrument is valid. The Reliability and Validity results in the table showed that the instrument was both reliable and valid since the variable coefficients were above 0.6 in both cases.

Pilot Test

Sixty-five respondents at Taylor's University are approached to answer questionnaire online in the pilot test. Data collected is then analyzed using SPSS data analysis (See Appendix 1). A cover letter is attached detailing the relevance of the study. In addition, anonymity of the respondents is guaranteed. Respondents are requested to fill up the questionnaire based on their free will. The constructs used in this study are adopted from various other research, and in order to validate them in the context of Malaysia, we perform reliability tests, with references to the Cronbach's alpha statistics (Tavakol and Dennick, 2011). As a general rule of thumb, 0.6 is the minimum acceptable value of Cronbach alpha for internal consistency. (Tavakol and Dennick, 2011; Eiras et al., 2014).

REFERENCES

Aharony, N. (2015). Whats App: A social capital perspective. *Online Information Review*, *39*(1), 26–42. doi:10.1108/OIR-08-2014-0177

Aharony, N. (2015). Why do students use Whats App? – an exploratory study. *Aslib Journal of Info Mgmt.*, *67*(2), 136–158. doi:10.1108/AJIM-11-2014-0148

Ahmed, E., & Akhlaq, A. (2015). Digital commerce in emerging economies. *Int Journal of Emerging Mkts.*, *10*(4), 634–647. doi:10.1108/IJoEM-01-2014-0051

Akroush, M., & Al-Debei, M. (2015). An integrated model of factors affecting consumer attitudes towards online shopping. *Business Process Management Journal*, *21*(6), 1353–1376. doi:10.1108/BPMJ-02-2015-0022

Al-Debei, M., Akroush, M., & Ashouri, M. (2015). Consumer attitudes towards online shopping. *Internet Research*, *25*(5), 707–733. doi:10.1108/IntR-05-2014-0146

Aldás-Manzano, J., Lassala-Navarré, C., Ruiz-Mafé, C., & Sanz-Blas, S. (2009). Key drivers of internet banking services use. *Online Information Review*, *33*(4), 672–695. doi:10.1108/14684520910985675

Amin, M., Rezaei, S., & Abolghasemi, M. (2014). User satisfaction with mobile websites: The impact of perceived usefulness (PU), perceived ease of use (PEOU) and trust. *Nankai Business Review International*, *5*(3), 258–274. doi:10.1108/NBRI-01-2014-0005

Amin, M., Rezaei, S., & Tavana, F. S. (2015). Gender differences and consumers repurchase intention: The impact of trust propensity, usefulness and ease of use for implication of innovative online retail. *International Journal of Innovation and Learning*, *17*(2), 217–233. doi:10.1504/IJIL.2015.067409

Anderl, E., Schumann, J., & Kunz, W. (2016). Helping Firms Reduce Complexity in Multichannel Online Data: A New Taxonomy-Based Approach for Customer Journeys. *Journal of Retailing*, *92*(2), 185–203. doi:10.1016/j.jretai.2015.10.001

Atkinson, J., Mitchell, J., Rio, M., & Matich, G. (2016). Your WiFi is leaking: What do your mobile App gossip about you? *Future Generation Computer Systems*. doi:10.1016/j.future.2016.05.030

Blut, M., Chowdhry, N., Mittal, V., & Brock, C. (2015). E-Service Quality: A Meta-Analytic Review. *Journal of Retailing*, *91*(4), 679–700. doi:10.1016/j.jretai.2015.05.004

Böhm, S., & Constantine, G. (2016). Impact of contextuality on mobile learning acceptance. *Interactive Technology and Smart Education*, *13*(2), 107–122. doi:10.1108/ITSE-02-2016-0003

Carter, S., & Yeo, A. (2016). Mobile App usage by Malaysian business undergraduates and postgraduates. *Internet Research*, *26*(3), 733–757. doi:10.1108/IntR-10-2014-0273

Casaló, L., Flavián, C., & Guinalíu, M. (2007). The role of security, privacy, usability and reputation in the development of online banking. *Online Information Review*, *31*(5), 583–603. doi:10.1108/14684520710832315

Chang, S., Chih, W., Liou, D., & Yang, Y. (2016). The mediation of cognitive attitude for online shopping. *Information Technology & People*, *29*(3), 618–646. doi:10.1108/ITP-08-2014-0172

Chiu, C., Chang, C., Cheng, H., & Fang, Y. (2009). Determinants of customer repurchase intention in online shopping. *Online Information Review*, *33*(4), 761–784. doi:10.1108/14684520910985710

Chung, S. (2014). An empirical analysis of usage dynamics in a mobile music App: Evidence from large-scale data. *Internet Research*, *24*(4), 436–456. doi:10.1108/IntR-05-2013-0088

Cluley, R. (2016). The depiction of marketing and marketers in the news media. *European Journal of Marketing*, *50*(5/6), 752–769. doi:10.1108/EJM-02-2015-0076

Ding, Y., & Chai, K. (2015). Emotions and continued usage of mobile Applications. [Accessed 8 August 2016]. *Industr Mngmnt & Data Systems., 115*(5), 833–852. doi:10.1108/IMDS-11-2014-0338

Feigi, H. (2016). Positivism. In Encyclopedia Britannica. Britannica.

Giovanis, A., Binioris, S., & Polychronopoulos, G. (2012). An extension of TAM model with IDT and security/privacy risk in the adoption of internet banking services in Greece. *EuroMed Journal of Business, 7*(1), 24–53. doi:10.1108/14502191211225365

Han Rebekah Wong, S. (2012). Which platform do our users prefer: Website or mobile App? *RSR. Reference Services Review, 40*(1), 103–115. doi:10.1108/00907321211203667

Harrison, R., Flood, D., & Duce, D. (2013). Usability of mobile Applications: Literature review and rationale for a new usability model. *J Interact Sci., 1*(1), 1. doi:10.1186/2194-0827-1-1

Hinsz, V. and Nickell, G. (2015). The prediction of workers' food safety intentions and behavior with job attitudes and the reasoned action. *Approach, 31*(2), 91-100.

Hirsh-Pasek, K., Zosh, J., Golinkoff, R., Gray, J., Robb, M., & Kaufman, J. (2015). Putting Education in Educational App: Lessons From the Science of Learning. *Psychological Science in the Public Interest, 16*(1), 3–34. doi:10.1177/1529100615569721 PMID:25985468

Honore Petnji Yaya, L., Marimon, F., & Casadesus, M. (2011). Customers loyalty and perception of ISO 9001 in online banking. *Industr Mngmnt & Data Systems, 111*(8), 1194–1213. doi:10.1108/02635571111170767

Hoppner, J., & Griffith, D. (2015). Looking Back to Move Forward: A Review of the Evolution of Research in International Marketing Channels. *Journal of Retailing, 91*(4), 610–626. doi:10.1016/j.jretai.2015.04.005

Hsu, M., Chuang, L., & Hsu, C. (2014). Understanding online shopping intention: The roles of four types of trust and their antecedents. *Internet Research, 24*(3), 332–352. doi:10.1108/IntR-01-2013-0007

Kotler, P. & Kotler, P. (2010). *Marketing*. Frenchs Forest, Australia: Pearson Australia.

Kozlenkova, I., Hult, G., Lund, D., Mena, J., & Kekec, P. (2015). The Role of Marketing Channels in Supply Chain Management. *Journal of Retailing, 91*(4), 586–609. doi:10.1016/j.jretai.2015.03.003

Krafft, M., Goetz, O., Mantrala, M., Sotgiu, F., & Tillmanns, S. (2015). The Evolution of Marketing Channel Research Domains and Methodologies: An Integrative Review and Future Directions. *Journal of Retailing*, *91*(4), 569–585. doi:10.1016/j.jretai.2015.05.001

Lada, S., Harvey Tanakinjal, G., & Amin, H. (2009). Predicting intention to choose halal products using theory of reasoned action. *I J Islam Mid East Fin and Mgt.*, *2*(1), 66–76. doi:10.1108/17538390910946276

Lee, G., & Lin, H. (2005). Customer perceptions of e-service quality in online shopping. *International Journal of Retail & Distribution Management*, *33*(2), 161–176. doi:10.1108/09590550510581485

Lee, N., & Lings, I. (2008). *Doing business research*. Los Angeles, CA: SAGE.

Li, M., Dong, Z., & Chen, X. (2012). Factors influencing consumption experience of mobile commerce. *Internet Research*, *22*(2), 120–141. doi:10.1108/10662241211214539

Liu, X., He, M., Gao, F., & Xie, P. (2008). An empirical study of online shopping customer satisfaction in China: A holistic perspective. *International Journal of Retail & Distribution Management*, *36*(11), 919–940. doi:10.1108/09590550810911683

Lorenzo-Blanco, E., Schwartz, S., Unger, J., Zamboanga, B., Des Rosiers, S., Baezconde-Garbanati, L., & Pattarroyo, M. et al. (2016). Alcohol use among recent immigrant Latino/a youth: Acculturation, gender, and the Theory of Reasoned Action. *Ethnicity & Health*, 1–19. PMID:27220730

Lu, L., Chang, H., & Yu, S. (2013). Online shoppers perceptions of e-retailers ethics, cultural orientation, and loyalty. *Internet Research*, *23*(1), 47–68. doi:10.1108/10662241311295773

Lu, Q., Pattnaik, C., & Shi, M. (2016). Spillover effects of marketing expertise on market performance of domestic firms and MNEs in emerging markets. *Management Decision*, *54*(1), 107–129. doi:10.1108/MD-12-2014-0667

Madan, K., & Yadav, R. (2016). Behavioural intention to adopt mobile wallet: A developing country perspective. *Jnl of Indian Business Res*, *8*(3), 227–244. doi:10.1108/JIBR-10-2015-0112

Mitchell, A., Madill, J., & Chreim, S. (2015). Marketing and social enterprises: Implications for social marketing. *Journal of Social Marketing.*, *5*(4), 285–306. doi:10.1108/JSOCM-09-2014-0068

Mkansi, M., & Acheampong, E. (2016). Research Philosophy Debates and Classifications: Students' Dilemma. *Electronic Journal of Business Research Methods, 10*(2), 132-134.

Mohseni, S., Jayashree, S., Rezaei, S., Kasim, A., & Okumus, F. (2016). Attracting tourists to travel companies websites: The structural relationship between website brand, personal value, shopping experience, perceived risk and purchase intention. *Current Issues in Tourism*, 1–30. doi:10.1080/13683500.2016.1200539

Mustaffa, N., Ibrahim, F., Mahmud, W. A. W., Ahmad, F., Kee, C. P., & Mahbob, M. H. (2011). Diffusion of innovations: The adoption of Facebook among youth in Malaysia. *The Public Sector Innovation Journal, 16*(3), 1–15.

Otieno, O., Liyala, S., Odongo, B., & Abeka, S. (2016). Theory of Reasoned Action as an Underpinning to Technological Innovation Adoption Studies. *World Journal of Computer Application and Technology*. Available at: http://www.hrpub.org

Page, C., & Luding, Y. (2003). Bank managers direct marketing dilemmas – customers attitudes and purchase intention. *International Journal of Bank Marketing, 21*(3), 147–163. doi:10.1108/02652320310469520

Paswan, A., Blankson, C., & Guzman, F. (2011). Relationalism in marketing channels and marketing strategy. *European Journal of Marketing, 45*(3), 311–333. doi:10.1108/03090561111107212

Pelser, J., de Ruyter, K., Wetzels, M., Grewal, D., Cox, D., & van Beuningen, J. (2015). B2B Channel Partner Programs: Disentangling Indebtedness from Gratitude. *Journal of Retailing, 91*(4), 660–678. doi:10.1016/j.jretai.2015.05.006

Peng, K., Chen, Y., & Wen, K. (2014). Brand relationship, consumption values and branded App adoption. *Industr Mngmnt & Data Systems., 114*(8), 1131–1143. doi:10.1108/IMDS-05-2014-0132

Picot-Coupey, K., Huré, E., & Piveteau, L. (2016). Channel design to enrich customers shopping experiences. *International Journal of Retail & Distribution Management, 44*(3), 336–368. doi:10.1108/IJRDM-04-2015-0056

Pookulangara, S., Hawley, J., & Xiao, G. (2011). Explaining multi-channel consumers channel migration intention using theory of reasoned action. *International Journal of Retail & Distribution Management, 39*(3), 183–202. doi:10.1108/09590551111115024

Rezaei, S. (2015). Segmenting consumer decision-making styles (CDMS) toward marketing practice: A partial least squares (PLS) path modeling approach. *Journal of Retailing and Consumer Services, 22*, 1–15. doi:10.1016/j.jretconser.2014.09.001

Rezaei, S., Ali, F., Amin, M., & Jayashree, S. (2016a). Online impulse buying of tourism products: The role of web site personality, utilitarian and hedonic web browsing. *Journal of Hospitality and Tourism Technology*, *7*(1), 60–83. doi:10.1108/JHTT-03-2015-0018

Rezaei, S., & Amin, M. (2013). Exploring online repurchase behavioural intention of university students in Malaysia. *Journal for Global Business Advancement*, *6*(2), 92–119. doi:10.1504/JGBA.2013.053561

Rezaei, S., Amin, M., & Khairuzzaman Wan Ismail, W. (2014). Online repatronage intention: An empirical study among Malaysian experienced online shoppers. *International Journal of Retail & Distribution Management*, *42*(5), 390–421. doi:10.1108/IJRDM-03-2012-0026

Rezaei, S., Amin, M., Moghaddam, M., & Mohamed, N. (2016b). 3G post adoption users experience with telecommunications services. *Nankai Business Review International*, *7*(3), 361–394. doi:10.1108/NBRI-01-2016-0007

Rezaei, S., & Ghodsi, S. S. (2014). Does value matters in playing online game? An empirical study among massively multiplayer online role-playing games (MMORPGs). *Computers in Human Behavior*, *35*, 252–266. doi:10.1016/j.chb.2014.03.002

Rezaei, S., Shahijan, M. K., Amin, M., & Ismail, W. K. W. (2016c). Determinants of App Stores Continuance Behavior: A PLS Path Modelling Approach. *Journal of Internet Commerce*, *15*(4), 408–440. doi:10.1080/15332861.2016.1256749

Saunders, M., Lewis, P., & Thornhill, A. (2016). Research methods for business students (7th ed.). Academic Press.

Schmitz Weiss, A. (2013). Exploring News App and Location-Based Services on the Smartphone. *Journalism & Mass Communication Quarterly*, *90*(3), 435–456. doi:10.1177/1077699013493788

Seock, Y., & Norton, M. (2007). Attitude toward internet web sites, online information search, and channel choices for purchasing. *Journal of Fashion Marketing and Management: An International Journal*, *11*(4), 571–586. doi:10.1108/13612020710824616

Sikdar, P., Kumar, A., & Makkad, M. (2015). Online banking adoption. *International Journal of Bank Marketing*, *33*(6), 760–785. doi:10.1108/IJBM-11-2014-0161

Susanto, A., Chang, Y., & Ha, Y. (2016). Determinants of continuance intention to use the smartphone banking services. *Industr Mngmnt & Data Systems.*, *116*(3), 508–525. doi:10.1108/IMDS-05-2015-0195

Tan, E., & Leby Lau, J. (2016). Behavioural intention to adopt mobile banking among the millennial generation. *Young Consumers*, *17*(1), 18–31. doi:10.1108/YC-07-2015-00537

Tanusondjaja, A., Greenacre, L., Banelis, M., Truong, O., & Andrews, T. (2015). International brands in emerging markets: The myths of segmentation. *International Marketing Review*, *32*(6), 783–796. doi:10.1108/IMR-08-2014-0286

Taylor, & Levin. (2014). Predicting mobile App usage for purchasing and information-sharing. *International Journal of Retail & Distribution Management*, *42*(8), 759–774. doi:10.1108/IJRDM-11-2012-0108

Tollin, K., & Schmidt, M. (2015). Marketings contribution from the perspective of marketing executives. *Marketing Intelligence & Planning*, *33*(7), 1047–1070. doi:10.1108/MIP-07-2014-0136

Tran, H., & Corner, J. (2016). The impact of communication channels on mobile banking adoption. *International Journal of Bank Marketing*, *34*(1), 78–109. doi:10.1108/IJBM-06-2014-0073

Valaei, N., Rezaei, S., & Ismail, W. K. W. (2017). Examining learning strategies, creativity, and innovation at SMEs using fuzzy set Qualitative Comparative Analysis and PLS path modeling. *Journal of Business Research*, *70*, 224–233. doi:10.1016/j.jbusres.2016.08.016

Valos, M., Haji Habibi, F., Casidy, R., Driesener, C., & Maplestone, V. (2016). Exploring the integration of social media within integrated marketing communication frameworks. *Marketing Intelligence & Planning*, *34*(1), 19–40. doi:10.1108/MIP-09-2014-0169

Venkatesan, R., Farris, P., Guissoni, L., & Neves, M. (2015). Consumer Brand Marketing through Full- and Self-Service Channels in an Emerging Economy. *Journal of Retailing*, *91*(4), 644–659. doi:10.1016/j.jretai.2015.04.003

Vos, A., Marinagi, C., Trivellas, P., Eberhagen, N., Giannakopoulos, G., & Skourlas, C. (2014). Electronic service quality in online shopping and risk reduction strategies. *J of Systems and Info Tech*, *16*(3), 170–186. doi:10.1108/JSIT-01-2014-0008

Walliman, N., Buckler, S., & Walliman, N. (2008). *Your dissertation in education*. Los Angeles, CA: SAGE.

Watson, G. IV, Worm, S., Palmatier, R., & Ganesan, S. (2015). The Evolution of Marketing Channels: Trends and Research Directions. *Journal of Retailing*, *91*(4), 546–568. doi:10.1016/j.jretai.2015.04.002

Wilson, J. (2010). *Essentials of business research*. Los Angeles, CA: Sage Publications.

Yan, L.K. (2015). *Factors influencing the adoption of mobile Application among tourism organizations in Malaysia* (Doctoral dissertation). Universiti Tunku Abdul Rahman.

Yang, S., Lu, Y., & Chau, P. (2013). Why do consumers adopt online channel? An empirical investigation of two channel extension mechanisms. *Decision Support Systems*, *54*(2), 858–869. doi:10.1016/j.dss.2012.09.011

Yee-Loong Chong, A., Ooi, K., Lin, B., & Tan, B. (2010). Online banking adoption: An empirical analysis. *International Journal of Bank Marketing*, *28*(4), 267–287. doi:10.1108/02652321011054963

Yen, C., & Lu, H. (2008). Factors influencing online auction repurchase intention. *Internet Research*, *18*(1), 7–25. doi:10.1108/10662240810849568

Yeo, V. C. S., Goh, S.-K., & Rezaei, S. (2017). Consumer experiences, attitude and behavioral intention toward online food delivery (OFD) services. *Journal of Retailing and Consumer Services*, *35*, 150–162. doi:10.1016/j.jretconser.2016.12.013

Zarzuela, P., & Antón, C. (2015). Determinants of social commitment in the young. Applying the Theory of Reasoned Action. *Revista Española de Investigación en Marketing ESIC*, *19*(2), 83–94. doi:10.1016/j.reimke.2015.05.001

Zhang, L., & Chung, D. (2016). *Strategic Channel Selection with Online Platforms: An Empirical Analysis of the Daily Deal Industry*. Harvard Business School.

Zhikun, D., & Fungfai, N. (2009). Knowledge sharing among architects in a project design team. *Chinese Management Studies.*, *3*(2), 130–142. doi:10.1108/17506140910963639

KEY TERMS AND DEFINITIONS

Apps Privacy: The extent to which Apps shopping channel is secure in safeguarding customers' personal information.

Marketing Research: The function that links the marketing research to consumer, customer and public to generate, refine and evaluate marketing actions of the marketing process.

Perceived Online Service Quality: The difference between customers' expectations for service performance prior to the service encounter and their perceptions of the service received.

Relative Benefits of Apps Channels: consumer's overall view regarding the positive effect or behavioural response towards a specific threat.

APPENDIX

Table 1. Research variables and measurement scales

Variable name	Type of variable	Items	Source	Reliability results (Cronbach's alpha)
1. App Channel Selection	Dependent Variable	OCS1 By shopping through the Apps, I save a lot of time OCS2 I'm ordering more things via the Apps channel OCS3 I do like shopping via the Apps channel OCS4 I love to surf the Apps shopping channels OCS5 I use the App channel to order because I can't find what I want in the local store OCS6 App channel shopping is more convenient than going to the store	(Rezaei and Ismail, 2014)	0.8930
2. Privacy	Independent Variable	P1 App Channel protects information about my channel P2 Apps do not share my personal information with others P3 Apps protects the information about my credit card and debit card P4 I feel secure giving out credit card information to Apps P5 The App has adequate security features P6 I feel I can trust this App P7 I feel safe in my transaction with this App	(Honore Petnji Yaya, Marimon and Casadesus, 2011; Liu *et al.*, 2008)	0.9481
3. Fulfilment	Independent Variable	FLF1 App delivers orders when promised FLF2 App quickly delivers what I order. FLF3 The App is truthful about its offerings FLF4 The App makes accurate promises FLF5 App promises to do something by a certain time, they do it	(Honore Petnji Yaya, Marimon and Casadesus, 2011; Lu, Chang and Yu, 2013)	0.9160

continued on following page

Table 1. Continued

Variable name	Type of variable	Items	Source	Reliability results (Cronbach's alpha)
4. Relative Benefits of App Channel	Independent Variable	RB1 App channel selection has more advantages than normal day-to-day activities because services are not limited by location. RB2 Using Apps channel is more convenient than normal day-to-day activities RB3 Apps Channel is more efficient than normal day-to-day activities RB4 Apps Channel is more effective than normal day-to-day activities RB5 By using this Apps Channel, I can get my work done in privacy of home RB6 I can use this App whenever I want RB7 Buying from this App can save me the effort of buying what I want from offline/ traditional stores	Kim *et al.* 2009; Al-Debei, Akroush and Ashouri, 2015; Yang, Lu and Chau, 2013)	0.9165
5. Perceived App Service Quality	Independent Variable	PAQ1 App Channel presents visually attractive PAQ2 App service is dependable PAQ3 Apps can respond to customer requests promptly. PAQ4 You can feel safe in your transactions with App PAQ5 App channel have your best interests at heart.	Cronin and Taylor 1992; Yang, Lu and Chau, 2013)	0.8395

Chapter 13
Value and Risk:
Dual Pillars of Apps Usefulness

Gu Manli
Taylor's University, Malaysia

Sajad Rezaei
Taylor's University, Malaysia

ABSTRACT

The rapid expansion of Apps and subsequently Apps marketing have now entered into a post-adoption stage, where technical characteristics and qualities such as visual design, user interfaces, and navigation become the determinants of consumer's intentions. However, very few studies have looked into the perceptions related to usefulness and "post-adoption" or acceptance of Apps-commerce. Building on risk and value concept, the aim of this chapter is to expand an understanding of the decision-making of those potential Apps customers to adopt Apps usage for the first time and also re-purchase decisions of experienced e-customers. As the concept of customer value has received increasing attention from both marketing, mangers, researchers and practitioners, more originalities are encouraged to start incorporating the elements of Apps value, Apps risk, Apps usefulness elements in their strategies to sustain their core businesses activities. Besides, customers are likely to perceive a higher level of risk in using Apps than in traditional in-store setting. Thus, this chapter proposes that the risk concern of user information given to the vendors has an impact on the amount of consumption in Apps market. The practical and conceptual implications are discussed.

DOI: 10.4018/978-1-5225-2449-6.ch013

Copyright ©2017, IGI Global. Copying or distributing in print or electronic forms without written permission of IGI Global is prohibited.

INTRODUCTION

E-commerce has benefited retailers by way of increasing access to customers and information and also reducing the cost of operation and procurement (Rotem-Mindali, 2010). Over the past few years, electronic commerce (EC) has also enhanced the financial performance of organizations, removed some of the barriers to market entry, improved business efficiency and effectiveness, streamlined inventory management and brought down the cost (Liu, Marchewka, Lu, & Yu, 2005). From a retailer's perspective, how E-commerce is likely to reshape their markets and business processes is crucial (Ellis-Chadwick, Doherty, & Hart, 2002).

Notwithstanding of the millions of dollars spent on creating and maintaining corporate websites, many corporations have failed to reach the organization's goals (Hausman & Siekpe, 2009). One crucial principle, according to Butler & Peppard (1998), which holds true in the market space, is that marketers must understand the behavior intention of consumers before they can effectively respond to their demands. These phenomena open the room to for managers and academicians to emphasize and focus on the implementation of Apps as a core marketing and business activities. Regardless of the economic downturn since 2005 which has stricken the Internet and telecommunication sectors, it is predicted that electronic commerce (EC) will continue to grow (Liu et al., 2005). The increasing international competition has raised the question of how firms can effectively manage the new economic order in their domestic markets as well as other international markets (Lindman, 2010). This is crucial for all kinds of industry. Retail functions have been discussed in an academic debate with regard to retailers' justification and their contribution to economic welfare and prosperity (Madlberger, 2004). Economic theory argue that purchased via would occur if the channel minimize the transactions costs (Ward, 2001). This could be the overwhelming reason why all vendors are starting to embrace the digital transformation such as Apps and related technologies.

The economic transformation in Asia in the last two decades has created a new generation of well-educated middle class consumers in the region who are becoming impatient about certain products that they want but cannot purchase conveniently locally because local retail stores tend to move slower than this group of dynamic and aspiring consumers (Lee & Cheung, 2004). According to Hannah & Lybecker (2010) internet shopping appears to be most strongly associated with the notion of convenience in addition to recreation and economic advantages as discussed before. The economy at this age could be described as "experience economy", "attention economy", and also "trust economy", in which the buyer's psychological factors play a crucial role in initiating a transaction (Chun-hui & Jun, 2008). Therefore, the digital era affects people's lifestyles and buying habits in that customers are starting to look for maximization of self-perceived value (Jingdong & Xiaoqian, 2010).

From an economic perspective, Apps retailing has led to higher consumption that stimulates growths in a country's economic prosperity. Online shopping has increasingly received attention from every social community as a new type of consumption mode with regard to the application of Internet (Dan & Xu, 2011). According to Stern (1999) consumer expenditures account for most of GDP, and that therefore changing consumer behavior can go a long way toward reducing environmental degradation. In fact, the emergence of internet economy offers customers easy access to many different options to purchase. Eighty-two million people aged between 18 to 31 could account for as much as ''half the spending in the economy to spend $200 billion in annual spending (Djamasbi, Siegel, & Tullis, 2010). Therefore, this cohort has become the most important participant in internet retailing, where the percentage of total retail sales increases from less than 1% in 1999 to 3.3% by the end of 2006 (Cai & Cude, 2008).

There is a steady, continuous increase in Apps retailing sale from the first quarter of 2014 till the third quarter in 2016. Retailers are trying to continue to offer improved web site's features in order to enhance the shopping experience, differentiate between shopping sites, and to further improve online sales performance (Jeong, Fiore, Niehm, & Lorenz, 2009). The aim of doing so is to gain more market shares in online retailing and also to make more profits. Given the technology-oriented and fast-changing nature of online retailing, this new form of retailing has shifted from its early stage in the 1990s to growth or even maturity stage in today's market (Grewal, Iyer, & Levy, 2004).

It might beg attention for online marketers to understand the importance that has been created by the emergence of the internet for online retailer vendors. The fact is online purchase has a significant effect on the offline purchase, so forgetting the internet even for offline retailers is a big mistake. An important aspect of the history of retailing is the notion of convenience. Chao-Min, Hua-Yang, et al., (2009) found that as compared to the traditional in-store retailing, web retailing entails a higher level of inherent uncertainty in that the physical assurance is missing when one experiences online transactions. Online shopping, on one hand, has a number of advantages such as offering a variety of product information, overcoming time and spatial obstacles, and more importantly, enabling faster processing of customer orders and delivery of products. On the other hand, it is facing many challenges such as designing user-friendly interface, coordinating various online activities like order fulfillment, payment methods, and safeguarding customer information (Vijayasarathy, 2004). According to (McEleny, 2010), internet retail had remained largely unaffected by the last recession. It is on its way to maturity, which leads to the stalling of growth rates. Therefore, consumers' internet shopping intention is highly correlated with their online shopping behaviors and attitudes (Chang & Zhu, 2007).

Apps Marketing Strategy and Online Consumer Behavior Intention

Consumers' post-purchase behavioral intention or repurchase intention processes is a dominant theme in the consumer behavior literature (Rezaei, Amin, Moghaddam, & Mohamed, 2016b; Rezaei, Shahijan, Valaei, Rahimi, & Ismail, 2016e; Thong, Hong, & Tam, 2006; Yeo, Goh, & Rezaei, 2017). According to Butler & Peppard (1998), online marketers need to re-examine the traditional models of consumer behavior and their underlying assumptions, and also the extent of validity of those models in the light of digital era. Those developments, to name a few, include the global spread of the internet and subsequently, the digitization of information products and information attributes of non-information products (Varadarajan & Yadav, 2009). E-commerce and internet shopping are transforming the retailing industry by enabling businesses to reach consumers directly beyond national borders (Talal, Charles, & Sue Vaux, 2011). He & Chai (2009) found that the future growth of E-commerce depends heavily on how customers view the relatively new cyber-retail medium. Therefore, a number of rapid developments over the past decade have prompted business to re-evaluate their Apps marketing strategies and also to implement major changes in implementing those strategies.

Apps Usefulness

In the Technology Acceptance Model (TAM), perceived usefulness (PU) and perceived ease of use (PEOU) are two distinct factors influencing the degree of acceptance of technology (Yuan, 2009). Perceived usefulness is the degree to which one believes that using the technology will enhance user performance (Peng, Wang, & Cai, 2008). People may decide to continue with the same internet service which they find useful, even though they are not happy with their prior use (Talal et al., 2011). Perceived usefulness can also be defined "as the extent to which a consumer believes that online shopping will enhance his or her transaction performance" (Chai Har, Uchenna Cyril, & Nelson Oly, 2011). According to Gefen, et al., (2003), as in the case of other information technology, the decision to adopt and then to continue using the website also depends on its perceived usefulness (PU) and indirectly on its perceived ease of use (PEOU). In TAM, PU is found to be the strongest predictor of usage intention and customer continuance intention (Talal et al., 2011). According to Pitt, Parent, Steyn, Berthon, & Money (2010) TAM originates in Ajzen and Fishbein's theory of reasoned action (TRA). It replaces many of TRA's attitude measures with the two simple technology acceptance dimensions, which are ease of use and usefulness. Perceived usefulness as explained before is defined as "the degree to which a person believes that using a particular system would enhance his or her job performance" (Badrinarayanan, Becerra, Kim, & Madhavaram, 2010; Chao-Min, Chen-Chi, Hsiang-Lan, & Yu-Hui, 2009).

There is a wealth of empirical literature showing that perceived ease of use has a strong, direct influence on shopper behavioral intention and an indirect influence on intentions through perceived usefulness (Juan Carlos, Juan José, & Juan José de la, 2009). Gefen, et al., (2003) suggests that the relationship between perceived usefulness and behavioral intent should become stronger as individuals become more acquainted with information technology. In a similar recent study conducted by Talal, et al., (2011) it is suggested that it is more logical to have usefulness as a predictor or substitute for post-adoption expectations in future research when measuring repurchase behavior intention.

Apps Perceived Value

As the concept of customer value has received increasing attention from both marketing researchers and practitioners, more enterprises have started incorporating this element in their strategies to sustain their core businesses (Tang & Zhang, 2010). According to Lindman (2010), in contemporary business management, value creation for target customers has become an important element, therefore, knowledge about customer perceived value is vital to gaining strategic competitiveness. One of the keys to the success of a firm is how much consumers value the product offering (Caruana & Ewing, 2010). Honesty, honor, trust and justice are cornerstone values in contemporary business (Maaja & Krista, 2011). To enhance customer overall satisfaction, value is an important concept for Apps stores to construct their competitive advantages (Ren & Zhang, 2010; Rezaei, Shahijan, Amin, & Ismail, 2016d; Valaei & Rezaei, 2016; Valaei, Rezaei, Ismail, & Moi, 2016; Valaei, Rezaei, & Shahijan, 2016; Yeo et al., 2017). A value could be defined as "a recommendable quality that has an impact on the choice of objectives, means, and manners available, and is used as a criterion in assessing various phenomena" and "personal values are the basis of preferences or modality of selective orientation" (Maaja & Krista, 2011). Customer value, however, is not a simple and clear concept, because the notion of value estimation itself has some degree of the subjectivity and uncertainty (Ye, Zhang, & Zan, 2009).

According to previous studies, value has been shown to have an impact on important outcomes such as preference, satisfaction, and loyalty. However, this finding is applicable largely in the context of "offline" consumer behavior (Overby & Lee, 2006). Customer perceived value could be a key factor leading to the preference of online store (Chai Har et al., 2011; Ren & Zhang, 2010). Customer value creation is frequently referred to as a firm side activity (Lindman, 2010; Rezaei, Emami, & Valaei, 2016c; Rezaei et al., 2016d; Rezaei et al., 2016e; Shahijan, Rezaei, & Amin,

2016; Valaei & Rezaei, 2016). Ismail, Abdullah, & Parasuraman (2009) found that customers satisfactions are insignificantly correlated with the interaction between perceive value and responsiveness. Yet, the concept of customer perceived value has not gotten a unified conclusion so far. The reason is that values have been conceptualized "as the enduring beliefs people hold about specific modes of conduct they believe are important and as the guiding principles in a person's life" (Limon, Kahle, & Orth, 2009).

Maaja & Krista (2011) suggested that "values are neither attitudes nor behaviors but rather the building blocks of the behavior and choices made by individuals". According to the previous studies, perceived value strongly affects trust and satisfaction (Tao, 2008). When making a purchase decision in online shopping, consumers wants information regarding product attribute-value and also recommendations from a variety of information sources, either in the market-place or market space (Lee, Park, & Han, 2008). Creating higher customer value for the enterprise nowadays has become the only way to achieve profits (Jingdong & Xiaoqian, 2010). It is generally believed that Customer Perceived Value (CPV) should be studied from the standpoint of both enterprises and customers (Wang & Feng, 2010). Dwayne, et al., (2004) found that perceived value has a direct impact on customer satisfaction. Perceived value is defined "as the ratio between perceived profits and perceived lost". "Perceived value is the overall assessment of product or service utility and can be measured with the trade-off between benefits and costs" i.e. Benefits could be tangible (e.g. performance improvement) or intangible (e.g. entertainment). Costs include financial costs such as price and non-financial costs such as time and effort (Tao, 2008). Koo (2006) identified two different kinds of values which are as follows:

1. **Instrumental Values**: General beliefs concerning desirable modes of conduct
2. **Terminal Values**: Enduring beliefs concerning desirable end-states of existence.

The majority of the existing empirical work suggest a direct effect of value on loyalty (Caruana & Ewing, 2010). It is logical that since consumers select and return to retailers who offer superior perceived value, online retailers should aim to design and ultimately deliver a value proposition that is most attractive to the online customers (Alavi, Rezaei, Valaei, & Wan Ismail, 2016; Mohseni, Jayashree, Rezaei, Kasim, & Okumus, 2016; Overby & Lee, 2006; Rezaei, Ali, Amin, & Jayashree, 2016a; Rezaei et al., 2016b). Perceive value could be defined as customer recognition and appreciation of a product that is given by a service provider which may fulfill his/her expectation (Ismail et al., 2009). To strengthen the perceived value of a website, retailers could present their products or services in a more informative, enjoyable and organized manner, so that users perceive the interface to be useful and easy to navigate (Yuan, 2009).

Because perceived value is a form of subjective value judgment by the consumers, it is often also difficult to quantify factors influencing customer perceived values (Ren & Zhang, 2010). According to previous researchers (Baker, 2006; Overby & Lee, 2006) found two main types of value which include utilitarian and hedonic value:

1. **Utilitarian Value**: Overall assessment (i.e., judgment) of functional benefits and sacrifices which is relevant for the task-specific use of online shopping, such as purchase deliberation (i.e., considering the product, service, and price features before actual purchase).
2. **Hedonic Value**: Overall assessment (i.e., judgment) of experiential benefits and sacrifices, such as entertainment and escapism and consumers often shop for an appreciation of the experience rather than simply for task completion.

A study by Talal and his colleagues (2011) confirms that e-shopping continuance intention consists of both hedonic and utilitarian values (Talal et al., 2011). While it has been acknowledged that consumers may receive utilitarian and/or hedonic value from a given shopping experience, research continues to study satisfaction as an overall outcome primarily (Jones & Reynolds, 2006). In business-to-consumer transactions, an online shopper is not only a consumer but also a computer user who engages in a social exchange (Alavi et al., 2016; Mohseni et al., 2016; Rezaei, 2015; Rezaei et al., 2016a; Rezaei et al., 2016b; Rezaei & Ghodsi, 2014). Therefore, the cognitive perceptions of the shopper, in such an environment, could influence his or her perception of Apps usage and thus the vendor who operates using the digital way.

Although the factors influencing customer perceived value are not easy to be quantified, they can be prioritized, however, those factors can be used by online stores for the enhancement of customer perceived value and for advancing their competitive advantages, which would eventually help to promote customers' purchases (Ren & Zhang, 2010). According to Lindman (2010), little has been written on how to manage value creation. A clear management gap in this respect exists. In fact, the consumer's behavior toward online shopping is explained by their beliefs about the contents and the perceived values (both utilitarian and hedonic) of the website. These would consequently result in a positive attitude toward, and trust of, online shopping. Therefore, the customer perceived value plays an important role in the Apps intention model as a predictor.

Perceived Risk of Apps

Perceived risk refers to the uncertainty that consumers face when they cannot foresee the consequences of their online transaction behavior (Lu, Cao, Wang, & Yang, 2011). Existing literature suggest that perceived risk plays a key role in influencing purchase and repurchase intention of online shoppers (Peng et al., 2008). This is obvious that all users are concerned about risk issue because they are going to put their money to make a purchase. Risk consideration during purchase decision process is a crucial construct in marketing and particularly in studies of internet consumer behavior. Besides, customers are likely to perceive a higher level of risk in Apps purchase than in traditional in-store purchase (Sonia San, Carmen, & Rebeca San, 2011). It is safe to say that the privacy concern of user information given to the vendors has an impact on the amount of consumption in online market (Shouming & Jie, 2009). In the cultures that the people prefer more risk taking they are more likely to purchase more.

In the context of online purchase behavior, perceived risk first was studied as early as the 1960s and it has also been examined in the research of information systems adoption (Lu et al., 2011). The impact of perceived risk on online consumer behavior received further attention since the commercial development of the internet in the 1990s. The "analysis of this variable is still very much a topic of interest" (Sonia San et al., 2011). As mentioned, consumers associate higher risks and uncertainties in online shopping, especially when dealing with an unknown seller (Jumin, Do-Hyung, & Ingoo, 2011). Therefore, the major concerns on internet security and privacy would be the transfer of personal data to the third party without consent, the risk of personal information being hacked and the insecurity of transactions.

Some other relevant studies also claim that there are differences between privacy and security, that "Privacy is related to what a company consciously decides to do with consumer data, while security is concerned with any inadvertent compromises of consumer data to a third party" (Peng et al., 2008). While considering online shopping, a potential consumer would take into consideration two types of perceived risks, which are the product risk and the security risk (Amin, Rezaei, & Tavana, 2015; Kalantari Shahijan, Rezaei, Nigel Preece, & Khairuzzaman Wan Ismail, 2014; Rezaei, 2015; Rezaei, Amin, & Ismail, 2014; Rezaei & Ismail, 2014; Rotem-Mindali, 2010).

It is suggested by prior studies (Rezaei et al., 2014; Rezaei et al., 2016b; Rezaei et al., 2016d) that perceived risk mediates the relationship between trust and purchase intention, especially when customers are not very experienced in online shopping or when they have to deal with various websites less well known (Gefen et al., 2003). Sim & Koi (2002) argue that the first-timers of online shopping are mainly concerned with the fact that they are not able to physically examine the products and to verify how reliable the sellers, who are often unknown to the shoppers. According to Sonia San, et al., (2011) there are different kinds of risk perception which include:

1. Risk associated with purchase channel,
2. Risk perceived during the purchase of products/services,
3. And social risk, linked to the social influence of the group which the subjects belong to.

In addition, consumer perception towards security has a strong effect on online purchase intention. This could be due to the fact that the actual interaction which they are used to in traditional in-store shopping with the salesperson is missing when it is done in a digital way. That online shopping has to rely on electronic payment also increases the perceived risk of shoppers (Chang & Chen, 2009). According to Brent Lynn Selby, et al., (2011), self-confidence in performing a given task may influence a person's perception of risk toward the online purchase. Once a risk perception is formed, it is suggested that subsequently, consumer behavior would be shaped by such perception (Shouming & Jie, 2009). Lu, et al., (2011) shows that perceived risk affects online purchase intention in a strong, negative way. Sim and Koi (2002) suggest that off-line or non-online shoppers tend to be more risk-averse in that they have less trust in the quality of the products. Others question the security of online transaction and payment modes and the worthiness of the sellers. It could be said that traditional shoppers can see the sellers and also their products in person, therefore there is a higher risk associated with online shopping as compared to the traditional way.

Peng, et al., (2008) points out another interesting aspect of the role of perceived risk. It is suggested that perceived risk has an impact on word-of-mouth communications among customers, and hence it influences the final Apps purchase intentions. The impact of perceived risk on online purchase behavior can also be moderated by a list of other factors such as the frequency of purchase, satisfaction with earlier purchase experiences or the degree of involvement in the purchase decision (Sonia San et al., 2011).

CONCLUSION AND FUTURE RESEARCH DIRECTIONS

A brief review of the literature suggests terms such interactive marketing, e-commerce, online marketing, digital marketing and internet marketing are often used in an interchangeable way. In a similar fashion, with reference to marketing strategy, the terms e-commerce strategy, digital marketing strategy, interactive marketing strategy, internet marketing strategy, and online marketing strategy are often used to refer to more or less the same thing. Apps marketing is an exciting, emerging and quickly growing in marketing strategy that runs the spectrum from cyber brochures, to email, to electronic commerce" (Frost, 2007). All kind of organizations from for-profit to non-profit organizations are using Apps and related technologies in their marketing efforts to target their market all around the market segments. In addition, there is an evolution among consumers who increasingly rely on the internet as a purchasing medium, known as the phenomenon of e-purchasing or online shopping. Rajshekhar, Lori, Glenna, & Rober (2005) in their finding mentioned that it is not possible to achieve outstanding performance without understanding decision-making behavior of consumers who engage in online shopping. The results shown by Wei, et al., (2010) indicate how satisfaction about internet marketing strategy has a great impact on the improvement of the product value to consumers.

The terms e-commerce and internet marketing are often used in the business context, however, they both refer to the phenomenon of what we call internet-enabled marketing, which has to gain increasing prominence in many organizations worldwide. There is a handful of emerging journals whose scope is dedicated to e-commerce and internet marketing. We have, to name a few, *The Journal of Interactive Marketing, International Journal of Electronic Commerce, Electronic Commerce Research, and the Journal of Electronic Commerce Research.* The information system (IS) literature has also conducted studies in parallel which capture the interest of marketers, such as purchasing behavior, channel preferences or customer satisfaction. It has served as a useful source of information, where marketers extract a wealth of information on the topic of internet marketing.

A substantial body of researcher shows that this amount will increase in both developed and developing economics dramatically because of expansion of technology (Varadarajan & Yadav, 2009). It seems that the Internet has brought a crucial opportunity for both manufacturers to sell and for buyers to purchase their products. From the perspectives of firms, an effective integration of the Apps into the marketing strategy and operations allow them to gain a competitive edge. Not only firms can track the online behavior of individual customer for a better targeting of market segments, the post-purchase behavior of the retailers would also influence consumer judgments and loyalty subsequently.

Therefore, the spread of internet and subsequently digital marketing and online purchase have now entered into a post-adoption stage, where technical attributes such as visual design, user interfaces, and navigation become the determinants of purchase intentions of online shoppers. However, very few studies have looked into the perceptions related to adoption and "post-adoption" or acceptance of Apps-commerce. The aim of this chapter is to expand an understanding pf the decision-making of those potential Apps customers to adopt Apps usage for the first time, and also re-purchase decisions the experienced e-customers. It is commonly agreed by both industrialist and academics that the capturing and retaining a group of satisfied, loyal customers is the key to achieving business success in today's marketplace (Baker, 2006). With the aid of information technology, firms are now able to offer consumers products and promotions based on their past online purchase behavior (Amin, Rezaei, & Abolghasemi, 2014; Daliri, Rezaei, & Ismail, 2014; Rezaei et al., 2014; Rezaei & Ghodsi, 2014; Varadarajan & Yadav, 2009).

REFERENCES

Alavi, S. A., Rezaei, S., Valaei, N., & Wan Ismail, W. K. (2016). Examining shopping mall consumer decision-making styles, satisfaction and purchase intention. *International Review of Retail, Distribution and Consumer Research*, *26*(3), 272–303. doi:10.1080/09593969.2015.1096808

Amin, M., Rezaei, S., & Abolghasemi, M. (2014). User satisfaction with mobile websites: The impact of perceived usefulness (PU), perceived ease of use (PEOU) and trust. *Nankai Business Review International*, *5*(3), 258–274. doi:10.1108/NBRI-01-2014-0005

Amin, M., Rezaei, S., & Tavana, F. S. (2015). Gender differences and consumers repurchase intention: The impact of trust propensity, usefulness and ease of use for implication of innovative online retail. *International Journal of Innovation and Learning*, *17*(2), 217–233. doi:10.1504/IJIL.2015.067409

Badrinarayanan, V., Becerra, E., Kim, C.-H., & Madhavaram, S. (2010). Transference and congruence effects on purchase intentions in online stores of multi-channel retailers: Initial evidence from the U.S. and South Korea. *Journal of the Academy of Marketing Science*, 1–19. doi:10.1007/s11747-010-0239-9

Baker, S. M. (2006). Consumer normalcy: Understanding the value of shopping through narratives of consumers with visual impairments. *Journal of Retailing*, *82*(1), 37–50. doi:10.1016/j.jretai.2005.11.003

Butler, P., & Peppard, J. (1998). Consumer purchasing on the Internet: Processes and prospects. *European Management Journal*, *16*(5), 600–610. doi:10.1016/S0263-2373(98)00036-X

Cai, Y., & Cude, B. J. (2008). Online Shopping. In J. J. Xiao (Ed.), *Handbook of Consumer Finance Research* (pp. 137–159). Springer New York. doi:10.1007/978-0-387-75734-6_9

Caruana, A., & Ewing, M. T. (2010). How corporate reputation, quality, and value influence online loyalty. *Journal of Business Research, 63*(9-10), 1103–1110. doi:10.1016/j.jbusres.2009.04.030

Chai Har, L., Uchenna Cyril, E., & Nelson Oly, N. (2011). Analyzing key determinants of online repurchase intentions. *Asia Pacific Journal of Marketing and Logistics, 23*(2), 200–221. doi:10.1108/13555851111120498

Chang, H. H., & Chen, S. W. (2009). Consumer perception of interface quality, security, and loyalty in electronic commerce. *Information & Management, 46*(7), 411–417. doi:10.1016/j.im.2009.08.002

Chang, Y.-p., & Zhu, D.-h. (2007). Factors Influencing New and Repeated Buyers' Intention to Shop Online in China: A Comparatively Empirical Study. *Wireless Communications, Networking and Mobile Computing, 2007. WiCom 2007. International Conference on* (pp. 3494-3497).

Chao-Min, C., Chen-Chi, C., Hsiang-Lan, C., & Yu-Hui, F. (2009). Determinants of customer repurchase intention in online shopping. *Online Information Review, 33*(4), 761–784. doi:10.1108/14684520910985710

Chao-Min, C., Hua-Yang, L., Szu-Yuan, S., & Meng-Hsiang, H. (2009). Understanding customers loyalty intentions towards online shopping: An integration of technology acceptance model and fairness theory. *Behaviour & Information Technology, 28*(4), 347–360. doi:10.1080/01449290801892492

Chun-hui, T., & Jun, W. (2008). The Model of Online Purchasing Behavior Based on Website's Credibility and Its Inspiration for Enterprises. *Information Management, Innovation Management and Industrial Engineering, 2008. ICIII '08. International Conference on* (Vol. 2, pp. 506-511).

Daliri, E., Rezaei, S., & Ismail, W. K. W. (2014). Online social shopping: The impact of attitude, customer information quality, effectiveness of information content and perceived social presence. *International Journal of Business Environment, 6*(4), 426–450. doi:10.1504/IJBE.2014.064995

Dan, S., & Xu, H. (2011). Research on Online Shopping Intention of Undergraduate Consumer in China--Based on the Theory of Planned Behavior. *International Business Research, 4*(1), 86–92.

Djamasbi, S., Siegel, M., & Tullis, T. (2010). Generation Y, web design, and eye tracking. *International Journal of Human-Computer Studies, 68*(5), 307–323. doi:10.1016/j.ijhcs.2009.12.006

Dwayne, B., Pedro Simões, C., & Alexandra, M. (2004). The role of communication and trust in explaining customer loyalty: An extension to the ECSI model. *European Journal of Marketing*, *38*(9), 1272–1293.

Ellis-Chadwick, F., Doherty, N., & Hart, C. (2002). Signs of change? A longitudinal study of Internet adoption in the UK retail sector. *Journal of Retailing and Consumer Services*, *9*(2), 71–80. doi:10.1016/S0969-6989(01)00030-3

Gefen, D., Karahanna, E., & Straub, D. W. (2003). Inexperience and experience with online stores: The importance of TAM and trust. *Engineering Management. IEEE Transactions on*, *50*(3), 307–321.

Grewal, D., Iyer, G. R., & Levy, M. (2004). Internet retailing: Enablers, limiters and market consequences. *Journal of Business Research*, *57*(7), 703–713. doi:10.1016/S0148-2963(02)00348-X

Hannah, B., & Lybecker, K. M. (2010). Determinants of Recent Online Purchasing and the Percentage of Income Spent Online. *International Business Research*, *3*(4), 60–71. doi:10.5539/ibr.v3n4p60

Hausman, A. V., & Siekpe, J. S. (2009). The effect of web interface features on consumer online purchase intentions. *Journal of Business Research*, *62*(1), 5–13. doi:10.1016/j.jbusres.2008.01.018

He, W., & Chai, J. (2009). Study on Mechanism and Models of Customer Segmentation of C2C Shopping. *Information Science and Engineering (ICISE), 2009 1st International Conference on* (pp. 3073-3076).

Ismail, A., Abdullah, M. M., & Parasuraman, B. (2009). Effect of Service Quality and Perceive Value on Customer Satisfaction. *International Journal of Management Perspectives*, *1*(3), 29–44.

Jeong, S. W., Fiore, A. M., Niehm, L. S., & Lorenz, F. O. (2009). The role of experiential value in online shopping: The impacts of product presentation on consumer responses towards an apparel web site. *Internet Research*, *19*(1), 105–124. doi:10.1108/10662240910927858

Jingdong, C., & Xiaoqian, G. (2010). The Theory and Empirical Research of Network Profit Based on the Perceived Value. *Computer Modeling and Simulation, 2010. ICCMS '10. Second International Conference on* (Vol. 3, pp. 104-108).

Jones, M. A., & Reynolds, K. E. (2006). The role of retailer interest on shopping behavior. *Journal of Retailing*, *82*(2), 115–126. doi:10.1016/j.jretai.2005.05.001

Juan Carlos, R., & Juan José, G. (2009). The importance of perceived trust, security and privacy in online trading systems. *Information Management & Computer Security*, *17*(2), 96–113. doi:10.1108/09685220910963983

Jumin, L., Do-Hyung, P., & Ingoo, H. (2011). The different effects of online consumer reviews on consumers purchase intentions depending on trust in online shopping malls: An advertising perspective. *Internet Research*, *21*(2), 187–206. doi:10.1108/10662241111123766

Kalantari Shahijan, M., Rezaei, S., Nigel Preece, C., & Khairuzzaman Wan Ismail, W. (2014). Examining retailers behaviour in managing critical points in Halal meat handling: A PLS analysis. *Journal of Islamic Marketing*, *5*(3), 446–472. doi:10.1108/JIMA-10-2013-0070

Koo, D.-M. (2006). The fundamental reasons of e-consumers loyalty to an online store. *Electronic Commerce Research and Applications*, *5*(2), 117–130. doi:10.1016/j.elerap.2005.10.003

Lee, J., Park, D.-H., & Han, I. (2008). The effect of negative online consumer reviews on product attitude: An information processing view. *Electronic Commerce Research and Applications*, *7*(3), 341–352. doi:10.1016/j.elerap.2007.05.004

Lee, M. K. O., & Cheung, C. M. K. (2004). Internet Retailing Adoption by Small-to-Medium Sized Enterprises (SMEs): A Multiple-Case Study. *Information Systems Frontiers*, *6*(4), 385–397. doi:10.1023/B:ISFI.0000046379.58029.54

Limon, Y., Kahle, L. R., & Orth, U. R. (2009). Package Design as a Communications Vehicle in Cross-Cultural Values Shopping. *Journal of International Marketing*, *17*(1), 30–57. doi:10.1509/jimk.17.1.30

Lindman, M. (2010). Extending customer knowledge: The value of customer value-based approach. *Journal of Global Business & Technology*, *6*(2), 48–63.

Liu, C., Marchewka, J. T., Lu, J., & Yu, C.-S. (2005). Beyond concerna privacy-trust-behavioral intention model of electronic commerce. *Information & Management*, *42*(2), 289–304. doi:10.1016/j.im.2004.01.003

Lu, Y., Cao, Y., Wang, B., & Yang, S. (2011). A study on factors that affect users behavioral intention to transfer usage from the offline to the online channel. *Computers in Human Behavior*, *27*(1), 355–364. doi:10.1016/j.chb.2010.08.013

Maaja, V., & Krista, J. (2011). The dual value of honesty among Russians in selected former Soviet countries. *Cross Cultural Management: An International Journal*, *18*(1), 55–70. doi:10.1108/13527601111104296

Madlberger, M. (2004). Strategies and business models in electronic retailing: indications from the U.S. and the UK.*Proceedings of the 6th international conference on Electronic commerce*. doi:10.1145/1052220.1052258

McEleny, C. (2010). Article. Centaur Communications Ltd.

Mohseni, S., Jayashree, S., Rezaei, S., Kasim, A., & Okumus, F. (2016). Attracting tourists to travel companies websites: The structural relationship between website brand, personal value, shopping experience, perceived risk and purchase intention. *Current Issues in Tourism*, 1–30. doi:10.1080/13683500.2016.1200539

Overby, J. W., & Lee, E.-J. (2006). The effects of utilitarian and hedonic online shopping value on consumer preference and intentions. *Journal of Business Research, 59*(10-11), 1160–1166. doi:10.1016/j.jbusres.2006.03.008

Peng, H., Wang, C., & Cai, J. (2008). An Empirical Investigation on the Adoption of Online Shopping of University Students in China. *Business and Information Management, 2008. ISBIM '08. International Seminar on* (Vol. 1, pp. 498-501).

Pitt, L., Parent, M., Steyn, P., Berthon, P., & Money, A. (2010). The Social Media Release as a Corporate Communications Tool for Bloggers. *Professional Communication, IEEE Transactions on.*

Rajshekhar, G. J., Lori, P. R., Glenna, P., & Robert, F. S. (2005). Sustainable competitive advantage of internet firms: A strategic framework and implications for global marketers. *International Marketing Review, 22*(6), 658–672. doi:10.1108/02651330510630276

Ren, L., & Zhang, Y. (2010). Research of Customer Perceived Value on eStores. *E-Business and E-Government (ICEE), 2010 International Conference on* (pp. 2237-2240).

Rezaei, S. (2015). Segmenting consumer decision-making styles (CDMS) toward marketing practice: A partial least squares (PLS) path modeling approach. *Journal of Retailing and Consumer Services, 22*, 1–15. doi:10.1016/j.jretconser.2014.09.001

Rezaei, S., Ali, F., Amin, M., & Jayashree, S. (2016a). Online impulse buying of tourism products: The role of web site personality, utilitarian and hedonic web browsing. *Journal of Hospitality and Tourism Technology*, *7*(1), 60–83. doi:10.1108/JHTT-03-2015-0018

Rezaei, S., Amin, M., & Ismail, W. K. W. (2014). Online repatronage intention: An empirical study among Malaysian experienced online shoppers. *International Journal of Retail & Distribution Management*, *42*(5), 390–421. doi:10.1108/IJRDM-03-2012-0026

Rezaei, S., Amin, M., Moghaddam, M., & Mohamed, N. (2016b). 3G post adoption users experience with telecommunications services. *Nankai Business Review International*, *7*(3), 361–394. doi:10.1108/NBRI-01-2016-0007

Rezaei, S., Emami, M., & Valaei, N. (2016c). *The moderating impact of product classification on the relationship between online trust, satisfaction, and repurchase intention. In Encyclopedia of E-Commerce Development, Implementation, and Management* (p. 1692). IGI Global.

Rezaei, S., & Ghodsi, S. S. (2014). Does value matters in playing online game? An empirical study among massively multiplayer online role-playing games (MMORPGs). *Computers in Human Behavior*, *35*, 252–266. doi:10.1016/j.chb.2014.03.002

Rezaei, S., & Ismail, W. K. W. (2014). Examining online channel selection behaviour among social media shoppers: A PLS analysis. *International Journal of Electronic Marketing and Retailing*, *6*(1), 28–51. doi:10.1504/IJEMR.2014.064876

Rezaei, S., Shahijan, M. K., Amin, M., & Ismail, W. K. W. (2016d). Determinants of App Stores Continuance Behavior: A PLS Path Modelling Approach. *Journal of Internet Commerce*, *15*(4), 408–440. doi:10.1080/15332861.2016.1256749

Rezaei, S., Shahijan, M. K., Valaei, N., Rahimi, R., & Ismail, W. K. W. (2016e). Experienced international business traveller's behaviour in Iran: A partial least squares path modelling analysis. *Tourism and Hospitality Research.*

Rotem-Mindali, O. (2010). E-tail versus retail: The effects on shopping related travel empirical evidence from Israel. *Transport Policy*, *17*(5), 312–322. doi:10.1016/j.tranpol.2010.02.005

Selby, C., Jeremy, A., & Beverley, H. (2011). Measuring Internet Product Purchase Risk. *European Journal of Marketing*, *45*(7), 6–6.

Shahijan, M. K., Rezaei, S., & Amin, M. (2016). International students course satisfaction and continuance behavioral intention in higher education setting: An empirical assessment in Malaysia. *Asia Pacific Education Review*, *17*(1), 41–62. doi:10.1007/s12564-015-9410-9

Shouming, C., & Jie, L. (2009). Factors Influencing the Consumers' Willingness to Buy in E-Commerce. *E-Business and Information System Security, 2009. EBISS '09. International Conference on* (pp. 1-8).

Sim, L. L., & Koi, S. M. (2002). Singapores Internet shoppers and their impact on traditional shopping patterns. *Journal of Retailing and Consumer Services*, *9*(2), 115–124. doi:10.1016/S0969-6989(01)00029-7

Sonia San, M., Carmen, C., & Rebeca San, J. (2011). Dual effect of perceived risk on cross-national e-commerce. *Internet Research*, *21*(1), 46–66. doi:10.1108/10662241111104875

Stern, P. C. (1999). Information, Incentives, and Proenvironmental Consumer Behavior. *Journal of Consumer Policy*, *22*(4), 461–478. doi:10.1023/A:1006211709570

Talal, A., Charles, D., & Sue Vaux, H. (2011). Antecedents of continuance intentions towards e-shopping: The case of Saudi Arabia. *Journal of Enterprise Information Management*, *24*(1), 85–111. doi:10.1108/17410391111097447

Tang, S., & Zhang, M. (2010). Differences and Impact Factors between Customer Expected Value and Customer Perceived Value. *E-Product E-Service and E-Entertainment (ICEEE), 2010 International Conference on* (pp. 1-4).

Tao, Z. (2008). The Impact of Perceived Value on User Acceptance of Mobile Commerce. *Electronic Commerce and Security, 2008 International Symposium on* (pp. 237-240).

Thong, J. Y. L., Hong, S.-J., & Tam, K. Y. (2006). The effects of post-adoption beliefs on the expectation-confirmation model for information technology continuance. *International Journal of Human-Computer Studies*, *64*(9), 799–810. doi:10.1016/j.ijhcs.2006.05.001

Valaei, N., & Rezaei, S. (2016). Does Web 2.0 utilisation lead to knowledge quality, improvisational creativity, compositional creativity, and innovation in small and medium-sized enterprises? A sense-making perspective. *Technology Analysis and Strategic Management*, 1–14. doi:10.1080/09537325.2016.1213806

Valaei, N., Rezaei, S., Ismail, W. K. W., & Moi, O. Y. (2016). Cultural effect on attitude toward online advertising and online brands: Applying Hofstedes cultural factors to Internet marketing. *International Journal of Internet Marketing and Advertising*, *10*(4), 270. doi:10.1504/IJIMA.2016.081346

Valaei, N., Rezaei, S., & Shahijan, M. K. (2016). CouQual: Assessing overall service quality in courier service industry and the moderating impact of age, gender and ethnicity. *International Journal of Management Concepts and Philosophy*, *9*(2), 144–169. doi:10.1504/IJMCP.2016.077770

Varadarajan, R., & Yadav, M. S. (2009). Marketing Strategy in an Internet-Enabled Environment: A Retrospective on the First Ten Years of JIM and a Prospective on the Next Ten Years. *Journal of Interactive Marketing*, *23*(1), 11–22. doi:10.1016/j.intmar.2008.10.002

Vijayasarathy, L. R. (2004). Predicting consumer intentions to use on-line shopping: The case for an augmented technology acceptance model. *Information & Management*, *41*(6), 747–762. doi:10.1016/j.im.2003.08.011

Wang, S.-j., & Feng, C. (2010). Ways to maximize customer perceived value in E-commerce age. *Networking and Digital Society (ICNDS), 2010 2nd International Conference on* (Vol. 1, pp. 298-301).

Ward, M. R. (2001). Will Online Shopping Compete More with Traditional Retailing or Catalog Shopping? *NETNOMICS: Economic Research and Electronic Networking*, *3*(2), 103–117. doi:10.1023/A:1011451228921

Wei, Z., Jingdong, C., & Wei, H. (2010). The internet marketing strategies theory and empirical research based on product value. *Information Management and Engineering (ICIME), 2010 The 2nd IEEE International Conference on* (pp. 203-206).

Ye, J.-h., Zhang, M.-l., & Zan, J.-y. (2009). Study on Customer Satisfaction in Benefit/Sacrifice Hierarchy. *Fuzzy Systems and Knowledge Discovery, 2009. FSKD '09. Sixth International Conference on* (Vol. 7, pp. 379-385).

Yeo, V. C. S., Goh, S.-K., & Rezaei, S. (2017). Consumer experiences, attitude and behavioral intention toward online food delivery (OFD) services. *Journal of Retailing and Consumer Services*, *35*, 150–162. doi:10.1016/j.jretconser.2016.12.013

Yuan, G. (2009). Factors Influencing Perceived Value of and Attitude toward E-commerce among Online Shoppers in China. *Information Engineering, 2009. ICIE '09. WASE International Conference on* (Vol. 2, pp. 330-332).

KEY TERMS AND DEFINITIONS

Apps Hedonic Value: Overall assessment or decision of Apps experiential benefits and disadvantages in order to obtain the feeling of escapism in order to obtain an appreciation of the experience rather than simply for task completion such as the purchase of a product.

Apps Usefulness: Consumers confidence of usage usefulness in Apps commerce to perform transaction.

Apps Utilitarian Value: Overall assessment or judgment of functional benefits and sacrifices of Apps usage which is relevant for the task-specific use of online shopping.

Perceived Risk of Apps: Consumers uncertainty when they are not able to predict the consequences of their Apps transaction outcomes.

Chapter 14
The Future of Apps: A Smart Investment for Business

Cathrine Linnes
Østfold University College, Norway

Brian R. Metcalf
Hawaii Pacific University, USA

Milad Kalantari Shahijan
Universiti Teknologi Malaysia, Malaysia

ABSTRACT

Apps have the solutions for many things and consumers have them right in their pocket. Just think about a holiday. From the booking of flight tickets, making a hotel reservation, sharing it with your friends, ordering a rental car, paying for apparel, and so on. You can use your smartphone for almost everything these days and most apps are connected with social media sites. Even though many users do not want to pay lots of money for apps, experts still forecast huge growth. There is a big different on how consumers used apps 5 years ago and how they use apps today. Today consumers are demanding apps that can fulfil many different needs and are much more individualized. This high and consuming demand forces the developers the use large amounts of data before they can be able to meet these needs.

DOI: 10.4018/978-1-5225-2449-6.ch014

Copyright ©2017, IGI Global. Copying or distributing in print or electronic forms without written permission of IGI Global is prohibited.

INTRODUCTION

The word "application" is so ubiquitous. What is an application, or app for short? An app is a type of software that allows the end user to perform particular tasks. Applications for desktop or laptop computers are sometimes referred to as desktop applications, and those for mobile devices are known as mobile apps (GCFLearnFree.org, 2015). The end user task can be as simple as a traditional calculator or as complex as a word processing software system. Nevertheless, the core mission will be the same, to perform a specific task for the end user. Applications have a rich history. Specifically, apps are being developed for mobile devices in conjunction with aspects of Big Data. Many mobile applications are free but are they truly at no cost to the end user? The cost must be absorbed elsewhere. Privacy is also a concern which is often overlooked when selecting a mobile app.

Today's Millennials are very clever at computer usage. The majority of the millennials have always had internet access. The concept of using applications is as second nature as riding a bicycle. However, the rise of applications in a mobile environment is a relatively new venture. The Apple App Store launched in July 2008, a year after the first iPhone was released. The App Store had 500 apps and, to many, this was an eye-opener. It also signaled the dominance of the native mobile application. An astonishing 10 million applications were downloaded during the first weekend (Rowinski, 2012). Today Android users are able to select between 2.2 million apps, followed by the App Store at 2 million apps and Windows Store at 669,000, Amazon App store at 600,000 and BlackBerry World at 234, 500 (Statista, 2016b).

Not long after, Google Android followed this successful scheme. Research In Motion, the manufacturers of the Blackberry, and Microsoft, producers of the Windows Phone, also adapted the app store concept. The idea itself is simplistic genius. It allows the delivery of software without the need for any physical medium that requires a store front and/or mailing and distribution costs for installation. The app store concept was not the first interpretation. First generation mobile phones were designed and developed by the handset manufacturers (Clark, 2015). The software and apps for these early models were written in-house. As the usage and concept of a mobile phone changed so did the deployment or development of applications.

Moreover, applications are created for a specific task. To many users, apps are simply useful and entertaining tools. As well as providing users with information, however, these mobile software applications are also limitless data-gatherers. Even the most mundane apps often collect a surprising amount from handsets just to do the work (Guess, 2011). The data that is subsequently created and analyzed can of course be used to enhance the experience of the app. By analyzing feature usage, the developers can determine the more popular items. This information can be used to determine retention rates within the same category of apps. It can also be used to conclude how the app is performing to a comparable competitor's app (Business Insider, 2013). Long term usage will reveal unique patterns which may show the developers the ways in which the app is being used. The app may be used in a way which is unintended thus spurring further development of the app or a new application entirely. These factors are important development tools for an alarming reason. For all their flexibility app users are a very fickle bunch. The average user spends 70% of app time in their three most-frequently-used apps. Most users have approximately 30 apps installed and only three are getting prime time usage. Of those apps that are actually used about 52% lose at least half of their peak users after three months. The most shocking statistic is less than 0.01% of mobile apps will be considered financially successful by 2018 (Gartner, 2014; Hickman, 2015; Varshneya, 2015).

Cell phones have enacted a dynamic change. Going back a few years, in 2010 fully eight in ten adults (82%) were cell phone users, and about one-quarter of adults (23%) lived in a household that has a cell phone but no landline phone. Of that 82% who own cell phones, 43% of them have apps. Often these apps cannot be uninstalled without resorting to rooting the device. This is not limited to cell phones. Tablets, smart watches, and other items which belong to the genre of the Internet of Things (IoT) are also preconfigured with apps. Twenty-nine percent of mobile device owners download new apps to the device. Twenty percent of owners under the age of thirty download apps habitually. It is estimated that 53% of these individuals download an app within the past 30 days, while 33% of those may have installed a new app within the last seven days. These statistics are reflective of the United States population. Taken upon a global scale the end result is obvious; a lot of data is being generated by these apps (Purcewll, Entner, & Henderson, 2010).

The objective of this chapter is to look at the implications apps have on society. Current apps are not going to be around forever, so future potential modifications will be discussed as changes are needed to keep the users engaged. Benefits, challenges, and solutions will be discussed along with examples.

BACKGROUND

People around the world are creating an unprecedented amount of data. In 2015, the annual data center traffic accumulated to approximately 3.9 zettabytes (1 zettabyte is equal to 1 billion terabytes) and it is estimated to increase to 14.1 zettabytes by the end of 2020 (Cisco, 2015). Statistics show that in most developing countries, mobile phone reached over 100% per capita with individuals owning more than one device (Hoehle & Venkatesh, 2015). In 2015, annual smartphone sales accumulated approximately 1.4 billion units compared to 1.2 in 2014. According to a Gartner report, that is an increase of 9.7% over the same period in 2014 (Goasduff & Rivera, 2015; Woods & van der Meulen, 2016). A trend that people use more data volume can also be seen by comparing data plans offered by various providers. According to Ericsson, the average smartphone user in 2021 is projected to go through 8.9GB of data every month compared to 1.4GB of data per month today. In addition, phone carriers will start to roll out 5G speeds by 2020 and the data traffic is expected to increase ten-fold by the end of 2021 (Heisler, 2016). The combination of a cell phone, personal digital assistant (PDA), media player and GPS navigation unit led to a popular form of mobile device: the smartphone. We will soon move towards intelligent phones.

The top 10 countries for ownership of smart phones are South Korea at 88%, followed by Australia at 77%, Israel 74%, United States 72%, Spain 71%, United Kingdom 68%, Canada 67%, Chile 65%, Malaysia 65% and Germany 60%. Once online, 76% of the users across the globe use social networking sites such as Facebook and Twitter (Poushter, 2016). It is estimated that U.S. adults spend approximately 12 hours a day using various digital media per day. This is up 5 minutes from 2015 (eMarketer, 2016). It is multitasking on smartphones that help drive this increase. Traditional TV watching is still popular where the average American spends more than 4 hours of watching programs daily. However, the trend is shifting and according to eMarketer (2016), the average viewing is expected to go down by more than two hours by 2018 due to new ways of living.

There are great benefits to utilize mobile phone applications for business such as building relationships and loyalty with clients, reinforcing brand loyalty, increasing visibility and accessibility, generating repeat business, and enhancing social networking strategies. Mobile apps also have the capability to function even while offline. These apps are referred to as native mobile apps. As well as they offer constant visibility on the screen and push notifications that websites lack. Industry leading companies such as Amazon, Target, and Macys are using mobile apps to promote their brand and merchandise. There are more and more industries adopting these functionalities.

According to Statista (2017), $81,069 million were spent on digital advertising in 2016 and the market is expected to grow to $198,657 million in 2021. There is an immense market for businesses to utilize smart phone applications to enhance their business operations. A study shows that 62% of smartphone users utilize their devices for health information, 57% for banking, 44% for real estate, 43% for job information, 40% for information on government services, 30% for educational content, and 18% for submitting job applications (Smith, 2015a). Numbers like these are useful information for mobile phone developers as well as industries on potential market opportunities.

Native Mobile Apps vs. Mobile Web Apps

Apps that continue to work while offline can be important for businesses. A sales person can enter his or her data while on the road and when returning to the office the information is automatically synced with the server. It is possible to develop a mobile web app that is ready to go offline that meets the need of the user. However, it depends upon the offline capabilities and data needed. Mobile web apps can be built with three core functionalities and part of the HTML5 standard:

- Browser application caching of pages
- Local storage
- Local database

With an application cache it is easy to make an offline version of the web application by creating a cache manifest file. Setting up an application cache manifest tells the browser how it can use pages already downloaded to the user's mobile device instead off displaying an error when there is no longer a network connection. Advantages to browser application caching of pages are, the user can continue to use the application which offline, the cached resources load faster, and the browser will only download updated/changed resources from the server. Local storage is a standard that holds local web application data, even when offline. It is very similar to a cookie. However, there are some differences, cookies are resent to the server with every HTTP request, and it uses a lot of bandwidth to resend all offline data when the server doesn't need it. Further, cookies can max out at 4MB of data, while applications are given 5MB of data to work with per domain. A local database removes the 5MB limit of local storage and allows data to be indexed so that multiple properties can be queried faster.

Other terms frequently referred to in the media are "hybrid apps" which combine elements from both the native and web applications. One can often see this term being mentioned in the context of mobile computing. "Killer app" is another term being used and it is a program that purposely or unintentionally gets the user to buy the system the application runs on. Finally, "legacy app" is referred to apps that has been inherited from languages, platforms, and techniques earlier than current technology

HTML Cache Manifest Example

The example below shows an HTML document with a cache manifest used for offline user browsing. Once the file is cached, the browser will continue to show the cached version, even if the user changes the file on the server. To ensure the browser updates the cache, the user need to change the manifest file. If the manifest attribute is not specified, the page will not be attached (unless the page is specified directly in the manifest file). The recommended file extension for manifest files is ".appcache".

```
<!DOCTYPE HTML>
<html manifest="demo.appcache">

<body>
The content of the document......
</body>

</html>
```

The manifest file has three sections: "cache manifest," is a file listed under the header will be cached after the page is downloaded for the first time, "network" files listed under the header require a connection to the server, and will never be cached, and "fallback" files listed under the header specifies fallback pages if a page is inaccessible.

Privacy Issues

Similar to all modern software, applications are usually accompanied by the standard end user license agreement. Navigating to the appropriate app store for software installation invariably produces the end users license agreement prior to installation. Most consumers rarely read the fine print which is detailed in the written statement but all users should. Apps can make phone calls, take photos, track the user's location, monitor the user's web browsing habits, read files and transmit the user's contact list to advertisers, all without the user noticing a thing. Perhaps this might not seem like such a big problem at the given time, however, once the user discovers that the flashlight app just installed on their smart phone is designed to do location tracking, read their calendar, use their camera, or gain access to unique numbers that identify the phone and then share this data with a number of ad agencies, then it might become a problem for the user. In most cases the consumer can simply uninstall the app and find a substitute. However, there are those apps which are pre-installed onto the device. Normally, these are uninstall-able unless the device is rooted. Not all apps are like this. There are paid versions which do not have such invasive features. Of course, those which are free have to produce income for the developers somehow. In this case the currency in exchange for free apps is information comprimising privacy.

OVERVIEW AND IMPACT OF SMAC TECHNOLOGIES

Previous in this chapter, we have accounted for apps and how the introduction of them managed to create, what is known as, the mobile revolution. Not only did it impact the way we use our mobile devices, but also how we live our everyday lives. When we start to count the hours in a day it is amazing how many hours social media and mobile games are taking up in people's lives.

In the beginning, apps were typically small arcade games, ring tone editors, calculators, calendars, etc. Already from the beginning, the suppliers experienced a big demand for these apps, which makes more and more companies see the opportunity in the app market (Clark, 2014). Companies and individuals have introduced more and more apps and are trying to make the apps more interesting and more attractive to the consumers. In the beginning, many app developers had challenges because the phone's technology limited the app developers' options. But the app developers did not give up, and when Juniper Research estimated in 2010 that the revenues from sales of apps would be $25 billion in 2014, they saw a big and potential lucrative market (Clark, 2014). For app developers, this is a true Eldorado of opportunities and it may even be too much for some, as was seen in the Flappy Bird case. For those not familiar with Flappy Bird, it was the most popular game on the Internet, consisting of a simple one button game where the user has to navigate the bird past various obstacles. The Flappy Bird game was found to be addictive so the creator decided to pull the App from the market as people were getting obsessed with the gamc (Abigail, 2014). But others like King, have seized the opportunities and turned their company into word famous brands and a revenue-generating machine. King is a London-based Swedish social games company, King (or formerly known as King.com)

The most popular application category is games at 24.85% of all apps. Business apps are the second most popular category with a share of 9.96% followed by education (8.55%), lifestyle (8.44%), entertainment (6.16%), utilities (4.9%), travel (3.88%), books (3.03%), health and fitness (2.97%), food and drink (2.86%), productivity (2.63%), music (2.58%), finance (2.24%), reference (2.24%), photo and video (2.22%), sports (2.22%), social networking (2.12%), news (2.02%), medical (1.9%) and shopping (1.25%) (Statista, 2016a). As of summer of 2016, more than 130 billion apps were downloaded from the App Store (Statista, 2016a). For this chapter we have chosen to highlight some of the many popular apps: health, games, financial, social network, professional network, and dating apps in order to get a better understanding of the impact these apps are having upon society.

Health Apps

Companies around the world benefit from customer insight with the help of app technology. Two industries that are using the opportunities from the rapid growth in the use of smartphones are medical and behavioral health care. The number of health care applications available to consumers is over 165,000 and the popularity continues to grow (Chain Drug Review, 2015). Apps are available for a variety of useful tasks to include symptom assessment, self-monitoring and psychoeducation, resource location, and tracking treatment progress. Also, developers incorporate innovative data collection features linked to sensors and wearables. One in ten apps now has the ability of connecting a device or sensor, providing biofeedback and physiological function data from the patient. This increases the accuracy and convenience of data collection (Chain Drug Review, 2015).

The Mobile Health, or "mHealth" Apps are divided into three categories: Disease & Treatment Management, Wellness Management, and Other. Wellness Management is the biggest category and includes fitness, lifestyle and stress, and diet and nutrition. Medical professionals have long been some of the earliest adopters of personal mobile technology for assisting with daily routine of their practice. Although handheld mobile platforms and smartphones have been used in the medical industry for some time, the adoption of the specific technology for the behavioral health care has been slow. Smartphone apps provide a useful function that can be integrated with the conventional manualized treatment. For example, apps designed for self-assessments that can help the patients assess and monitor their own symptoms. These results can be shared with the healthcare provider. Furthermore, the healthcare apps can also keep track of hours of sleep, anxiety levels, and medication used that can be sent to family members, caregiver or clinician (Luxton & McCann, 2011).

According to Berg Insight (n.d.) around 2.8 million patients worldwide were using a home monitoring service based on equipment with integrated connectivity at the end of 2012. These numbers do not include patients that use monitoring devices connected to a PC or mobile phone. It only includes systems that rely on monitors with integrated connectivity or systems that use monitoring hubs with integrated cellular or fixed-line modems. One can clearly see the growth potential of the healthcare app market. Berg Insight has forecasted that the number of home monitoring systems with integrated communication capabilities will grow at a compound annual growth rate (CAGR) of 26.9 percent between 2011 and 2017, reaching 9.4 million connections globally by the end of the forecast period. In 2015, Berg Insight reported that the number of remotely monitored patients had reached 4.9 million (IoT Business News, 2015).

Mental health apps (MHapps) are being developed at a fast pace and are now available to smartphone users in recent years. The goal of these apps is to boost mental health and well-being. They range from guiding recovery of mental illness to facilitating beneficial habits to improve emotional health (Donker, Petrie, Proudfoot, Clarke, Birch, & Christensen, 2013). These certainly have the potential to play a large role in the future of mental health care. As yet, there is no clear guidelines for the development of evidence-based MHapps, however and many lack features that would greatly enhance their functionality. Many also lack features that are optimized. MHapp and mHealth developers all too rarely conduct or provide evidence-based experimental validation of their effectiveness (Bakker, Kazantzis, Rickwood, & Rickard, 2016). Nevertheless, MHapps have great potential to play a key role in the future of behavioral and mental health care (Simon & Ludman, 2009), to make mental health care more accessible to more people, and to reduce stigma and other barriers to people seeking help (Watts & Andrews, 2014).

All-in-all, current and emerging smartphone technology offers numerous capabilities and benefits for consumers and providers of medical and behavioral health care. These technological advantages, however, are outpacing many policies regarding the delivery of tele mental health care. These type of apps allow patients to have a follow up in between their doctor appointments which can be very important for the client.

Game Apps

In a more frivolous use of the technology, games, especially, play an increasingly large role in the app universe. Facebook has a game section where the users spend 927 million hours per month (Smith, 2015d). There are many game apps available in the app stores around the world, but the most successful of them are the ones that manage to properly integrate a social aspect to the mobile games that can be played wherever and whenever. A good example of this is the London-based Swedish social games company, King (or formerly known as King.com). While King has been developing games even before the introduction of mobile apps, it was not until the release of their first mobile app game that King became a super successful game developer. In 2012, King had 7 million daily active users, which is a lot, but only one year later (after releasing their first mobile app game) they had 50 million daily active users. The game they released was the world famous Candy Crush Saga which quickly became the top Facebook game in 2013. Today, Candy Crush is still one of the best Facebook integrated games in terms of daily active users, and in particular, it is the integration with Facebook that has made the game so popular. King has managed to make a simple, casual game like Candy Crush Saga, into an addictive, entertaining, and social game. This is the goal for all King's games and one of the key things that make King so successful is their focus on making their games mobile. Alex Dale, the chief marketing officer of King, says that:

King's games sync across Facebook on the desktop, iPhone, iPad and Android devices, so that you can pick up your game of Candy Crush on different devices throughout the day. King has made it a point to make it the exact same game across all devices. And when users play more than one device, they have much more engagement and monetization (Geron, 2013).

The augmented reality game from Nintendo, Pokemon Go is another app that gained viral popularity among its users. Not only is the game very social, but it requires users to be outdoors and active while playing it. Lights and vibration on the phone would alert the user there was a Pokemon hiding nearby. User would then push the button to try to catch it and then continue on their way. Pokemon Go was launched in July of 2016 and has 20 million daily active users (and growing) in the U.S. alone. The estimated number of Pokemon Go downloads to date are 500 million downloads and the average user spent 26 minutes daily on the game. It is quite amazing how powerful one game can become (Smith, 2017).

Financial Apps

In October of 2014 Apple introduced Apple Pay. Apple Pay is a mobile payment platform through which users with compatible devices can make payments in retail stores and also inside of apps. It allows anyone with the device and a compatible debit or credit card account to make contactless payments simply by hovering their device over an NFC compatible payment terminal (Grothaus, 2016). According to (Rogowsky, 2014), the service will replace the traditional credit card swipe; it also introduces ID verification with a Touch ID sensor of an iPhone. According to Bloomberg Technology, the three biggest mobile payment competitors are Apple Pay, Samsung Pay, and Android Pay. Apple Pay is the clear winner with 12 million users, followed by Android and Samsung with 5 million users each (Kharif, 2016). Furthermore, smartphone owners frequently embrace mobile payment apps from PayPal, Mobile app, Google Wallet, McDonald's app, Starbucks app, gas station apps, parking apps, etc. No need to remember your wallet when shopping at your favorite places, and no reason to get a parking ticket when you can pay for more parking without returning to the meter or fumbling with coins or payment machines.

Despite the interest and convenience, there are still retailers who cannot accept mobile payments (also referred to as mobile money, mobile wallet) and some countries use their own local banks payment apps. This is creating some confusion for consumers and some countries will lag behind others. Some people might not see the advantage of a mobile wallet over plastic credit and debit cards and some may never trust the technology to be secure enough. Forrester Research (2014) estimates mobile payments will top $142 billion a year by 2019 and peer-to-peer payments will reach $17 billion in 2019. Society is certainly moving in a wallet-less direction.

Social Apps

To make these individualized apps that help the consumers make their everyday life a little bit easier requires a lot of data, and especially personal data, which can be a challenge. Social media such as Facebook, Twitter and Instagram have a lot of personal information, which many app developers take advantage of. An increased number of apps require a login through, for example, Facebook, because a social media platform like Facebook has a big amount of personal data which many apps use (Larson, 2014). A login through Facebook makes it easy for both the consumers and the app developers, which makes this a very popularly way for the app developers to create an individualized app. The app developers can use the consumer's pictures, names, friends and other personal information to make a fast and easy individualized app but also use the information to send targeted advertisements to the consumers (Clifford, 2014). As of January 2017, there are over 1.79 billion monthly active Facebook users on which 4.5 billion "likes" are generated daily (Zephoria, 2017). Twitter is reported to have approximately 400 million users, however there has been some decrease over the last year due to advertisement and brand noise (Social Times, 2016). Advertisement and brand noise can become a problem on all social media sites. It can be great receiving advertisement, however, it can become too much.

Snapchat was launched in 2011 and has become one of the most used apps across the world with more 100 million daily active users. Snapchat is basically an app where you can share pictures or videos called "snaps", and it makes it really easy to share moments with your friends. Approximately 8,796 snaps are sent every second (Smith, 2015c) and together with the many million users, Snapchat is an extremely attractive app for thousands of companies, that are looking for accessible advertising options. In Snapchat, you can see advertising, live snap opportunities based on your location, and a chance to discover things from different companies in the target group such as MTV, CNN, Cosmopolitan, and National Geographic. However, studies show that advertisers have to be better to get the viewers' attention within the first two seconds of the ad, because if not, the users will just skip the ad by clicking the screen. Besides location Snapchat also gets access to contacts and a relatively new feature with facial recognition, which Snap acquired from Looksery for what is said to be around $150 million (TechCrunch, 2015). Some experts have earlier said that users should watch out what content in the pictures and videos they allow Snapchat to save, and now some claim that Snapchat with their facial recognition have the opportunity to save your facial features and use them as they want.

Professional Network Apps

Another useful category for companies are recruiting apps to help find the best candidate for their organization. The market for corporate recruiting software has reached $1.5 billion and 65% of applicants are looking for jobs on mobile devices. A recruiting app allows companies to bypass the middlemen and headhunters to talk to candidates directly (Tantry, 2015). Downloading apps that are focused on recruitment can enable users to become more efficient when it comes to their organizations workflow. Apps like these can help companies find more qualified employees, even at a distance. The current top five apps are:

- LinkedIn
- Instajob
- WhatsApp
- Interview Assistant
- Smart Recruiters Mobile Hiring App

LinkedIn is the number one and world's largest professional network app on the Internet. The app has over 467 million members in over 200 countries and territories and it is currently available in 24 languages. Their fastest growing demographics are students and recent graduates with around 40 million users (LinkedIn, 2017). This app allows the user to stay updated with the latest development of the candidate. Instajob is an app that allows employers to take pictures and turn them into visual job adds. Instajob can be a good tool to give candidates an insight into what it is like to work for a certain company. This app allows for employment branding through pictures. WhatsApp is a messaging system that offers messaging and calling for free all over the world. Interview assistant is an interview scheduling app which allows for company branding, candidate tracking and ad-free content. The app looks professional and the company offers several plans. Smart Recruiters mobile hiring app can assist companies in finding, attracting, and hiring good employees. The app is easy to use, is scalable, and it offers marketing, hiring and analytics all in one package.

In addition, mobile apps can help to improve employee productivity and enhance customer satisfaction. Companies have started to incorporate mobile strategies into their business plan. There are several in-house popular features any business can benefit from such as:

- Absence Request
- Team Calendar
- Employee Profile
- Employee Directory
- Quick Access

Enabling the absence request feature allows managers to view employees leave request and process it from any mobile device. A team calendar allows managers and co-workers to view other employees' leave requests. This can help improve collaboration. Employee profile allows employees to modify their own profile. This feature provides employees with more flexibility as well as it helps HR to keep record of latest employee details like changes of address and so on. An employee directory allows employees to contact co-workers on the go. Quick asses to paystubs can help improve employee satisfaction. Employees can easily click on a link to access their latest payment which can save the HR team some time.

Dating Apps

Tinder is a dating app that was introduced in 2012, and since its introduction it has grown tremendously. The basic thing is that the user sees a picture of the gender they have chosen, and then they use their finger to swipe either left (nope) or to the right (like). If both users liked each other, they can begin to chat in the app. Simple as that. Tinder was the first app that saw the increasing demand for "fun-dating" without responsibilities and consequences (Arce, 2015). New research shows that there are 50 million active users on Tinder who check their accounts 11 times per day, spend an average of 90 minutes per day on the app, and there are more than 16,000 swipes per second on Tinder (Smith, 2015b). The typical user is a male, single, and between 25-44 years old. But the diversity on Tinder is actually quite broad. To connect with Tinder, it asks permission to use the user's Facebook data and their exact location. First, location processing takes place on the user side, so precise location data for matched users in a 25-mile radius is delivered directly to the user's device, unmediated by the Tinder servers. Second, that data is incredibly accurate, within 100 ft. or less (Kosner, 2015). The app basically follows the user 24/7 and produces tons of data ready for companies to use. Tinder allows advertising based on their Facebook information and the location they have, which is a huge advantage for companies such as Budweiser and Coors Light, which are some of the advertisers on Tinder. However, one can clearly see users across the world are giving away way quite a bit of information just for the convenience of fun. It is impossible to get this information back again. One needs to think twice before signing up for all these apps.

Travel Apps

A great example of an app that really understood how to meet the consumer's need is Uber. The developers of Uber understood the expression "Consumers is Boss", and thought of the consumer as their boss and knew that unique consumer insights and meeting their needs was the future (Ryan, 2015). The technology is allowing companies to make significant improvements in meeting and exceeding consumers' needs and expectations like never before – which was exactly what Uber did. Uber saw a potential opportunity in the Taxi market that before Uber was an old and not-developed market. Uber offers the consumers an easy and available tool, that helps them to get a taxi in a faster, easier, and cheaper way than the originally taxi companies offer. Uber has the opportunity to give the consumers all these things because of all the data that are available (Ryan, 2015). Consumers can login through Facebook, so Uber can use a lot of personal information like picture, name, and location, which make it easy for the consumer. Furthermore, Uber also uses location data, so the app can register where the consumers is, which makes it even easier for the consumer. The app also saves the users credit card information, which addresses the consumer's desire for frictionless payment. Payment happens automatically and a receipt is sent to the consumer's email (Ryan, 2015).

Travelocity is also another great app designed to assist travelers shopping for their perfect get away or help hotels improve their service. The app prominently displays consumers' ratings and comments about the businesses they have patronized. As a business, one should take an app like this very serious as the free publicity can be either very beneficial or damaging. Travelocity is owned by Expedia and they also run Hotels.com (De La Merced, 2015).

SOLUTIONS AND RECOMMENDATIONS

The app store is a marvelous invention for the dissemination of applications. However, as with all technology, changes are constantly happening. The introduction of the "Internet of Things" will once again change the perceived notion of mobile. Consumerism will continue to merge and be accepted in the enterprise. As such mobile apps may never disappear, but the traditional app, obtained from a platform app store (such as Google Play or the Apple store) and installed onto a mobile device (such as a smartphone), will become just one of a wide range of ways that functionality and services will be delivered (Jones, 2015).

There will be a paradigm shift. Companies will need to create multi-purpose apps. When creating apps, it is important to ask why would a consumer use my app and what will make them come back when there are so many apps out there that can do the same thing. Take for example an electric vehicle charging station app. Having a generic app makes more sense as users can see all stations nearby. If companies choose to create their own app they need to offer more features such as a loyalty program, social engagement as well as incorporate other features from other parts of the business. Another major development in mobile (and stationary) devices is voice-activated commands. First made popular by Apple with Siri, but now being widely used by Google and Amazon and others, this way of interacting with our devices in our pockets, on our wrists, and throughout our homes and in our vehicles will no doubt have an impact on app development and use. We are now beginning to expect that rather than open an app to find information or perform a function, we can just speak to our devices in plain and flexible wording. This emergent technology will greatly impact the app universe.

FUTURE RESEARCH DIRECTIONS

The public, both private individuals and businesses are relying more and more on mobile applications as they provide great convenience. In addition, to providing convenient feature for both employers and employees, apps allow users to have 24/7 access and mobility that is nearly limitless. Both app developers and businesses can take great advantage of this fact to respond to the market demand as well as advancing their business processes. Looking into the impact technology has upon people's health, financial, work, and social lives is an important avenue for virtually all businesses. Too often we all see families or friends sit at Starbucks or various restaurants all staring into their various devices without speaking one word to each other. The lack of socialization certainly depicts an upcoming problem for families, friends and society. Social scientists, like Philip Zimbardo, lament the negative social and emotional impact "screens" are having on young people, particulalry boys and men, and how we are being "digitally rewired." The average boy has spent 10,000 hours playing games on devices by the time he is 19, not even including other activity on the Internet. And they are not alone. Girls and young women are increasingly using and depending upon devices for social contact and entertainment. More research needs to be done on the impact this will have and for solutions to whatever problems may develop (Zimbardo & Coulombe, 2016).

CONCLUSION

Applications were initially created to do a specific task. They continue to fulfill this role in the modern age. Typically, apps are installed upon mobile devices. They may be preinstalled by the service provider or installed by the end user. The apps may be purchased or offered for free. As we have learned, care should be taken to read the permissions which are given to apps upon installation. In particular free apps are aggressive with the permissions that are allowed. This is a tradeoff of privacy in exchange for usage of the product. The developers of free applications typically sell the collected data to ad agencies in exchange for free usage of their product. The only thing is as the number of free apps increase the developers who crease apps for sale decreases. It is therefore important for developers to find new ways of getting in revenue.

From apps to virtual reality and analytics, society is becoming more and more connected. There are apps in all forms and shapes. Virtual reality is here and will most likely become widespread and standard within the next year or two. The cost is getting more affordable and the technology is getting better. One can clearly see that consumer brands are moving in the VR direction. Volvo among many others is one brand that has incorporated VR in their corporate adds. In addition, everything and everyone is connected these days. One device can control multiple devices in people's homes and billions of dollars are being spent on digital ads. There is a huge market and exciting times.

Data creation with mobile devices and accompanying apps is able to generate benefits in everyday life, but on the other hand it can have a negative impact for individuals or society. Since smartphone applications provide solutions for almost every problem of human life, they can be beneficial for consumers (Cygnis Media, 2015). In fact, this new technology enables individuals to use their time in a more efficient way. More precisely, it gives users the opportunity to learn whenever they want, e.g. when they go to work and school by train. On the other hand, electronic communication has the potential for users of reducing their ability to concentrate and socialize, because of extensive smartphone and mobile app usage, respectively. According to thedoormouse (2008), in-person communication gave way to electronic communication, because of three main offenders: instant messaging, email and text messaging applications.

REFERENCES

Abigail, E. (2014). *Flappy Bird Game Deleted: Creator Pulled App Because It Was An Addictive Product.* Retrieved from: http://www.ibtimes.com/flappy-bird-game-deleted-creator-pulled-app-because-it-was-addictive-product-1554708

Arce, N. (2015). *Here are the best dating apps to help you find a date*. Retrieved from: http://www.techtimes.com/articles/29741/20150131/here-are-the-best-dating-apps-to-help-you-find-a-date-for-valentines-day-2015.htm

Bakker, D., Kazantzis, N., Rickwood, D., & Rickard, N. (2016). Mental health smartphone apps: Review and evidence-based recommendations for future developments. *JMIR Mental Health, 3*(1), e7. Retrieved from https://www.ncbi.nlm.nih.gov/pmc/articles/PMC4795320/

Bergin Insight. (n.d.). *mHealth and Home Monitoring*. Retrieved from: http://www.berginsight.com/reportpdf/productsheet/bi-mhealth5-ps.pdf

Business Insider. (2013). *How Big Data Is Transforming The Mobile Industry*. Retrieved from http://www.businessinsider.com/big-data-will-transform-mobile-industry-2013-6

Chain Drug Review. (2015). *Apps promise to transform health care*. Retrieved from: https://www.highbeam.com/publications/chain-drug-review-p168/october-2015

Cisco. (2015). *Cisco Global Cloud Index: Forecast and Methodology, 2015-2020*. Retrieved from: http://www.cisco.com/c/dam/en/us/solutions/collateral/service-provider/global-cloud-index-gci/white-paper-c11-738085.pdf

Clark, J. F. (2015). *History of Mobile Applications*. Retrieved from http://www.uky.edu/~jclark/mas490apps/History%20of%20Mobile%20Apps.pdf

Clifford, C. (2014). *By 2017, the App Market Will be a $77 billion Industry*. Retrieved from: https://www.entrepreneur.com/article/236832

De La Merced, M. J. (2015). *Expedia Buys Travelocity for $280 Million in Cash*. Retrieved from: https://dealbook.nytimes.com/2015/01/23/expedia-buys-travelocity-for-280-million-in-cash/?_r=1

Donker, T., Petrie, K., Proudfoot, J., Clarke, J., Birch, M., & Christensen, H. (2013). Smartphones for smarter delivery of mental health programs: A systematic review. *Journal of Medical Internet Research, 15*(11), e247. doi:10.2196/jmir.2791 PMID:24240579 eMarketer. (2016). *US Time Spent with Media: eMarketer's Updated Estimates and Forecast for 2013-2018*. Retrieved from: https://www.emarketer.com/Report/US-Time-Spent-with-Media-eMarketers-Updated-Estimates-Forecast-20132018/2001933

Forrester. (2014). *US Mobile Payments to Reach $142 Billion by 2019*. Retrieved from: https://www.forrester.com/US+Mobile+Payments+To+Reach+142+Billion+By+2019/-/E-PRE7454

Gartner. (2014). *Gartner Says Less Than 0.01 Percent of Consumer Mobile Apps Will Be Considered a Financial Success by Their Developers Through 2018*. Retrieved from: http://www.gartner.com/newsroom/id/2648515

GCF LearnFree.org. (2015). *What is an application?* Retrieved from http://www.gcflearnfree.org/computerbasics/3

Geron, T. (2013). *How King.com Zoomed Up The Social Gaming Charts*. Retrieved from: http://www.forbes.com/sites/tomiogeron/2013/03/26/howkingcomzoomedupthesocialga mingcharts/

Goasduff, L., & Rivera, J. (2015). *Gartner Says Smartphone Sales Surpassed One Billion Units in 2014*. Retrieved from http://www.gartner.com/newsroom/id/2996817

Grothaus, M. (2016). *Apple Pay Leads mobile Payments With 12 Million Monthly Users*. Retrieved from: https://www.fastcompany.com/3057353/fast-feed/apple-pay-leads-mobile-payments-with-12-million-monthly-users

Guess, A. R. (2011). *Smartphone Apps and Big Data*. Retrieved from http://www.dataversity.net/smartphone-apps-and-big-data/

Heisler, Y. (2016). *By 2021, the average smartphone user will plow through 8.9GB of data per month*. Retrieved from: http://bgr.com/2016/06/02/smartphone-data-usage-2021-gigabytes-erricson/

Hickman, G. (2015). *The Rise and Fall of Mobile Apps: What the Media Isn't Telling You*. Retrieved from http://mobilemarketingengine.com/rise-and-fall-mobile-apps-what-media-isnt-telling/

Hoehle, H., & Venkatesh, V. (2015). Mobile Application Usability: Conceptualization and Instrument Development. *Management Information Systems Quarterly*, *39*(2), 435–472.

IoT Business News. (2015). *Berg Insight says 4.9 million patients worldwide are remotely monitored*. Retrieved from: https://iotbusinessnews.com/2015/12/07/81959-berg-insight-says-4-9-million-patients-worldwide-are-remotely-monitored/

Jones, N. (2015). *Preparing for the Post-App Era*. Retrieved from: https://www.gartner.com/doc/3135321/preparing-postapp-era

Kharif, O. (2016). *Samsung Gunning for Apple in Race to Dominate Mobile Payments*. Retrieved from: https://www.bloomberg.com/news/articles/2016-03-01/samsung-gunning-for-apple-in-race-to-dominate-mobile-payments

Kosner, A. W. (2014). *Tinder Dating App Users Are Playing With Privacy Fire*. Retrieved from: http://www.forbes.com/sites/anthonykosner/2014/02/18/tinder-dating-app-users-are-playing- with-privacy-fire/

Larson, S. (2014). *Users Are Growlin About Apps That Require Facebook*. Retrieved rom: http://readwrite.com/2014/05/27/facebook-login-required-apps-lyft-barkbuddy/

LinkedIn. (2017). *About LinkedIn*. Retrieved from: https://press.linkedin.com/about-linkedin?

Luxton, D. D., McCann, R. A., Bush, N. E., Mishkind, M. C., & Reger, G. M. (2011). mHealth for Mental Health: Integrating Smartphone Technology in bahavioral Healthcare. *Professional Psychology, Research and Practice*, *42*(6), 505–512. doi:10.1037/a0024485

Media, C. (2015). *Role of Smartphone Applications in Education*. Retrieved from: http://www.cygnismedia.com/blog/smartphone-apps-in-education/

Poushter, J. (2016). *Smartphone Ownership and Internet Usage Continues to Climb in Emerging Economics*. Retrieved from: http://www.pewglobal.org/2016/02/22/smartphone-ownership-and-internet-usage-continues-to-climb-in-emerging-economies/

Purcewll, K., Entner, R., & Henderson, N. (2010). *The Rise of Apps Culture*. Retrieved from http://www.pewinternet.org/2010/09/14/the-rise-of-apps-culture/?beta=true&utm_expid=53098246-2.Lly4CFSVQG2lphsg-KopIg.1&utm_referrer=https%3A%2F%2Fwww.google.com%2F

Rowinski, D. (2012). *History of Mobile App Stores*. Retrieved from http://readwrite.com/2012/02/07/infographic_history_of_mobile_app_stores

Ryan, P. (2015). *Uber vs. Taxis: Meeting and Exceeding Consumer Needs*. Retrieved from: http://www.denneen.com/2015/09/04/uber-vs-taxis-meeting-and-exceeding-consumer-needs/

Simon, G. E., & Ludman, E. J. (2009). Its time for disruptive innovation in psychotherapy. *Lancet*, *374*(9690), 594–595. doi:10.1016/S0140-6736(09)61415-X PMID:19699995

Smith, A. (2015a). *US. Smartphone Use in 2015*. Retrieved from: http://pewinternet.org/2015/04/01/us-smartphone-use-in-2015/?beta=true&utm_expid=53098246-2.Lly4CFSVQG21phsg-KopIg.1&utm_referrer=https://www.google.com/

Smith, C. (2015b). *By The Number: 20 Impressive Tinder Statistics*. Retrieved from: http://expandedramblings.com/index.php/tinder-statistics/

Smith, C. (2015c). *By The Number: 60 Impressive Snapchat Statistics*. Retrieved from: http://expandedramblings.com/index.php/snapchat-statistics/

Smith, C. (2015d). *By the Numbers: 60+ Amazing Facebook Mobile Stats, Expanded Ramblings*. Retrieved from: http://expandedramblings.com/index.php/facebookmobileappstatistics/

Smith, C. (2017). *75 Incredible Pokemon Go Statistics*. Retrieved from: http://expandedramblings.com/index.php/pokemon-go-statistics/

SocialTimes. (2016). *Here's How any People Are on Facebook, Instagram, Twitter and Other Big Social Networks*. Retrieved from: http://www.adweek.com/socialtimes/heres-how-many-people-are-on-facebook-instagram-twitter-other-big-social-networks/637205

Statista. (2016a). *Most popular Apple App Store categories in December 2016, by share of available apps*. Retrieved from: https://www.statista.com/statistics/270291/popular-categories-in-the-app-store/

Statista. (2016b). *Number of apps available in leading app stores as of June 2016*. Retrieved from: https://www.statista.com/statistics/276623/number-of-apps-available-in-leading-app-stores/

Statista. (2017). *Digital Advertising*. Retrieved from https://www.statista.com

Tantry, S. (2015). *Why Smart Entrepreneurs Are Swiping 'Right§ on Recruiting Apps*. Retrieved from: https://www.entrepreneur.com/article/250421

thedoormouse. (2008). *Technological Desocialization*. Retrieved from: https://thedmouse.wordpress.com/2008/09/30/technological-desocialization/

Varshneya, R. (2015). *What stops your apps from becoming financially successful?* Retrieved from: http://thenextweb.com/entrepreneur/2015/03/01/what-stops-your-apps-from-becoming-financially-successful/

Watts, S. E., & Andrews, G. (2014). Internet access is NOT restricted globally to high income countries: So why are evidenced based prevention and treatment programs for mental disorders so rare? *Asian Journal of Psychiatry*, *10*, 71–74. doi:10.1016/j.ajp.2014.06.007 PMID:25042956

Woods, V., & van der Meulen, R. (2016). *Gartner Says Worldwide Smartphone Sales Grew 9.7 Percent in Fourth Quarter of 2015*. Retrieved from: http://www.gartner.com/newsroom/id/3215217

Zephoria. (2017). *The Top 20 Valuable Facebook Statistics*. Retrieved from: https://zephoria.com/top-15-valuable-facebook-statistics/how

Zimbardo, P. G., & Coulombe, N. (2016). *Man interrupted: Why young men are struggling & what we can do about it*. Newburyport, MA: Conari Press.

KEY TERMS AND DEFINITIONS

Apps: An application, usually a small, defined program that is downloadable to the user's mobile device.

Hybrid Apps: An app that combines elements from both native and web applications. Native apps are developed for a specific platform and installed on a computer.

Internet of Things: (IoT) is a computing concept that describes how everyday physical objects will be connected to the Internet and be able to identify themselves to other devices.

Mobile apps: Software applications designed to run on mobile devices.

Mobile Platform: A mobile platform is also described as an operating system. Example mobile platforms are Windows, BlackBerry, and OS X.

Mobile Wallet: An electronic payment service in which businesses and individuals can received and send money via their mobile devices.

Native Apps: Native app is an application that has been designed for use on a particular platform or mobile device.

Social Media: A computer mediated technology that allow users to share information via virtual communities and networks.

VR Technology: Virtual reality technology is software creating realistic images, sounds and other sensations that replicate the real world.

Compilation of References

Aaker, J. (1997). Dimensions of Brand Personality. *JMR, Journal of Marketing Research, 34*(3), 347–356. doi:10.2307/3151897

Abigail, E. (2014). *Flappy Bird Game Deleted: Creator Pulled App Because It Was An Addictive Product.* Retrieved from: http://www.ibtimes.com/flappy-bird-game-deleted-creator-pulled-app-because-it-was-addictive-product-1554708

Ackx, S. (2014). Emerging Technologies, Disrupt or be Disrupted. In ISSE 2014 Securing Electronic Business Processes (pp. 177-187). Springer Fachmedien Wiesbaden.

Adukaite, A., Reimann, A. M., Marchiori, E., & Cantoni, L. (2013). *Hotel mobile apps. The case of 4 and 5 star hotels in european german-speaking countries. In Information and communication technologies in tourism 2014* (pp. 45–57). Springer.

Aharony, N. (2015). Whats App: A social capital perspective. *Online Information Review, 39*(1), 26–42. doi:10.1108/OIR-08-2014-0177

Aharony, N. (2015). Why do students use Whats App? – an exploratory study. *Aslib Journal of Info Mgmt., 67*(2), 136–158. doi:10.1108/AJIM-11-2014-0148

Ahmad, W., Arshad, H., Sabir, R., & Ashraf, R. (2013). Antecedents of Purchase Intention for Foreign Apparel Products among Pakistani University Students: Implications for Market Entry Strategy. *Middle-East Journal of Scientific Research, 16*(9), 1255–1263.

Ahmed, E., & Akhlaq, A. (2015). Digital commerce in emerging economies. *Int Journal of Emerging Mkts., 10*(4), 634–647. doi:10.1108/IJoEM-01-2014-0051

Ahmed, M., & Hossain, M. A. (2014). Cloud computing and security issues in the cloud. *International Journal of Network Security & Its Applications, 6*(1), 25–36. doi:10.5121/ijnsa.2014.6103

Ajzen, I., Heilbroner, R. L., Fishbein, M., & Thurow, L. C. (1980). *Understanding attitudes and predicting social behaviour*. Prentice Hall PTR.

Akman, I., & Mishra, A. (2010). Gender, age and income differences in internet usage among employees in organizations. *Computers in Human Behavior, 26*(3), 482–490. doi:10.1016/j.chb.2009.12.007

Akroush, M., & Al-Debei, M. (2015). An integrated model of factors affecting consumer attitudes towards online shopping. *Business Process Management Journal, 21*(6), 1353–1376. doi:10.1108/BPMJ-02-2015-0022

Alahuhta, P., Löthman, H., Helaakoski, H., Koskela, A., & Röning, J. (2005). *Apricot agent platform for user-friendly mobile service development. In Systems aspects in organic and pervasive computing-arcs 2005* (pp. 65–78). Springer. doi:10.1007/978-3-540-31967-2_5

Alavi, S. A., Rezaei, S., Valaei, N., & Wan Ismail, W. K. (2016). Examining shopping mall consumer decision-making styles, satisfaction and purchase intention. *International Review of Retail, Distribution and Consumer Research, 26*(3), 272–303. doi:10.1080/09593969.2015.1096808

Aldás-Manzano, J., Lassala-Navarré, C., Ruiz-Mafé, C., & Sanz-Blas, S. (2009). Key drivers of internet banking services use. *Online Information Review, 33*(4), 672–695. doi:10.1108/14684520910985675

Al-Debei, M., Akroush, M., & Ashouri, M. (2015). Consumer attitudes towards online shopping. *Internet Research, 25*(5), 707–733. doi:10.1108/IntR-05-2014-0146

Allameh, S. M., Khazaei Pool, J., Jaberi, A., Salehzadeh, R., & Asadi, H. (2015). Factors influencing sport tourists revisit intentions: The role and effect of destination image, perceived quality, perceived value and satisfaction. *Asia Pacific Journal of Marketing and Logistics, 27*(2), 191–207. doi:10.1108/APJML-12-2013-0159

Al-Subaihin, A., Finkelstein, A., Harman, M., Jia, Y., Martin, W., Sarro, F., & Zhang, Y. (2015). App Store Mining and Analysis. In *Proceedings of the 3rd International Workshop on Software Development Lifecycle for Mobile* (pp. 1–2). New York, NY: ACM. doi:10.1145/2804345.2804346

Ama.org. (2015). *Dictionary*. Available from: https://www.ama.org/resources/pages/dictionary.aspx?dLetter=B

Amatulli, C., & Guido, G. (2011). Determinants of purchasing intention for fashion luxury goods in the Italian market. *Journal of Fashion Marketing and Management. An International Journal, 15*(1), 123–136. doi:10.1108/13612021111112386

Amazon Web Services. (2016). *What is Cloud Computing?* Retrieved January 31, 2016, from https://aws.amazon.com/what-is-cloud-computing/

Amazon.com. (2011). *Server Said to Have Been Used in Sony Attack*. Retrieved from http://www.bloomberg.com/news/2011-05-13/sony-network-said-to-have-been-invaded- by-hackers-using-amazon-com-server.html

Amin, M., Rezaei, S., & Abolghasemi, M. (2014). User satisfaction with mobile websites: The impact of perceived usefulness (pu), perceived ease of use (peou) and trust. *Nankai Business Review International, 5*(3), 258–274. doi:10.1108/NBRI-01-2014-0005

Amin, M., Rezaei, S., & Tavana, F. S. (2015). Gender differences and consumers repurchase intention: The impact of trust propensity, usefulness and ease of use for implication of innovative online retail. *International Journal of Innovation and Learning*, *17*(2), 217–233. doi:10.1504/IJIL.2015.067409

Andaleeb, S. S. (1995). Dependence relations and the moderating role of trust: Implications for behavioral intentions in marketing channels. *International Journal of Research in Marketing*, *12*(2), 157–172. doi:10.1016/0167-8116(94)00020-O

Andel, C., Davidow, S. L., Hollander, M., & Moreno, D. A. (2012). The economics of health care quality and medical errors. *Journal of Health Care Finance*, *39*(1), 39–50. PMID:23155743

Anderl, E., Schumann, J., & Kunz, W. (2016). Helping Firms Reduce Complexity in Multichannel Online Data: A New Taxonomy-Based Approach for Customer Journeys. *Journal of Retailing*, *92*(2), 185–203. doi:10.1016/j.jretai.2015.10.001

Andreas, H., Lan, X., Kent, B. M., & Frank, H. (2007). The influence of price fairness on customer satisfaction: An empirical test in the context of automobile purchases. *Journal of Product and Brand Management*, *16*(1), 49–58. doi:10.1108/10610420710731151

Anwar, M. A., Carmody, P., Surborg, B., & Corcoran, A. (2014). *The diffusion and impacts of information and communication technology on tourism in the western cape, south africa.* Paper presented at the Urban Forum. doi:10.1007/s12132-013-9210-4

Apache. (n.d.). *Apache Cordova*. Retrieved April 28, 2016, from https://cordova.apache.org/

AppCelerator. (n.d.). *AppCelerator*. Retrieved April 30, 2016, from http://www.appcelerator.com/

Applause. (n.d.). *Applause Repository*. Retrieved April 29, 2016, from https://github.com/applause/applause

Apple Inc. (n.d.). *iOS Human Interface Guidelines*. Retrieved April 21, 2016, from https://developer.apple.com/library/ios/documentation/UserExperience/Conceptual/MobileHIG/index.html

Apple. (n.d.). *Apple iOS*. Retrieved April 30, 2016, from http://www.apple.com/de/ios/

Aral, S., & Walker, D. (2011). Creating social contagion through viral product design: A randomized trial of peer influence in networks. *Management Science*, *57*(9), 1623–1639. doi:10.1287/mnsc.1110.1421

Arce, N. (2015). *Here are the best dating apps to help you find a date*. Retrieved from: http://www.techtimes.com/articles/29741/20150131/here-are-the-best-dating-apps-to-help-you-find-a-date-for-valentines-day-2015.htm

Ariffin, A. A. M., & Maghzi, A. (2012). A preliminary study on customer expectations of hotel hospitality: Influences of personal and hotel factors. *International Journal of Hospitality Management*, *31*(1), 191–198. doi:10.1016/j.ijhm.2011.04.012

Armbrust, M. (2009). *Above the clouds: A Berkeley view of cloud computing*. Technical report EECS-2009-28, UC Berkeley.

Armesh, H., Salarzehi, H., & Yaghoobi, N. M. (2010b). Impact of online/internet marketing on computer industry in malaysia in enhancing consumer experience. *International Journal of Marketing Studies*, *2*(2), 75–86. doi:10.5539/ijms.v2n2p75

Armesh, H., Salarzehi, H., Yaghoobi, N. M., Heydari, A., & Nikbin, D. (2010a). The effects of security and privacy information on trust & trustworthiness and loyalty in online marketing in malaysia. *International Journal of Marketing Studies*, *2*(2), 223–234. doi:10.5539/ijms.v2n2p223

Arnold, M. J., Reynolds, K. E., Ponder, N., & Lueg, J. E. (2005). Customer delight in a retail context: Investigating delightful and terrible shopping experiences. *Journal of Business Research*, *58*(8), 1132–1145. doi:10.1016/j.jbusres.2004.01.006

Assaker, G., Vinzi, V. E., & OConnor, P. (2011). Examining the effect of novelty seeking, satisfaction, and destination image on tourists return pattern: A two factor, non-linear latent growth model. *Tourism Management*, *32*(4), 890–901. doi:10.1016/j.tourman.2010.08.004

Asur, S., & Huberman, B. A. (2010). *Predicting the future with social media*. HP Labs. Retrieved January 31, 2016, from http://www.hpl.hp.com/research/scl/papers/ socialmedia/socialmedia.pdf

Atchariyachanvanich, K., Okada, H., & Sonehara, N. (2007). *Theoretical model of purchase and repurchase in internet shopping: Evidence from japanese online customers*. Paper presented at the Proceedings of the ninth international conference on Electronic commerce, Minneapolis, MN. doi:10.1145/1282100.1282146

Atkinson, J., Mitchell, J., Rio, M., & Matich, G. (2016). Your WiFi is leaking: What do your mobile App gossip about you? *Future Generation Computer Systems*. doi:10.1016/j.future.2016.05.030

avart. (2015). *How Augmented Reality Works*. Retrieved from: http://www.avart.com.tr/medya/interaktifvitrin.aspx (in Turkish)

Azim, R., & Hassan, A. (2013). Impact Analysis of Wireless and Mobile Technology on Business Management Strategies. *Journal of Information and Knowledge Management*, *2*(2), 141–150.

Badrinarayanan, V., Becerra, E., Kim, C.-H., & Madhavaram, S. (2010). Transference and congruence effects on purchase intentions in online stores of multi-channel retailers: Initial evidence from the u.S. And south korea. *Journal of the Academy of Marketing Science*, 1–19. doi:10.1007/s11747-010-0239-9

Baker, S. M. (2006). Consumer normalcy: Understanding the value of shopping through narratives of consumers with visual impairments. *Journal of Retailing*, *82*(1), 37–50. doi:10.1016/j.jretai.2005.11.003

Bakker, D., Kazantzis, N., Rickwood, D., & Rickard, N. (2016). Mental health smartphone apps: Review and evidence-based recommendations for future developments. *JMIR Mental Health*, *3*(1), e7. Retrieved from https://www.ncbi.nlm.nih.gov/pmc/articles/PMC4795320/

Balachandra, R. K., Ramakrishna, P. V., & Rakshit, A. (2009). Cloud security issues. *PROC'09 IEEE International Conference on Services Computing*, 517–520.

Barnett, S., Avazpour, I., Vasa, R., & Grundy, J. (2015). A Multi-view Framework for Generating Mobile Apps. *IEEE Symposium on Visual Languages and Human-Centric Computing (VL/HCC)*, (1), 305–306. http://doi.org/ doi:10.1109/VLHCC.2015.7357239

Barnett, S., Vasa, R., & Grundy, J. (2015). Bootstrapping Mobile App Development. *Proceedings - International Conference on Software Engineering, 2*, 657–660. http://doi.org/ doi:10.1109/ICSE.2015.216

Basescu, C., Carpen-Amarie, A., Leordeanu, C., Leordeanu, C., Costan, A., & Antoniu, G. (2011). Managing Data Access on Clouds: A Generic Framework for Enforcing Security Policies. *International Conference on Advanced Information Networking and Applications (AINA)*. doi:10.1109/AINA.2011.61

Basole, R. C., & Karla, J. (2011). On the evolution of mobile platform ecosystem structure and strategy. *Business and Information Systems Engineering*, *3*(5), 313–322. doi:10.1007/s12599-011-0174-4

Bastič, M., & Gojčič, S. (2012). Measurement scale for eco-component of hotel service quality. *International Journal of Hospitality Management*, *31*(3), 1012–1020. doi:10.1016/j.ijhm.2011.12.007

Bellman, S., Potter, R. F., Treleaven-Hassard, S., Robinson, J. A., & Varan, D. (2011). The effectiveness of branded mobile phone apps. *Journal of Interactive Marketing*, *25*(4), 191–200. doi:10.1016/j.intmar.2011.06.001

Benitez, J. M., Martín, J. C., & Román, C. (2007). Using fuzzy number for measuring quality of service in the hotel industry. *Tourism Management*, *28*(2), 544–555. doi:10.1016/j.tourman.2006.04.018

Bergin Insight. (n.d.). *mHealth and Home Monitoring*. Retrieved from: http://www.berginsight.com/reportpdf/productsheet/bi-mhealth5-ps.pdf

Berl, A. (2010). *Energy-Efficient Cloud Computing*. Retrieved January 31, 2016 from: https://www.researchgate.net/publication/46116227_Energy-Efficient_Cloud_Computing

Berthon, P. R., Pitt, L. F., Plangger, K., & Shapiro, D. (2012). Marketing meets web 2.0, social media, and creative consumers: Implications for international marketing strategy. *Business Horizons*, *55*(3), 261–271. doi:10.1016/j.bushor.2012.01.007

Bhadauria, R. (2011). A survey on security issues in cloud computing. IEEE Communications Surveys and Tutorial, 1–15.

Bhat, S. A., & Shah, M. A. (2014). Diffusion of internet technology in the tourism sector: An empirical study. *Journal of Transnational Management*, *19*(2), 152–164. doi:10.1080/15475778.2014.904674

Biedenbach, G., Bengtsson, M., & Wincent, J. (2011). Brand equity in the professional service context: Analyzing the impact of employee role behavior and customer–employee rapport. *Industrial Marketing Management*, *40*(7), 1093–1102. doi:10.1016/j.indmarman.2011.09.007

Bigné, E., Ruiz, C., & Sanz, S. (2007). Key Drivers of Mobile Commerce Adoption. An Exploratory Study of Spanish Mobile Users. *Journal of Theoretical and Applied Electronic Commerce Research*, *2*(2), 48–60.

Bijani, C., Vilrokx, M., & White, B. K. (2013). Giving voice to enterprise mobile applications. In *Proceedings of the 15th International Conference on Human-Computer Interaction with Mobile Devices and Services* (pp. 428-433). ACM Press.

Blanca, H., Julio, J., & Martín, M. J. (2011). Age, gender and income: Do they really moderate online shopping behaviour? *Online Information Review*, *35*(1), 113–133. doi:10.1108/14684521111113614

Blery, E. K., Andreas, D., Anna, B., Anna, E., Efi, K., Nertilda, T., & Ioanna, R. (2009). Customer retention in the greek internet market. *International Journal of Business and Management*, *3*(1), 35–48.

Blut, M., Chowdhry, N., Mittal, V., & Brock, C. (2015). E-Service Quality: A Meta-Analytic Review. *Journal of Retailing*, *91*(4), 679–700. doi:10.1016/j.jretai.2015.05.004

Böhm, S., & Constantine, G. (2016). Impact of contextuality on mobile learning acceptance. *Interactive Technology and Smart Education*, *13*(2), 107–122. doi:10.1108/ITSE-02-2016-0003

Bonaguro, J. (2015). *Data in San Francisco: Meeting supply, spurring demand* (FY2015-16). Retrieved January 31, 2016, from https://docs.google.com/document/d/1mqunsT9wXRt-mBbO-mY3WcEJmsWSpMOISotZ1WHZ1_IU/edit?usp=embed_facebook

Bootstrap. (2016). *Bootstrap - The world's most popular mobile first and responsive front end framework*. Retrieved June 5, 2016, from http://getbootstrap.com/

Bowater, J. (2016). *Welcome to the Chief Data Officer Forum, Government*. Retrieved February 10, 2016, from http://www.chiefdataofficergovernment.com

Boyd, D., & Ellison, N. B. (2007). Social network sites: Definition, history, and scholarship. *Journal of Computer-Mediated Communication*, *13*(1), 210–230. doi:10.1111/j.1083-6101.2007.00393.x

Boyraz, B. (2013). Museum Technologies and Exhibition Differences. *Journal of Academic View, 39*. (in Turkish)

Brady, M. K., Cronin, J. J. Jr, Fox, G. L., & Roehm, M. L. (2008). Strategies to offset performance failures: The role of brand equity. *Journal of Retailing*, *84*(2), 151–164. doi:10.1016/j.jretai.2008.04.002

Brambilla, M., Mauri, A., & Umuhoza, E. (2014). Extending the Interaction Flow Modeling Language (IFML) for Model Driven Development of Mobile Applications Front End. *MobiWIS, 2000*, 176–191. Retrieved from http://dblp.org/db/conf/mobiwis/mobiwis2014.html#BrambillaMU14

Brown, M., Pope, N., & Voges, K. (2003). Buying or browsing? *European Journal of Marketing*, *37*(11/12), 1666–1684. doi:10.1108/03090560310495401

Brunelle, E., & Lapierre, J. (2008). *Testing media richness theory to explain consumers' intentions of buying online*. Paper presented at the 10th international conference on Electronic commerce, Innsbruck, Austria. doi:10.1145/1409540.1409582

Buhalis, D., & Law, R. (2008). Progress in information technology and tourism management: 20 years on and 10 years after the internet—the state of etourism research. *Tourism Management*, *29*(4), 609–623. doi:10.1016/j.tourman.2008.01.005

Buhalis, D., & Wagner, R. (2013). eDestination: International best practices of tourism technologies and application. *Tourism Tribune*, *28*(1), 3–6.

Buil, I., de Chernatony, L., & Martínez, E. (2013). Examining the role of advertising and sales promotions in brand equity creation. *Journal of Business Research*, *66*(1), 115–122. doi:10.1016/j.jbusres.2011.07.030

Buschmann, F., Meunier, R., Rohnert, H., Sommerlad, P., & Stal, M. (1996). *A System of Patterns: Pattern-Oriented Software Architecture*. Wiley.

Business Insider. (2013). *How Big Data Is Transforming The Mobile Industry*. Retrieved from http://www.businessinsider.com/big-data-will-transform-mobile-industry-2013-6

Busold, C., Heuser, S., Rios, J., Sadeghi, A. R., & Asokan, N. (2015). Smart and secure cross-device Apps for the Internet of advanced things. Lecture Notes in Computer Science, 8975, 272–290. http://doi.org/ doi:10.1007/978-3-662-47854-7_17

Butler, P., & Peppard, J. (1998). Consumer purchasing on the internet: Processes and prospects. *European Management Journal*, *16*(5), 600–610. doi:10.1016/S0263-2373(98)00036-X

Cai, S., & Xu, Y. (2006). Effects of outcome, process and shopping enjoyment on online consumer behaviour. *Electronic Commerce Research and Applications*, *5*(4), 272–281. doi:10.1016/j.elerap.2006.04.004

Cai, Y., & Cude, B. J. (2008). Online shopping. In J. J. Xiao (Ed.), *Handbook of consumer finance research* (pp. 137–159). Springer New York. doi:10.1007/978-0-387-75734-6_9

Callarisa, L., García, J. S., Cardiff, J., & Roshchina, A. (2012). Harnessing social media platforms to measure customer-based hotel brand equity. *Tourism Management Perspectives*, *4*, 73–79. doi:10.1016/j.tmp.2012.04.005

Capgemini Consulting. (2014). *Cracking the Data Conundrum: How Successful Companies Make Big Data Operational*. Retrieved February 10, 2016, from http://www.datascienceassn.org/sites/default/files/Cracking%20the%20Data%20Conundrum%20-%20How%20Successful%20Companies%20Make%20Big%20Data%20Operational.pdf

Carr, A. (2010). *Foursquare's business chief on revenue plans, google adwords, and why marketers shouldn't delay on geo-location.* Retrieved July 28, 2010, from http://www.fastcompany.com/1675626/

Carter, S., & Yeo, A. (2016). Mobile App usage by Malaysian business undergraduates and postgraduates. *Internet Research*, *26*(3), 733–757. doi:10.1108/IntR-10-2014-0273

Caruana, A., & Ewing, M. T. (2010). How corporate reputation, quality, and value influence online loyalty. *Journal of Business Research*, *63*(9-10), 1103–1110. doi:10.1016/j.jbusres.2009.04.030

Carver, S. (2013). *How the City of San Francisco uses Social Media to Connect with Citizens.* Retrieved February 10, 2016, from http://www.exacttarget.com/blog/how-the-city-of-san-francisco-uses-social-media/

Casado, R., & Younas, M. (2014). Emerging trends and technologies in big data processing. *Concurrency and Computation*, *27*(8), 2078–2209. doi:10.1002/cpe.3398

Casaló, L., Flavián, C., & Guinalíu, M. (2007). The role of security, privacy, usability and reputation in the development of online banking. *Online Information Review*, *31*(5), 583–603. doi:10.1108/14684520710832315

Castro, C. B., Martín Armario, E., & Martín Ruiz, D. (2007). The influence of market heterogeneity on the relationship between a destinations image and tourists future behaviour. *Tourism Management*, *28*(1), 175–187. doi:10.1016/j.tourman.2005.11.013

Chai Har, L., Uchenna Cyril, E., & Nelson Oly, N. (2011). Analyzing key determinants of online repurchase intentions. *Asia Pacific Journal of Marketing and Logistics*, *23*(2), 200–221. doi:10.1108/13555851111120498

Chain Drug Review. (2015). *Apps promise to transform health care*. Retrieved from: https://www.highbeam.com/publications/chain-drug-review-p168/october-2015

Chang, Y.-p., & Zhu, D.-h. (2007). Factors Influencing New and Repeated Buyers' Intention to Shop Online in China: A Comparatively Empirical Study. *Wireless Communications, Networking and Mobile Computing, 2007. WiCom 2007. International Conference on* (pp. 3494-3497).

Chang, H. H., & Chen, S. W. (2008). The impact of customer interface quality, satisfaction and switching costs on e-loyalty: Internet experience as a moderator. *Computers in Human Behavior*, *24*(6), 2927–2944. doi:10.1016/j.chb.2008.04.014

Chang, H. H., & Chen, S. W. (2008). The impact of online store environment cues on purchase intention trust and perceived risk as a mediator. *Online Information Review*, *32*(6), 818–841. doi:10.1108/14684520810923953

Chang, H. H., & Chen, S. W. (2009). Consumer perception of interface quality, security, and loyalty in electronic commerce. *Information & Management*, *46*(7), 411–417. doi:10.1016/j.im.2009.08.002

Chang, J., & Samuel, N. (2004). Internet shopper demographics and buying behaviour in australia. *Journal of American Academy of Business, Cambridge*, *5*(1/2), 171–176.

Chang, S., Chih, W., Liou, D., & Yang, Y. (2016). The mediation of cognitive attitude for online shopping. *Information Technology & People*, *29*(3), 618–646. doi:10.1108/ITP-08-2014-0172

Chao-Min, C., Hua-Yang, L., Szu-Yuan, S., & Meng-Hsiang, H. (2009). Understanding customers loyalty intentions towards online shopping: An integration of technology acceptance model and fairness theory. *Behaviour & Information Technology*, *28*(4), 347–360. doi:10.1080/01449290801892492

Charles, K., Hurst, E., & Roussanov, N. (2009). Conspicuous Consumption and Race. *The Quarterly Journal of Economics*, *124*(2), 425–467. doi:10.1162/qjec.2009.124.2.425

Chauhan, J., Mahanti, A., & Kaafar, M. A. (2014). Towards the Era of Wearable Computing? In *Proceedings of the 2014 CoNEXT on Student Workshop* (pp. 24–25). New York, NY: ACM. http://doi.org/ doi:10.1145/2680821.2680833

Chen, C.-C., Huang, W.-J., & Petrick, J. F. (2016). Holiday recovery experiences, tourism satisfaction and life satisfaction–is there a relationship? *Tourism Management*, *53*, 140–147. doi:10.1016/j.tourman.2015.09.016

Chen, C.-F., & Phou, S. (2013). A closer look at destination: Image, personality, relationship and loyalty. *Tourism Management*, *36*, 269–278. doi:10.1016/j.tourman.2012.11.015

Chen, C.-F., & Tsai, M.-H. (2008). Perceived value, satisfaction, and loyalty of tv travel product shopping: Involvement as a moderator. *Tourism Management*, *29*(6), 1166–1171. doi:10.1016/j.tourman.2008.02.019

Cheng, Q., Fang, L., & Chen, H. (2015). Visitors' brand loyalty to a historical and cultural theme park: A case study of hangzhou songcheng, china. *Current Issues in Tourism*, 1–8.

Cheng, T.-M., & Lu, C.-C. (2013). Destination image, novelty, hedonics, perceived value, and revisiting behavioral intention for island tourism. *Asia Pacific Journal of Tourism Research*, *18*(7), 766–783. doi:10.1080/10941665.2012.697906

Chen, H., Chiang, R. H., & Storey, V. C. (2012). Business Intelligence and Analytics: From Big Data to Big Impact. *Management Information Systems Quarterly*, *36*(4), 1165–1188.

Chen, H.-J., Chen, P.-J., & Okumus, F. (2013). The relationship between travel constraints and destination image: A case study of brunei. *Tourism Management*, *35*, 198–208. doi:10.1016/j.tourman.2012.07.004

Chen, S.-H., & Lee, K.-P. (2008). The Role Of Personality Traits And Perceived Values In Persuasion: An Elaboration Likelihood Model Perspective On Online Shopping. *Social Behavior & Personality: An International Journal*, *36*(10), 1379–1400. doi:10.2224/sbp.2008.36.10.1379

Chevalier, J. A., & Mayzlin, D. (2006). The effect of word of mouth on sales: Online book reviews. *JMR, Journal of Marketing Research*, *43*(3), 345–354. doi:10.1509/jmkr.43.3.345

Chia, P. H., Yamamoto, Y., & Asokan, N. (2012). Is This App Safe?: A Large Scale Study on Application Permissions and Risk Signals. In *Proceedings of the 21st International Conference on World Wide Web* (pp. 311–320). New York, NY: ACM. http://doi.org/ doi:10.1145/2187836.2187879

Chi, C. G.-Q., & Qu, H. (2008). Examining the structural relationships of destination image, tourist satisfaction and destination loyalty: An integrated approach. *Tourism Management*, *29*(4), 624–636. doi:10.1016/j.tourman.2007.06.007

Chiou, J.-S., & Pan, L.-Y. (2009). Antecedents of Internet Retailing Loyalty: Differences Between Heavy Versus Light Shoppers. *Journal of Business and Psychology*, *24*(3), 327–339. doi:10.1007/s10869-009-9111-7

Chiu, C., Chang, C., Cheng, H., & Fang, Y. (2009). Determinants of customer repurchase intention in online shopping. *Online Information Review*, *33*(4), 761–784. doi:10.1108/14684520910985710

Choen, H. (2015). *2015 Mobile Marketing – 19 Research Charts*. Retrieved February 10, 2016, from http://heidicohen.com/2015-mobile-marketing/

Cho, H., & Schwarz, N. (2012). I like your product when i like my photo: Misattribution using interactive virtual mirrors. *Journal of Interactive Marketing*, *26*(4), 235–243. doi:10.1016/j.intmar.2012.03.003

Choo, K.K.R. (2010). Cloud computing: Challenges and future directions. *Trends & Issues in Crime and Criminal Justice, 6*, 1-6.

Choo, H., Ahn, K., & Petrick, F., J. (. (2016). An integrated model of festival revisit intentions: Theory of planned behavior and festival quality/satisfaction. *International Journal of Contemporary Hospitality Management*, *28*(4), 818–838. doi:10.1108/IJCHM-09-2014-0448

Christodoulides, G., & Michaelidou, N. (2011). Shopping motives as antecedents of e-satisfaction and e-loyalty. *Journal of Marketing Management*, *27*(1-2), 181–197. doi:10.1080/0267257X.2010.489815

Christodoulides, G., & Michaelidou, N. (2011). Shopping motives as antecedents of e-satisfaction and e-loyalty. *Journal of Marketing Management*, *27*(1/2), 181–197.

Chuanlan, L., & Sandra, F. (2010). Post-adoption online shopping continuance. *International Journal of Retail & Distribution Management*, *38*(2), 97–114. doi:10.1108/09590551011020110

Chu, J., Arce-Urriza, M., Cebollada-Calvo, J.-J., & Chintagunta, P. K. (2010). An empirical analysis of shopping behavior across online and offline channels for grocery products: The moderating effects of household and product characteristics. *Journal of Interactive Marketing*, *24*(4), 251–268. doi:10.1016/j.intmar.2010.07.004

Chung, S. (2014). An empirical analysis of usage dynamics in a mobile music App: Evidence from large-scale data. *Internet Research*, *24*(4), 436–456. doi:10.1108/IntR-05-2013-0088

Chun-hui, T., & Jun, W. (2008). The Model of Online Purchasing Behavior Based on Website's Credibility and Its Inspiration for Enterprises. *Information Management, Innovation Management and Industrial Engineering, 2008. ICIII '08. International Conference on* (Vol. 2, pp. 506-511).

Cialdini, R. (1984). *Influence, the psychology of Persuasion.* Collins Business Essentials.

CISCO. (2014). *Cisco Global Cloud Index: Forecast and Methodology, 2013–2018.* Retrieved February 10, 2016, from https://www.terena.org/mail-archives/storage/pdfVVqL9tLHLH.pdf

Cisco. (2015). *Cisco Global Cloud Index: Forecast and Methodology, 2015-2020.* Retrieved from: http://www.cisco.com/c/dam/en/us/solutions/collateral/service-provider/global-cloud-index-gci/white-paper-c11-738085.pdf

Clark, J. F. (2015). *History of Mobile Applications.* Retrieved from http://www.uky.edu/~jclark/mas490apps/History%20of%20Mobile%20Apps.pdf

Clifford, C. (2014). *By 2017, the App Market Will be a $77 billion Industry.* Retrieved from: https://www.entrepreneur.com/article/236832

Close, A. G., & Kukar-Kinney, M. (2010). Beyond buying: Motivations behind consumers online shopping cart use. *Journal of Business Research, 63*(9-10), 986–992. doi:10.1016/j.jbusres.2009.01.022

Cloud Security Alliance. (2010). *Security guidance for critical areas of focus in cloud computing v2.1. Technical report.* Cloud Security Alliance.

Cloud Security Alliance. (2010). *Top Threats to Cloud Computing V 1.0.* Author.

Cloud Security. (2012). *What security lessons can be learned from LinkedIn?* Retrieved February 10, 2016, from http://www.cloudcomputing-news.net/news/2012/jun/18/security-lessons-learned-from-linkedin/

Cluley, R. (2016). The depiction of marketing and marketers in the news media. *European Journal of Marketing, 50*(5/6), 752–769. doi:10.1108/EJM-02-2015-0076

Cognizant. (2013). Keep on Smacking: Taking Social, Mobile, Analytics and Cloud to the Bottom Line. *Cognizanti, 6*(1). Retrieved February 10, 2016, from: https://www.cognizant.com/InsightsWhitepapers/Cognizanti-Journal-XaaS-Code-Halos-SMAC-and-the-Future-of-Work.pdf

Connolly, R., & Hoar, R. (2015). *Fundamentals of Web Development.* Boston: Pearson. Retrieved March 5, 2016, from: https://scanlibs.com/fundamentals-of-web-development/

Consolvo, S. et al.. (2005). Location disclosure to social relations: Why, when, and what people want to share. In *Proceedings of the SIGCHI Conference on Human Factors in Computing Systems* (pp. 81-90). ACM Press. doi:10.1145/1054972.1054985

Cooney, M. (2013). *Gartner: Top 10 future strategic IT predictions.* Retrieved March 5, 2016, from http://www.networkworld.com/article/2225521/malware-cybercrime/gartner--top-10-future-strategic-it-predictions.html

Craig, S. (2015). *By the numbers: 17 important foursquare stats.* Retrieved December 23, 2015, from http://expandedramblings.com/index.php/by-the-numbers-interesting-foursquare-user-stats/

Cronin, J. J. Jr, Brady, M. K., & Hult, G. T. M. (2000). Assessing the effects of quality, value, and customer satisfaction on consumer behavioral intentions in service environments. *Journal of Retailing, 76*(2), 193–218. doi:10.1016/S0022-4359(00)00028-2

Cuadrado, F., & Dueñas, J. (2012). Mobile application stores: Success factors, existing approaches, and future developments. *IEEE Communications Magazine, 50*(11), 160–167. doi:10.1109/MCOM.2012.6353696

Curty, R. G., & Zhang, P. (2011). Social commerce: looking back and forward. *Proceedings of the American Society for Information Science and Technology (ASIST) Annual Conference, 48*(1), 1-10.

Dadwal, S., & Hassan, A. (2105). The Augmented Reality Marketing: A Merger of Marketing and Technology in Tourism. In N. Ray (Ed.), *Emerging innovative marketing strategies in the tourism industry* (pp. 78–96). IGI Global.

Dageförde, J. C., Reischmann, T., Majchrzak, T. A., & Ernsting, J. (2016). Generating App Product Lines in a Model-Driven Cross-Platform Development Approach. In *Proceedings of the 2016 49th Hawaii International Conference on System Sciences* (pp. 5803–5812). http://doi.org/ doi:10.1109/HICSS.2016.718

Daliri, E., Rezaei, S., & Ismail, W. K. W. (2014). Online social shopping: The impact of attitude, customer information quality, effectiveness of information content and perceived social presence. *International Journal of Business Environment, 6*(4), 426–450. doi:10.1504/IJBE.2014.064995

Dan, S., & Xu, H. (2011). Research on online shopping intention of undergraduate consumer in china--based on the theory of planned behavior. *International Business Research, 4*(1), 86–92.

Dan, S., & Xu, H. (2011). Research on Online Shopping Intention of Undergraduate Consumer in China--Based on the Theory of Planned Behavior. *International Business Research, 4*(1), 86–92.

Data, S. F. (n.d.). *About.* Retrieved March 5, 2016, from http://datasf.org/about/

Dawei, S. (2011) Surveying and analyzing security, privacy and trust issues in cloud computing environments. CEIS, 15, 2852–2856.

Dawoud, W., Takouna, I., & Meinel, C. (2010). Infrastructure as a service security: Challenges and solutions. *The 7th International Conference on Informatics and Systems (INFOS)*, 1–8.

De La Merced, M. J. (2015). *Expedia Buys Travelocity for $280 Million in Cash.* Retrieved from: https://dealbook.nytimes.com/2015/01/23/expedia-buys-travelocity-for-280-million-in-cash/?_r=1

De Vries, L., Gensler, S., & Leeflang, P. S. H. (2012). Popularity of brand posts on brand fan pages: An investigation of the effects of social media marketing. *Journal of Interactive Marketing, 26*(2), 83–91. doi:10.1016/j.intmar.2012.01.003

Debata, B. R., Patnaik, B., Mahapatra, S. S., & Sree, K. (2015). Interrelations of service quality and service loyalty dimensions in medical tourism: A structural equation modelling approach. *Benchmarking: An International Journal*, *22*(1), 18–55. doi:10.1108/BIJ-04-2013-0036

Deloitte. (2016). *SMAC: Better together Improving health care efficiency with social, mobile, analytics, and cloud technologies*. Retrieved September 28, 2016, from https://www2.deloitte.com/content/dam/Deloitte/us/Documents/life-sciences-health-care/us-lshc-smac-better-together.pdf

Dennis, C., Morgan, A., Wright, L. T., & Jayawardhena, C. (2010). The influences of social e-shopping in enhancing young womens online shopping behaviour. *Journal of Customer Behaviour*, *9*(2), 151–174. doi:10.1362/147539210X511353

Dens, N., & Pelsmacker, D. P. (2016). Does poor fit always lead to negative evaluations? Extension advertising and perceived brand quality. *International Journal of Advertising*, *35*(3), 465–485.

Dewan, B., & Jena, S. R. (2014, December). The State-Of-The-Art of Social, Mobility, Analytics and Cloud Computing an Empirical Analysis. In *High Performance Computing and Applications (ICHPCA), 2014 International Conference on* (pp. 1-6). IEEE.

Dickinson, J. E., Ghali, K., Cherrett, T., Speed, C., Davies, N., & Norgate, S. (2014). Tourism and the smartphone app: Capabilities, emerging practice and scope in the travel domain. *Current Issues in Tourism*, *17*(1), 84–101. doi:10.1080/13683500.2012.718323

Diehl, K., & Poynor, C. (2010). Great Expectations?! Assortment Size, Expectations, and Satisfaction. *JMR, Journal of Marketing Research*, *47*(2), 312–322. doi:10.1509/jmkr.47.2.312

Din, D., & Sahn, F. (2013). Measuring the factors affecting Egyptian consumers` intentions to purchase global luxury fashion brands. *The Business and Management Review*, *3*(4), 44–59.

Dinev, T., & Hart, P. (2005). Internet privacy concerns and social awareness as determinants of intention to transact. *International Journal of Electronic Commerce*, *10*(2), 7–29. doi:10.2753/JEC1086-4415100201

Ding, Y., & Chai, K. (2015). Emotions and continued usage of mobile Applications.[Accessed 8 August 2016]. *Industr Mngmnt & Data Systems.*, *115*(5), 833–852. doi:10.1108/IMDS-11-2014-0338

Dittmar, H., Long, K., & Meek, R. (2004). Buying on the internet: Gender differences in on-line and conventional buying motivations. *Sex Roles*, *50*(5), 423–444. doi:10.1023/B:SERS.0000018896.35251.c7

Djamasbi, S., Siegel, M., & Tullis, T. (2010). Generation y, web design, and eye tracking. *International Journal of Human-Computer Studies*, *68*(5), 307–323. doi:10.1016/j.ijhcs.2009.12.006

Dobie, A. (2012). *Why you'll never have the latest version of Android.* Retrieved April 30, 2016, from http://www.androidcentral.com/why-you-ll-never-have-latest-version-android

Donker, T., Petrie, K., Proudfoot, J., Clarke, J., Birch, M., & Christensen, H. (2013). Smartphones for smarter delivery of mental health programs: A systematic review. *Journal of Medical Internet Research, 15*(11), e247. doi:10.2196/jmir.2791 PMID:24240579

Donmezoglu, D. (2013). *Exhibition Technical with Support of Virtual Technology in our Present Day's Museology and Application Examples* (Unpublished Thesis). Turkish Republic Ministry of Culture and Tourism Genereal Directorate of Cultural Assets and Museums, Ankara, Turkey. (in Turkish)

Dortyol, I. T., Varinli, I., & Kitapci, O. (2014). How do international tourists perceive hotel quality? An exploratory study of service quality in antalya tourism region. *International Journal of Contemporary Hospitality Management, 26*(3), 470–495. doi:10.1108/IJCHM-11-2012-0211

Dr. Brent Lynn Selby, C., Dr. Nicholas Jeremy, A., & Dr. Beverley, H. (2011). Measuring internet product purchase risk. *European Journal of Marketing, 45*(7), 6–6.

Duggan, M., Ellison, N. B., Lampe, C., Lenhart, A., & Madden, M. (2015). *Social Media Update 2014*. Retrieved March 5, 2016, from http://www.pewinternet.org/files/2015/01/ PI_SocialMediaUpdate20144.pdf

Durvasula, S., & Lysonski, S. (2008). A double edged sword: Understanding vanity across cultures. *Journal of Consumer Marketing, 25*(4), 230–244. doi:10.1108/07363760810882425

Durvasula, S., Lysonski, S., & Watson, J. (2001). Does Vanity Describe Other Cultures? A Cross-Cultural Examination of the Vanity Scale. *The Journal of Consumer Affairs, 35*(1), 180–199. doi:10.1111/j.1745-6606.2001.tb00108.x

Dwayne, B., Pedro Simões, C., & Alexandra, M. (2004). The role of communication and trust in explaining customer loyalty: An extension to the ecsi model. *European Journal of Marketing, 38*(9), 1272–1293.

Dwayne, B., Pedro Simões, C., & Alexandra, M. (2004). The role of communication and trust in explaining customer loyalty: An extension to the ECSI model. *European Journal of Marketing, 38*(9), 1272–1293.

Dwivedi, Y., Williams, M., & Lal, B. (2008). The diffusion of research on the adoption and diffusion of information technology. In G. León, A. Bernardos, J. Casar, K. Kautz, & J. De Gross (Eds.), Open it-based innovation: Moving towards cooperative it transfer and knowledge diffusion (Vol. 287, pp. 3-22). Springer Boston. doi:10.1007/978-0-387-87503-3_1

Dzisah, W., & Ocloo, C. (2013). Celebrity Endorsement and Consumer Buying Behaviour; Enhancing the Promotion Function of Marketing in the Central Business Area of Accra, Ghana. *European Journal of Business and Management, 5*(25), 197–209.

Eastman, J., Goldsmith, R., & Flynn, L. R. (1999). Status Consumption in Consumer Behavior: Scale Development and Validation. *Journal of Marketing Theory and Practice, 7*(3), 41–51. doi:10.1080/10696679.1999.11501839

Efthymios, C., Carlota, L.-R., & Miguel, A. G. (2010). Effects of web experience on consumer choice: A multicultural approach. *Internet Research, 20*(2), 188–209. doi:10.1108/10662241011032245

Eid, R. (2015). Integrating muslim customer perceived value, satisfaction, loyalty and retention in the tourism industry: An empirical study. *International Journal of Tourism Research, 17*(3), 249–260. doi:10.1002/jtr.1982

Ekatalog. (2015). *Who we are?* Retrieved from: http://www.ekatalog.com.tr/ (in Turkish)

Ekinci, Y., Dawes, P. L., & Massey, G. R. (2008). An extended model of the antecedents and consequences of consumer satisfaction for hospitality services. *European Journal of Marketing, 42*(1/2), 35–68. doi:10.1108/03090560810840907

Ellis-Chadwick, F., Doherty, N., & Hart, C. (2002). Signs of change? A longitudinal study of Internet adoption in the UK retail sector. *Journal of Retailing and Consumer Services, 9*(2), 71–80. doi:10.1016/S0969-6989(01)00030-3

Ellison, N. B., & Boyd, D. (2013). Sociality through Social Network Sites. In W. H. Dutton (Ed.), *The Oxford Handbook of Internet Studies*. Oxford, UK: Oxford University Press.

Emam, A. H. M. (2013). Additional authentication and authorization using registered email-id for cloud computing. *International Journal of Soft Computing and Engineering, 3*(2), 110–113.

eMarketer. (2016). *US Time Spent with Media: eMarketer's Updated Estimates and Forecast for 2013-2018*. Retrieved from: https://www.emarketer.com/Report/US-Time-Spent-with-Media-eMarketers-Updated-Estimates-Forecast-20132018/2001933

Emmanaouilidis, C., Koutsiamanis, R. A., & Tasidou, A. (2013). Mobile Guides: Taxonomy of Architectures, Context Awareness, Technologies and Applications. *Journal of Network and Computer Applications, 36*(1), 103–125. doi:10.1016/j.jnca.2012.04.007

Empson, R. (2012). *Clouds & APIs: Mayor Lee Unveils The San Francisco Open Data Cloud*. Retrieved March 5, 2016, from http://techcrunch.com/2012/03/09/san-francisco-open-data/

ENISA. (2010). *Cloud computing: benefits, risks and recommendations for information security*. Technical report, ENISA. Retrieved from http://www.enisa.europa.eu/act/rm/files/deliverables/cloud-computingrisk-assessment

Eralp, E. E. (2009). *Mobile Tour Guidance* (Unpublished Master Thesis). Ege University Institute of Science Department of Computer Engineering, Izmır, Turkey. (in Turkish)

Ernsting, J., Rieger, C., Wrede, F., & Majchrzak, T. A. (2016). Refining a Reference Architecture for Model-Driven Business Apps. *WEBIST 2016 - Proceedings of the 12th International Conference on Web Information Systems and Technologies*.

Esdorlion. (2015). *Digital Course*. Retrieved from: www.esdorlion.com (in Turkish)

Esper, F. S., & Rateike, J. Á. (2010). Tourism destination image and motivations: The spanish perspective of mexico. *Journal of Travel & Tourism Marketing*, *27*(4), 349–360. doi:10.1080/10548408.2010.481567

Euromonitor. (2015). Luxury Goods in Malaysia. *Euromonitor International.*

Evers, S., Ernsting, J., & Majchrzak, T. A. (2016). *Towards a Reference Architecture for Model-Driven Business Apps*. http://doi.org/10.1109/HICSS.2016.708

Facebook. (2015). Facebook reports second quarter 2015 results. *Facebook Investor Relations*. Retrieved from http://investor.fb.com/releasedetail.cfm?ReleaseID=924562

Facebook. (2015). *Our Mission*. Retrieved March 5, 2016, from http://newsroom. fb.com/company-info/

Farag, S., Schwanen, T., Dijst, M., & Faber, J. (2007). Shopping online and/or in-store? A structural equation model of the relationships between e-shopping and in-store shopping. *Transportation Research Part A, Policy and Practice*, *41*(2), 125–141. doi:10.1016/j.tra.2006.02.003

FDC Servers. (2016). *The Bandwidth Authority*. Retrieved September 27, 2016, from https://fdcservers.net

Feigi, H. (2016). Positivism. In Encyclopedia Britannica. Britannica.

Ferns, B. H., & Walls, A. (2012). Enduring travel involvement, destination brand equity, and travelers visit intentions: A structural model analysis. *Journal of Destination Marketing & Management*, *1*(1–2), 27–35. doi:10.1016/j.jdmm.2012.07.002

Filios, G., Nikoletseas, S., & Pavlopoulou, C. (2015). Efficient Parameterized Methods for Physical Activity Detection Using Only Smartphone Sensors. In *Proceedings of the 13th ACM International Symposium on Mobility Management and Wireless Access* (pp. 97–104). New York, NY: ACM. http://doi.org/ doi:10.1145/2810362.2810372

Finn, A., Wang, L., & Frank, T. (2009). Attribute Perceptions, Customer Satisfaction and Intention to Recommend E-Services. *Journal of Interactive Marketing*, *23*(3), 209–220. doi:10.1016/j.intmar.2009.04.006

Fletcher, N. (2007). *Apple: "we plan to have an iPhone SDK in developers' hands in February"*. Retrieved April 30, 2016, from http://www.engadget.com/2007/10/17/apple-we-plan-to-have-an-iphone-sdk-in-developers-hands-in-fe/

Forrester. (2014). *US Mobile Payments to Reach $142 Billion by 2019*. Retrieved from: https://www.forrester.com/US+Mobile+Payments+To+Reach+142+Billion+By+2019/-/E-PRE7454

Foster, I., Zhao, Y., Raicu, I., & Lu, S. (2008). *Cloud Computing and Grid Computing 360-Degree Compared*. Retrieved March 5, 2016, from https://arxiv.org/pdf/0901.0131.pdf

Freling, T., & Forbes, L. (2005). An empirical analysis of the brand personality effect. *Journal of Product and Brand Management*, *14*(7), 404–413. doi:10.1108/10610420510633350

Fritz, F., Susperregui, A., & Linaza, M. T. (2005). Enhancing Cultural Tourism Experiences with Augmented Reality Technologies. *The 6th International Symposium on Virtual Reality, Archaeology and Cultural Heritage (VAST).*

Fu, B., Lin, J., Li, L., Faloutsos, C., Hong, J., & Sadeh, N. (2013). Why People Hate Your App: Making Sense of User Feedback in a Mobile App Store. In *Proceedings of the 19th ACM SIGKDD International Conference on Knowledge Discovery and Data Mining* (pp. 1276–1284). New York, NY: ACM. http://doi.org/ doi:10.1145/2487575.2488202

Fulgoni, G. M. (2015). How Brands Using Social Media Ignite Marketing and Drive Growth. *Journal of Advertising Research*, 235–236.

Gallego, D., Woerndl, W., & Huecas, G. (2013). Evaluating the impact of proactivity in the user experience of a context-aware restaurant recommender for Android smartphones. *Journal of Systems Architecture*, *59*(9), 748–758. doi:10.1016/j.sysarc.2013.02.004

Gallegos, J. A. (2016, April). *The Best Social Media Campaigns of 2016.* Retrieved September 28, 2016, from http://www.tintup.com/blog/the-best-social-media-campaigns-of-2016-so-far/

Ganesh, J., Reynolds, K. E., Luckett, M., & Pomirleanu, N. (2010). Online shopper motivations, and e-store attributes: An examination of online patronage behavior and shopper typologies. *Journal of Retailing*, *86*(1), 106–115. doi:10.1016/j.jretai.2010.01.003

Garau, C. (2014). From Territory to Smartphone: Smart Fruition of Cultural Heritage for Dynamic Tourism Development. *Planning Practice and Research*, *29*(3), 238–255. doi:10.1080/02697459.2014.929837

Gartner, BJ. (2009). *Seven cloud-computing security risks.* Technical report.

Gartner. (2014). *Gartner Says Less Than 0.01 Percent of Consumer Mobile Apps Will Be Considered a Financial Success by Their Developers Through 2018.* Retrieved from: http://www.gartner.com/newsroom/id/2648515

Gartner. (2015a). *Gartner's 2015 Hype Cycle for Emerging Technologies Identifies the Computing Innovations That Organizations Should Monitor*. Retrieved March 5, 2016 from http://www.gartner.com/newsroom/id/3114217

Gartner. (2015b). *Gartner Says 6.4 Billion Connected "Things" Will Be in Use in 2016, Up 30 Percent From 2015.* Retrieved March 5, 2016 from http://www.gartner.com/newsroom/ id/3165317

GCF LearnFree.org. (2015). *What is an application?* Retrieved from http://www.gcflearnfree.org/computerbasics/3

Gefen, D., Karahanna, E., & Straub, D. W. (2003). Inexperience and experience with online stores: The importance of tam and trust. *Engineering Management. IEEE Transactions on*, *50*(3), 307–321.

Gefen, D., Karahanna, E., & Straub, D. W. (2003). Inexperience and experience with online stores: The importance of TAM and trust. *Engineering Management. IEEE Transactions on*, *50*(3), 307–321.

Gens, F. (2009). *New IDC IT cloud services survey: Top benefits and challenges*. Technical report, IDC eXchange. Retrieved from http://blogs.idc.com/ie/?p=730

Geron, T. (2013). *How King.com Zoomed Up The Social Gaming Charts*. Retrieved from: http://www.forbes.com/sites/tomiogeron/2013/03/26/howkingcomzoomedupthesocialga mingcharts/

Ghosh, A., & Riccardi, G. (2014). Recognizing Human Activities from Smartphone Sensor Signals. In *Proceedings of the 22Nd ACM International Conference on Multimedia* (pp. 865–868). New York, NY: ACM. http://doi.org/ doi:10.1145/2647868.2655034

Giovanis, A., Binioris, S., & Polychronopoulos, G. (2012). An extension of TAM model with IDT and security/privacy risk in the adoption of internet banking services in Greece. *EuroMed Journal of Business*, *7*(1), 24–53. doi:10.1108/14502191211225365

Goasduff, L., & Pettey, C. (2012). *Gartner Says Worldwide Smartphone Sales Soared in Fourth Quarter of 2011 With 47 Percent Growth*. Retrieved April 30, 2016, from http://www.gartner.com/newsroom/id/1924314

Goasduff, L., & Rivera, J. (2015). *Gartner Says Smartphone Sales Surpassed One Billion Units in 2014*. Retrieved from http://www.gartner.com/newsroom/id/2996817

Goldsmith, R., & Goldsmith, E. (2012). Brand Personality and Brand Engagement. *American Journal of Management*, *12*(1), 11–20.

Goody, J. (2006). From Misery to Luxury. *Social Sciences Information. Information Sur les Sciences Sociales*, *45*(3), 341–348. doi:10.1177/0539018406066526

Google. (2013). *Mobile In-Store Research: how in-store shoppers are using mobile devices*. Google Shopper Marketing Council.

Google. (2016a). *Android*. Retrieved April 30, 2016, from https://www.android.com/

Google. (2016b). *Android Auto*. Retrieved April 28, 2016, from https://www.android.com/intl/de_de/auto/

Google. (2016c). *Google Play Store*. Retrieved April 30, 2016, from https://play.google.com/

Goswami, A., Chung, S. H., Chittar, N., & Islam, A. (2012). *Assessing product image quality for online shopping*. Paper presented at the IS&T/SPIE Electronic Imaging. doi:10.1117/12.906982

Grewal, D., Iyer, G. R., & Levy, M. (2004). Internet retailing: Enablers, limiters and market consequences. *Journal of Business Research*, *57*(7), 703–713. doi:10.1016/S0148-2963(02)00348-X

Grewal, D., & Levy, M. (2007). Retailing research: Past, present, and future. *Journal of Retailing*, *83*(4), 447–464. doi:10.1016/j.jretai.2007.09.003

Grobauer, B., Walloschek, T., & Stocker, E. (2011). Understanding cloud computing vulnerabilities. *Security & Privacy*, *9*(2), 50–57. doi:10.1109/MSP.2010.115

Grønli, T.-M., Hansen, J., & Ghinea, G. (2010). Android vs Windows Mobile vs Java ME: A Comparative Study of Mobile Development Environments. In *Proceedings of the 3rd International Conference on Pervasive Technologies Related to Assistive Environments* (pp. 45:1–45:8). New York, NY: ACM. http://doi.org/ doi:10.1145/1839294.1839348

Grothaus, M. (2016). *Apple Pay Leads mobile Payments With 12 Million Monthly Users*. Retrieved from: https://www.fastcompany.com/3057353/fast-feed/apple-pay-leads-mobile-payments-with-12-million-monthly-users

Guan, H.-L., & Cheng, B.-D. (2009). *Analysis on the consumer's online information search behavior.* Paper presented at the E-Business and Information System Security, 2009. EBISS '09. International Conference on.

Guess, A. R. (2011). *Smartphone Apps and Big Data*. Retrieved from http://www.dataversity.net/smartphone-apps-and-big-data/

Hair, J. F., Hult, G. T. M., Ringle, C., & Sarstedt, M. (2013). *A primer on partial least squares structural equation modeling (pls-sem)*. SAGE Publications.

Hallmann, K., Zehrer, A., & Müller, S. (2013). Perceived destination image: An image model for a winter sports destination and its effect on intention to revisit. *Journal of Travel Research, 54*(1), 94–106. doi:10.1177/0047287513513161

Hamid, R. M. N., Bryan, S., & Sharad, S. (2009). Outsourcing business to cloud computing services: Opportunities and challenges. IEEE Internet Computing.

Hamlen, K., Kantarcioglu, M., Khan, L., & Thuraisingham, B. (2010). Security Issues for Cloud Computing. *International Journal of Information Security and Privacy*, *4*(2), 36–48. doi:10.4018/jisp.2010040103

Han Rebekah Wong, S. (2012). Which platform do our users prefer: Website or mobile App? *RSR. Reference Services Review*, *40*(1), 103–115. doi:10.1108/00907321211203667

Han, H., & Hyun, S. S. (2015). Customer retention in the medical tourism industry: Impact of quality, satisfaction, trust, and price reasonableness. *Tourism Management*, *46*, 20–29. doi:10.1016/j.tourman.2014.06.003

Han, H., & Ryu, K. (2009). The roles of the physical environment, price perception, and customer satisfaction in determining customer loyalty in the restaurant industry. *Journal of Hospitality & Tourism Research (Washington, D.C.)*, *33*(4), 487–510. doi:10.1177/1096348009344212

Hannah, B., & Lybecker, K. M. (2010). Determinants of recent online purchasing and the percentage of income spent online. *International Business Research*, *3*(4), 60–71. doi:10.5539/ibr.v3n4p60

Hardiman, N. (2013). *Cloud computing and the rise of big data*. Retrieved March 5, 2016, from http://www.techrepublic.com/blog/the-enterprise-cloud/cloud-computing-and-the-rise-of-big-data/

Harris, L. C., & Goode, M. M. H. (2004). The four levels of loyalty and the pivotal role of trust: A study of online service dynamics. *Journal of Retailing*, *80*(2), 139–158. doi:10.1016/j.jretai.2004.04.002

Harrison, R., Flood, D., & Duce, D. (2013). Usability of mobile Applications: Literature review and rationale for a new usability model. *J Interact Sci.*, *1*(1), 1. doi:10.1186/2194-0827-1-1

Hart, M. (2008). *Do online buying behaviour and attitudes to web personalization vary by age group?* Paper presented at the 2008 annual research conference of the South African Institute of Computer Scientists and Information Technologists on IT research in developing countries: riding the wave of technology, Wilderness, South Africa. doi:10.1145/1456659.1456670

Hassan, Q. F. (2011). *Demystifying cloud computing*. Retrieved March 5, 2016, from http://static1.1.sqspcdn.com/static/f/702523/10181434/1294788395300/201101-Hassan.pdf

Hassan, A. (2012). bc). Rationalization of Business Planning Through the Current Dynamics of Tourism. *International Journal of Management and Development Studies*, *2*(1), 61–63.

Hassan, A. (2012a). Key Components for an Effective Marketing Planning: A Conceptual Analysis. *International Journal of Management and Development Studies*, *2*(1), 68–70.

Hassan, A. (in press). Destination Image Formation: The Function Analysis of Augmented Reality Application. In M. Khosrow-Pour (Ed.), *The Encyclopaedia of Information Science and Technology*. IGI Global.

Hassan, A., & Jung, T. (2016). Augmented Reality as an Emerging Application in Tourism Education. In D. H. Choi, A. Dailey-Hebert, & J. S. Estes (Eds.), *Emerging Tools and Applications of Virtual Reality in Education* (pp. 168–185). IGI Global. doi:10.4018/978-1-4666-9837-6.ch008

Hassan, A., & Rahimi, R. (in press). Consuming 'Innovation': Augmented Reality as an Innovation Tool in Digital Tourism Marketing. In P. Nikolaos & I. Bregoli (Eds.), *Global Dynamics in Travel, Tourism, and Hospitality*. IGI Global. doi:10.4018/978-1-5225-0201-2.ch008

Hassan, A., & Rahimi, R. (in press). Insights and Rumination in Human Resource Management Practices of SMEs: Case of a Family Run Tour Operator in London. In P. O. de Pablos & R. D. Tennyson (Eds.), *Handbook of Research on Human Resources Strategies for the New Millennial Workforce*. IGI Global. doi:10.4018/978-1-5225-0948-6.ch012

Hassell, J. (2015, May 4). *Talking SMAC: Revisiting social, mobile, analytics and cloud.* Retrieved September 26, 2016 from http://www.cio.com/article/2918194/cloud-computing/taking-smac-revisiting-social-mobile-analytics-and-cloud.html

Hausman, A. V., & Siekpe, J. S. (2009). The effect of web interface features on consumer online purchase intentions. *Journal of Business Research*, *62*(1), 5–13. doi:10.1016/j.jbusres.2008.01.018

Haverila, M. (2011). Mobile phone feature preferences, customer satisfaction and repurchase intent among male users. *Australasian Marketing Journal*, *19*(4), 238–246. doi:10.1016/j.ausmj.2011.05.009

Haytko, D. L., & Baker, J. (2004). Its all at the mall: Exploring adolescent girls experiences. *Journal of Retailing*, *80*(1), 67–83. doi:10.1016/j.jretai.2004.01.005

He, W., & Chai, J. (2009). Study on Mechanism and Models of Customer Segmentation of C2C Shopping. *Information Science and Engineering (ICISE), 2009 1st International Conference on* (pp. 3073-3076).

He, W., & Chai, J. (2009). *Study on mechanism and models of customer segmentation of c2c shopping*. Paper presented at the Information Science and Engineering (ICISE), 2009 1st International Conference on.

Heinemann, G., & Schwarzl, C. (2010a). *New online retailing — what does it mean? In New online retailing* (pp. 19–91). Gabler.

Heinemann, G., & Schwarzl, C. (2010a). *New online retailing — what does it mean?. In New online retailing* (pp. 19–91). Gabler.

Heinemann, G., & Schwarzl, C. (2010b). *Online retailing in transition – revolution, not evolution. In New online retailing* (pp. 1–18). Gabler.

Heinonen, K., & Strandvik, T. (2007). Consumer responsiveness to mobile marketing. *International Journal of Mobile Communications*, *5*(6), 603–617. doi:10.1504/IJMC.2007.014177

Heisler, Y. (2016). *By 2021, the average smartphone user will plow through 8.9GB of data per month*. Retrieved from: http://bgr.com/2016/06/02/smartphone-data-usage-2021-gigabytes-erricson/

Heitkötter, H., Hanschke, S., & Majchrzak, T. A. (2012). Comparing Cross-platform Development Approaches for Mobile Applications. In *Proceedings of the 8th International Conference on Web Information Systems and Technologies (WEBIST)* (pp. 299–311). http://doi.org/doi:10.5220/0003904502990311

Heitkötter, H., Majchrzak, T. A., Ruland, B., & Weber, T. (2013). Evaluating Frameworks for Creating Mobile Web Apps. In K.-H. Krempels & A. Stocker (Eds.), *WEBIST 2013 - Proceedings of the 9th International Conference on Web Information Systems and Technologies* (pp. 209–221). SciTePress.

Heitkötter, H., Majchrzak, T. A., Wolffgang, U., & Kuchen, H. (2012). *Business Apps: Grundlagen und Status quo*. Münster: Förderkreis der Angewandten Informatik an der Westfälischen Wilhelms-Universität Münster e.V.

Heitkötter, H., Kuchen, H., & Majchrzak, T. A. (2015). Extending a Model-Driven Cross-Platform Development Approach for Business Apps. *Science of Computer Programming*, *97*(Part 1), 31–36. doi:10.1016/j.scico.2013.11.013

Heitkötter, H., & Majchrzak, T. A. (2013). Cross-Platform Development of Business Apps with MD2. In *Proc. of the 8th Int. Conf. on Design Science at the Intersection of Physical and Virtual Design (DESRIST)* (Vol. 7939, pp. 405–411). Springer. doi:10.1007/978-3-642-38827-9_29

Heitkötter, H., Majchrzak, T. A., & Kuchen, H. (2013). Cross-Platform Model-Driven Development of Mobile Applications with MD2. In *Proc. 28th SAC* (pp. 526–533). ACM. doi:10.1145/2480362.2480464

Helal, A. (2002). *Anytime, Anywhere Computing: Mobile Computing Concepts and Technology*. New York, NY: The Springer International Series in Engineering and Computer Science.

Hemel, Z., & Visser, E. (2011). Declaratively Programming the Mobile Web with Mobl. In *Proceedings of the 2011 ACM International Conference on Object Oriented Programming Systems Languages and Applications* (pp. 695–712). New York, NY: ACM. http://doi.org/ doi:10.1145/2048066.2048121

Henderson, S. J., & Feiner, S. K. (2007). *Augmented Reality for Maintenance and Repair (ARMAR)*. Retrieved from: http://graphics.cs.columbia.edu/projects/armar/pubs/henderson_feiner_AFRL_RH-WP-TR-2007-0112.pdf

Hendricks, D. (2013). *Complete History of Social Media: Then and Now*. Retrieved March 5, 2016, from http://smallbiztrends.com/2013/05/the-complete-history-of-social-media-infographic.html

Hernandez, B., Jimenez, J., & Jose Martin, M. (2009). The impact of self-efficacy, ease of use and usefulness on e-purchasing: An analysis of experienced e-shoppers. *Interacting with Computers*, *21*(1-2), 146–156. doi:10.1016/j.intcom.2008.11.001

Hernández-Lobato, L., Solis-Radilla, M. M., Moliner-Tena, M. A., & Sánchez-García, J. (2006). Tourism destination image, satisfaction and loyalty: A study in ixtapa-zihuatanejo, mexico. *Tourism Geographies*, *8*(4), 343–358. doi:10.1080/14616680600922039

Hickman, G. (2015). *The Rise and Fall of Mobile Apps: What the Media Isn't Telling You*. Retrieved from http://mobilemarketingengine.com/rise-and-fall-mobile-apps-what-media-isnt-telling/

Hinchcliffe, D. (2013). *2013 predictions for enterprise social media*. Retrieved January 18, 2013, from http://www.zdnet.com/2013-predictions-for-enterprise-social-media-7000009964/

Hinckley, K., Pierce, J., Sinclair, M., & Horvitz, E. (2000). Sensing techniques for mobile interaction. In *Proceedings of the 13th annual ACM symposium on User interface software and technology* (pp. 91-100). ACM Press. doi:10.1145/354401.354417

Hinsz, V. and Nickell, G. (2015). The prediction of workers' food safety intentions and behavior with job attitudes and the reasoned action. *Approach, 31*(2), 91-100.

Hirsh-Pasek, K., Zosh, J., Golinkoff, R., Gray, J., Robb, M., & Kaufman, J. (2015). Putting Education in Educational App: Lessons From the Science of Learning. *Psychological Science in the Public Interest*, *16*(1), 3–34. doi:10.1177/1529100615569721 PMID:25985468

Hoehle, H., & Venkatesh, V. (2015). Mobile Application Usability: Conceptualization and Instrument Development. *Management Information Systems Quarterly*, *39*(2), 435–472.

Hoffman, D. L. T. P. N., & Novak, T. P. (1996). Marketing in hypermedia computer-mediated environments: Conceptual foundations. *Journal of Marketing*, *60*(July), 50–68. doi:10.2307/1251841

Ho, H. Y., & Syu, L. Y. (2010). Uses and gratifications of mobile application users. In *Proceeding of the 2010 international conference on electronics and information engineering* (pp. 315-319). IEEE Press. doi:10.1109/ICEIE.2010.5559869

Holbrook, M. B., & Hirschman, E. C. (1982). The experimental aspects of consumption: Consumer fantasies, feelings, and fun. *The Journal of Consumer Research*, *9*(2), 132–140. doi:10.1086/208906

Hollerer, T. H., & Feiner, S. K. (2004). Mobile Augmented Reality. In H. Karinzi & A. Hammand (Eds.), Telegeoformatics: Location-based computing services. Taylor and Francis Books Ltd.

Hong-Youl, H., Swinder, J., & Siva, K. M. (2010). A new understanding of satisfaction model in e-re-purchase situation. *European Journal of Marketing*, *44*(7), 997–1016.

Honore Petnji Yaya, L., Marimon, F., & Casadesus, M. (2011). Customers loyalty and perception of ISO 9001 in online banking. *Industr Mngmnt & Data Systems*, *111*(8), 1194–1213. doi:10.1108/02635571111170767

Hoppner, J., & Griffith, D. (2015). Looking Back to Move Forward: A Review of the Evolution of Research in International Marketing Channels. *Journal of Retailing*, *91*(4), 610–626. doi:10.1016/j.jretai.2015.04.005

Horng, J.-S., Liu, C.-H., Chiu, H.-Y., & Tsai, C.-Y. (2012). The role of international tourist perceptions of brand equity and travel intention in culinary tourism. *Service Industries Journal*, *32*(16), 2607–2621. doi:10.1080/02642069.2011.594879

Hsin Hsin, C., Yao-Hua, W., & Wen-Ying, Y. (2009). The impact of e-service quality, customer satisfaction and loyalty on e-marketing: Moderating effect of perceived value. *Total Quality Management & Business Excellence*, *20*(4), 423–443. doi:10.1080/14783360902781923

Hsu, C. H. C., Wolfe, K., & Kang, S. K. (2004). Image Assessment for a Destination with Limited Comparative Advantages. *Tourism Management*, *25*(1), 121–126. doi:10.1016/S0261-5177(03)00062-1

Hsu, C. H., Oh, H., & Assaf, A. G. (2011). A customer-based brand equity model for upscale hotels. *Journal of Travel Research*.

Hsu, M., Chuang, L., & Hsu, C. (2014). Understanding online shopping intention: The roles of four types of trust and their antecedents. *Internet Research*, *24*(3), 332–352. doi:10.1108/IntR-01-2013-0007

Hu, Y., Wu, W., & Cheng, D. (2012). Towards law-aware semantic cloud policies with exceptions for data integration and protection. *2nd International Conference on Web Intelligence, Mining and Semantics*. doi:10.1145/2254129.2254162

Hughes, J. (2014). *Data breaches in the cloud: Who's responsible?* Retrieved March 5, 2016, from http://www.govtech.com/security/Data-Breaches-in-the-Cloud-Whos-Responsible.html

Hui, S.K., Inman, J., Huang, Y., & Suher, J. (2013). The effect of in-store travel distance on unplanned spending: applications to mobile promotion strategies. *Journal of Marketing*, *77*, 1-16.

Hung, K., Huiling Chen, A., Peng, N., Hackley, C., Amy Tiwsakul, R., & Chou, C. (2011). Antecedents of luxury brand purchase intention. *Journal of Product and Brand Management*, *20*(6), 457–467. doi:10.1108/10610421111166603

Hyun, S. S. (2009). Creating a model of customer equity for chain restaurant brand formation. *International Journal of Hospitality Management*, *28*(4), 529–539. doi:10.1016/j.ijhm.2009.02.006

Hyun, S. S., & Kim, W. (2011). Dimensions of brand equity in the chain restaurant industry. *Cornell Hospitality Quarterly*, *52*(4), 429–437. doi:10.1177/1938965510397533

Ibrahim, A. S. Hamlyn-Harris, J. & Grundy, J. (2010). Emerging security challenges of cloud virtual infrastructure. *The Asia Pacific Software Engineering Conference 2010 Cloud Workshop*.

IDC. (2016). *Smartphone OS Market Share*. Retrieved April 30, 2016, from http://www.idc.com/prodserv/smartphone-os-market-share.jsp

Ieva, A., & Gaile-Sarkane, E. (2009). Behavioral differences in consumer purchasing behavior between online and traditional shopping: Case of latvia. *Economics & Management*, 345-352.

Ieva, A., & Gaile-Sarkane, E. (2009). Behavioral differences in consumer purchasing behavior between online and traditional shopping: Case of Latvia. *Economics & Management*, 345-352.

IFML. (n.d.). *IFML: The Interaction Flow Modeling Language*. Retrieved April 30, 2016, from http://www.ifml.org/

Im, H. H., Kim, S. S., Elliot, S., & Han, H. (2012). Conceptualizing destination brand equity dimensions from a consumer-based brand equity perspective. *Journal of Travel & Tourism Marketing*, *29*(4), 385–403. doi:10.1080/10548408.2012.674884

Indexmundi.com. (2015). *Malaysia Demographics Profile 2014*. Available from: http://www.indexmundi.com/malaysia/demographics_profile.html

Institute of Medicine. (1999). *To err is human: Building a safer health system*. Retrieved March 5, 2016, from https://www.nationalacademies.org/hmd/~/media/ Files/Report% 20Files/ 1999/To-Err-is Human/To%20Err%20is%20Human%201999%20% 20report%20brief.pdf

IoT Business News. (2015). *Berg Insight says 4.9 million patients worldwide are remotely monitored*. Retrieved from: https://iotbusinessnews.com/2015/12/07/81959-berg-insight-says-4-9-million-patients-worldwide-are-remotely-monitored/

Ismail, A., Abdullah, M. M., & Parasuraman, B. (2009). Effect of Service Quality and Perceive Value on Customer Satisfaction. *International Journal of Management Perspectives*, *1*(3), 29–44.

ISO. (2009). *Information technology? security techniques information security risk management*. Technical report. ISO.

Jaiswal, A. K., Niraj, R., & Venugopal, P. (2010). Context-general and Context-specific Determinants of Online Satisfaction and Loyalty for Commerce and Content Sites. *Journal of Interactive Marketing*, *24*(3), 222–238. doi:10.1016/j.intmar.2010.04.003

Jamal, A., & Goode, M. (2001). Consumers and Brands: A study of the impact of self congruence on brand preferance and satisfaction. *Marketing Intelligence & Planning*, *19*(7), 482–492. doi:10.1108/02634500110408286

Jang, S. S., & Feng, R. (2007). Temporal destination revisit intention: The effects of novelty seeking and satisfaction. *Tourism Management*, *28*(2), 580–590. doi:10.1016/j.tourman.2006.04.024

Jani, D., & Han, H. (2014). Personality, satisfaction, image, ambience, and loyalty: Testing their relationships in the hotel industry. *International Journal of Hospitality Management*, *37*, 11–20. doi:10.1016/j.ijhm.2013.10.007

Jenamani, M., Mohapatra, P. K. J., & Ghose, S. (2003). A stochastic model of e-customer behavior. *Electronic Commerce Research and Applications*, *2*(1), 81–94. doi:10.1016/S1567-4223(03)00010-3

Jeong, S. W., Fiore, A. M., Niehm, L. S., & Lorenz, F. O. (2009). The role of experiential value in online shopping: The impacts of product presentation on consumer responses towards an apparel web site. *Internet Research*, *19*(1), 105–124. doi:10.1108/10662240910927858

Jingdong, C., & Xiaoqian, G. (2010). The Theory and Empirical Research of Network Profit Based on the Perceived Value. *Computer Modeling and Simulation, 2010. ICCMS '10. Second International Conference on* (Vol. 3, pp. 104-108).

Jingdong, C., & Xiaoqian, G. (2010). *The Theory and Empirical Research of Network Profit Based on the Perceived Value.* Paper presented at the Computer Modeling and Simulation, 2010. ICCMS '10. Second International Conference on.

Ji-Seok, Y., Jae-Nam, L., & Hoffmann, J. (2008). *Trust in Online Shopping: The Korean Student Experience.* Paper presented at the Hawaii International Conference on System Sciences.

Jones, C., & Jia, X. (2015). Using a Domain Specific Language for Lightweight Model-Driven Development. In ENASE 2014, CCIS 551 (pp. 46–62). http://doi.org/ doi:10.1007/978-3-319-27218-4_4

Jones, N. (2015). *Preparing for the Post-App Era.* Retrieved from: https://www.gartner.com/doc/3135321/preparing-postapp-era

Jones, M. A., & Reynolds, K. E. (2006). The role of retailer interest on shopping behavior. *Journal of Retailing*, *82*(2), 115–126. doi:10.1016/j.jretai.2005.05.001

Joorabchi, M. E., Mesbah, A., & Kruchten, P. (2013). Real challenges in mobile app development. In *International Symposium on Empirical Software Engineering and Measurement* (pp. 15–24). http://doi.org/ doi:10.1109/ESEM.2013.9

Joseph, P. (2000). How Personality Makes a Difference. *Journal of Advertising Research*, *40*(6), 79–83. doi:10.2501/JAR-40-6-79-83

Jouini, M., & Ben Arfa Rabai, L. (2014). Surveying and Analyzing Security Problems in Cloud Computing Environments. *The 10th International Conference on Computational Intelligence and Security (CIS 2014),* 689–493.

Jouini, M., Ben Arfa Rabai, L., & Ben Aissa, A. (2014). Classification of security threats in information systems. *ANT/SEIT 2014*, *32*, 489–496.

Jouini, M., Ben Arfa Rabai, L., & Khedri, R. (2015). A Multidimensional Approach Towards a Quantitative Assessment of Security Threats. *ANT/SEIT 2015*, *52*, 507-514.

JSR 68. (2011). *JSR 68: J2ME Platform Specification.* Retrieved April 30, 2016, from https://www.jcp.org/en/jsr/detail?id=68

Juan Carlos, R., & Juan José, G. (2009). The importance of perceived trust, security and privacy in online trading systems. *Information Management & Computer Security*, *17*(2), 96–113. doi:10.1108/09685220910963983

Julian, C. C., Rezaei, S., & Amin, M. (2014). *14 The impact of knowledge management, brand orientation and global marketing strategy on performance. In Research Handbook on Export Marketing* (pp. 305–333). Edward Elgar Publishing.

Jumin, L., Do-Hyung, P., & Ingoo, H. (2011). The different effects of online consumer reviews on consumers purchase intentions depending on trust in online shopping malls: An advertising perspective. *Internet Research*, *21*(2), 187–206. doi:10.1108/10662241111123766

Jung, T., Chung, N., & Leue, M. C. (2015). The Determinants of Recommendations to Use Augmented Reality Technologies: The Case of a Korean Theme Park. *Tourism Management*, *49*, 75–86. doi:10.1016/j.tourman.2015.02.013

JWT NEW YORK. (2012). *Johnson & Johnson Band-Aid Magic Vision.* Retrieved September, 2012, from https://www.thinkwithgoogle.com/campaigns/band-aid-brand-adhesive bandages-johnson-johnson-band-aid-magic-vision.html

Kalantari Shahijan, M., Rezaei, S., Nigel Preece, C., & Khairuzzaman Wan Ismail, W. (2014). Examining retailers behaviour in managing critical points in halal meat handling: A pls analysis. *Journal of Islamic Marketing*, *5*(3), 446–472. doi:10.1108/JIMA-10-2013-0070

Kandampully, J., Juwaheer, T. D., & Hu, H.-H. (2011). The influence of a hotel firms quality of service and image and its effect on tourism customer loyalty. *International Journal of Hospitality & Tourism Administration*, *12*(1), 21–42. doi:10.1080/15256480.2011.540976

Kang, J. Y. M., Mun, J. M., & Johnson, K. K. P. (2015). In-store mobile usage: Downloading and usage intention toward mobile location-based retail apps. *Computers in Human Behavior*, *46*, 210–217. doi:10.1016/j.chb.2015.01.012

Kaplan, A. M., & Haenlein, M. (2009). The fairyland of Second Life: About virtual social worlds and how to use them. *Business Horizons*, *52*(6), 563–572. doi:10.1016/j.bushor.2009.07.002

Kaplan, A. M., & Haenlein, M. (2010). Users of the world, unite! The challenges and opportunities of social media. *Business Horizons*, *53*(1), 59–68. doi:10.1016/j.bushor.2009.09.003

Kaplan, A. M., & Haenlein, M. (2012). Social media: Back to the roots and back to the future. *Journal of Systems and Information Technology*, *14*(2), 101–104. doi:10.1108/13287261211232126

Kaur, A., Chauhan, A., & Medury, Y. (2016). Destination image of indian tourism destinations: An evaluation using correspondence analysis. *Asia Pacific Journal of Marketing and Logistics*, *28*(3), 499–524. doi:10.1108/APJML-05-2015-0074

Kautonen, T., Karjaluoto, H., Jayawardhena, C., & Kuckertz, A. (2007). Permission-based mobile marketing and sources of trust in selected european markets. *Journal of Systems and Information Technology*, *9*(2), 104–123. doi:10.1108/13287260710839201

Kejriwal, A. A. (2009). MobiDSL - a Domain Specific Language for Mobile Web Applications: developing applications for mobile platform without web programming.*Proceedings of the 9th OOPSLA Workshop on Domain-Specific Modeling*.

Keller, K. L. (1993). Conceptualizing, measuring, and managing customer-based brand equity. *Journal of Marketing*, *57*(1), 1. doi:10.2307/1252054

Kennedy-Eden, H., & Gretzel, U. (2012). A Taxonomy of Mobile Applications in Tourism. *eReview of Tourism Research*, *10*(2), 47-50.

Kepes, B. (2015). *New Stats from the State of Cloud Report*. Retrieved March 5, 2016, from http://www.forbes.com/sites/benkepes/2015/03/04/new-stats-from-the-state-of-cloud-report/

Khalid, H., Shihab, E., Nagappan, M., & Hassan, A. E. (2015). What do mobile app users complain about? *IEEE Software*, *32*(3), 70–77. doi:10.1109/MS.2014.50

Khalifa, M., & Limayem, M. (2003). Drivers of internet shopping. *Communications of the ACM*, *46*(12), 233–239. doi:10.1145/953460.953505

Khan, O. J. (2010). Understanding consumer transaction behaviour in web retailing. *International Journal of Business and Management*, *4*(2), 17–36.

Khansa, L., Zobel, C., & Goicochea, G. (2012). Creating a Taxonomy for Mobile Commerce Innovations Using Social Network and Cluster Analyses. *International Journal of Electronic Commerce*, *16*(4), 19–52. doi:10.2753/JEC1086-4415160402

Kharif, O. (2016). *Samsung Gunning for Apple in Race to Dominate Mobile Payments*. Retrieved from: https://www.bloomberg.com/news/articles/2016-03-01/samsung-gunning-for-apple-in-race-to-dominate-mobile-payments

Kietzman, J. H., Hermkens, K., McCarthy, I. P., & Silvestre, B. S. (2011). Social media? Get serious! Understanding the functional building blocks of social media. *Business Horizons*, *54*(3), 241–251. doi:10.1016/j.bushor.2011.01.005

Kim, A. J., & Ko, E. (2012). Do social media marketing activities enhance customer equity? An empirical study of luxury fashion brand. *Journal of Business Research*, *65*(10), 1480–1486. doi:10.1016/j.jbusres.2011.10.014

Kimbler, K. (2010). App store strategies for service providers. In *Intelligence in Next Generation Networks (ICIN), 2010 14th International Conference on* (pp. 1–5). http://doi.org/ doi:10.1109/ ICIN.2010.5640947

Kim, D. J., Ferrin, D. L., & Rao, H. R. (2008). A trust-based consumer decision-making model in electronic commerce: The role of trust, perceived risk, and their antecedents. *Decision Support Systems*, *44*(2), 544–564. doi:10.1016/j.dss.2007.07.001

Kim, E., Lin, J.-S., & Sung, Y. (2013). To app or not to app: Engaging consumers via branded mobile apps. *Journal of Interactive Advertising*, *13*(1), 53–65. doi:10.1080/15252019.2013.782780

Kim, J., Park, Y., Kim, C., & Lee, H. (2013). Mobile application service networks: Apples App Store. *Service Business*, *8*(1), 1–27. doi:10.1007/s11628-013-0184-z

Kim, K. H., Kim, K. S., Kim, D. Y., Kim, J. H., & Kang, S. H. (2008). Brand equity in hospital marketing. *Journal of Business Research*, *61*(1), 75–82. doi:10.1016/j.jbusres.2006.05.010

Kim, M.-J., Chung, N., & Lee, C.-K. (2011). The effect of perceived trust on electronic commerce: Shopping online for tourism products and services in south korea. *Tourism Management*, *32*(2), 256–265. doi:10.1016/j.tourman.2010.01.011

Kim, S. H., Holland, S., & Han, H. S. (2013). A structural model for examining how destination image, perceived value, and service quality affect destination loyalty: A case study of orlando. *International Journal of Tourism Research*, *15*(4), 313–328. doi:10.1002/jtr.1877

Kim, S. J., Wang, R. J.-H., & Malthouse, E. C. (2015). The effects of adopting and using a brands mobile application on customers subsequent purchase behavior. *Journal of Interactive Marketing*, *31*, 28–41. doi:10.1016/j.intmar.2015.05.004

Kim, W. G., Ma, X., & Kim, D. J. (2006). Determinants of Chinese hotel customers e-satisfaction and purchase intentions. *Tourism Management*, *27*(5), 890–900. doi:10.1016/j.tourman.2005.05.010

Kim, Y. H., Kim, D. J., & Wachter, K. (2013). A study of mobile user engagement (MoEN): Engagement motivations, perceived value, satisfaction, and continued engagement intention. *Decision Support Systems*, *56*, 361–370. doi:10.1016/j.dss.2013.07.002

Klais, B. (2013, June). *Research: Two-Thirds of the Fortune 100 are not Mobile-Optimized for Google*. Retrieved September 26, 2016, from http://pureoxygenlabs.com/research-two-thirds-of-the-fortune-100-are-not-mobile-optimized-for-google/

Kobialka, D. (2015). *7 Worst Cloud Outages of 2015 (So Far)*. Retrieved March 5, 2016, from http://talkincloud.com/cloud-computing/06172015/7-worst-cloud-outages-2015-so-far#slide-0-field_images-46431

Koo, D.-M. (2006). The fundamental reasons of e-consumers loyalty to an online store. *Electronic Commerce Research and Applications*, *5*(2), 117–130. doi:10.1016/j.elerap.2005.10.003

Koren, A., Stash, N., & Andreev, A. (2011). A Proposal for Semantic Recommender for Outdoor Audio Tour Guides. *Workshop on Personalization in Mobile Applications at the 5th ACM Conference on Recommender Systems.*

Kosner, A. W. (2014). *Tinder Dating App Users Are Playing With Privacy Fire.* Retrieved from: http://www.forbes.com/sites/anthonykosner/2014/02/18/tinder-dating-app-users-are-playing-with-privacy-fire/

Kotler, P. & Kotler, P. (2010). *Marketing.* Frenchs Forest, Australia: Pearson Australia.

Kotler, P., & Armstrong, G. (2015). *Principles of marketing*. Pearson.

Kourouthanassis, P. E., & Giaglis, G. M. (2012). Introduction to the Special Issue Mobile Commerce: The Past, Present, and Future of Mobile Commerce Research. *International Journal of Electronic Commerce*, *16*(4), 5–18. doi:10.2753/JEC1086-4415160401

Kourouthanassis, P., Boletsis, C., Bardaki, C., & Chasanidou, D. (2015). Tourists Responses to Mobile Augmented Reality Travel Guides: The Role of Emotions on Adoption Behavior. *Pervasive and Mobile Computing*, *18*, 71–87. doi:10.1016/j.pmcj.2014.08.009

Kourouthanassis, P., Georgiadis, C., Zamani, E., & Giaglis, G. (2010). Explaining the adoption of mobile Internet applications. In *Proceedings of Mobile Business and 2010 Ninth Global Mobility Roundtable* (pp. 148-153). IEEE Press. doi:10.1109/ICMB-GMR.2010.70

Kozlenkova, I., Hult, G., Lund, D., Mena, J., & Kekec, P. (2015). The Role of Marketing Channels in Supply Chain Management. *Journal of Retailing*, *91*(4), 586–609. doi:10.1016/j.jretai.2015.03.003

KPMG. (2013). *The SMAC Code Embracing new technologies for future business.* Retrieved April 10, 2016, from https://www.kpmg.com/IN/en/IssuesAndInsights/ ArticlesPublications/Documents/The-SMAC-code-Embracing-new-technologies-for-future-business.pdf

Krafft, M., Goetz, O., Mantrala, M., Sotgiu, F., & Tillmanns, S. (2015). The Evolution of Marketing Channel Research Domains and Methodologies: An Integrative Review and Future Directions. *Journal of Retailing*, *91*(4), 569–585. doi:10.1016/j.jretai.2015.05.001

Krevelen, D. W. F., & Poelman, R. (2010). A Survey of Augmented Reality Technologies, Applications and Limitations. *The International Journal of Virtual Reality*, *9*(2), 1–20.

Kuyoro, S. O., Ibikunle, F., & Awodele, O. (2011). Cloud computing security issues and challenges. *International Journal of Computer Networks*, *3*(5), 247–255.

Kwek Choon, L., Lau Teck, C., & Tan Hoi, P. (2010). The effects of shopping orientations, online trust and prior online purchase experience toward customers' online purchase intention. *International Business Research*, *3*(3), 63–76.

Labrecque, L. I., vor dem Esche, J., Mathwick, C., Novak, T. P., & Hofacker, C. F. (2013). Consumer Power: Evolution in the Digital Age. *Journal of Interactive Marketing*, *27*(4), 257–269. doi:10.1016/j.intmar.2013.09.002

Lada, S., Harvey Tanakinjal, G., & Amin, H. (2009). Predicting intention to choose halal products using theory of reasoned action. *I J Islam Mid East Fin and Mgt.*, *2*(1), 66–76. doi:10.1108/17538390910946276

Lai, W.-H., & Vinh, N. Q. (2013). Online promotion and its influence on destination awareness and loyalty in the tourism industry. *Advances in Management and Applied Economics*, *3*(3), 15.

Lane, N. D., Miluzzo, E., Lu, H., Peebles, D., Choudhury, T., & Campbell, A. (2010). A Survey of Mobile Phone Sensing. *IEEE Communications Magazine*, *48*(9), 140–150. doi:10.1109/MCOM.2010.5560598

Lao, G., & Hu, S. (2005). *Strategic enlightenment from retailing to e-tailing*. Paper presented at the 7th international conference on Electronic commerce, Xi'an, China. doi:10.1145/1089551.1089554

Laroche, M. (2010a). Advances in internet consumer behavior and marketing strategy: Introduction to the special issue. *Journal of Business Research*, *63*(9-10), 1015–1017. doi:10.1016/j.jbusres.2009.06.010

Laroche, M. (2010b). New developments in modeling internet consumer behavior: Introduction to the special issue. *Journal of Business Research*, *63*(9-10), 915–918. doi:10.1016/j.jbusres.2008.12.013

Larson, S. (2014). *Users Are Growlin About Apps That Require Facebook*. Retrieved rom: http://readwrite.com/2014/05/27/facebook-login-required-apps-lyft-barkbuddy/

Lawton, R. (2015). *SMAC – Social, Mobile, Analytics, Cloud: A Guide*. Retrieved March 20, 2016, from http://www.arrkgroup.com/thought-leadership/smac-social-mobile-analytics-cloud-a-guide/

Lee, K., Joshi, K., & McIvor, R. (2007). *Understanding multicultural differences in online satisfaction*. Paper presented at the 2007 ACM SIGMIS CPR conference on Computer personnel research: The global information technology workforce, St. Louis, MO. doi:10.1145/1235000.1235048

Lee, G., & Lin, H. (2005). Customer perceptions of e-service quality in online shopping. *International Journal of Retail & Distribution Management*, *33*(2), 161–176. doi:10.1108/09590550510581485

Lee, J., Park, D.-H., & Han, I. (2008). The effect of negative online consumer reviews on product attitude: An information processing view. *Electronic Commerce Research and Applications*, *7*(3), 341–352. doi:10.1016/j.elerap.2007.05.004

Lee, J.-S., & Back, K.-J. (2008). Attendee-based brand equity. *Tourism Management*, *29*(2), 331–344. doi:10.1016/j.tourman.2007.03.002

Lee, J.-S., & Back, K.-J. (2010). Reexamination of attendee-based brand equity. *Tourism Management*, *31*(3), 395–401. doi:10.1016/j.tourman.2009.04.006

Lee, M. K. O., & Cheung, C. M. K. (2004). Internet Retailing Adoption by Small-to-Medium Sized Enterprises (SMEs): A Multiple-Case Study. *Information Systems Frontiers*, *6*(4), 385–397. doi:10.1023/B:ISFI.0000046379.58029.54

Lee, N., & Lings, I. (2008). *Doing business research*. Los Angeles, CA: SAGE.

Lee, S., Jeon, S., & Kim, D. (2011). The impact of tour quality and tourist satisfaction on tourist loyalty: The case of chinese tourists in korea. *Tourism Management*, *32*(5), 1115–1124. doi:10.1016/j.tourman.2010.09.016

Lee, Y.-K., Back, K.-J., & Kim, J.-Y. (2009). Family restaurant brand personality and its impact on customers emotion, satisfaction, and brand loyalty. *Journal of Hospitality & Tourism Research (Washington, D.C.)*, *33*(3), 305–328. doi:10.1177/1096348009338511

Leskovec, J. (2011). *Social Media Analytics: Tracking, Modeling and Predicting the Flow of Information through Networks*. Retrieved March 10, 2016, from https://pdfs.semanticscholar.org/7ec6/c63dc0b12cb7e00122ffe08daf1cbd28cba9.pdf

Li, N. (2014). *The antecedents and consequences of brand commitment towards luxury brand buying behaviour: A study of mainland China* (Doctoral Thesis). University of Northumbria.

Lian, J.-W., & Lin, T.-M. (2008). Effects of consumer characteristics on their acceptance of online shopping: Comparisons among different product types. *Computers in Human Behavior*, *24*(1), 48–65. doi:10.1016/j.chb.2007.01.002

Liao, S., & Cheng, C. C. J. (2014). Brand equity and the exacerbating factors of product innovation failure evaluations: A communication effect perspective. *Journal of Business Research*, *67*(1), 2919–2925. doi:10.1016/j.jbusres.2012.10.001

Liao, Z., & Cheung, M. T. (2001). Internet-based e-shopping and consumer attitudes: An empirical study. *Information & Management*, *38*(5), 299–306. doi:10.1016/S0378-7206(00)00072-0

Liat, C. B., Mansori, S., & Huei, C. T. (2014). The associations between service quality, corporate image, customer satisfaction, and loyalty: Evidence from the malaysian hotel industry. *Journal of Hospitality Marketing & Management*, *23*(3), 314–326. doi:10.1080/19368623.2013.796867

Li, H., Ye, Q., & Law, R. (2013). Determinants of customer satisfaction in the hotel industry: An application of online review analysis. *Asia Pacific Journal of Tourism Research*, *18*(7), 784–802. doi:10.1080/10941665.2012.708351

Li, J., & Yang, Y. (2015). Describing and testing gender as moderator: Illustrated substantively with a hypothesized relation between image, satisfaction, and behavioural intentions. *Anatolia*, *26*(2), 258–268. doi:10.1080/13032917.2014.939203

Li, M., Dong, Z., & Chen, X. (2012). Factors influencing consumption experience of mobile commerce. *Internet Research*, *22*(2), 120–141. doi:10.1108/10662241211214539

Limon, Y., Kahle, L. R., & Orth, U. R. (2009). Package Design as a Communications Vehicle in Cross-Cultural Values Shopping. *Journal of International Marketing*, *17*(1), 30–57. doi:10.1509/jimk.17.1.30

Lindman, M. (2010). Extending customer knowledge: The value of customer value-based approach. *Journal of Global Business & Technology*, *6*(2), 48–63.

Lindqvist, J., Cranshaw, J., Wiese, J., Hong, J., & Zimmmerman, J. (2011). I'm the mayor of my house: examining why people use foursquare: A social-driven location sharing application. In *Proceedings of the SIGCHI Conference on Human Factors in Computing Systems* (pp. 2409-2418). ACM Press. doi:10.1145/1978942.1979295

Line, N. D., & Runyan, R. C. (2012). Hospitality marketing research: Recent trends and future directions. *International Journal of Hospitality Management*, *31*(2), 477–488. doi:10.1016/j.ijhm.2011.07.006

LinkedIn. (2017). *About LinkedIn*. Retrieved from: https://press.linkedin.com/about-linkedin?

Linnes, C., Viwatmanitsakul, B., Ladegaard, M., Cheng, F., Alamran, S., & Befus, N. … Tabor, R. (2013). *Welcome to Open Data for Hawaii*. Retrieved March 10, 2016, from http://data.hpu.edu/index.html

Liu, H. (2014). *How to Mine Social Media*. Retrieved March 10, 2016, from http://theinstitute.ieee.org/ieee-roundup/members/achievements/how-to-mine-social-media

Liu, X., Li, J. J., & Kim, W. G. (2015). The role of travel experience in the structural relationships among tourists' perceived image, satisfaction, and behavioral intentions. *Tourism and Hospitality Research*.

Liu, C., Marchewka, J. T., Lu, J., & Yu, C.-S. (2005). Beyond concerna privacy-trust-behavioral intention model of electronic commerce. *Information & Management*, *42*(2), 289–304. doi:10.1016/j.im.2004.01.003

Liu, M. T., Wong, I. A., Shi, G., Chu, R., & Brock, J. L. (2014). The impact of corporate social responsibility (csr) performance and perceived brand quality on customer-based brand preference. *Journal of Services Marketing*, *28*(3), 181–194. doi:10.1108/JSM-09-2012-0171

Liu, X., He, M., Gao, F., & Xie, P. (2008). An empirical study of online shopping customer satisfaction in China: A holistic perspective. *International Journal of Retail & Distribution Management*, *36*(11), 919–940. doi:10.1108/09590550810911683

Liu, Y.-D. (2014). Image-based segmentation of cultural tourism market: The perceptions of taiwans inbound visitors. *Asia Pacific Journal of Tourism Research*, *19*(8), 971–987. doi:10.1080/10941665.2013.833124

Liu, Y., & Jang, S. S. (2009). Perceptions of chinese restaurants in the us: What affects customer satisfaction and behavioral intentions? *International Journal of Hospitality Management*, *28*(3), 338–348. doi:10.1016/j.ijhm.2008.10.008

Lorenzo, C., Constantinides, E., Geurts, P., & Gómez, M. (2007). Impact of web experience on e-consumer responses. In G. Psaila & R. Wagner (Eds.), E-commerce and web technologies (Vol. 4655, pp. 191-200). Springer Berlin / Heidelberg. doi:10.1007/978-3-540-74563-1_19

Lorenzo-Blanco, E., Schwartz, S., Unger, J., Zamboanga, B., Des Rosiers, S., Baezconde-Garbanati, L., & Pattarroyo, M. et al. (2016). Alcohol use among recent immigrant Latino/a youth: Acculturation, gender, and the Theory of Reasoned Action. *Ethnicity & Health*, 1–19. PMID:27220730

Loureiro, S. M. C., & González, F. J. M. (2008). The importance of quality, satisfaction, trust, and image in relation to rural tourist loyalty. *Journal of Travel & Tourism Marketing*, *25*(2), 117–136. doi:10.1080/10548400802402321

Lu, J., Mao, Z., Wang, M., & Hu, L. (2015). Goodbye maps, hello apps? Exploring the influential determinants of travel app adoption. *Current Issues in Tourism*, 1-21.

Lu, Y., & Smith, S. (2007). Augmented Reality E-Commerce Assistant System: Trying While Shopping. In J. A. Jacko (Ed.), *Human-Computer Interaction. Interaction Platforms and Techniques:12th International Conference* (pp. 643–652). Berlin: Springer Berlin Heidelberg. http://doi.org/ doi:10.1007/978-3-540-73107-8_72

Lu, A. C. C., Gursoy, D., & Lu, C. Y. (2015). Authenticity perceptions, brand equity and brand choice intention: The case of ethnic restaurants. *International Journal of Hospitality Management*, *50*, 36–45. doi:10.1016/j.ijhm.2015.07.008

Lucía Melián, A., & Víctor Padrón, R. (2010). The impact of pre-sale and post-sale factors on online purchasing satisfaction: A survey. *International Journal of Quality & Reliability Management*, *27*(2), 121–137. doi:10.1108/02656711011014267

Lu, L., Chang, H., & Yu, S. (2013). Online shoppers perceptions of e-retailers ethics, cultural orientation, and loyalty. *Internet Research*, *23*(1), 47–68. doi:10.1108/10662241311295773

Luo, S. (2011). Virtualization security for cloud computing services. Inter Conf on Cloud and Service Computing, 174–179. doi:10.1109/CSC.2011.6138516

Lu, Q., Pattnaik, C., & Shi, M. (2016). Spillover effects of marketing expertise on market performance of domestic firms and MNEs in emerging markets. *Management Decision*, *54*(1), 107–129. doi:10.1108/MD-12-2014-0667

Luxton, D. D., McCann, R. A., Bush, N. E., Mishkind, M. C., & Reger, G. M. (2011). mHealth for Mental Health: Integrating Smartphone Technology in bahavioral Healthcare. *Professional Psychology, Research and Practice*, *42*(6), 505–512. doi:10.1037/a0024485

Lu, Y., Cao, Y., Wang, B., & Yang, S. (2011). A study on factors that affect users behavioral intention to transfer usage from the offline to the online channel. *Computers in Human Behavior*, *27*(1), 355–364. doi:10.1016/j.chb.2010.08.013

Maaja, V., & Krista, J. (2011). The dual value of honesty among Russians in selected former Soviet countries. *Cross Cultural Management: An International Journal*, *18*(1), 55–70. doi:10.1108/13527601111104296

Macedonia, M. (2007). iPhones Target the Tech Elite. *Computer*, *40*(6), 94–95. doi:10.1109/MC.2007.212

Madan, K., & Yadav, R. (2016). Behavioural intention to adopt mobile wallet: A developing country perspective. *Jnl of Indian Business Res*, *8*(3), 227–244. doi:10.1108/JIBR-10-2015-0112

Madlberger, M. (2004). *Strategies and business models in electronic retailing: Indications from the u.S. And the uk.* Paper presented at the 6th international conference on Electronic commerce, Delft, The Netherlands. doi:10.1145/1052220.1052258

Maehle, N., & Shneor, R. (2010). On congruence between brand and human personalities. *Journal of Product and Brand Management*, *19*(1), 44–53.

Ma, J. X., Buhalis, D., & Song, H. (2003). Icts and internet adoption in chinas tourism industry. *International Journal of Information Management*, *23*(6), 451–467. doi:10.1016/j.ijinfomgt.2003.09.002

Majchrzak, T. A., & Ernsting, J. (2015). Reengineering an Approach to Model-Driven Development of Business Apps. In 8th SIGSAND/PLAIS EuroSymposium (pp. 15–31). http://doi.org/doi:10.1007/978-3-319-24366-5_2

Majchrzak, T. A., & Heitkötter, H. (2014). Status Quo and Best Practices of App Development in Regional Companies. In K.-H. Krempels & A. Stocker (Eds.), *Revised Selected Papers WEBIST 2013* (Vol. 189, pp. 189–206). Springer. doi:10.1007/978-3-662-44300-2_12

Majchrzak, T. A., & Schulte, M. (2015). Context-Dependent Testing of Applications for Mobile Devices. *Open Journal of Web Technologies, 2*(1), 27–39. Retrieved from http://www.ronpub.com/ojwt

Majchrzak, T. A., Ernsting, J., & Kuchen, H. (2015). Achieving Business Practicability of Model-Driven Cross-Platform Apps. *OJIS*, *2*(2), 3–14.

Majchrzak, T. A., Wolf, S., & Abbassi, P. (2015). Comparing the Capabilities of Mobile Platforms for Business App Development. In S. Wrycza (Ed.), *Information Systems: Development, Applications, Education: 8th SIGSAND/PLAIS EuroSymposium 2015* (pp. 70–88). Cham: Springer International Publishing; doi:10.1007/978-3-319-24366-5_6

Makanyeza, C. (2015). Consumer awareness, ethnocentrism and loyalty: An integrative model. *Journal of International Consumer Marketing*, *27*(2), 167–183. doi:10.1080/08961530.2014.980927

Malik, A., & Nazir, M. M. (2012). Security Framework for Cloud Computing Environment: A Review. *Journal of Emerging Trends in Computing and Information Sciences*, *3*(3), 390–394.

Mansfield-Devine, S. (2012). Paranoid Android: Just how insecure is the most popular mobile platform? *Network Security*, (9): 5–10. doi:10.1016/S1353-4858(12)70081-8

Mardsen, P. (2010). *Social Commerce: monetizing social media*. Hamburg, Germany: Syzygy Deutschland Gmbh.

Marinho, E. H., & Resende, R. F. (2015). Native and Multiple Targeted Mobile Applications. In O. Gervasi, B. Murgante, S. Misra, L. M. Gavrilova, C. A. M. A. Rocha, C. Torre, … O. B. Apduhan (Eds.), *Computational Science and Its ApplicationsICCSA 2015: 15th International Conference* (pp. 544–558). Springer International Publishing. http://doi.org/ doi:10.1007/978-3-319-21410-8_42

Martin, D., Vicente, O., Vicente, S., Ballesteros, J., & Maynar, M. (2014). I Will Prescribe You an App. In *Proceedings of the 2014 Summer Simulation Multiconference* (pp. 58:1–58:8). San Diego, CA: Society for Computer Simulation International. Retrieved from http://dl.acm.org/citation.cfm?id=2685617.2685675

Martin, J. A. (2015). *11 most memorable social media marketing successes of 2015*. Retrieved March 10, 2016 from http://www.cio.com/article/2988313/social-networking/11-most-memorable-social-media-marketing-successes-of-2015.html#slide4

Mary Ann, E., & Sherry, L. (2011). Cognitive and institutional predictors of initial trust toward an online retailer. *International Journal of Retail & Distribution Management*, *39*(4), 234–255. doi:10.1108/09590551111117527

McCabe, S., Sharples, M., & Foster, C. (2012). Stakeholder engagement in the design of scenarios of technology-enhanced tourism services. *Tourism Management Perspectives*, *4*, 36–44. doi:10.1016/j.tmp.2012.04.007

McCole, P., Ramsey, E., & Williams, J. (2010). Trust considerations on attitudes towards online purchasing: The moderating effect of privacy and security concerns. *Journal of Business Research*, *63*(9-10), 1018–1024. doi:10.1016/j.jbusres.2009.02.025

McEleny, C. (2010). Article. Centaur Communications Ltd.

McGuire, W. (1974). Psychological motives and communication gratification. In J. F. Blumler & J. Katz (Eds.), *The uses of mass communications: Current perspectives on gratification research* (pp. 106–167). Beverly Hills, CA: Sage.

McKinsey & Company. (2015). *The Internet of Things: Mapping the Value Beyond the Hype (Tech. Rep.)*. Mc Kinsey Global Institute.

McLellan, C. (2014). *Enterprise mobility in 2014: App-ocalypse Now?* Retrieved April 30, 2016, from http://www.zdnet.com/article/enterprise-mobility-in-2014-app-ocalypse-now

McMillan, D. W., & Chavis, D. M. (1986). Sense of community: A definition and theory. *Journal of Community Psychology*, *14*(1), 6–23. doi:10.1002/1520-6629(198601)14:1<6::AID-JCOP2290140103>3.0.CO;2-I

Media, C. (2015). *Role of Smartphone Applications in Education*. Retrieved from: http://www.cygnismedia.com/blog/smartphone-apps-in-education/

Meunier, B. (2015, January). *82% Of Sites Use Responsive Web Design In 2015? Try 11.8%?* Retrieved September 26, 2016 from http://marketingland.com/82-sites-use-responsive-web-design-2015-try-11-8-114050

Minelli, M., Chambers, M., & Dhiraj, A. (2013). *Big Data Technology. Big Data, Big Analytics: Emerging Business Intelligence and Analytic Trends for Today's Businesses*. Hoboken, NJ: John Wiley & Sons. doi:10.1002/9781118562260

Min, Y. G., Shin, H. J., & Bang, Y. H. (2012). Cloud computing security issues and access control solutions. SERSC. *Journal of Security Engineering*, *9*, 135–142.

Mitchell, A., Madill, J., & Chreim, S. (2015). Marketing and social enterprises: Implications for social marketing. *Journal of Social Marketing.*, *5*(4), 285–306. doi:10.1108/JSOCM-09-2014-0068

Mkansi, M., & Acheampong, E. (2016). Research Philosophy Debates and Classifications: Students' Dilemma. *Electronic Journal of Business Research Methods*, *10*(2), 132-134.

MobileHTML5. (n.d.). *Mobile HTML5 compatibility*. Retrieved April 29, 2016, from http://mobilehtml5.org/

Moghaddam, H. A., Rezaei, S., & Amin, M. (2015). Examining job seekers perception and behavioural intention toward online recruitment: A pls path modelling approach. *Journal for Global Business Advancement*, *8*(3), 305–325. doi:10.1504/JGBA.2015.071331

Mohapatra, B., Parisa, V., & Banerjee, J. (2014). *The Value of Big Data Analytics to the Business* (Vol. 5). ISACA Journal.

Mohd Safar, H., & Ali, S. (2010). Factors affecting sustainability of internet usage among youth. *The Electronic Library*, *28*(2), 300–313. doi:10.1108/02640471011033657

Mohseni, S., Jayashree, S., Rezaei, S., Kasim, A., & Okumus, F. (2016). Attracting tourists to travel companies websites: The structural relationship between website brand, personal value, shopping experience, perceived risk and purchase intention. *Current Issues in Tourism*, 1–30. doi:10.1080/13683500.2016.1200539

Moliner, M. A., Sánchez, J., Rodríguez, R. M., & Callarisa, L. (2007). Relationship quality with a travel agency: The influence of the postpurchase perceived value of a tourism package. *Tourism and Hospitality Research*, *7*(3-4), 194–211. doi:10.1057/palgrave.thr.6050052

Moore, S. A., Rodger, K., & Taplin, R. (2015). Moving beyond visitor satisfaction to loyalty in nature-based tourism: A review and research agenda. *Current Issues in Tourism*, *18*(7), 667–683. doi:10.1080/13683500.2013.790346

Moyse, I. (2015). *Big data, Cloud, Mobility, and Why IT Needs to Move at the Speed of Business*. Retrieved March 15, 2016, from http://www.cloudcomputing-news.net/news/2015/aug/25/big-data-cloud-mobility-and-why-it-needs-move-speed-business

Muhammad Najib, R., Zaharah, M., & Azlina Mohd, Y. (2010). Internet business strategies by property companies in asia. *Property Management*, *28*(4), 270–289. doi:10.1108/02637471011065692

Mukhopadhyay, T., Kekre, S., & Kalathur, S. (1995). Business Value of Information Technology: A Study of Electronic Data Interchange. *Management Information Systems Quarterly*, *19*(2), 137–156. doi:10.2307/249685

Mulyanegara, R., & Tsarenko, Y. (2009). Predicting brand preferences. *Journal of Fashion Marketing and Management: An International Journal, 13*(3), 358–371. doi:10.1108/13612020910974492

Mulyanegara, R., Tsarenko, Y., & Anderson, A. (2007). The Big Five and brand personality: Investigating the impact of consumer personality on preferences towards particular brand personality. *Journal of Brand Management, 16*(4), 234–247. doi:10.1057/palgrave.bm.2550093

Mummalaneni, V. (2005). An empirical investigation of web site characteristics, consumer emotional states and on-line shopping behaviors. *Journal of Business Research, 58*(4), 526–532. doi:10.1016/S0148-2963(03)00143-7

Murphy, J. (1990). Assessing the Value of Brands. *Long Range Planning, 23*(3), 23–29. doi:10.1016/0024-6301(90)90049-A

Murray, A., & Kline, C. (2015). Rural tourism and the craft beer experience: Factors influencing brand loyalty in rural north carolina, USA. *Journal of Sustainable Tourism, 23*(8-9), 1198–1216. doi:10.1080/09669582.2014.987146

Mustaffa, N., Ibrahim, F., Mahmud, W. A. W., Ahmad, F., Kee, C. P., & Mahbob, M. H. (2011). Diffusion of innovations: The adoption of Facebook among youth in Malaysia. *The Public Sector Innovation Journal, 16*(3), 1–15.

Nam, J., Ekinci, Y., & Whyatt, G. (2011). Brand equity, brand loyalty and consumer satisfaction. *Annals of Tourism Research, 38*(3), 1009–1030. doi:10.1016/j.annals.2011.01.015

Namkung, Y., & Jang, S. (2013). Effects of restaurant green practices on brand equity formation: Do green practices really matter? *International Journal of Hospitality Management, 33*(0), 85–95. doi:10.1016/j.ijhm.2012.06.006

Nash, R., Thyne, M., & Davies, S. (2006). An investigation into customer satisfaction levels in the budget accommodation sector in scotland: A case study of backpacker tourists and the scottish youth hostels association. *Tourism Management, 27*(3), 525–532. doi:10.1016/j.tourman.2005.01.001

Neistat, M. (2013). *What is the 3rd Platform and How Will It Affect Business?* Retrieved March 15, 2016, from https://technologyfirst.org/magazine-articles/124-may-2013/843-mark-neistat-us-signal-company.html

Netemeyer, R., Burton, S., & Lichtenstein, D. (1995). Trait Aspects of Vanity: Measurement and Relevance to Consumer Behavior. *The Journal of Consumer Research, 25*(4), 612–626.

Ng, C. F. (2003). Satisfying shoppers psychological needs: From public market to cyber-mall. *Journal of Environmental Psychology, 23*(4), 439–455. doi:10.1016/S0272-4944(02)00102-0

Nielsen. (2012). *Social media report 2012: Social media comes of age*. Retrieved March 12, 2012, from http://www.nielsen.com/us/en/insights/news/2012/social-media-report-2012-social-media-comes-of-age.html

Nyadzayo, M. W., Matanda, M. J., & Ewing, M. T. (2011). Brand relationships and brand equity in franchising. *Industrial Marketing Management*, *40*(7), 1103–1115. doi:10.1016/j.indmarman.2011.09.004

O'Cass, A., & Frost, H. (2002). Status brands: Examining the effects of non product related brand associations on status and conspicuous consumption. *Journal of Product and Brand Management*, *11*(2), 67–88.

O'Cass, A., & McEwen, H. (2004). Exploring Consumer Status and Conspicuous Consumption. *Journal of Consumer Behaviour*, *4*(1), 25–39. doi:10.1002/cb.155

O'Cass, A., & Siahtiri, V. (2014). Are young adult Chinese status and fashion clothing brand conscious? *Journal of Fashion Marketing and Management: An International Journal*, *18*(3), 284–300. doi:10.1108/JFMM-03-2012-0013

O'Toole, J. (2014). *Mobile apps overtake PC Internet usage in U.S.* Retrieved March 5, 2016, from http://money.cnn.com/2014/02/28/technology/mobile/mobile-apps-internet/

Obama, B. (2014). *Remarks by the President in Q&A with TechShop Workers*. Presented at the Address at TechShop, Pittsburgh, PA. Retrieved March 11, 2016, from https://www.whitehouse.gov/the-press-office/2014/06/17/remarks-president-qa-techshop-workers

OCass, A., & Fenech, T. (2003). Web retailing adoption: Exploring the nature of internet users web retailing behaviour. *Journal of Retailing and Consumer Services*, *10*(2), 81–94. doi:10.1016/S0969-6989(02)00004-8

O'Cass, A., & Lim, K. (2001). The influence of Brand Associations on Brand Preference and Purchase Intention: An Asian Perspective on Brand Associations. *Journal of International Consumer Marketing*, *14*(2/3), 1–10.

Ogden, H., & Venkat, R. (2001). Social comparison and possessions: Japan vs Canada. *Asia Pacific Journal of Marketing and Logistics*, *13*(2), 72–84. doi:10.1108/13555850110764775

Oh, H., & Hsu, C. H. C. (2014). Assessing equivalence of hotel brand equity measures in cross-cultural contexts. *International Journal of Hospitality Management*, *36*(0), 156–166. doi:10.1016/j.ijhm.2013.09.002

Ohrt, J., & Turau, V. (2012). Cross-Platform Development Tools for Smartphone Applications. *IEEE Computer*, *45*(9), 72–79. doi:10.1109/MC.2012.121

Oinas-Kukkonen, H., & Kurkela, V. (2003). Developing successful mobile applications. *Proceedings of Computer Science and Technology*, 19–21.

Okyle, C. (2015). *Password statistics: The bad, the worse and the ugly (infographic)*. Retrieved March 11, 2016, from http://www.entrepreneur.com/article/246902

Olalı, H., & Timur. (1988). *Turizm Ekonomisi*. Izmir: Ofis Ticaret Matbaacılık. (in Turkish)

Olalı, H. (1982). *Turizm Politikası ve Planlaması*. Izmir: Ege Üniversitesi Matbaası. (in Turkish)

Olbrich, R., & Holsing, C. (2011). Modeling consumer purchasing behavior in social shopping communities with clickstream data. *International Journal of Electronic Commerce*, *16*(2), 15–40. doi:10.2753/JEC1086-4415160202

Oliver, R. L. (1977). Effect of expectation and disconfirmation on postexposure product evaluations: An alternative interpretation. *The Journal of Applied Psychology*, *62*(4), 480–486. doi:10.1037/0021-9010.62.4.480

Oliver, R. L. (1980). A cognitive model of the antecedents and consequences of satisfaction decisions. *JMR, Journal of Marketing Research*, *17*(4), 460–469. doi:10.2307/3150499

Olsson, T., & v Salo, M. (2012). Narratives of satisfying and unsatisfying experiences of current mobile augmented reality applications. In *Proceedings of the SIGCHI Conference on Human Factors in Computing Systems* (pp. 2779-2788). ACM Press. doi:10.1145/2207676.2208677

Open Handset Alliance. (2007). Industry Leaders Announce Open Platform for Mobile Devices. *Open Handset Alliance*. Retrieved from http://www.openhandsetalliance.com/press_110507.html

ORegan, M., & Chang, H. (2015). Smartphone adoption amongst chinese youth during leisure-based tourism: Challenges and opportunities. *Journal of China Tourism Research*, *11*(3), 238–254. doi:10.1080/19388160.2015.1077181

Otieno, O., Liyala, S., Odongo, B., & Abeka, S. (2016). Theory of Reasoned Action as an Underpinning to Technological Innovation Adoption Studies. *World Journal of Computer Application and Technology*. Available at: http://www.hrpub.org

Overby, J. W., & Lee, E.-J. (2006). The effects of utilitarian and hedonic online shopping value on consumer preference and intentions. *Journal of Business Research*, *59*(10-11), 1160–1166. doi:10.1016/j.jbusres.2006.03.008

Page, S. (1995). Urban Tourism. Oxon, UK: Academic Press.

Page, C., & Luding, Y. (2003). Bank managers direct marketing dilemmas – customers attitudes and purchase intention. *International Journal of Bank Marketing*, *21*(3), 147–163. doi:10.1108/02652320310469520

Pan, S., Lee, J., & Tsai, H. (2014). Travel photos: Motivations, image dimensions, and affective qualities of places. *Tourism Management*, *40*, 59–69. doi:10.1016/j.tourman.2013.05.007

Pantano, E., & Viassone, M. (2014). Demand pull and technology push perspective in technology-based innovations for the points of sale: The retailers evaluation. *Journal of Retailing and Consumer Services*, *21*(1), 43–47. doi:10.1016/j.jretconser.2013.06.007

Park, H., Rabolt, N., & Sook Jeon, K. (2008). Purchasing global luxury brands among young Korean consumers. *Journal of Fashion Marketing and Management: An International Journal*, *12*(2), 244–259. doi:10.1108/13612020810874917

Paswan, A., Blankson, C., & Guzman, F. (2011). Relationalism in marketing channels and marketing strategy. *European Journal of Marketing*, *45*(3), 311–333. doi:10.1108/03090561111107212

Patricia, S., Victor, P., & Stanley, W. (2005). Attitude and age differences in online buying. *International Journal of Retail & Distribution Management*, *33*(2), 122–132. doi:10.1108/09590550510581458

Payton, T. (2014). *Will SMAC Hit You in the Face?* Retrieved March, 15, 2016, from http://www.fortalicesolutions.com/blog/2014/10/27/will-smac-hit-you-in-the-face/

Pearce, D. G., & Schänzel, H. A. (2013). Destination management: The tourists perspective. *Journal of Destination Marketing and Management*, *2*(3), 137–145. doi:10.1016/j.jdmm.2013.06.001

Pelser, J., de Ruyter, K., Wetzels, M., Grewal, D., Cox, D., & van Beuningen, J. (2015). B2B Channel Partner Programs: Disentangling Indebtedness from Gratitude. *Journal of Retailing*, *91*(4), 660–678. doi:10.1016/j.jretai.2015.05.006

Peng, H., Wang, C., & Cai, J. (2008). An Empirical Investigation on the Adoption of Online Shopping of University Students in China. *Business and Information Management, 2008. ISBIM '08. International Seminar on* (Vol. 1, pp. 498-501).

Peng, H., Wang, C., & Cai, J. (2008). *An empirical investigation on the adoption of online shopping of university students in china.* Paper presented at the Business and Information Management, 2008. ISBIM '08. International Seminar on.

Peng, K., Chen, Y., & Wen, K. (2014). Brand relationship, consumption values and branded App adoption. *Industr Mngmnt & Data Systems.*, *114*(8), 1131–1143. doi:10.1108/IMDS-05-2014-0132

Pesonen, J., & Horster, E. (2012). Near field communication technology in tourism. *Tourism Management Perspectives*, *4*, 11–18. doi:10.1016/j.tmp.2012.04.001

Peterson, R. A., & Balasubramanian, S. (2002). Retailing in the 21st century: Reflections and prologue to research. *Journal of Retailing*, *78*(1), 9–16. doi:10.1016/S0022-4359(01)00062-8

Picot-Coupey, K., Huré, E., & Piveteau, L. (2016). Channel design to enrich customers shopping experiences. *International Journal of Retail & Distribution Management*, *44*(3), 336–368. doi:10.1108/IJRDM-04-2015-0056

Picoto, W. N., Palma-dos-Reis, A., & Belanger, F. (2010). How does mobile business create value for firms? In *Proceedings of Mobile Business and 2010 Ninth Global Mobility Roundtable* (pp. 9-16). IEEE Press. doi:10.1109/ICMB-GMR.2010.19

Pitt, L., Parent, M., Steyn, P., Berthon, P., & Money, A. (2010). The Social Media Release as a Corporate Communications Tool for Bloggers. *Professional Communication, IEEE Transactions on.*

Pookulangara, S., Hawley, J., & Xiao, G. (2011). Explaining multi-channel consumers channel migration intention using theory of reasoned action. *International Journal of Retail & Distribution Management*, *39*(3), 183–202. doi:10.1108/09590551111115024

Popper, B. (2016, April). *Netflix passes 81 million subscribers, but predicts slower growth ahead.* Retrieved September 27, 2016, from http://www.theverge.com/2016/4/18/11454362/netflix-q1-2016-earnings-81-million-subscribers

Poushter, J. (2016). *Smartphone Ownership and Internet Usage Continues to Climb in Emerging Economics*. Retrieved from: http://www.pewglobal.org/2016/02/22/smartphone-ownership-and-internet-usage-continues-to-climb-in-emerging-economies/

Pousttchi, K., Tilson, D., Lyytinen, K., & Hufenbach, Y. (2015). Introduction to the Special Issue on Mobile Commerce: Mobile Commerce Research Yesterday, Today, Tomorrow - What Remains to Be Done? *International Journal of Electronic Commerce*, *19*(4), 1–20. doi:10.1080/10864415.2015.1029351

Pousttchi, K., & Wiedemann, D. G. (2007). Success factors in mobile viral marketing: A multi-case study approach. In *Proceedings of the 6th International Conference on Management of Mobile Business*. IEEE Press. doi:10.1109/ICMB.2007.61

Power, D. J., Sohal, A. S., & Rahman, S.-U. (2001). Critical success factors in agile supply chain management-an empirical study. *International Journal of Physical Distribution & Logistics Management*, *31*(4), 247–265. doi:10.1108/09600030110394923

PR Newswire. (2009). *MMA Updates Definition of Mobile Marketing*. Retrieved from: http://www.mmaglobal.com/news/mma-updates-definition-mobile-marketing

Prayag, G., Hosany, S., Muskat, B., & Del Chiappa, G. (2015). Understanding the relationships between tourists' emotional experiences, perceived overall image, satisfaction, and intention to recommend. *Journal of Travel Research*.

Prayag, G., & Ryan, C. (2012). Antecedents of tourists loyalty to mauritius the role and influence of destination image, place attachment, personal involvement, and satisfaction. *Journal of Travel Research*, *51*(3), 342–356. doi:10.1177/0047287511410321

PricewaterhouseCoopers. (2015). *The connected workforce is talking SMAC. Are you ready?* Retrieved March 10, 2016, from: https://www.pwc.com/us/en/people-management/publications/assets/ connected-workforce.pdf

Primoz, J., Maja, B., Tanja, M., Barbara, P., & Darko, M. (2006). Who says that old dogs cannot learn new tricks?: A survey of internet/web usage among seniors. *New Library World*, *107*(7), 332–345.

Priyadharshini, A. (2013). A survey on security issues and countermeasures in cloud computing storage and a tour towards multi-clouds. *International Journal of Research in Engineering & Technology*, *1*(2), 1–10.

Purcewll, K., Entner, R., & Henderson, N. (2010). *The Rise of Apps Culture*. Retrieved from http://www.pewinternet.org/2010/09/14/the-rise-of-apps-culture/?beta=true&utm_expid=53098246-2.Lly4CFSVQG2lphsg-KopIg.1&utm_referrer=https%3A%2F%2Fwww.google.com%2F

Qaisar, S., & Khawaja, K. F. (2012). Cloud computing: network/ security threats and counter-measures. *Interdisciplinary Journal of Contemporary Research in Business*, *3*(9), 1323-1329.

Rageh Ismail, A., & Spinelli, G. (2012). Effects of brand love, personality and image on word of mouth. *Journal of Fashion Marketing and Management: An International Journal, 16*(4), 386–398. doi:10.1108/13612021211265791

Rajshekhar, G. J., Lori, P. R., Glenna, P., & Robert, F. S. (2005). Sustainable competitive advantage of internet firms: A strategic framework and implications for global marketers. *International Marketing Review, 22*(6), 658–672. doi:10.1108/02651330510630276

Ramadianti, N., Medard, P., & Mganga, C. (2011). *Enhancing information security in cloud computing services using sla based metrics* (Master's thesis). School of Computing, Blekinge Institute of Technology SE-371 79, Karlskrona, Sweden.

Ramaseshan, B., & Tsao, H. (2007). Moderating effects of the brand concept on the relationship between brand personality and perceived quality. *Journal Of Brand Management, 14*(6), 458–456. doi:10.1057/palgrave.bm.2550090

Rana, A., Bhat, A., & Rani, L. (2015). A classificatory scheme for antecedents of the sources of online brand equity. *Journal of Research in Interactive Marketing, 9*(4), 262–298. doi:10.1108/JRIM-02-2014-0008

Randall, T., Ulrich, K., & Reibstein, D. (1998). Brand equity and vertical product line extent. *Marketing Science, 17*(4), 356–379. doi:10.1287/mksc.17.4.356

Reddy, V. K. (2011). Research issues in cloud computing. *Global Journal of Computer Science and Technology, 11*(11).

Ren, L., & Zhang, Y. (2010). Research of Customer Perceived Value on eStores. *E-Business and E-Government (ICEE), 2010 International Conference on* (pp. 2237-2240).

Reo-tek. (2015). *Ana Sayfa*. Retrieved from: http://www.Reo-Tek.Com/Tr/Hakkimizda/ (in Turkish)

Reynolds, K. E., Ganesh, J., & Luckett, M. (2002). Traditional malls vs. Factory outlets: Comparing shopper typologies and implications for retail strategy. *Journal of Business Research, 55*(9), 687–696. doi:10.1016/S0148-2963(00)00213-7

Rezaei, S., Shahijan, M. K., Valaei, N., Rahimi, R., & Ismail, W. K. W. (2016). Experienced international business traveller's behaviour in Iran: A partial least squares path modelling analysis. *Tourism and Hospitality Research.*

Rezaei, S., Shahijan, M. K., Valaei, N., Rahimi, R., & Ismail, W. K. W. (2016e). Experienced international business traveller's behaviour in Iran: A partial least squares path modelling analysis. *Tourism and Hospitality Research.*

Rezaei, S. (2015). Segmenting consumer decision-making styles (cdms) toward marketing practice: A partial least squares (pls) path modeling approach. *Journal of Retailing and Consumer Services, 22*, 1–15. doi:10.1016/j.jretconser.2014.09.001

Rezaei, S., Ali, F., Amin, M., & Jayashree, S. (2016). Online impulse buying of tourism products: The role of web site personality, utilitarian and hedonic web browsing. *Journal of Hospitality and Tourism Technology*, *7*(1), 60–83. doi:10.1108/JHTT-03-2015-0018

Rezaei, S., & Amin, M. (2013). Exploring online repurchase behavioural intention of university students in malaysia. *Journal for Global Business Advancement*, *6*(2), 92–119. doi:10.1504/JGBA.2013.053561

Rezaei, S., Amin, M., & Ismail, W. K. W. (2014). Online repatronage intention: An empirical study among malaysian experienced online shoppers. *International Journal of Retail & Distribution Management*, *42*(5), 390–421. doi:10.1108/IJRDM-03-2012-0026

Rezaei, S., Amin, M., Moghaddam, M., & Mohamed, N. (2016). 3g post adoption users experience with telecommunications services. *Nankai Business Review International*, *7*(3), 361–394. doi:10.1108/NBRI-01-2016-0007

Rezaei, S., Emami, M., & Valaei, N. (2016). *The moderating impact of product classification on the relationship between online trust, satisfaction, and repurchase intention. In Encyclopedia of e-commerce development, implementation, and management* (p. 1692). IGI Global.

Rezaei, S., Emami, M., & Valaei, N. (2016). *The moderating impact of product classification on the relationship between online trust, satisfaction, and repurchase intention. In Encyclopedia of E-Commerce Development, Implementation, and Management* (p. 1692). IGI Global.

Rezaei, S., & Ghodsi, S. S. (2014). Does value matters in playing online game? An empirical study among massively multiplayer online role-playing games (mmorpgs). *Computers in Human Behavior*, *35*, 252–266. doi:10.1016/j.chb.2014.03.002

Rezaei, S., & Ismail, W. K. W. (2014). Examining online channel selection behaviour among social media shoppers: A pls analysis. *International Journal of Electronic Marketing and Retailing*, *6*(1), 28–51. doi:10.1504/IJEMR.2014.064876

Rezaei, S., Shahijan, M. K., Amin, M., & Ismail, W. K. W. (2016). Determinants of app stores continuance behavior: A pls path modelling approach. *Journal of Internet Commerce*, *15*(4), 408–440. doi:10.1080/15332861.2016.1256749

Rittinghouse, J. W., & Ransome, J. F. (2010). *Cloud computing: Implementation, management, and security*. Boca Raton, FL: CRC Press.

Rivera, J., & van der Meulen, R. (2014a). *Gartner Says Annual Smartphone Sales Surpassed Sales of Feature Phones for the First Time in 2013*. Retrieved April 30, 2016, from http://www.gartner.com/newsroom/id/2665715

Rivera, J., & van der Meulen, R. (2014b). *Gartner Says Sales of Smartphones Grew 20 Percent in Third Quarter of 2014*. Retrieved April 30, 2016, from http://www.gartner.com/newsroom/id/2944819

Romanov, A. (2012). The near and far of proximity marketing: The future of marketing exists at the nexus of digital signage and mobility. *IJMM Canada Issue*, *7*(1), 31–33.

Rotem-Mindali, O. (2010). E-tail versus retail: The effects on shopping related travel empirical evidence from israel. *Transport Policy*, *17*(5), 312–322. doi:10.1016/j.tranpol.2010.02.005

Rouse, M. (2014). *SMAC (social, mobile, analytics and cloud) definition*. Retrieved March 10, 2016, from http://searchcio.techtarget.com/definition/SMAC-social-mobile-analytics-and-cloud

Rowinski, D. (2012). *History of Mobile App Stores*. Retrieved from http://readwrite.com/2012/02/07/infographic_history_of_mobile_app_stores

Rozwell, C., Sallam, L, R., & Sussin, J. (2013, September 27). *Who's who in Social Analytics*. Gartner.

Ryan, P. (2015). *Uber vs. Taxis: Meeting and Exceeding Consumer Needs*. Retrieved from: http://www.denneen.com/2015/09/04/uber-vs-taxis-meeting-and-exceeding-consumer-needs/

Salo, M., Olsson, T., Makkonen, M., Hautamaki, A. & Frank, L. (2013). Consumer value of camera-based mobile interaction with the real world. *Journal of Pervasive and Mobile Computing*, *9*, 258-268.

Saunders, M., Lewis, P., & Thornhill, A. (2016). Research methods for business students (7th ed.). Academic Press.

Schechter, S. E. (2004). *Computer Security Strength & Risk: A Quantitative Approach* (PhD thesis). Harvard University DEAS.

Schmitz Weiss, A. (2013). Exploring News App and Location-Based Services on the Smartphone. *Journalism & Mass Communication Quarterly*, *90*(3), 435–456. doi:10.1177/1077699013493788

Schooler, C. (2013). *Social Class and Social Status*. Oxford Bibliographies. doi:10.1093/OBO_dataset_home

Schwinger, W., Grün, Ch., Pröll, B., Retschitzegger, W., & Schauerhuber, A. (2005). *Context-awareness in Mobile Tourism Guides - A Comprehensive Survey*. Retrieved from: http://publik.tuwien.ac.at/files/PubDat_177481.pdf

Selby, C., Jeremy, A., & Beverley, H. (2011). Measuring Internet Product Purchase Risk. *European Journal of Marketing*, *45*(7), 6–6.

Seneviratne, S., Seneviratne, A., Kaafar, M. A., Mahanti, A., & Mohapatra, P. (2015). Early Detection of Spam Mobile Apps. In *Proceedings of the 24th International Conference on World Wide Web* (pp. 949–959). New York, NY: ACM. http://doi.org/ doi:10.1145/2736277.2741084

Seock, Y., & Norton, M. (2007). Attitude toward internet web sites, online information search, and channel choices for purchasing. *Journal of Fashion Marketing and Management: An International Journal*, *11*(4), 571–586. doi:10.1108/13612020710824616

Seo, S., & Jang, S. (2013). The roles of brand equity and branding strategy: A study of restaurant food crises. *International Journal of Hospitality Management*, *34*(0), 192–201. doi:10.1016/j.ijhm.2013.02.014

Shahijan, M. K., Rezaei, S., & Amin, M. (2016). International students course satisfaction and continuance behavioral intention in higher education setting: An empirical assessment in malaysia. *Asia Pacific Education Review*, *17*(1), 41–62. doi:10.1007/s12564-015-9410-9

Shahijan, M. K., Rezaei, S., & Preece, C. N. (2016). Developing a framework of internationalisation for higher education institutions in Malaysia: A SWOT analysis. *International Journal of Management in Education*, *10*(2), 145–173. doi:10.1504/IJMIE.2016.075556

Shahijan, M. K., Rezaei, S., Preece, C. N., & Ismail, W. K. W. (2015). International medical travelers behavioral intention: An empirical study in iran. *Journal of Travel & Tourism Marketing*, *32*(5), 475–502. doi:10.1080/10548408.2014.916248

Shankar, V., & Balasubramanian, S. (2009). Mobile marketing: A synthesis and prognosis. *Journal of Interactive Marketing*, *23*(2), 118–129. doi:10.1016/j.intmar.2009.02.002

Shankar, V., Kleijnen, M., Ramanathan, S., Rizley, R., Holland, S., & Morrissey, S. (2016). Mobile Shopper Marketing: Key Issues, Current Insights, and Future Research Avenues. *Journal of Interactive Marketing*, *34*, 37–48. doi:10.1016/j.intmar.2016.03.002

Shankar, V., Smith, A. K., & Rangaswamy, A. (2003). Customer satisfaction and loyalty in online and offline environments. *International Journal of Research in Marketing*, *20*(2), 153–175. doi:10.1016/S0167-8116(03)00016-8

Shankar, V., Venkatesh, A., Hofacker, C., & Naik, P. (2010). Mobile marketing in the retailing environment: Current insights and future research avenues. *Journal of Interactive Marketing*, *24*(2), 111–120. doi:10.1016/j.intmar.2010.02.006

Shelton, T. (2013). Appendix: PwC thought leadership on social, mobile, analytics, cloud (SMAC). Business Models for the Social Mobile Cloud: Transform Your Business Using Social Media. In *Mobile Internet, and Cloud Computing*, (pp. 165-216). Retrieved March 10, 2016, from http://adnanalhashmi.weebly.com/uploads/2/3/7/6/23764062/business_models_for_the_social_mobile_cloud.pdf

Shen, G. C.-C. (2015). Users adoption of mobile applications: Product type and message framings moderating effect. *Journal of Business Research*, *68*(11), 2317–2321. doi:10.1016/j.jbusres.2015.06.018

Sheng, M. L., & Teo, T. S. H. (2012). Product attributes and brand equity in the mobile domain: The mediating role of customer experience. *International Journal of Information Management*, *32*(2), 139–146. doi:10.1016/j.ijinfomgt.2011.11.017

Shen, K. N., & Khalifa, M. (2008). Exploring multidimensional conceptualization of social presence in the context of online communities. *International Journal of Human-Computer Interaction*, *24*(7), 722–774. doi:10.1080/10447310802335789

Sherman, E., & Topol, M. T. (1996). Anticipating the impact of new technologies on retailing. *Journal of Retailing and Consumer Services*, *3*(2), 107–111. doi:10.1016/0969-6989(95)00070-4

Shi, F., & Marini, J. (2016). Can e-Commerce Recommender Systems be More Popular with Online Shoppers if they are Mood-aware? *WEBIST*, *2*, 173–180.

Shih, H.-P. (2004). An empirical study on predicting user acceptance of e-shopping on the web. *Information & Management*, *41*(3), 351–368. doi:10.1016/S0378-7206(03)00079-X

Shin, D.-H., & Shin, Y.-J. (2011). Consumers trust in virtual mall shopping: The role of social presence and perceived security. *International Journal of Human-Computer Interaction*, *27*(5), 450–475. doi:10.1080/10447318.2011.552060

Shouming, C., & Jie, L. (2009). Factors Influencing the Consumers' Willingness to Buy in E-Commerce. *E-Business and Information System Security, 2009. EBISS '09. International Conference on* (pp. 1-8).

Shueh, J. (2014). *San Francisco Announces Chief Data Officer Joy Bonaguro*. Retrieved February 5, 2016, from http://www.govtech.com/data/San-Francisco-Announces-Chief-Data-Officer-Joy-Bonaguro.html

Sigurðardóttir, I., & Helgadóttir, G. (2015). Riding high: Quality and customer satisfaction in equestrian tourism in iceland. *Scandinavian Journal of Hospitality and Tourism*, *15*(1-2), 105–121. doi:10.1080/15022250.2015.1015765

Sikdar, P., Kumar, A., & Makkad, M. (2015). Online banking adoption. *International Journal of Bank Marketing*, *33*(6), 760–785. doi:10.1108/IJBM-11-2014-0161

Sim, L. L., & Koi, S. M. (2002). Singapores internet shoppers and their impact on traditional shopping patterns. *Journal of Retailing and Consumer Services*, *9*(2), 115–124. doi:10.1016/S0969-6989(01)00029-7

Simon, G. E., & Ludman, E. J. (2009). Its time for disruptive innovation in psychotherapy. *Lancet*, *374*(9690), 594–595. doi:10.1016/S0140-6736(09)61415-X PMID:19699995

Singh, S., & Sonnenburg, S. (2012). Brand performances in social media. *Journal of Interactive Marketing*, *26*(4), 189–197. doi:10.1016/j.intmar.2012.04.001

Slater, S. F., Hult, G. T. M., & Olson, E. M. (2010). Factors influencing the relative importance of marketing strategy creativity and marketing strategy implementation effectiveness. *Industrial Marketing Management*, *39*(4), 551–559. doi:10.1016/j.indmarman.2008.03.007

Smith, A. (2015a). *US. Smartphone Use in 2015*. Retrieved from: http://pewinternet.org/2015/04/01/us-smartphone-use-in-2015/?beta=true&utm_expid=53098246-2.Lly4CFSVQG21phsg-KopIg.1&utm_referrer=https://www.google.com/

Smith, C. (2015b). *By The Number: 20 Impressive Tinder Statistics*. Retrieved from: http://expandedramblings.com/index.php/tinder-statistics/

Smith, C. (2015c). *By The Number: 60 Impressive Snapchat Statistics*. Retrieved from: http://expandedramblings.com/index.php/snapchat-statistics/

Smith, C. (2015d). *By the Numbers: 60+ Amazing Facebook Mobile Stats, Expanded Ramblings.* Retrieved from: http://expandedramblings.com/index.php/facebookmobileappstatistics/

Smith, C. (2017). *75 Incredible Pokemon Go Statistics.* Retrieved from: http://expandedramblings.com/index.php/pokemon-go-statistics/

Smith, M. (2015, February). *The White House Names Dr. DJ Patil as the First U.S. Chief Data Scientist.* Retrieved September 26, 2016, from https://www.whitehouse.gov/blog/2015/02/18 / white-house-names-dr-dj-patil-first-us-chief-data-scientist

SocialTimes. (2016). *Here's How any People Are on Facebook, Instagram, Twitter and Other Big Social Networks.* Retrieved from: http://www.adweek.com/socialtimes/heres-how-many-people-are-on-facebook-instagram-twitter-other-big-social-networks/637205

SocialTimes. (2016). *Here's How Many People Are on Facebook, Instagram, Twitter and Other Big Social Networks.* Retrieved September 5, 2016 from http://www.adweek.com/socialtimes/heres-how-many-people-are-on-facebook-instagram-twitter-other-big-social-networks/637205

Socrata. (2016). *Unleashing the Power of Government Data to Improve Society.* Retrieved September 26, 2016, from http://www.socrata.com/company-info/

So, K. K. F., King, C., Sparks, B. A., & Wang, Y. (2014). The role of customer engagement in building consumer loyalty to tourism brands. *Journal of Travel Research, 55*(1), 64–78. doi:10.1177/0047287514541008

Song, Z., Su, X., & Liaoning, L. (2013). The indirect effects of destination image on destination loyalty intention through tourist satisfaction and perceived value: The bootstrap approach. *Journal of Travel & Tourism Marketing, 30*(4), 386–409. doi:10.1080/10548408.2013.784157

Sonia San, M., Carmen, C., & Rebeca San, J. (2011). Dual effect of perceived risk on cross-national e-commerce. *Internet Research, 21*(1), 46–66. doi:10.1108/10662241111104875

Stahl, T., & Völter, M. (2006). *Model-Driven Software Development.* Chichester, UK: John Wiley & Sons.

Standing, C., Tang-Taye, J.-P., & Boyer, M. (2014). The impact of the internet in travel and tourism: A research review 2001–2010. *Journal of Travel & Tourism Marketing, 31*(1), 82–113. doi:10.1080/10548408.2014.861724

Statista. (2016a). *Most popular Apple App Store categories in December 2016, by share of available apps.* Retrieved from: https://www.statista.com/statistics/270291/popular-categories-in-the-app-store/

Statista. (2016a). *Number of apps available in the leading App stores as of June 2016.* Retrieved September 26, 2016, from https://www.statista.com/statistics/276623/number-of-apps-available-in-leading-app-stores/

Statista. (2016b). *Number of apps available in leading app stores as of June 2016.* Retrieved from: https://www.statista.com/statistics/276623/number-of-apps-available-in-leading-app-stores/

Statista. (2016b). *Numbers of LinkedIn members from 1st quarter 2009 to 2nd quarter 2016 (in millions).* Retrieved 26 September 2016 from, https://www.statista.com/ statistics/ 274050/ quarterly-numbers-of-linkedin-members/

Statista. (2016c). *Number of mobile app downloads worldwide from 2009 to 2017 (in millions).* Retrieved September 26, 2016, from https://www.statista.com/statistics/266488/forecast-of-mobile-app-downloads/

Statista. (2016d). *Number of monthly active Instagram users from January 2013 to June 2016 (in millions).* Retrieved September 26, 2016 from, https://www.statista.com/statistics/ 253577/ number-of-monthly-active-instagram-users/

Statista. (2016e). *Number of monthly active Twitter users worldwide from 1st quarter 2010 to 2nd quarter 2016 (in millions).* Retrieved 26 September, 2016 from https://www.statista.com/ statistics/282087/number-of-monthly-active-twitter-users/

Statista. (2016f). *Number of monthly active WhatsApp users worldwide from April 2013 to February 2016 (in millions).* Retrieved 26 September, 2016 from https://www.statista.com/ statistics/260819/number-of-monthly-active-whatsapp-users/

Statista. (2017). *Digital Advertising.* Retrieved from https://www.statista.com

Stephen, A. T., & Toubia, O. (2010). Deriving value from social commerce networks. *JMR, Journal of Marketing Research*, *47*(2), 215–228.

Stern, P. C. (1999). Information, Incentives, and Proenvironmental Consumer Behavior. *Journal of Consumer Policy*, *22*(4), 461–478. doi:10.1023/A:1006211709570

Su, Q.-Y., & Adams, C. (2005). *Will b2c e-commerce developed in one cultural environment be suitable for another culture: A cross-cultural study between amazon.co.uk (UK) and dangdang.com (China).* Paper presented at the 7th international conference on Electronic commerce, Xi'an, China. doi:10.1145/1089551.1089598

Subashini, S., & Kavitha, V. (2010). A survey on security issues in service delivery models of cloud computing. *Journal of Network and Computer Applications*, *34*(1), 1–11. doi:10.1016/j.jnca.2010.07.006

Su, L., Swanson, S. R., & Chen, X. (2016). The effects of perceived service quality on repurchase intentions and subjective well-being of chinese tourists: The mediating role of relationship quality. *Tourism Management*, *52*, 82–95. doi:10.1016/j.tourman.2015.06.012

Sun, D., Chang, G., Sun, L., Li, F., & Wang, X. (2012). A dynamic multi-dimensional trust evaluation model to enhance security of cloud computing environments. *International Journal of Innovative Computing and Applications*, *3*(4), 200–210. doi:10.1504/IJICA.2011.044529

Surdak, C. (2014). *Data Crush: How the Information Tidal Wave Is Driving New Business Opportunities.* New York: AMACOM.

Susanto, A., Chang, Y., & Ha, Y. (2016). Determinants of continuance intention to use the smartphone banking services. *Industr Mngmnt & Data Systems.*, *116*(3), 508–525. doi:10.1108/IMDS-05-2015-0195

Sussin, J., Rozwell, C., & Sallam, L, R. (2015, March 12). *Technology Overview for Social Analytics Applications*. Gartner.

Takabi, H., Joshi, J. B. D., & Ahn, G. J. (2010). Security and privacy challenges in cloud computing environments. *IEEE Security and Privacy*, *8*(6), 24–31. doi:10.1109/MSP.2010.186

Talal, A., Charles, D., & Sue Vaux, H. (2011). Antecedents of continuance intentions towards e-shopping: The case of saudi arabia. *Journal of Enterprise Information Management*, *24*(1), 85–111. doi:10.1108/17410391111097447

Tan, E., & Leby Lau, J. (2016). Behavioural intention to adopt mobile banking among the millennial generation. *Young Consumers*, *17*(1), 18–31. doi:10.1108/YC-07-2015-00537

Tan, F. b., Yan, L., & Urquhart, C. (2007). The effect of cultural differences on attitude, peer influence, external influence, and self-efficacy in actual online shopping behavior. *Journal of Information Science & Technology*, *4*(1), 3–23.

Tang, S., & Zhang, M. (2010). Differences and Impact Factors between Customer Expected Value and Customer Perceived Value. *E-Product E-Service and E-Entertainment (ICEEE), 2010 International Conference on* (pp. 1-4).

Tang, J. (2011). A locality analysis on purchasing helper at e-commerce webpage - the example in tw, cn, mo and hk. *Expert Systems with Applications*, *38*(1), 371–378. doi:10.1016/j.eswa.2010.06.074

Tang, K., Lin, J., Hong, J. I., Siewiorek, P., & Sadeh, N. (2010). Rethinking location sharing: Exploring the implications of social-driven vs. Purpose-driven location sharing. In *Proceedings of the 12th ACM international conference on Ubiquitous computing* (pp. 85-94). ACM Press. doi:10.1145/1864349.1864363

Tantry, S. (2015). *Why Smart Entrepreneurs Are Swiping 'Right§ on Recruiting Apps*. Retrieved from: https://www.entrepreneur.com/article/250421

Tanusondjaja, A., Greenacre, L., Banelis, M., Truong, O., & Andrews, T. (2015). International brands in emerging markets: The myths of segmentation. *International Marketing Review*, *32*(6), 783–796. doi:10.1108/IMR-08-2014-0286

Tao, Z. (2008). The Impact of Perceived Value on User Acceptance of Mobile Commerce. *Electronic Commerce and Security, 2008 International Symposium on* (pp. 237-240).

Tao, Z. (2008). *The Impact of Perceived Value on User Acceptance of Mobile Commerce*. Paper presented at the Electronic Commerce and Security, 2008 International Symposium on.

Tao, Z., Guijun, Z., & Yuanyuan, H. (2010). A literature review on the studies of internet retailing management. *Technology & Investment*, *1*(1), 19–25. doi:10.4236/ti.2010.11003

Tartaglia, S. (2006). A Preliminary Study for a New Model of Sense of Community. *Journal of Community Psychology, 34*(1), 25–36. doi:10.1002/jcop.20081

Tasci, A. D. A., & Gartner, W. C. (2007). Destination image and its functional relationships. *Journal of Travel Research, 45*(4), 413–425. doi:10.1177/0047287507299569

Tasci, A. D. A., Gartner, W. C., & Tamer Cavusgil, S. (2007). Conceptualization and operationalization of destination image. *Journal of Hospitality & Tourism Research (Washington, D.C.), 31*(2), 194–223. doi:10.1177/1096348006297290

Tauber, E. M. (1972). Why do people shop. *Journal of Marketing, 36*(4), 46–59. doi:10.2307/1250426

Taylor, D. G., & Levin, M. (2014). Predicting Mobile App Usage for Purchasing and Information-Sharing. *International Journal of Retail & Distribution Management, 42*(8), 759–774. doi:10.1108/IJRDM-11-2012-0108

Taylor, D. G., & Strutton, D. (2010). Has e-marketing come of age? Modeling historical influences on post-adoption era internet consumer behaviors. *Journal of Business Research, 63*(9-10), 950–956. doi:10.1016/j.jbusres.2009.01.018

TDMSZ. (2016). *keededves látogatóink!* Retrieved from: http://www.tdmszovetseg.e (in Turkish)

Teckst. (2015). *19 Texg Messaging Stats That Will Blow Your Mind.* Retrieved September 25, 2016, from https://teckst.com/19-text-messaging-stats-that-will-blow-your-mind/

Tekin, Ö., Bideci, M., & Aydın, A. (2015). Kültürel Mirasın Aktarımında Mobil Rehber Uygulamaları ile Turist rehberlerinin Yetkinliğinin Karşılaştırması (Konya Mevlana Müzesi Örneği). *Uluslararası Avrasya Turizm Kongresi.* (in Turkish)

Teng, C.-C. (2011). Commercial hospitality in restaurants and tourist accommodation: Perspectives from international consumer experience in scotland. *International Journal of Hospitality Management, 30*(4), 866–874. doi:10.1016/j.ijhm.2011.01.007

Thaichon, P., & Quach, T. N. (2015). From marketing communications to brand management: Factors influencing relationship quality and customer retention. *Journal of Relationship Marketing, 14*(3), 197–219. doi:10.1080/15332667.2015.1069523

The Economist. (2014). *Disillusioned hedonist shoppers.* Available from: http://www.economist.com/blogs/schumpeter/2014/02/luxury-goods-market

The New York Times. (2006). *Like shopping? Social networking? Try social shopping.* Retrieved June 2013, from www.nytimes.com/2006/09/11/technology/11ecom.html?_r1/41&adxnnl1/41& oref1/4 slogin&partner1/4rssnyt&emc1/4rss&adxnnlx1/41210267372-1HIJXtBN3gaeie1G/0HTcg

Thecka, S. (2014, May). Transforming fragmented industry into sustainable businesses with SMAC technologies. In *IST-Africa Conference Proceedings* (pp. 1-9). IEEE. doi:10.1109/ISTAFRICA.2014.6880615 thedoormouse. (2008). *Technological Desocialization*. Retrieved from: https://thedmouse.wordpress.com/2008/09/30/technological-desocialization/

Thong, J. Y. L., Hong, S.-J., & Tam, K. Y. (2006). The effects of post-adoption beliefs on the expectation-confirmation model for information technology continuance. *International Journal of Human-Computer Studies*, *64*(9), 799–810. doi:10.1016/j.ijhcs.2006.05.001

To, L. M. (2004). *Determinants affecting organizations' intent to adopt e-tailing: A study based on innovation theories*. Paper presented at the 9th annual SIGCSE conference on Innovation and technology in computer science education, Leeds, UK. doi:10.1145/1007996.1008074

Tollin, K., & Schmidt, M. (2015). Marketings contribution from the perspective of marketing executives. *Marketing Intelligence & Planning*, *33*(7), 1047–1070. doi:10.1108/MIP-07-2014-0136

tom Dieck, M. C., & Jung, T. (2015). A Theoretical Model of Mobile Augmented RealityAcceptance in Urban Heritage Tourism. *Current Issues in Tourism*, 1–21. doi:10.1080/13683500.2015.1070801

Toms Shoes. (2016). *About TOMS*. Retrieved September 27, 2016, from http://www.toms.com/about-toms#companyInfo

Toufaily, E., Ricard, L., & Perrien, J. (2013). Customer loyalty to a commercial website: Descriptive meta-analysis of the empirical literature and proposal of an integrative model. *Journal of Business Research*, *66*(9), 1436–1447. doi:10.1016/j.jbusres.2012.05.011

Tran, H., & Corner, J. (2016). The impact of communication channels on mobile banking adoption. *International Journal of Bank Marketing*, *34*(1), 78–109. doi:10.1108/IJBM-06-2014-0073

Tran, X., Dauchez, C., & Szemik, A.-M. (2013). Hotel brand personality and brand quality. *Journal of Vacation Marketing*, *19*(4), 329–341. doi:10.1177/1356766713481218

Tsai, J. Y., Kelley, P., Drielsma, P. H., Cranor, L. F., Hong, J. I., & Sadeh, N. (2009). Who's viewed you? The impact of feedback in a mobile location-sharing application. In *Proceedings of the SIGCHI Conference on Human Factors in Computing Systems* (pp. 2003-2012). ACM Press.

Tsai, S. (2005). Impact of personal orientation on luxury-brand purchase value An international investigation. *International Journal of Market Research*, *47*(4), 429–453.

tumblr. (2016). *Video Projection Mapping*. Retrieved from: http://videomapping.tumblr.com/

Ukil, A., Jana, D., & De Sarkar, A. (2013). A security framework in cloud computing infrastructure. *International Journal of Network Security & Its Applications*, *5*(5), 11–24. doi:10.5121/ijnsa.2013.5502

United Nations. (2014). *Status of Ratifications of the Kyoto Protocol*. Retrieved September 25, 2016, from http://unfccc.int/kyoto_protocol/status_of_ratification/items/2613.php

United States Environmental Protection Agency. (2014). *Climate Change Indicators in the United States*. Retrieved September 25, 2016, from: https://www3.epa.gov/climatechange/ pdfs/climateindicators-full-2014.pdf

Valaei, N., & Rezaei, S. (2016). Does web 2.0 utilisation lead to knowledge quality, improvisational creativity, compositional creativity, and innovation in small and medium-sized enterprises? A sense-making perspective. *Technology Analysis and Strategic Management*, 1–14. doi:10.1080/09537325.2016.1213806

Valaei, N., Rezaei, S., & Ismail, W. K. W. (2017). Examining learning strategies, creativity, and innovation at smes using fuzzy set qualitative comparative analysis and pls path modeling. *Journal of Business Research*, *70*, 224–233. doi:10.1016/j.jbusres.2016.08.016

Valaei, N., Rezaei, S., Ismail, W. K. W., & Moi, O. Y. (2016). Cultural effect on attitude toward online advertising and online brands: Applying hofstedes cultural factors to internet marketing. *International Journal of Internet Marketing and Advertising*, *10*(4), 270. doi:10.1504/IJIMA.2016.081346

Valaei, N., Rezaei, S., & Shahijan, M. K. (2016). Couqual: Assessing overall service quality in courier service industry and the moderating impact of age, gender and ethnicity. *International Journal of Management Concepts and Philosophy*, *9*(2), 144–169. doi:10.1504/IJMCP.2016.077770

Valos, M., Haji Habibi, F., Casidy, R., Driesener, C., & Maplestone, V. (2016). Exploring the integration of social media within integrated marketing communication frameworks. *Marketing Intelligence & Planning*, *34*(1), 19–40. doi:10.1108/MIP-09-2014-0169

Varadarajan, R., Srinivasan, R., Vadakkepatt, G. G., Yadav, M. S., Pavlou, P. A., Krishnamurthy, S., & Krause, T. (2010). Interactive technologies and retailing strategy: A review, conceptual framework and future research directions. *Journal of Interactive Marketing*, *24*(2), 96–110. doi:10.1016/j.intmar.2010.02.004

Varadarajan, R., & Yadav, M. S. (2009). Marketing Strategy in an Internet-Enabled Environment: A Retrospective on the First Ten Years of JIM and a Prospective on the Next Ten Years. *Journal of Interactive Marketing*, *23*(1), 11–22. doi:10.1016/j.intmar.2008.10.002

Varshneya, R. (2015). *What stops your apps from becoming financially successful?* Retrieved from: http://thenextweb.com/entrepreneur/2015/03/01/what-stops-your-apps-from-becoming-financially-successful/

Vazquez, P. M. (2011). *The fashion retailer launches its latest digital creation: A social fashion community to showcase the sartorial talent of its fans and customers*. Retrieved February 24, 2011, from http://www.psfk.com/2011/02/uniqlooks-uniqlos-new-fashion-community.html

Veasna, S., Wu, W.-Y., & Huang, C.-H. (2013). The impact of destination source credibility on destination satisfaction: The mediating effects of destination attachment and destination image. *Tourism Management*, *36*, 511–526. doi:10.1016/j.tourman.2012.09.007

Velázquez, B. M., Saura, I. G., & Molina, M. E. R. (2011). Conceptualizing and measuring loyalty: Towards a conceptual model of tourist loyalty antecedents. *Journal of Vacation Marketing*, *17*(1), 65–81. doi:10.1177/1356766710391450

Venkatesan, R., Farris, P., Guissoni, L., & Neves, M. (2015). Consumer Brand Marketing through Full- and Self-Service Channels in an Emerging Economy. *Journal of Retailing*, *91*(4), 644–659. doi:10.1016/j.jretai.2015.04.003

Vijayasarathy, L. R. (2004). Predicting consumer intentions to use on-line shopping: The case for an augmented technology acceptance model. *Information & Management*, *41*(6), 747–762. doi:10.1016/j.im.2003.08.011

Virtual Reality Site. (2016). *How Augmented Reality Works*. Retrieved from: http://www.vrs.org.uk/augmented-reality/invention.html

Voleti, S., & Ghosh, P. (2013). A non-parametric model of residual brand equity in hierarchical branding structures with application to us beer data. *Journal of the Royal Statistical Society: Series A (Statistics in Society)*. doi:10.1111/rssa.12004

Völter, M. (2013). *DSL engineering: Designing, implementing and using domain-specific languages*. Lexington, KY: CreateSpace Independent Publishing Platform.

Vos, A., Marinagi, C., Trivellas, P., Eberhagen, N., Giannakopoulos, G., & Skourlas, C. (2014). Electronic service quality in online shopping and risk reduction strategies. *J of Systems and Info Tech*, *16*(3), 170–186. doi:10.1108/JSIT-01-2014-0008

W3C. (2014). *HTML5: A vocabulary and associated APIs for HTML and XHTML, 28. October 2014*. Retrieved from https://www.w3.org/TR/html5/single-page.html

Wachter, K., Kim, Y. H., & Kim, D. J. (2012). Mobile users: Choosing to engage. *International Journal of Sales. Retailing and Marketing*, *1*(1), 3–13.

Wahab, S., & Elias, J. (2010). *The influence of trust on electronic banking adoption: Views of Malaysian university lecturers*. Paper presented at the Advanced Management Science (ICAMS), 2010 IEEE International Conference on.

Walker, M., Turnbull, R., & Sim, N. (2007). Future Mobile Devices: An Overview of Emerging Device Trends, and the Impact on Future Converged Services. *BT Technology Journal*, *25*(2), 120–125. doi:10.1007/s10550-007-0035-3

Wallace, D. W., Giese, J. L., & Johnson, J. L. (2004). Customer retailer loyalty in the context of multiple channel strategies. *Journal of Retailing*, *80*(4), 249–263. doi:10.1016/j.jretai.2004.10.002

Walliman, N., Buckler, S., & Walliman, N. (2008). *Your dissertation in education*. Los Angeles, CA: SAGE.

Wan, Y., Nakayama, M., & Sutcliffe, N. (2010). The impact of age and shopping experiences on the classification of search, experience, and credence goods in online shopping. *Information Systems and E-Business Management*, 1-14. doi:10.1007/s10257-010-0156-y

Wang, D., Xiang, Z., Law, R., & Ki, T. P. (2015). Assessing hotel-related smartphone apps using online reviews. *Journal of Hospitality Marketing & Management*.

Wang, S.-j., & Feng, C. (2010). Ways to maximize customer perceived value in E-commerce age. *Networking and Digital Society (ICNDS), 2010 2nd International Conference on* (Vol. 1, pp. 298-301).

Wang, S.-j., & Feng, C. (2010). *Ways to maximize customer perceived value in e-commerce age*. Paper presented at the Networking and Digital Society (ICNDS), 2010 2nd International Conference on.

Wang, T., Lu, K., Lu, L., Chung, S., & Lee, W. (2013). Jekyll on iOS: When Benign Apps Become Evil. In *22nd USENIX Security Symposium (USENIX Security 13)* (pp. 559–572). Washington, D.C.: USENIX. Retrieved from https://www.usenix.org/conference/usenixsecurity13/technical-sessions/presentation/wang_tielei

Wang, J.-C., & Chiang, M.-J. (2009). Social interaction and continuance intention in online auctions: A social capital perspective. *Decision Support Systems*, *47*(4), 466–476. doi:10.1016/j.dss.2009.04.013

Wang, Q., Wang, C., Ren, K., Lou, W., & Li, J. (2011). Enabling Public Auditability and Data Dynamics for Storage Security in Cloud Computing. *IEEE Transactions on Parallel and Distributed Systems*, *22*(5), 1–13. doi:10.1109/TPDS.2010.183

Wang, X., Yu, C., & Wei, Y. (2012). Social media peer communication and impacts on purchase intentions: A consumer socialization framework. *Journal of Interactive Marketing*, *26*(4), 198–208. doi:10.1016/j.intmar.2011.11.004

Wang, Y. J., Hernandez, M. D., & Minor, M. S. (2010). Web aesthetics effects on perceived online service quality and satisfaction in an e-tail environment: The moderating role of purchase task. *Journal of Business Research*, *63*(9-10), 935–942. doi:10.1016/j.jbusres.2009.01.016

Ward, M. R. (2001). Will Online Shopping Compete More with Traditional Retailing or Catalog Shopping? *NETNOMICS: Economic Research and Electronic Networking*, *3*(2), 103–117. doi:10.1023/A:1011451228921

Watson, G. IV, Worm, S., Palmatier, R., & Ganesan, S. (2015). The Evolution of Marketing Channels: Trends and Research Directions. *Journal of Retailing*, *91*(4), 546–568. doi:10.1016/j.jretai.2015.04.002

Watts, S. E., & Andrews, G. (2014). Internet access is NOT restricted globally to high income countries: So why are evidenced based prevention and treatment programs for mental disorders so rare? *Asian Journal of Psychiatry*, *10*, 71–74. doi:10.1016/j.ajp.2014.06.007 PMID:25042956

Wayne, J., & Timothy, G. (2011). *Guidelines on Security and Privacy in Public Cloud Computing*. Information Technology Laboratory.

WebDSL. (n.d.). *WebDSL Repository*. Retrieved January 1, 2016, from https://github.com/webdsl/webdsl

WebRatio. (n.d.). *WebRatio*. Retrieved April 30, 2016, from http://www.webratio.com/

Wei, Z., Jingdong, C., & Wei, H. (2010). The internet marketing strategies theory and empirical research based on product value. *Information Management and Engineering (ICIME), 2010 The 2nd IEEE International Conference on* (pp. 203-206).

Weiser, M. (1999). The Computer for the 21st Century. *SIGMOBILE Mob. Comput. Commun. Rev.*, *3*(3), 3–11. doi:10.1145/329124.329126

West, J., & Mace, M. (2010). Browsing as the killer app: Explaining the rapid success of Apples iPhone. *Telecommunications Policy*, *34*(5–6), 270–286. doi:10.1016/j.telpol.2009.12.002

William, M. (2010). *A Quick Start Guide to Cloud Computing: Moving Your Business Into the Cloud. New Tools for Business*. London: Kogan Page.

Williams, H., Williams, R. L., & Omar, M. (2014). Gastro-Tourism as Destination Branding in Emerging Markets. *International Journal of Leisure and Tourism Marketing*, *4*(1), 1–17. doi:10.1504/IJLTM.2014.059257

Wilson, J. (2010). *Essentials of business research*. Los Angeles, CA: Sage Publications.

Wong, I. A. (2013). Exploring customer equity and the role of service experience in the casino service encounter. *International Journal of Hospitality Management*, *32*, 91–101. doi:10.1016/j.ijhm.2012.04.007

Wong, J., Wu, H. C., & Cheng, C. C. (2015). An empirical analysis of synthesizing the effects of festival quality, emotion, festival image and festival satisfaction on festival loyalty: A case study of macau food festival. *International Journal of Tourism Research*, *17*(6), 521–536. doi:10.1002/jtr.2011

Woods, V., & van der Meulen, R. (2016). *Gartner Says Worldwide Smartphone Sales Grew 9.7 Percent in Fourth Quarter of 2015*. Retrieved April 30, 2016, from http://www.gartner.com/newsroom/id/3215217

Woods, V., & van der Meulen, R. (2016). *Gartner Says Worldwide Smartphone Sales Grew 9.7 Percent in Fourth Quarter of 2015*. Retrieved from: http://www.gartner.com/newsroom/id/3215217

Wooley, P. S. (2011). *Identifying cloud computing security risks* (Master's thesis). University of Oregon, Eugene, OR.

Wu, J.-J., & Chang, Y.-S. (2006). Effect of transaction trust on e-commerce relationships between travel agencies. *Tourism Management*, *27*(6), 1253–1261. doi:10.1016/j.tourman.2005.06.009

Xiao, T. (2010). A cross-national investigation of an extended technology acceptance model in the online shopping context. *International Journal of Retail & Distribution Management*, *38*(10), 742–759. doi:10.1108/09590551011076524

Xuan, Z., Nattapong, W., Hao, L., & Xuejie, Z. (2010). Information Security Risk Management Framework for the Cloud Computing Environments.*10th IEEE International Conference on Computer and Information Technology (CIT 2010)*, 1328 – 1334.

Yan, L.K. (2015). *Factors influencing the adoption of mobile Application among tourism organizations in Malaysia* (Doctoral dissertation). Universiti Tunku Abdul Rahman.

Yang, S., Lu, Y., & Chau, P. (2013). Why do consumers adopt online channel? An empirical investigation of two channel extension mechanisms. *Decision Support Systems*, *54*(2), 858–869. doi:10.1016/j.dss.2012.09.011

Yasuhiro, T. (2012). Tiering and Prioritizing Big Storage -In-House and in the Cloud. *Document News*, *30*(1), 2–4.

Ye, J.-h., Zhang, M.-l., & Zan, J.-y. (2009). Study on Customer Satisfaction in Benefit/Sacrifice Hierarchy. *Fuzzy Systems and Knowledge Discovery, 2009. FSKD '09. Sixth International Conference on* (Vol. 7, pp. 379-385).

Ye, J.-h., Zhang, M.-l., & Zan, J.-Y. (2009). *Study on Customer Satisfaction in Benefit/Sacrifice Hierarchy*. Paper presented at the Fuzzy Systems and Knowledge Discovery, 2009. FSKD '09. Sixth International Conference on.

Yee-Loong Chong, A., Ooi, K., Lin, B., & Tan, B. (2010). Online banking adoption: An empirical analysis. *International Journal of Bank Marketing*, *28*(4), 267–287. doi:10.1108/02652321011054963

Yen, C., & Lu, H. (2008). Factors influencing online auction repurchase intention. *Internet Research*, *18*(1), 7–25. doi:10.1108/10662240810849568

Yeo, V. C. S., Goh, S.-K., & Rezaei, S. (2017). Consumer experiences, attitude and behavioral intention toward online food delivery (ofd) services. *Journal of Retailing and Consumer Services*, *35*, 150–162. doi:10.1016/j.jretconser.2016.12.013

Yoo, M., & Bai, B. (2013). Customer loyalty marketing research: A comparative approach between hospitality and business journals. *International Journal of Hospitality Management*, *33*(0), 166–177. doi:10.1016/j.ijhm.2012.07.009

Yoon, Y.-S., Lee, J.-S., & Lee, C.-K. (2010). Measuring festival quality and value affecting visitors satisfaction and loyalty using a structural approach. *International Journal of Hospitality Management*, *29*(2), 335–342. doi:10.1016/j.ijhm.2009.10.002

Yuan, G. (2009). Factors Influencing Perceived Value of and Attitude toward E commerce among Online Shoppers in China. *Information Engineering, 2009. ICIE '09. WASE International Conference on* (Vol. 2, pp. 330-332).

Yuan, Y.-L., Gretzel, U., & Fesenmaier, D. R. (2003). Internet technology use by american convention and visitors bureaus. *Journal of Travel Research*, *41*(3), 240–255. doi:10.1177/0047287502239032

Yuksel, A., Yuksel, F., & Bilim, Y. (2010). Destination attachment: Effects on customer satisfaction and cognitive, affective and conative loyalty. *Tourism Management*, *31*(2), 274–284. doi:10.1016/j.tourman.2009.03.007

Zarzuela, P., & Antón, C. (2015). Determinants of social commitment in the young. Applying the Theory of Reasoned Action. *Revista Española de Investigación en Marketing ESIC, 19*(2), 83–94. doi:10.1016/j.reimke.2015.05.001

Zephoria. (2017). *The Top 20 Valuable Facebook Statistics*. Retrieved from: https://zephoria.com/top-15-valuable-facebook-statistics/how

Zhang, R., Wang, K., Chen, K., & Rong, R. (2007). *Customer Switching Intention in Service Industries and the Effect of Customer Perceived Value*. Paper presented at the Service Operations and Logistics, and Informatics, 2007. SOLI 2007. IEEE International Conference on.

Zhang, B., & Hwan Kim, J. (2013). Luxury fashion consumption in China: Factors affecting attitude and purchase intent. *Journal of Retailing and Consumer Services*, *20*(1), 68–79. doi:10.1016/j.jretconser.2012.10.007

Zhang, H., Fu, X., Cai, L. A., & Lu, L. (2014). Destination image and tourist loyalty: A meta-analysis. *Tourism Management*, *40*, 213–223. doi:10.1016/j.tourman.2013.06.006

Zhang, L., & Chung, D. (2016). *Strategic Channel Selection with Online Platforms: An Empirical Analysis of the Daily Deal Industry*. Harvard Business School.

Zhao, Z., & Balagué, C. (2014). A design framework of branded mobile applications. In *Proceedings of the 16th International Conference on Human-Computer Interaction with Mobile Devices and Services* (pp. 507-512). ACM Press. doi:10.1145/2628363.2634224

Zhao, Z., & Balagué, C. (2015). Designing branded mobile apps: Fundamentals and recommendations. *Business Horizons*, *58*(3), 305–315. doi:10.1016/j.bushor.2015.01.004

Zhikun, D., & Fungfai, N. (2009). Knowledge sharing among architects in a project design team. *Chinese Management Studies.*, *3*(2), 130–142. doi:10.1108/17506140910963639

Zhong, N., & Michahelles, F. (2013). Google play is not a long tail market: an empirical analysis of app adoption on the Google play app market.*Proceedings of the 28th Annual ACM*, 499–504. doi:10.1145/2480362.2480460

Zhou, T. (2011). An empirical examination of initial trust in mobile banking. *Internet Research*, *21*(5), 527–540. doi:10.1108/10662241111176353

Zhu, D.-S., Tsai, C.-H., & Huang, S.-S. (2010). An exploration of the intention to use online store. In R. Lee (Ed.), Computer and information science 2010 (Vol. 317, pp. 85-94). Springer Berlin / Heidelberg. doi:10.1007/978-3-642-15405-8_8

Zimbardo, P. G., & Coulombe, N. (2016). *Man interrupted: Why young men are struggling & what we can do about it*. Newburyport, MA: Conari Press.

Zissis, D., & Lekkas, D. (2012). Addressing cloud computing security issues. *Future Generation Computer Systems*, *28*(3), 583–592. doi:10.1016/j.future.2010.12.006

About the Contributors

Sajad Rezaei is a Lecturer in Marketing and Research Methods at Taylor's Business School, Taylor's University, Malaysia. His recent research has been published in refereed journals such as *Computers in Human Behavior, Journal of Business Research, Journal of Internet Commerce, Technology Analysis & Strategic Management, Journal ofRetailing andConsumer Services, The InternationalReview of Retail, Distribution and Consumer Research*, and *International Journal of Retail & Distribution Management,* among others. His research direction has extended from his background in BSc Business Administration, MBA dissertation and PhD. theses with two key research themes including e-commerce and marketing management. He serves as a reviewer for several refereed journals such as *Journal of Business Research, Online Information Review, Computers in Human Behavior* and *Current Issues in Tourism*, among others.

* * *

Christine Balagué is the Social Networks Chair holder at the Institut Mines-Télécom (http://www.mines-telecom.fr/en/) and Vice President of Digital National Council (http://www.cnnumerique.fr/en/) in France. At the Institut Mines-Télécom, her researches focus on economic and societal value created by social networks and internet of things, and how companies have to adapt their strategy to capture this value. In these researches, she manages different Big Data projects in partnership with multinational companies. She published more than 50 research articles and international conference proceedings as well as several books on society and economic digital metamorphosis. Within the Digital National Council, composed of 30 members appointed by a decree issued by the President of the French Republic, and regularly consulted by the french government, Christine Balagué contributed to different key reports on societal and economic impact of digital transformation (e-inclusion; e-education; web neutrality; platforms neutrality; fundamental rights and freedoms in a digital society; national consultation). Before 2013, she was during five years President of the Think Tank Renaissance Numérique and contributed to the development of a digital society in France. She is also president of services commission of Cap Digital, one of the major European clusters dedicated to the digital innovation, boosting digital R&D projects between big companies, start ups and research centers. Diploma: Habilitée à Diriger des Recherches, Ph Management at HEC, ESSEC, Master of econometry at ENSAE. She is also Chevalier de l'Ordre National du Mérite.

Jan Christoph Dageförde is a postgraduate researcher and PhD candidate at the Department of Information Systems, University of Münster. He received a B.Sc. and an M.Sc. in Information Systems from the University of Münster in 2014 and 2015, respectively. His M.Sc. focused around process management, business intelligence, and information systems development. During his studies he contributed to the effort of introducing advanced concepts into the MD^2 framework. His current research addresses the extension of established imperative programming languages with declarative concepts that are currently underrepresented in practice. He has been developing for the Web as well as for mobile devices since before starting his University studies.

Maryam (Mary) Emami received her Ph.D. from International Business School, Universiti Teknologi Malaysia in 2016. Her MBA is in strategic management from Universiti Teknologi Malaysia. Her area of research interest has been mainly focused on organizational behavior studies, including creativity in the business world. She has also been a reviewer in the Iranian Journal of Management Studies and she has made several publications in various journals. As a consultant, Emami is currently involved in change management projects in Houston, Texas.

Jan Ernsting is a researcher for Practical Computer Science at the Department of Information Systems, University of Münster, Germany. He received B.Sc. and M.Sc. degrees in Information Systems from the University of Münster. The group for Practical Computer Science has created a model-driven approach, the MD^2 framework, that facilitates the development of cross-platform business apps. His research extended the framework's capabilities to support the specification of interrelated apps, i.e. generate multiple apps from a single model archetype. In addition, his research explicated the architectural assumptions that the generated business apps make in order to assist generator developers in extending and maintaining platform support.

Azizul Hassan is a member of the Tourism Consultants Network of the UK Tourism Society, and is currently working towards a PhD at Cardiff Metropolitan University. His main areas of research are: technology-supported marketing in tourism; innovative marketing dynamics; destination branding in tourism; cultural heritage tourism; heritage interpretation; and sustainable management/marketing alternatives for cultural heritage industries. He is a regular reviewer of Tourism Analysis, the International Journal of Human Resource Management, the International Journal of Ecotourism, the eReview of Tourism Research (eRTR) and The International Interdisciplinary Business-Economics Advancement Journal.

Ree C. Ho has more than 10 years of teaching and administrative experiences in tertiary education for Malaysian, Australian and British universities. He has pioneered and involved in the development of course curriculum and learning materials for a number of offshore transnational programs. His academic portfolio includes the dean, head of the department, principal lecturer, and stream coordinator, etc. Prior to his academic career, Dr. Ho worked in the capacity of a business analyst for the development of corporate enterprise systems, particularly in the areas of banking, marketing real estate. He also served as the Asia Pacific regional manager for a US-based consultant firm.

Mouna Jouini is a PhD student in the Department of Computer Science at the Tunis University in the Higher Institute of Management (ISG). She received her Mastery diploma on computer science applied to management in 2008 from the University of Tunis in the Higher School of Economics and Management of Tunis (ESSECTT) and her master's degree in 2010 from the Tunis University in the Higher Institute of Management (ISG). Her research interest includes software engineering metrics, cloud computing, cyber security and security measurement and quantification. She has published. She has participated in several international conferences including topics related to the computer science, cloud computing, cyber security.

Cathrine Linnes is an Associate Professor in Computer Science at Østfold University College where she serves as a faculty member in the undergraduate and graduate programs. Her research focus is in software development, network analysis and business analytics. She received her Ph.D. from Nova Southeastern University.

Tim A. Majchrzak is an associate professor at the Department of Information Systems at the University of Agder in Kristiansand, Norway. He received BSc and MSc degrees in Information Systems and a PhD in economics (Dr. rer. pol.) from the University of Münster, Germany. His research comprises both technical and organizational aspects of software engineering, often in the context of Web technologies and Mobile Computing. He has also published work on several interdisciplinary Information Systems topics. Tim's research projects typically have an interface to industry or society. He is a member of the IEEE, the IEEE Computer Society, and the Gesellschaft für Informatik e.V.

Gu Manli is a lecturer in Taylor's Business School, Taylor's University Lakeside campus. She received her doctorate from Monash University. She is a reviewer for the Journal of Cross-cultural Psychology, The Sociological Quarterly and Asian Journal of Social Psychology. Her primary research interests are in the area of public opinion studies, cross-cultural management and comparative analysis of human values and attitudes.

Brian Metcalf is an Associate Professor in Psychology at Hawaii Pacific University where he serves as a faculty member in the psychology program. He is also a consultant for "Aetas Mind Developing Apps" (www.discoveraetas.com). His research focus is in Time Perpective Theory and Therapy, understanding and promoting Heroism and helping behavior, and consumer behavior. He received his Ph.D. from the University in Georgia.

Shanthi Bavani V. Raja Mohan is a Senior Lecturer in organizational studies at Taylor's Business School, Taylor's University, Malaysia. She has worked in the industries and was involved in project management. His recent research has been published in refereed journals and her areas of research interest are mainly in the studies of consumer behavior and marketing communications.

Roya Rahimi is a lecturer at the Business School, where she teaches across tourism, hospitality and events subject areas and supervises undergraduate/postgraduate dissertations and PhDs. Her research interests are Customer Relationship Management (CRM), Organizational Culture, Human Resource Management, Gender Equality and Tourism Higher Education. Her works has been published in leading journals such as Journal of Tourism and Hospitality Research, Journal of Travel & Tourism Marketing, International Journal of Contemporary Hospitality Management and Anatolia and has been presented at various international conferences and book chapters. She sits on the editorial board of Journal of Hospitality and Tourism Technology and serve as reviewer for different journals. Her industry experience includes seven years' experience working in the hotel industry in number of international hotels in various countries. Roya is fluent in three languages (English, Turkish and Persian) and has familiarity with European and Asian cultures. She believes that high quality teaching, strong research and industry partnership go hand in hand given the application aspect of the tourism and hospitality field. She was nominated for her cutting style of teaching in 2016 and nominated as the inspirational lecturer of the year in 2015 and 2016. Roya is the external examiner at Ulster University and acting as the director of the Visiting Scholar Scheme at the Faculty of Social Science.

Tobias Reischmann received a B.Sc. and a M.Sc. in Information Systems from the University of Münster in Germany in 2013 and 2015, respectively. During his studies, he focused on business intelligence and process management. Within a project seminar of his M.Sc. studies, he contributed to the MD^2 framework by working on the introduction of workflow elements. He started as a graduate student assistant at the University of Münster in 2014, administrating the central e-learning system of the University. Since October 2015, he continues this work at the Practical Computer Science Group of the University of Münster as a researcher and PhD candidate. His current research is about novel formative e-assessment approaches in combination with graph algorithms, especially error-tolerant subgraph isomorphisms. The foundation for this was laid during his master thesis, examining automated e-assessment of UML class diagrams.

Christoph Rieger is a postgraduate researcher and PhD candidate at the Department of Information Systems, University of Münster. He received a B.Sc. and an M.Sc. in Information Systems from the University of Münster in 2013 and 2015, respectively. His M.Sc. focused around business intelligence and business networks. In his Master's thesis he contributed to the MD^2 framework by developing a generator component for the iOS platform. This experience has increased his previous interest in the area of mobile apps. His current research focuses on model-driven software development and domain-specific languages, in particular regarding the abstract domain-oriented modelling of software in order to include business users in the development process.

Milad Kalantari Shahijan received his PhD in marketing management from Universiti Teknologi Malaysia. He obtained a Master of Business Administration in marketing management from Multimedia University, Malaysia. He has published his research papers in internationally refereed journals such as the Journal of Travel & Tourism Marketing and Journal of Islamic Marketing. His current research interests include Marketing Management, Tourism Marketing and Services Marketing.

Srikaanth Sivasubramaniam is a Senior Lecturer at Taylor's Business School, Taylor's University. He has more than 16 years of teaching experience in tertiary education in the areas of marketing and international business. Prior to his current teaching position, he has worked in the brand management and marketing communication department for an IT company and has consulted many small and medium enterprise. His areas of research interest are mainly in the studies of consumer behavior, retail marketing, brand management and marketing communications.

Naser Valaei is a Lecturer at Department of Marketing, Sunway University Business School (Partner with Lancaster University Management School), Sunway University. He holds a PhD in Business, Master of Business Administration in Information Technology, Bachelor of Software Engineering, and Associate Degree in Software Engineering. His research has been published or accepted in several journals such as *Journal of Business Research, Technology Analysis & Strategic Management, VINE, Information Technology and People, Business Process Management Journal, Journal of Management Development, the International Review of Retail, Distribution, and Consumer Research, Journal of Marketing Channels, Hospitality and Tourism Research, Management Research Review, Asia Pacific Journal of Marketing and Logistics*, among others.

Chew Hong Wee is a Senior Lecturer at Taylor's Business School, Taylor's University. He has more than 10 years of teaching experience in vocational and tertiary education in the areas of global business operations, transnational management and supervising dissertation students. He has held the position of Program Director of international business and marketing program from 2013 to 2014. He has worked in the management position in an Information Technology industries in Malaysia and Australia prior to joining the education industry. His areas of research interest are mainly in the studies of knowledge management.

Zhenzhen Zhao is a professor of marketing at Institut Supérieur du Commerce (ISC-Paris). She worked at the Institut Mines-Télécom as a digital marketing and user experience researcher, incorporating socio-scientific sensitivities for understanding the human experience into design practice. Her current research interests include crowd innovation, branded mobile applications, user-centered design etc. She has been publishing extensively in the areas of marketing and management, computing and human-computer interaction, serving a scientific committee member for several international conferences and workshops, delivering invited talks, guiding and supervising master students in their thesis. Zhenzhen received her joint PhD degree in Computer Science from the Télécom SudParis and the Université Pierre et Marie Curie (UPMC), France, and her M.S. in Communications and Information Systems from the Beijing University of Posts and Telecommunications (BUPT), China.

Index

C

D

E

F

G

H

I

L

M

Purchase Print + Free E-Book or E-Book Only*

Purchase a print book through the IGI Global Online Bookstore and receive the e-book for free or purchase the e-book only! Shipping fees apply.

www.igi-global.com

Recommended Reference Books

ISBN: 978-1-4666-5039-8
© 2014; 487 pp.
List Price: $260

ISBN: 978-1-4666-7476-9
© 2015; 508 pp.
List Price: $212

ISBN: 978-1-4666-6182-0
© 2014; 325 pp.
List Price: $180

ISBN: 978-1-4666-4474-8
© 2014; 735 pp.
List Price: $276

ISBN: 978-1-4666-5950-6
© 2014; 290 pp.
List Price: $156

ISBN: 978-1-4666-6595-8
© 2015; 406 pp.
List Price: $156

*IGI Global now offers the exclusive opportunity to receive a free e-book with the purchase of the publication in print, or purchase any e-book publication only. You choose the format that best suits your needs. This offer is only valid on purchases made directly through IGI Global's Online Bookstore and not intended for use by book distributors or wholesalers. Shipping fees will be applied for hardcover purchases during checkout if this option is selected.

Should a new edition of any given publication become available, access will not be extended on the new edition and will only be available for the purchased publication. If a new edition becomes available, you will not lose access, but you would no longer receive new content for that publication (i.e. updates). The free e-book is only available to single institutions that purchase printed publications through IGI Global. Sharing the free e-book is prohibited and will result in the termination of e-access.

Publishing Information Science and Technology Research Since 1988

IGI GLOBAL
DISSEMINATOR OF KNOWLEDGE

www.igi-global.com | Sign up at www.igi-global.com/newsletters | facebook.com/igiglobal | twitter.com/igiglobal

Stay Current on the Latest Emerging Research Developments

Become an IGI Global Reviewer for Authored Book Projects

The overall success of an authored book project is dependent on quality and timely reviews.

In this competitive age of scholarly publishing, constructive and timely feedback significantly decreases the turnaround time of manuscripts from submission to acceptance, allowing the publication and discovery of progressive research at a much more expeditious rate. Several IGI Global authored book projects are currently seeking highly qualified experts in the field to fill vacancies on their respective editorial review boards:

Applications may be sent to:
development@igi-global.com

Applicants must have a doctorate (or an equivalent degree) as well as publishing and reviewing experience. Reviewers are asked to write reviews in a timely, collegial, and constructive manner. All reviewers will begin their role on an ad-hoc basis for a period of one year, and upon successful completion of this term can be considered for full editorial review board status, with the potential for a subsequent promotion to Associate Editor.

If you have a colleague that may be interested in this opportunity, we encourage you to share this information with them.

www.igi-global.com

InfoSci®-Books

A Database for Progressive Information Science and Technology Research

Maximize Your Library's Book Collection!

Invest in IGI Global's InfoSci®-Books database and gain access to hundreds of reference books at a fraction of their individual list price.

The InfoSci®-Books database offers unlimited simultaneous users the ability to precisely return search results through more than 75,000 full-text chapters from nearly 3,400 reference books in the following academic research areas:

Business & Management Information Science & Technology • Computer Science & Information Technology
Educational Science & Technology • Engineering Science & Technology • Environmental Science & Technology
Government Science & Technology • Library Information Science & Technology • Media & Communication Science & Technology
Medical, Healthcare & Life Science & Technology • Security & Forensic Science & Technology • Social Sciences & Online Behavior

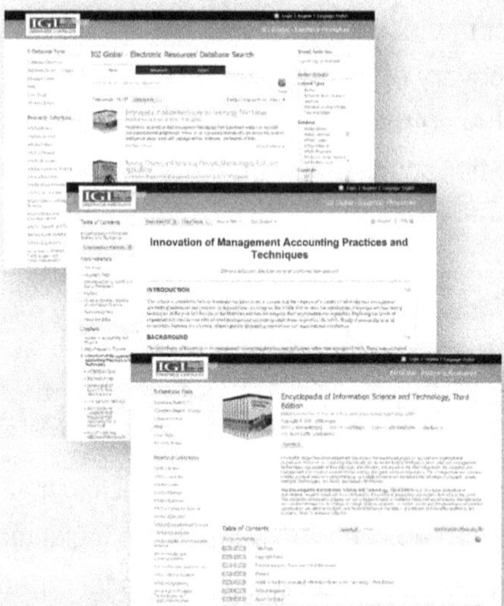

Peer-Reviewed Content:

- Cutting-edge research
- No embargoes
- Scholarly and professional
- Interdisciplinary

Award-Winning Platform:

- Unlimited simultaneous users
- Full-text in XML and PDF
- Advanced search engine
- No DRM

Librarian-Friendly:

- Free MARC records
- Discovery services
- COUNTER4/SUSHI compliant
- Training available

To find out more or request a free trial, visit: www.igi-global.com/eresources

IGI Global
DISSEMINATOR OF KNOWLEDGE
www.igi-global.com

IGI Global
Proudly Partners with
eContent Pro

eContent Pro specializes in the following areas:

Academic Copy Editing
Our expert copy editors will conduct a full copy editing procedure on your manuscript and will also address your preferred reference style to make sure your paper meets the standards of the style of your choice.

Expert Translation
Our expert translators will work to ensure a clear cut and accurate translation of your document, ensuring that your research is flawlessly communicated to your audience.

Professional Proofreading
Our editors will conduct a comprehensive assessment of your content and address all shortcomings of the paper in terms of grammar, language structures, spelling, and formatting.

IGI Global Authors, Save 10% on eContent Pro's Services!

Scan the QR Code to Receive Your 10% Discount

The 10% discount is applied directly to your eContent Pro shopping cart when placing an order through IGI Global's referral link. Use the QR code to access this referral link. eContent Pro has the right to end or modify any promotion at any time.

Email: customerservice@econtentpro.com

econtentpro.com

www.ingramcontent.com/pod-product-compliance
Lightning Source LLC
LaVergne TN
LVHW080341011026
849161LV00009B/2146